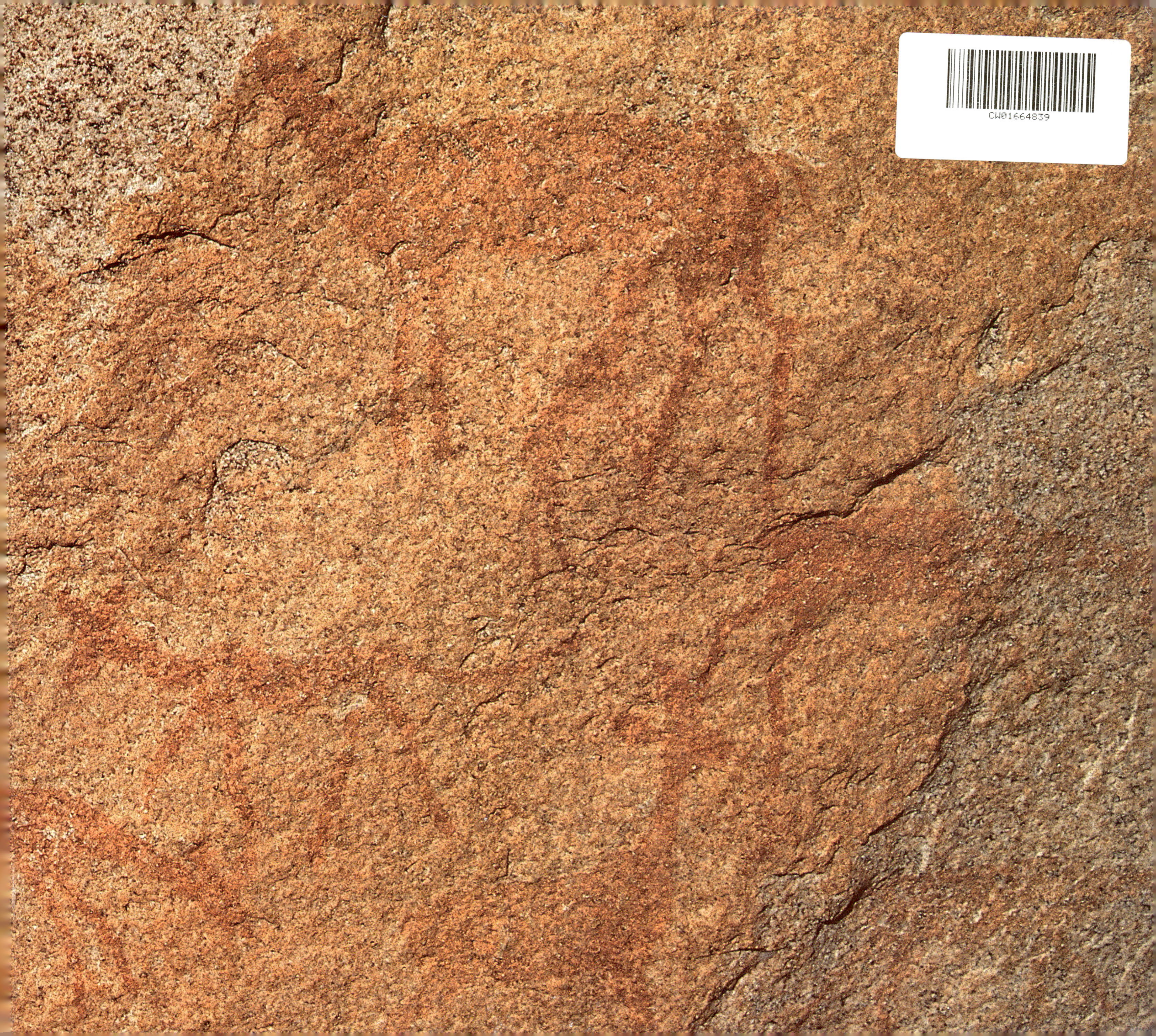

AFRICAN WILDLIFE
IN ART

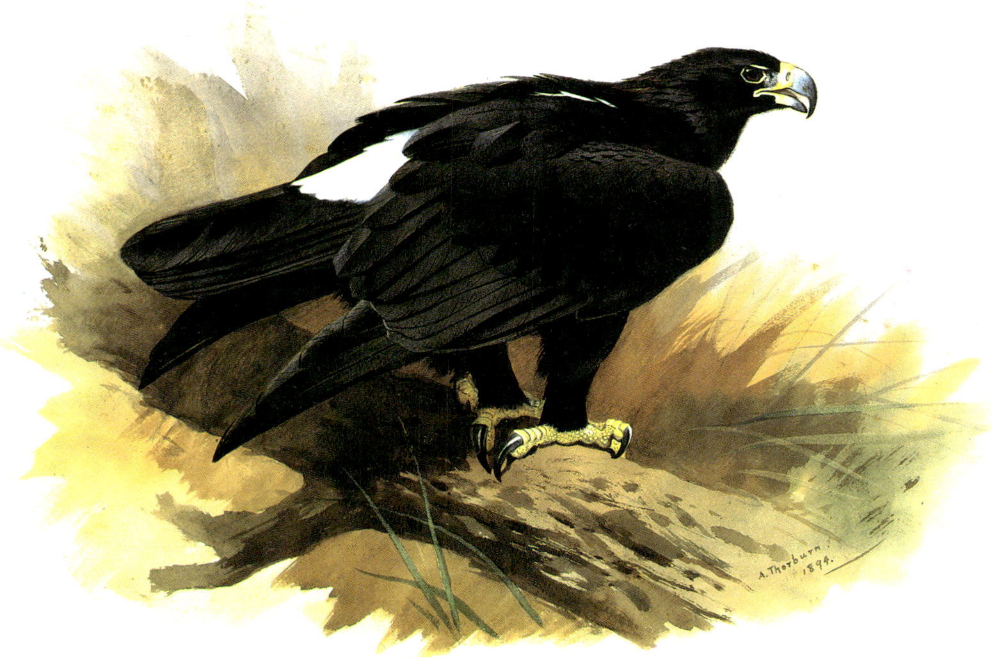

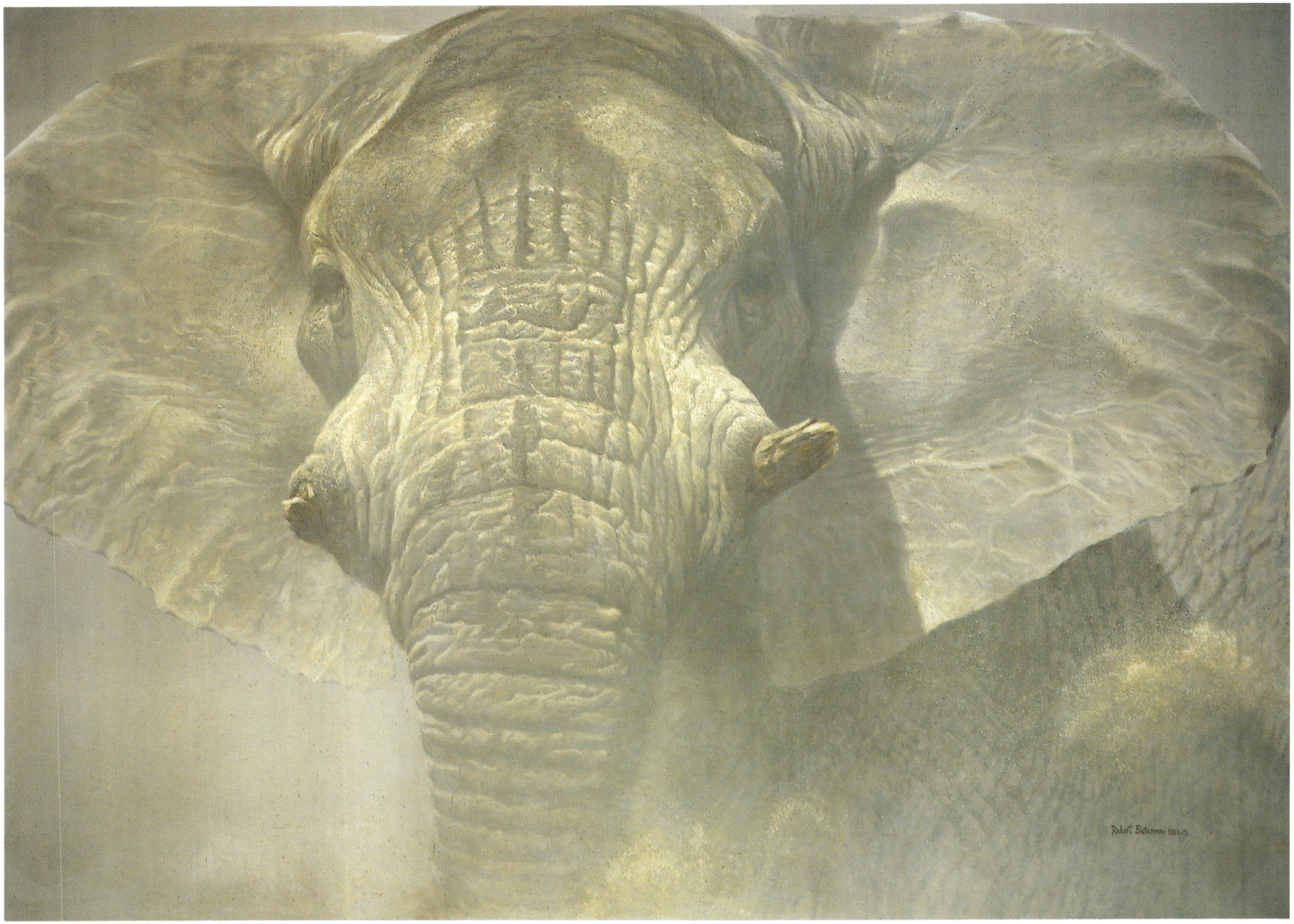

AFRICAN WILDLIFE IN ART

Master Painters of the Wilderness

WITH A COMMENTARY BY DAVID TOMLINSON

CLIVE HOLLOWAY BOOKS
LONDON

First published in Great Britain in 1991 by
Clive Holloway Books,
48 Baldry Gardens,
London SW16 3DJ

A CIP record for this book is available from the British Library

ISBN 0 907745 08 3

Designed by Nigel Partridge

Typeset by DP Photosetting, Aylesbury, Buckinghamshire
Colour separations by Columbia Offset, Singapore
Printed in Italy by New Interlitho S.p.A. - Milan

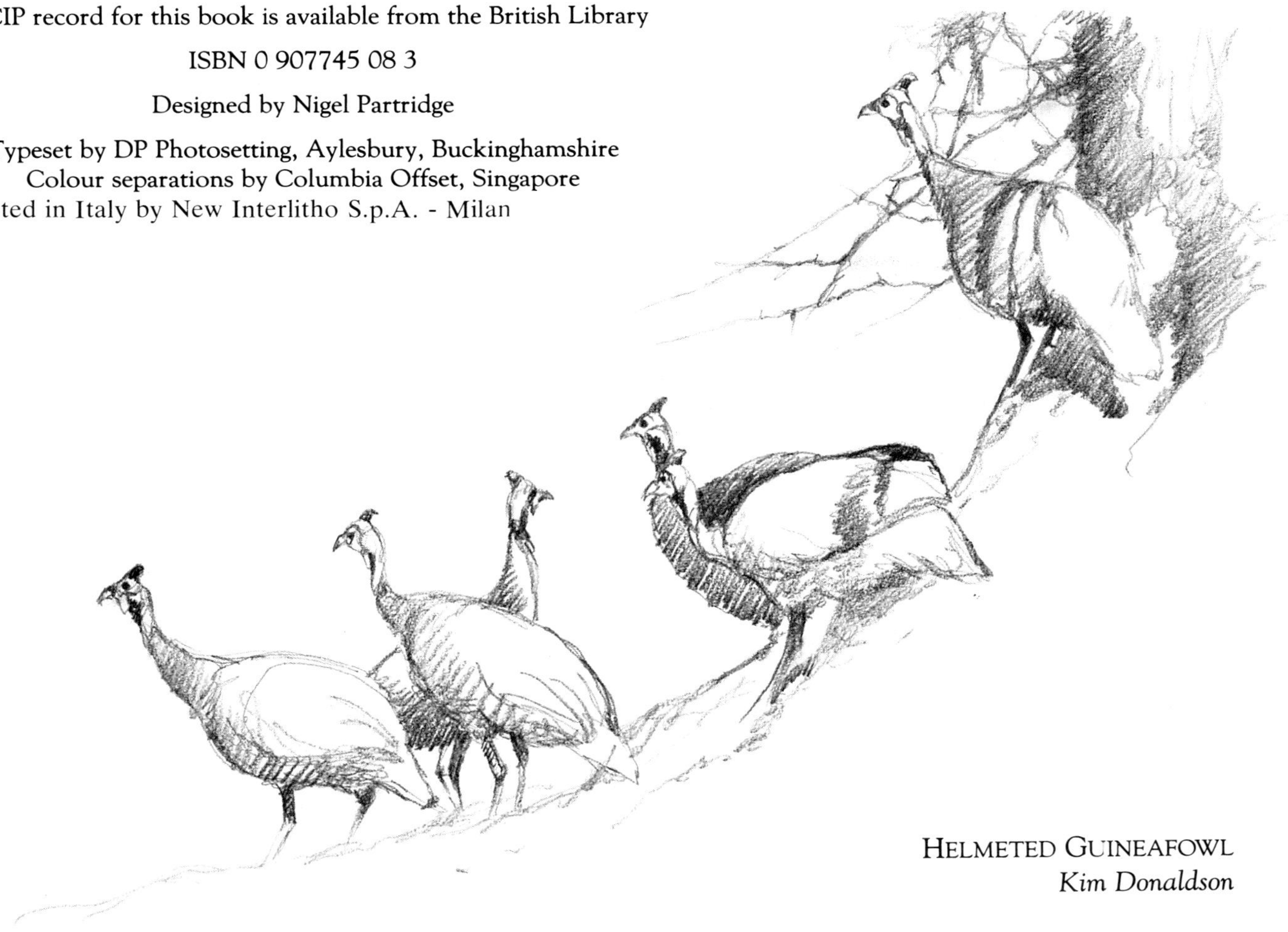

HELMETED GUINEAFOWL
Kim Donaldson

For John and Sheila McNeillie

Frontispiece: Of all African mammals, none is more impressive, nor more awe-inspiring, than the elephant. Robert Bateman's "The Wise One" depicts the matriarch of the herd, her tusks worn away after many years and many skirmishes. Painted in acrylic, this is fittingly Bateman's largest-ever work, some 71in × 95in. Bateman comments: "This is the face of a very old female, the acknowledged leader, or wise one, of the herd . . . It is a face you could look at for a very long time without ever getting tired of its variety." Elephants have a similar lifespan to man, so this female, portrayed in 1986, would have been born in the early twenties. She has lived through many changes, not least of which has been the massive reduction of the East African elephant population from hundreds of thousands to just thousands.

LILAC-BREASTED ROLLER
Mandy Shepherd

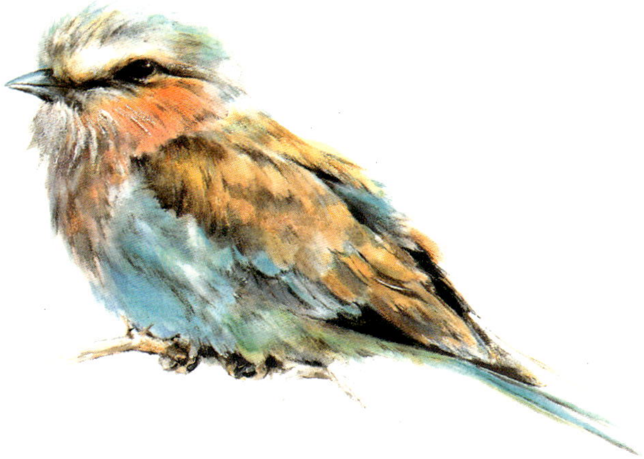

AFRICA'S PREHISTORIC ROCK ART

AN APPRECIATION BY DAVID COULSON

Scattered throughout the mountains of the African continent are innumerable crags and hidden valleys whose caves and boulders are vividly decorated with the art of prehistoric man. In the southern half of Africa most of this art is the work of Bushmen who are among Africa's earliest inhabitants. These hunter-gatherers have all but disappeared as a people after centuries of persecution at the hands of black and white pastoralists. Only in Western Botswana and Eastern Namibia can remnants of the true Bushmen be found. I have occasionally seen them here, and over the last ten years have been privileged to travel to many other remote areas where I have photographed their paintings and engravings. The last of the painters died out long ago, the surviving Bushmen having lost the knowledge and ability. Today they do not even remember that their ancestors painted.

In the early 1980s I worked on a book entitled *Mountain Odyssey* which took me to many wild regions of Southern Africa. In the course of my 30,000 mile journey I made several trips to the Drakensberg Mountains of Natal on the Lesotho/South African border. The Drakensberg is full of rock paintings but the richest site is the spectacular Ndedema Gorge which boasts a natural gallery of nearly 4,000 individual paintings. On the same expedition I visited Zimbabwe, a thousand miles further north, and explored its granite hills, known as "kopjes". Here on caves and overhangs I found the most delicate and sensitive rock paintings I have ever seen. The elegant giraffe, the stealthy leopard and the dainty bushbuck are all exquisitely portrayed in these kopjes. I have since travelled to Botswana's Tsodilo Hills in the Northern Kalahari, described by Laurens Van der Post as a veritable "Louvre" of rock art. Van der Post believes these hills were once a place of pilgrimage for the Bushmen, a form of sacred shrine. The Bushman was not just a painter, he was also an engraver, and I have twice visited Damaraland, Namibia, to see his engravings at Twyfelfontein (Doubtful Spring). Almost every boulder on this barren mountain side is covered with petraglyphs (engravings), meticulously pecked out of the granite surface using crude stone tools.

The Bushmen or "san" hunter-gatherers as they are more correctly known these days, may well have been the original inhabitants of Africa. They certainly seem to pre-date all the other inhabitants of Southern Africa. There is no group of people more indigenous than they. For tens of thousands of years they thrived in Africa's Eden. Their "herds" were wild animals tended by nature herself, and their fruit and vegetables were whatever nature cared to grow for them. In his classic book *The Lost World of the Kalahari* written in the 1950s, Laurens Van der Post gave us this beautiful picture of the bushman:

> They said he was a little man, not a dwarf or a pygmy, but just a little man about five feet in height. He was well, sturdily and truly made. His shoulders were broad, but his hands and feet were extraordinarily small and finely modelled. The oldest of our Suto servants told me that one had only to see his small, precise footprints in the sand never to forget them. His ankles were slim like a racehorse, his legs supple, his muscles loose and he ran like the wind, fast and long . . . When he laughed, which he did easily, his face broke into innumerable little folds and pleats of a most subtle and endearing criss-cross pattern.

At the end of the last century on the banks of the Orange River a lone Bushman fell splayed out on a boulder, a bullet through his back. From his zebra skin belt were suspended several tiny paint-filled antelope horns and, as he lay in the afternoon sun, his paint seeped out around him. Laurens Van der Post still remembers his father's description of this incident, which occurred during a raid on Bushmen cattle rustlers in which his grandfather participated. The dead Bushman was one of the last of a group of painters unparalleled in the history of art. When these painters died the secret of the ingredients they used for painting on rock died with them. That formula, which had no doubt been handed down over countless generations, had enabled their paintings to stand up to the wear and tear of untold centuries. Throughout Southern Africa Bushmen had been shot on sight by black and white farmers until as recently as World War I. In areas like the Drakensberg and the Cape, South Africa, they had been completely exterminated by the beginning of this century. It was not until the early 1900s in Bechuanaland, for example, that a government notice was issued advising that Bushmen were not game animals and should not be shot.

Although little is known about their technique and the exact materials they used, early reports suggest that some painters used brushes made from feathers. Others, we are told, used wildebeest tail and even hollow bone, tapered to a point at one end. The ingredients used for the paint itself must have varied according to what was available in the Bushmen's particular area. Haematite, for example, or oxidized red ochre, was used by many painters, either painted on as a liquid or first applied in a dry form. Blood

8

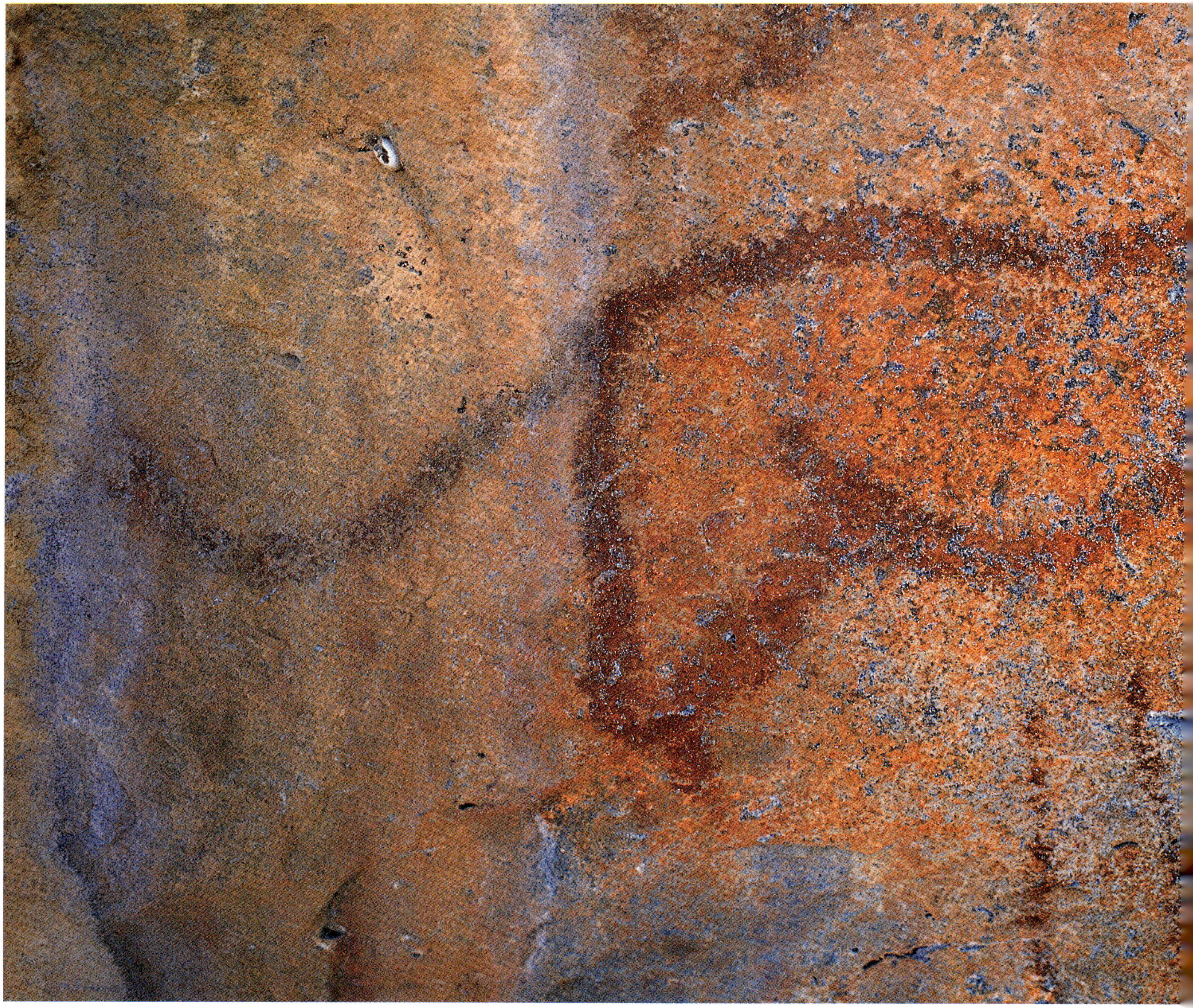

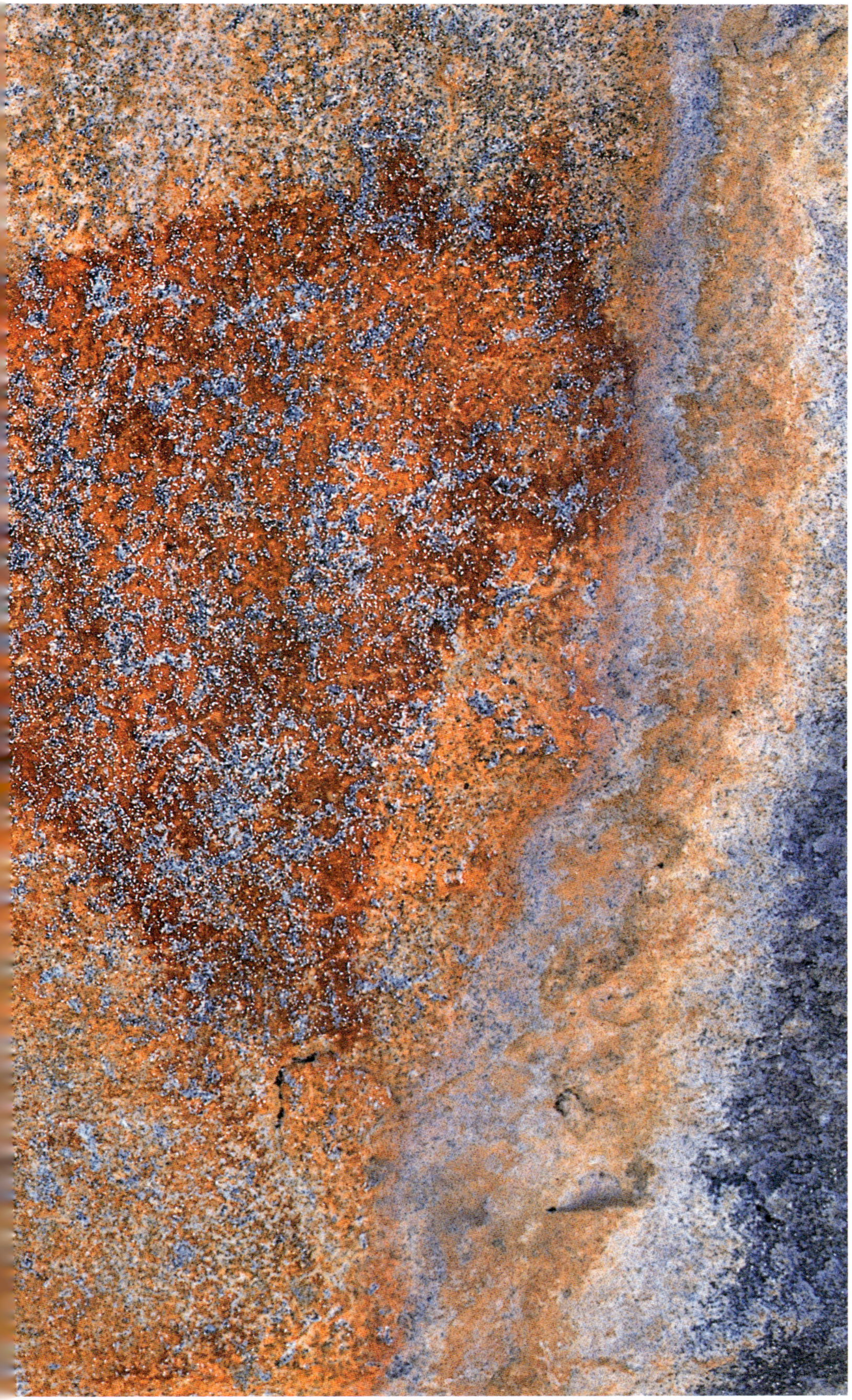

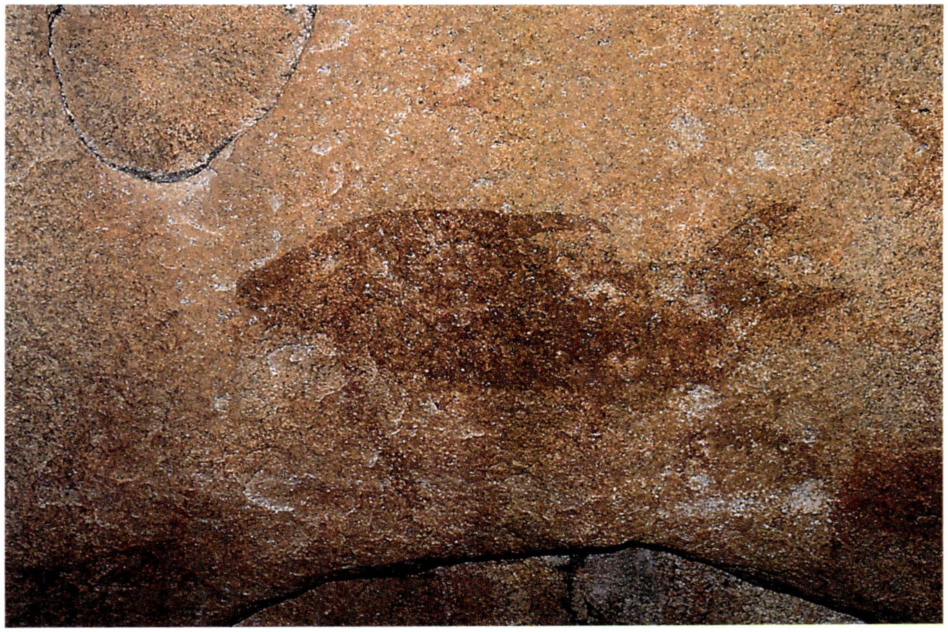

Above: Bushman painting of a fish, Tsodilo Hills, Botswana.
Left: Study of a lion, also from the Tsodilo Hills in Botswana.

and animal fat were commonly used as fixing agents. Despite differences in languages and geographical separation of hundreds of miles, the paintings of different groups demonstrated a similar style and spirit. This was the hallmark of their culture.

In 1987 I was working in the Kalahari on an illustrated edition of *The Lost World of the Kalahari* with Laurens Van der Post. This was the 30th anniversary edition of his original book to which he was adding an epilogue. My task was to try and recapture, this time with photographs, the "Lost World" that he had described in the 1950s while searching for the survivors of this vanished race of hunter-gatherers. I followed in his footsteps, travelling to the Okavango swamps and later to the Tsodilo Hills. The Kalahari is one of the world's flattest places, an ocean of bush under immense skies. The Tsodilo Hills are a tiny island in this ocean, a geological freak in an endless world of scrub and sand. Although only 1,300 feet high they are visible from a great distance. It is easy to see how important they must have been to the Bushmen whose own name for them was the "bracelet of the morning". There is permanent water in the hills.

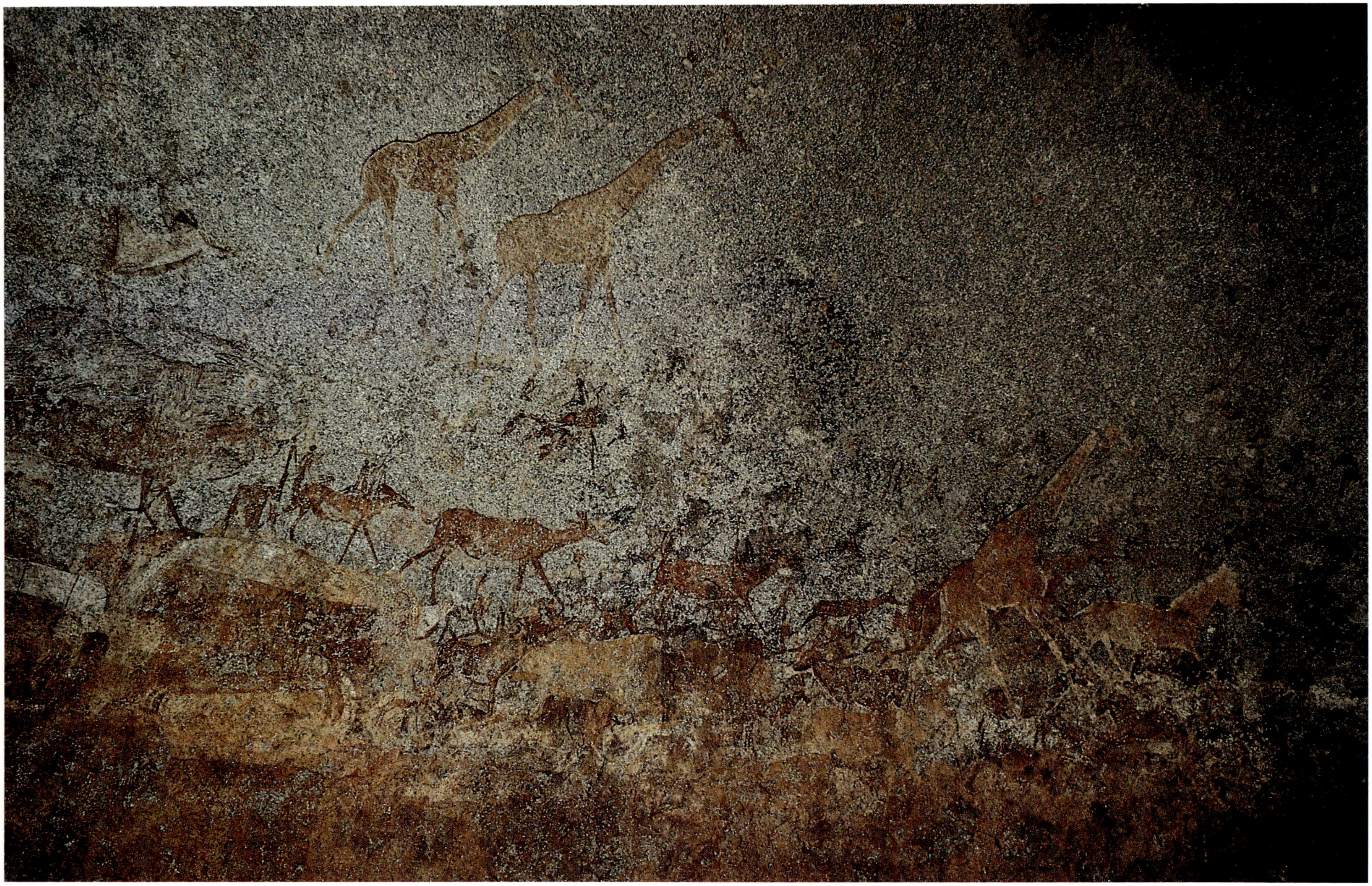

I spent 10 unforgettable days in these hills together with Alec Campbell, founder of the National Museum in Botswana, a great expert on the area and its rock art. During the last 24 years he and his helpers have discovered about 2,500 paintings at more than 250 different sites. Each time he returns he finds more. At the time of my visit he was conducting an archeological dig with Larry Robbins, Professor of Archeology at Michigan State University. While he and Larry laboured in their pit I walked for seven hours a day exploring the hills and looking for paintings. Through dense bush I made my way up secret valleys with solitary baobabs and cyclopean boulders scrutinizing their surfaces for paintings. All the time I was conscious of a spiritual atmosphere I had rarely known, even in a place of worship. Most of the paintings I saw were of animals and most of them were red on the orange-coloured granite. There were also a number of white paintings which were cruder, and Alec explained that these were thought to be more recent. The local Bushmen say that their ancestors made the white paintings but that the red ones were painted by God. This correlates with archaeological evidence that the red paintings are far older, in some cases thousands of years older than the others. Certainly the number of exceptionally high quality paintings at Tsodilo Hills seems to indicate that these hills may have witnessed the apex of the Bushman's art in Africa.

Above: A wonderful example of the Bushmen's artistic flair and draughtsmanship.

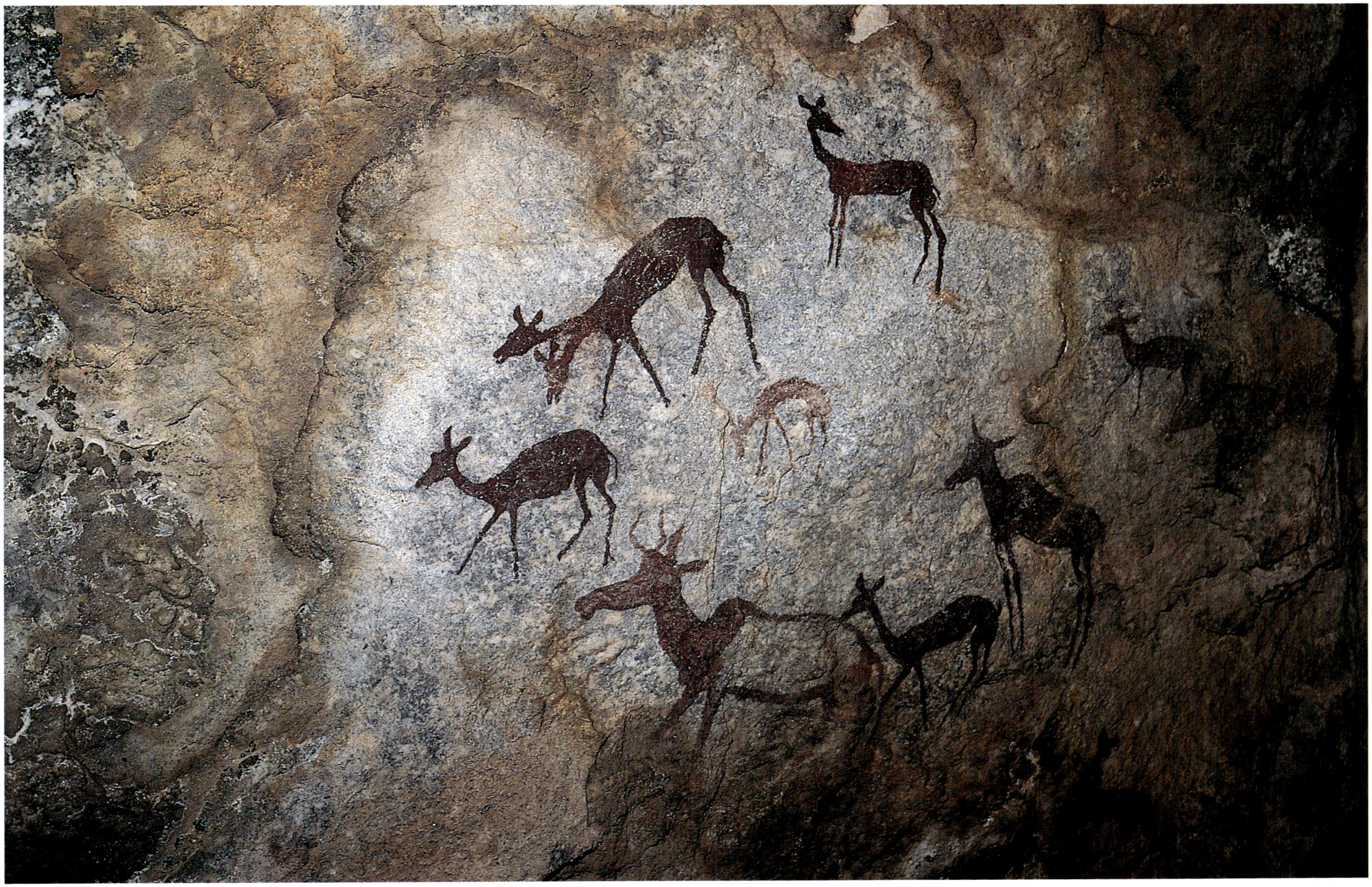

Above: Paintings of antelope, near Banket, Zimbabwe.

Different theories have been put forward as to why the Bushman painted animals and why he painted some animals more than others. Many archaeologists believe that the paintings were inspired by dreams, and were often executed by Shamaans, or medicine men. *Shamaan* is a Tungus word from Central Asia. In anthropological circles it means someone in a hunter-gathering society who enters a trance to heal people, control the weather, foretell the future, ensure good hunting, and so on. The theory is that the Bushmen Shamaans used the medium of rock art to communicate their spiritual visions, experienced in trances, to their people.

This helps to explain the paintings of mythical beasts, and people who look like bats and others wearing strange headdresses and masks. Whether it explains the abundance of representational and impressionist paintings of antelope and other creatures is open to question. Could this not merely have been an expression of the Bushman's love for the animals which surrounded him? As Van der Post wrote,

> He alone of all the races of Africa was so much of its earth and innermost being that he tried constantly to glorify it by adorning its stones and decorating its rocks with paintings. We other races went through Africa like locusts devouring and stripping the land for what we could get out of

12

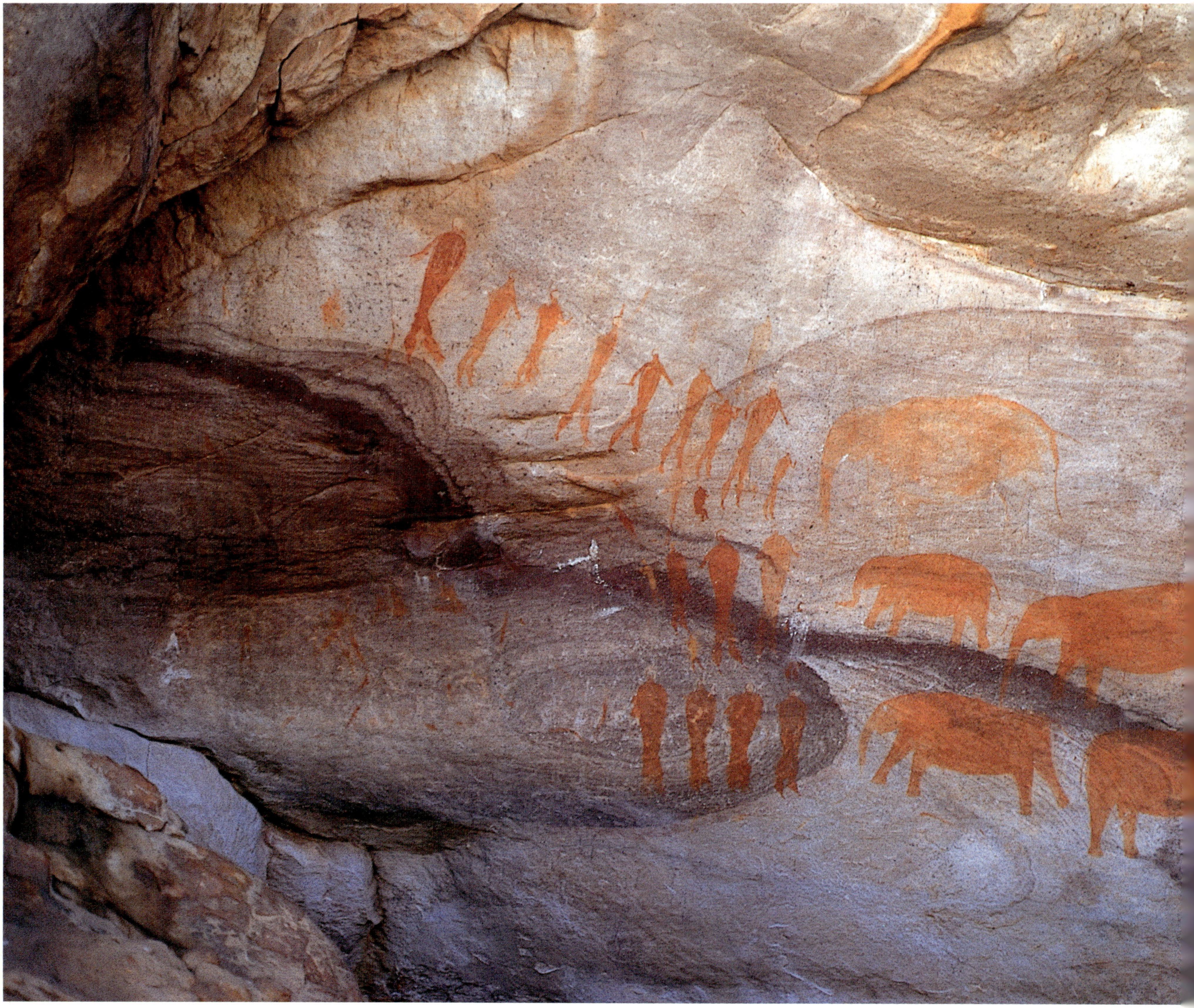

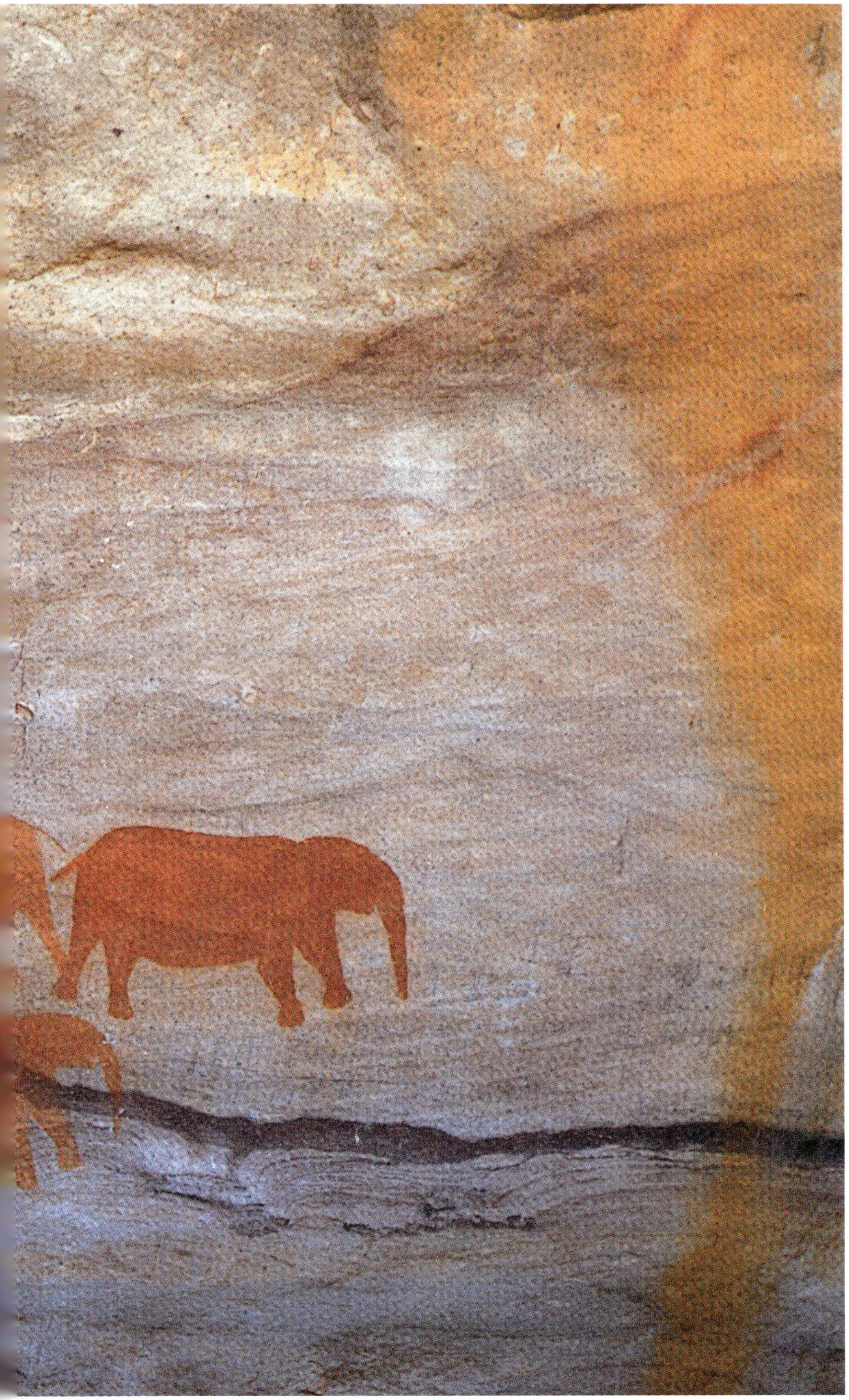

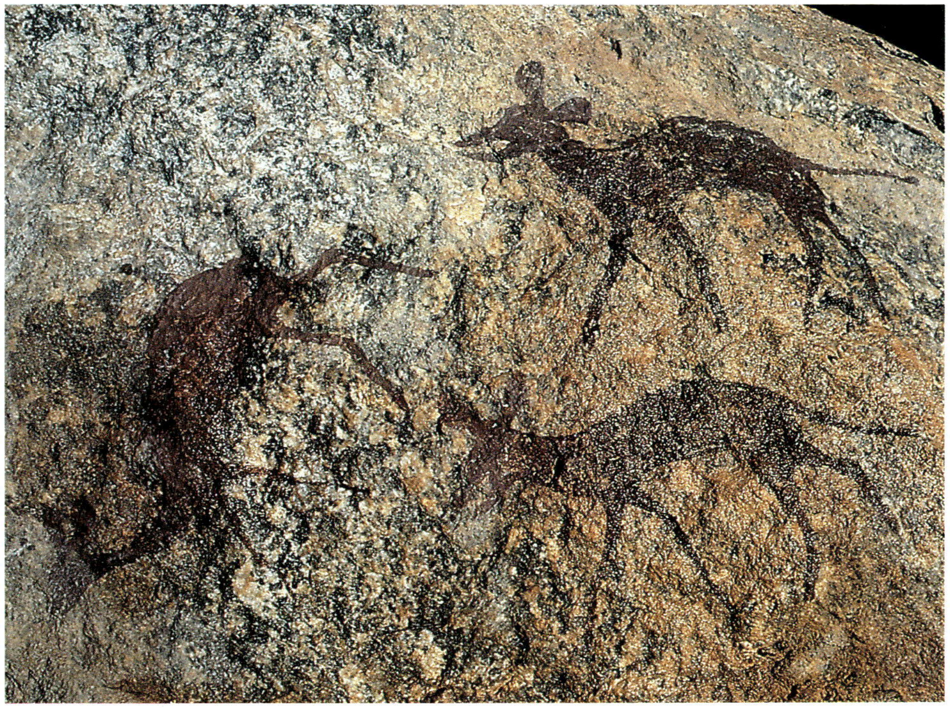

Above: Hunting dogs, from a cave in Zimbabwe.
Left: Well preserved paintings of elephants, at Sederberge in the Cape.

it. The Bushman was there solely because he belonged to it. Accordingly he endeavoured in many ways to express this feeling of belonging, which is love, but the greatest of them was in the manner of his painting.

On his original visit to Tsodilo, Van der Post was taken by his guide to the "Pool of Everlasting Water" in a bowl in the hills, next to which grew the "Tree of Knowledge". To reach it he was led up a track in a narrow gorge whose sides were richly decorated with animal paintings. Near the top, before arriving at the sacred pool, his guide knelt on a rock which bore two slight depressions with a round hole close by. These, said the guide, were the marks that the greatest spirit of all had made with his knees as he knelt to pray over his creation. The circular hole was where he had placed his cruse of water. I asked Alec Campbell if he knew where this gorge was, and he drew me a map showing me the way. The "Pool of Everlasting Water" had probably dried up, he said, but the gorge was worth a visit. It was only half a mile from our camp.

Following Alec's directions I located the bottom of the gorge and followed a narrow track steeply upwards through dense vegetation. The towering rock faces on either side were dappled with patches of sunlight but looking closely I could see paintings. Wherever the rocks were smooth enough they were painted with antelope, rhino, giraffe and other animals. I could see that this was no ordinary track. In the cool silence of the gorge I was acutely aware of a powerful spiritual atmosphere. Coming round corners I came face to face with kudu, eland and other majestic antelope standing out from the rock face. Eventually I reached an open area at the top where the pool had once been. Now everything was tinder dry and the "Tree of Knowledge" had disappeared. I retraced my steps along the track and looking carefully at all the rocks, I found one with marks exactly as Van der Post had described it, two circular depressions to fit a pair of knees and a round hole in the rock about four inches deep and the same wide, just right for a vessel of water. Sitting there I remembered Van der Post's description of a later trip he made here some years ago. Samutchao, the son of his original guide, took him back here to the pool, which was already dry. When asked what had happened to the water Samutchao had waved his arms and exclaimed: "All gone, gone, gone! All gone with the spirits back into the earth where they came from." Perhaps Samutchao had been right, but I had a definite feeling that the spirits of those ancient hunters were still around and would continue to frequent the hills.

Our camp site was under an overhanging crag with its own richly painted shelter. Alec Campbell and Larry Robbins had excavated a fifteen-foot pit nearby and had found stone tools at various levels associated with the shelter. Robbins subsequently took fragments of carbon back to America for investigation and has since established a date of 18,950 years for those taken from the halfway level. As they expected, the thermoluminescence tests on samples from the bottom levels revealed dates in excess of 30,000 years. In Namibia's Huns mountains similar paintings to those at Tsodilo have been dated at between 25,000 and 27,500 years of age, as old as, if not older than, the earliest rock art that has been discovered, to date, in Europe. The famous paintings at Tassili and other sites in North Africa's Sahara Desert are thought to be nearly 5,000 years old.

In recent years the problem of vandalism at rock art sites has raised its ugly head. Tourists have also discovered that if they wet these priceless paintings it brings out the colours for photography. Untold damage may already have been done this way. Some of the more accessible sites can be protected but most are too remote and difficult to police. Their remoteness makes them vulnerable, but it also helps protect them. Shielded from the elements in secret kloofs and valleys many of these paintings will survive untarnished for future generations to discover and rediscover.

Van der Post had the feeling right when he wrote:

> It is astonishing how, in this late hour, they still burn within the aubergine shadows of cave and overhang of cliff and krans, and what power they still possess to provoke an almost unbearable nostalgia for the vanished painter and for the spirit which possessed him.

David Coulson

AFRICAN WILDLIFE IN ART

INTRODUCTION BY DAVID TOMLINSON

One of the most significant moments of my life took place in June 1980: I visited the Okavango Delta, in northern Botswana. It was my first visit to Africa, and I was captivated. Watching television wildlife films may give you an idea of what to expect when you visit Africa for the first time, but nothing prepares you for the sights, sounds and smells of the bush. Experiencing wild Africa can be an overwhelming experience: it certainly was for me. Every minute of every hour was to be treasured and savoured, and I can still recall in vivid detail the excitement of my first lion in Chobe, my first encounters with elephants in Moremi, and watching (and listening to) fish eagles over the clean waters of the Okavango.

Since that unforgettable safari, I have been drawn back to Africa on many occasions. Each trip has produced its own unique experiences, whether watching wattled ibises in the Highlands of Ethiopia, gemsbok in the Namib desert, or lions in the Masai Mara. Africa has become a drug: an annual visit is needed just to hear the song of the emerald-spotted wood dove, the noisy bark of zebra, or the roar of a distant lion. Every day of each safari brings new experiences, exciting new encounters. Africa has cast its spell over me, and there is no escaping it.

There is, of course, nothing unusual about becoming addicted to Africa. Every artist whose work appears in this book will admit to a similar fixation to the Dark Continent, and for most of them visiting Africa for the first time was a changing point in their lives. Guy Coheleach, for example, first visited Africa as a result of winning the novice division of the 1966 Winchester National Trap and Skeet Championships. His prize was a trip to London, but London became the stepping stone on an unplanned trip to Africa. What he saw there changed his life and his career.

Bob Kuhn had a similar experience 10 years before, while Robert Bateman's initial visit to Africa was as a 27-year-old on a round-the-world trip in 1958. It was East Africa which left the most lasting impression, and to which he has returned many times since.

In contrast, several of the artists whose work appears in this book – such as Michael Ghaui and Kim Donaldson – were lucky enough to be born in Africa. Others, including Simon Combes and Dino Paravano, went there as children, and grew up surrounded by the delights and mystery of the bush.

There are many similarities between wine and art. Tastes differ, and though most critics will generally agree over the greatest vineyards, or the best vintages, it is rare to get two experts in total agreement. Just as some great vintages are not always obtainable, so one or two paintings we would like to have included were also impossible to track down and include, but we hope that neither their omission, nor the omission of any particular artist's work (whether by choice or not) will detract from the pleasure of such a feast of fine paintings.

Nearly all the artists represented are living, and this is a reflection on the fact that it is only in relatively recent years that Africa has become a favourite destination for wildlife painters, chiefly from North America and Northern Europe. The great pioneer of African wildlife art was Wilhelm Kuhnert, several of whose paintings appear here. What is remarkable about Kuhnert's work is the fact that he managed to produce so much despite the difficulties of travelling in East Africa at the turn of the century.

Kuhnert was born in 1865, winning a scholarship to Berlin's Academy of Arts at the age of 18. He first studied under Paul Meyerheim, an animal painter of some distinction, but who worked primarily from animals he saw in Berlin's zoological gardens. Meyerheim's place as professor of the Academy was later taken by Richard Friese, who is still regarded as one of the greatest animal artists of all time. Friese had considerable influence on the work of the young Kuhnert, and inspired him to go out and draw animals in their natural surroundings.

Thanks to the help and inspiration of Hans Meyer of the Bibliographical Institute of Leipzig, who had himself visited East Africa, Kuhnert was able to raise sufficient funds for his first African expedition in 1891, when he was 26. He visited South East Africa, then a German colonial territory, producing some fine work which showed a highly mature standard of draughtsmanship.

It was not until 1905 that Kuhnert returned to German East Africa, when he made a safari along the Ruhudji and Ruaha rivers, and hunted and sketched among the vast herds of game which roamed the Ulanga plains. His paintings remain as a reminder of the abundance of game at the turn of the century. On this safari Kuhnert travelled without any white companions, and took tremendous personal risks, but the results of his work speak for themselves. He produced huge numbers of sketches, which later formed the foundation for major pictures painted in his studio in Germany.

Kuhnert's third and final African safari was in 1911, when he accompanied King Frederick of Saxony on an expedition to the Sudan. He remained in Africa until the end of 1912.

There can be little doubt that Kuhnert's work has influenced every artist who has since attempted to paint African wildlife. Not only was he a superb draughtsman, but he also was an acute observer of wildlife. Working before the days of the long lens camera, he was forced to sketch from life, without even the comfort and security of a four-wheel-drive vehicle.

Modern wildlife artists have a much easier time. The great herds of game which so impressed Kuhnert may have gone, but many fine areas remain, and are easily accessible by vehicle or even plane. Though most artists still sketch in the field, nearly all also use a camera to record what they see. Bob Kuhn takes several thousand transparencies while on safari, and these later form the basis for his paintings. He admits that after a few weeks in Africa, he cannot wait to have his films developed and pore over the results in search of the few which might make the basis of a picture.

Kunhert was as skilled with a rifle as he was with a brush, and this link between hunting and art is especially strong in Africa. The majority of artists whose work appears here have hunted in Africa. It was a hunting safari which first took Bob Kuhn to Africa, while Simon Combes admits to an early passion for shooting: "In retrospect, I have often tried to analyze my passion for hunting during those teenage years. Why did I get such a kick out of killing animals? I do remember frequently feeling a fleeting sense of remorse but never enough to stop me doing the same thing the next day." He goes on to say he cannot remember any moral restrictions. "I was not conscious of any fervent desire to conserve; wild animals were plentiful, there was no television to bring us the wonderful wildlife documentaries that we see today and the talk among my peers on the ranch and at school was all of hunting. I hero-worshipped the legendary hunters of earlier times and avidly read every book I could about them."

Bob Kuhn only hunted on his first African safari, not giving up for moral reasons, but because he found it impossible to combine hunting and painting together. Instead of seeing the animals, he was assessing them as potential trophies.

Fellow American Guy Coheleach still hunts the occasional buffalo in Botswana, and points out that "I could never paint wild game as effectively if I hadn't also been a hunter and been hunted or stalked by lions and elephants in the field." The advantage most hunters have over their fellow artists who have never fired a rifle is a detailed knowledge of their subject's anatomy. Coheleach again: "I know a lot about anatomy from my hunting expeditions. While the other guys are hunting, I'm watching the skinners cutting the carcass."

There is a further connection between African wildlife art and hunting that cannot be ignored. For years, hunters have been the most important patrons of wildlife art, prepared to spend considerable sums on paintings that recapture for them the sights of the African bush. As a result, the great majority of African wildlife paintings are of what we loosely term game, or quarry species. When Kenya outlawed all hunting safaris in 1975, the demand for African paintings also diminished, especially in the important North American market. Today, sales have picked up once again, with more wildlife enthusiasts prepared to buy paintings of African wildlife. Hopefully, this will encourage more artists to turn their attention from such well-worn (but popular) subjects as lions and buffalo and portray instead other inhabitants of the bush. Here the most famous, or fashionable, artists have an advantage, for there is a strong demand for their work, regardless of the subject. Any painting by Robert Bateman, for example, is sure to sell, allowing him the indulgence of painting such a subject as rock hyrax, one of my favourites in this book.

One obvious omission from this volume is the absence of any paintings by black African artists. That many Africans are deeply artistic is not in doubt – but the problem is one of attitudes, even tradition. Few of the paintings you will see on the following pages have remained in Africa – nearly all are hung on the walls of collectors in Europe and North America. There is, as yet, little or no demand from Africans for paintings of wildlife, and it is a sobering thought that very few Kenyans, for example, have ever been in a national park, or seen a wild lion. For an African to become an established wildlife artist will be far from easy, but is sure to happen in the not too distant future.

Through their work, wildlife artists can do much to help and popularize the subjects that they paint. On the following pages you will find many superb images of African animals and birds. If these paintings are not to become memorials to what 20th-century man has all but destroyed, then we must give Africa as much help as we possibly can. African wildlife is a world heritage, and it is the responsibility of everyone to ensure that it survives. Many African countries now depend on tourism as their number one earner of foreign currency, and they are prepared to conserve wildlife simply because it attracts tourists. If this book persuades more people to go and see the splendours of African wildlife for themselves, then it will have succeeded.

THE PAINTINGS

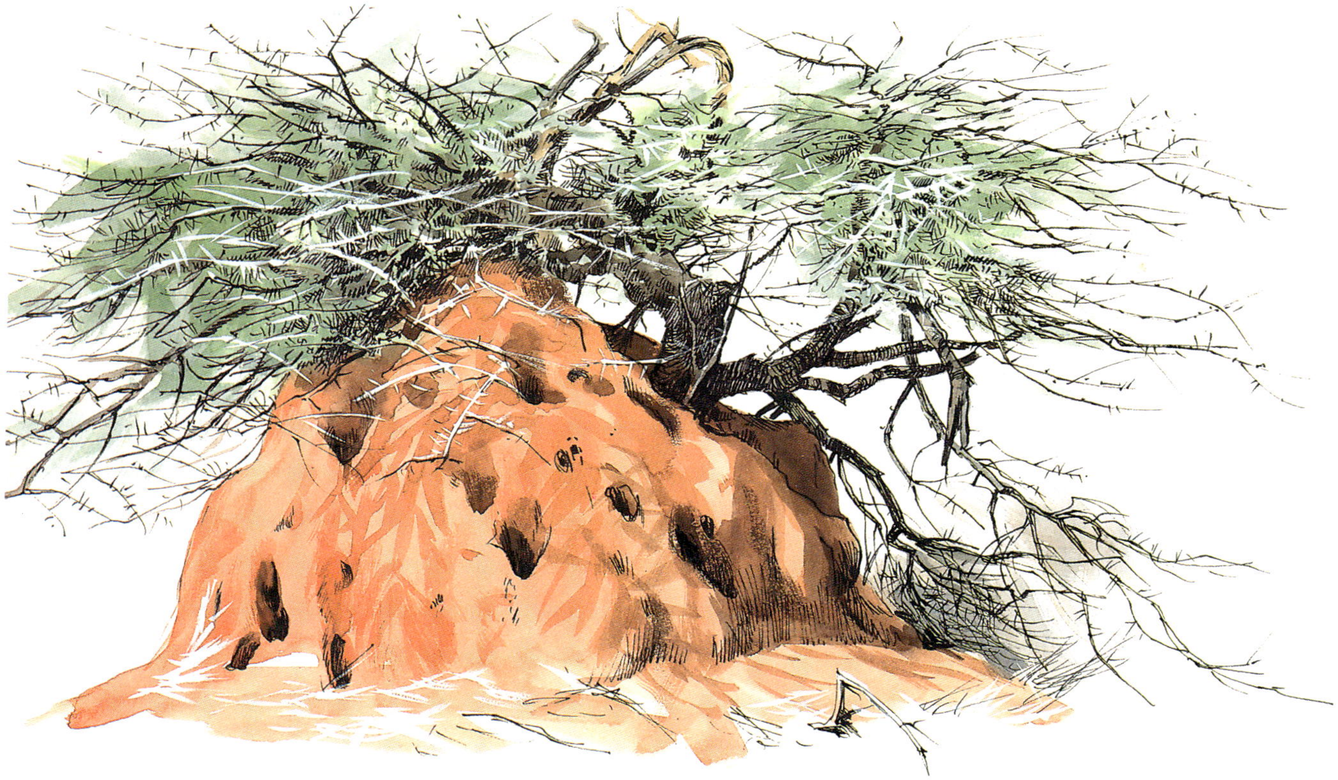

ANTHILL
Rena Fennessey

Zebras are nearly always in good condition, and even in times of drought they manage to look sleek and fat. Their stripes, which are never the same on any two animals, provide a fascinating pattern, especially when a group is bunched together. It is difficult to imagine the camouflage properties of these markings, but if the zebras in Ghaui's painting were to move a short distance away, they would first become greyish and would then blend into the surrounding bush, becoming almost impossible to see. Zebras are generally thought of as plains game – however, they do frequent thick bush as well, and it is here that he is most inspired to paint them.

Mike Ghaui lives on the shores of Lake Naivasha, in Kenya, but was born on a farm in the Southern Highlands of Tanganyika (now Tanzania), in 1950. He still makes what he calls his annual migration back to Tanzania's Ruaha Valley National Park, which provides the setting for this painting. He chose a burnt landscape for the background as the vegetation in this part of the world often turns to beautiful greens, reds and golds after a fire has been through the underlying grass. These colours, together with the rich, dark foreground of char and ash, make a subtle background for the bold black on white of the zebras.

BURNT BUSH – ZEBRAS
Michael Ghaui

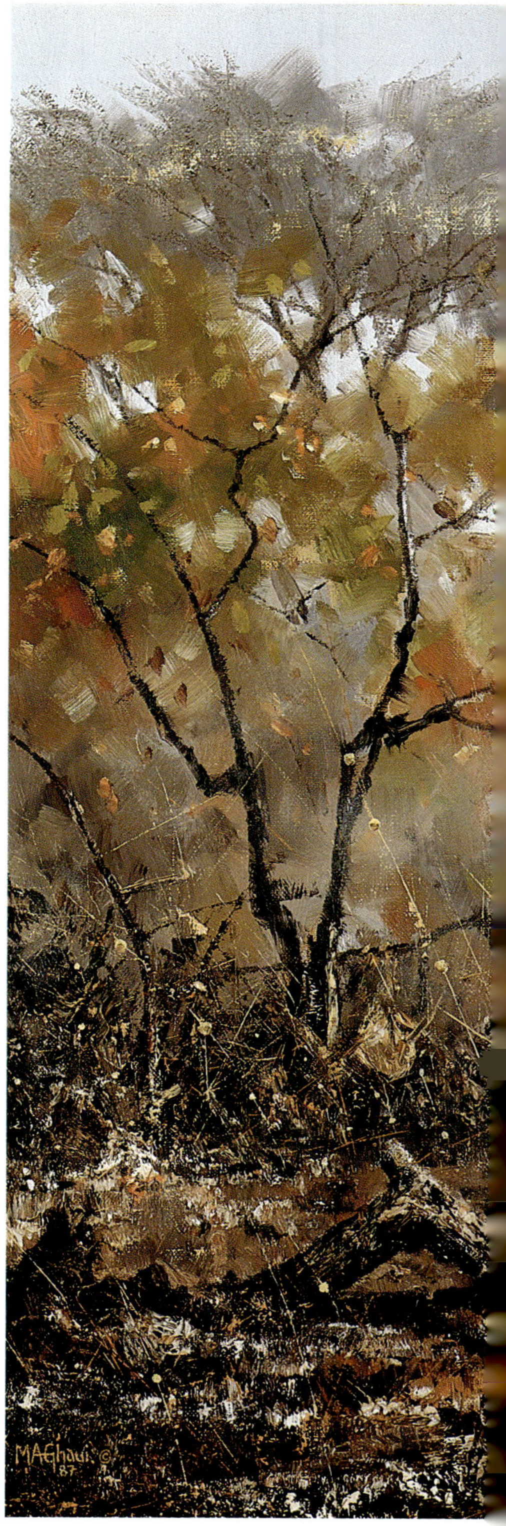

TSAVO FIVE – ZEBRA
Janet Heaton

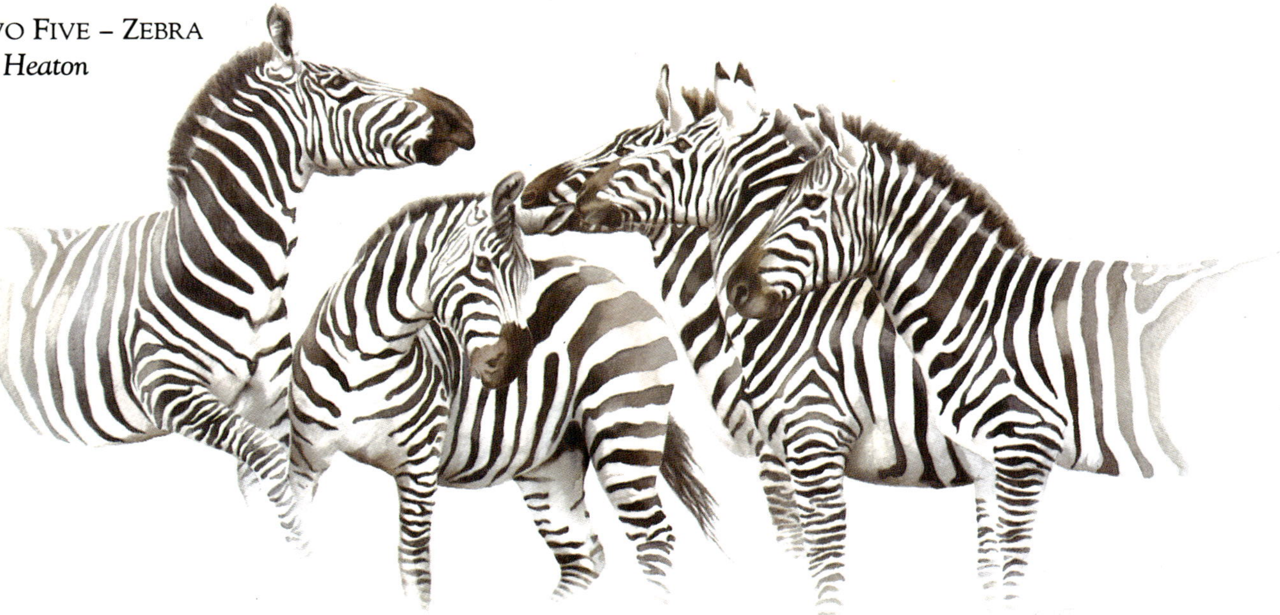

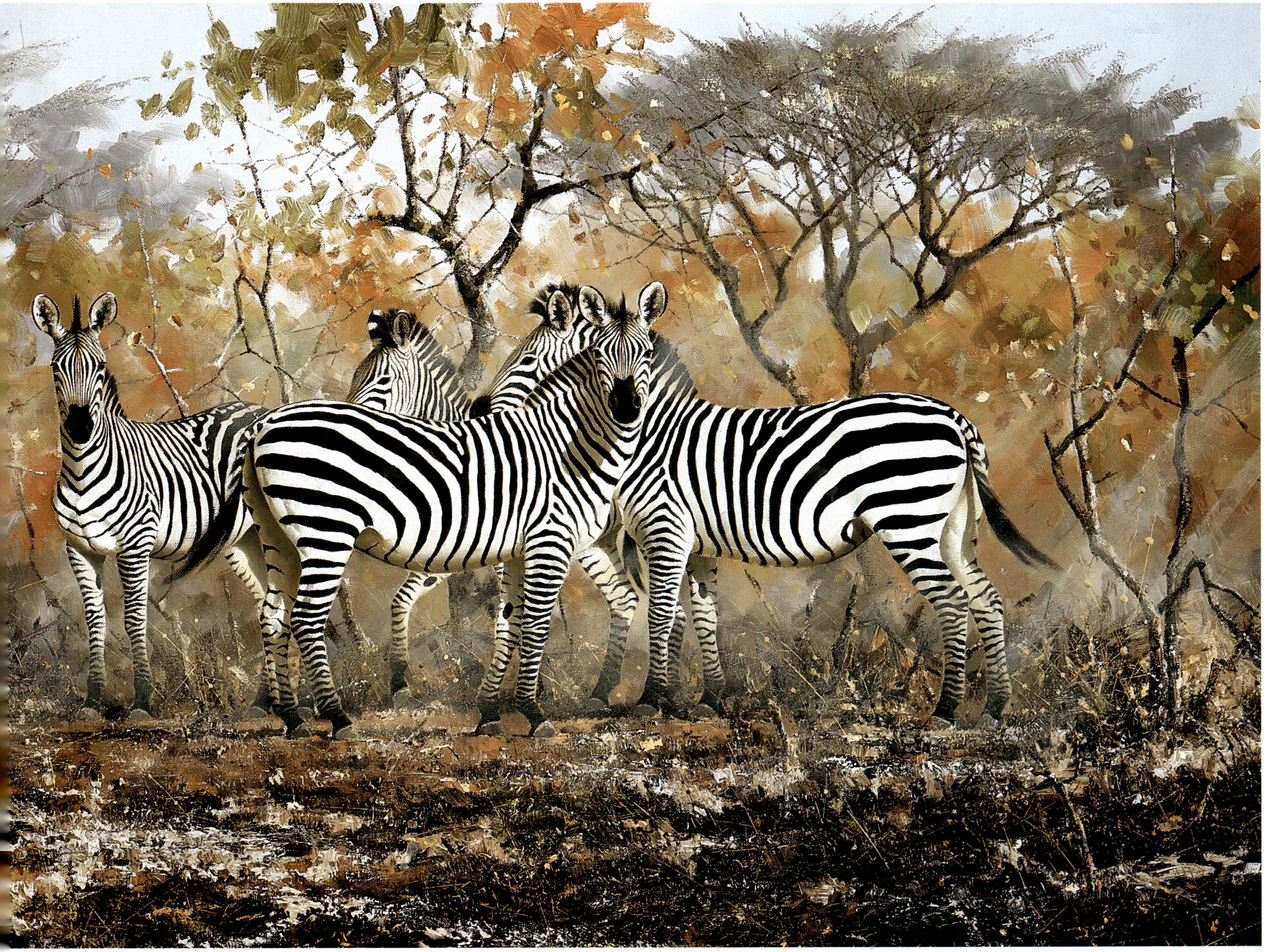

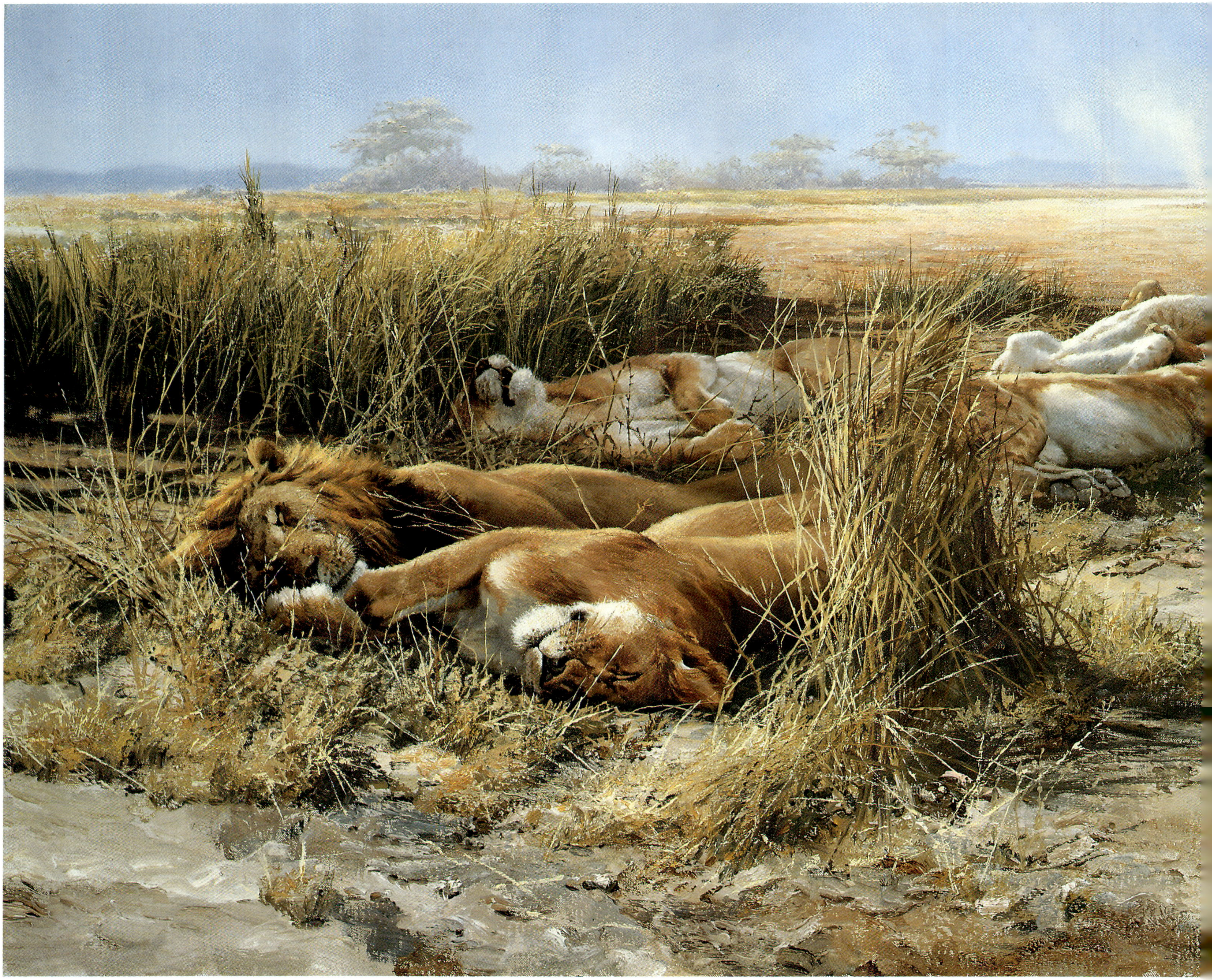

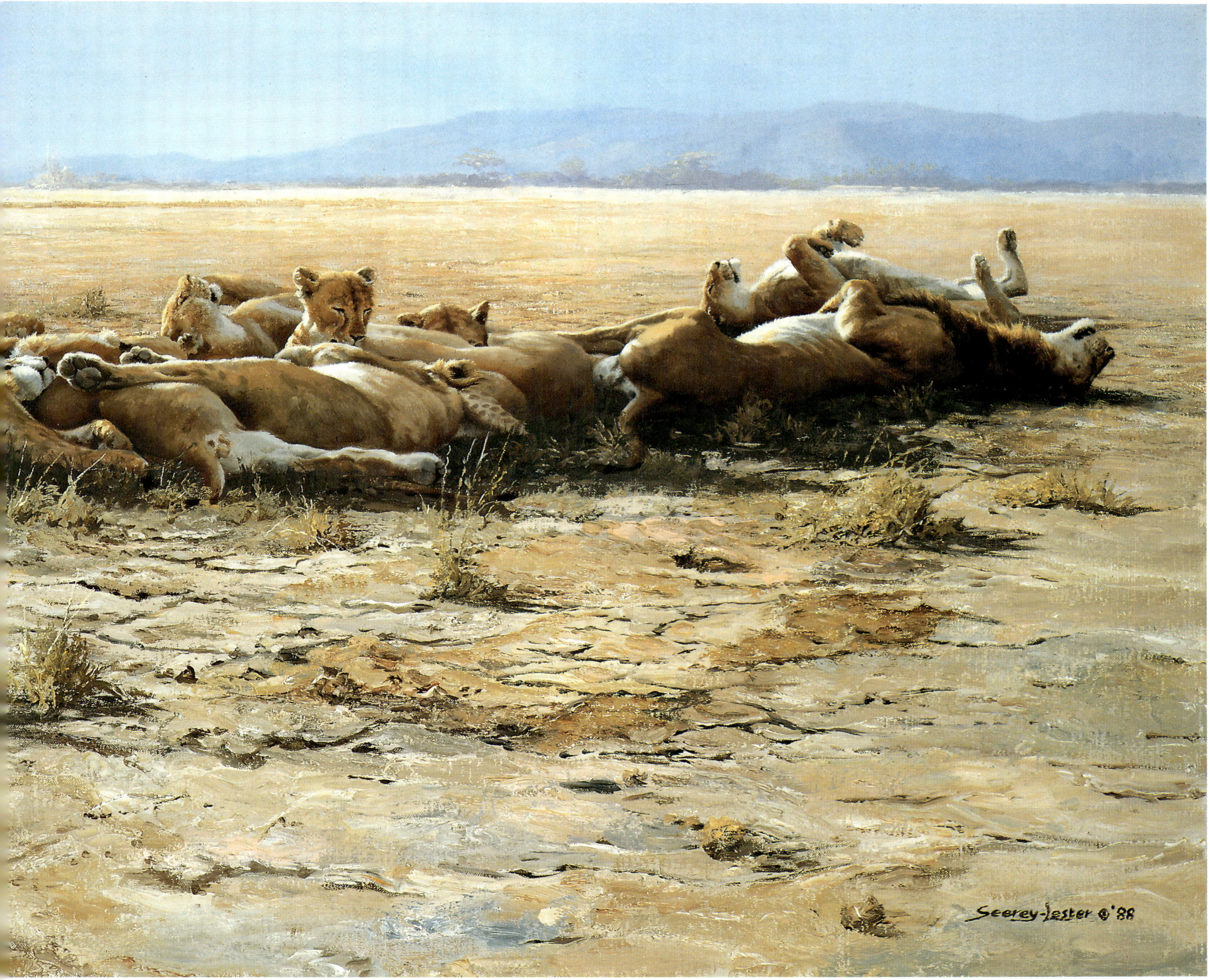
Seerey-Lester ©'88

22 John Seerey-Lester (*previous page*) first visited East Africa in 1980: what he saw fired him with enthusiasm, and he has been painting African wildlife scenes ever since. Before this he had concentrated on painting nostalgia, "like the old street scenes of my native city, Manchester, England". There is a touch of nostalgia here: Seerey-Lester has captured so well the mood of a hot, lazy African afternoon. This is how most tourists see lions: sprawled out, fast asleep, and apparently without a care in the world. Seerey-Lester found this pride in Amboseli on his first African visit, and was intrigued by the vulnerable positions some of the lions had struck, and how similar their poses were to those of a domestic cat. There are, indeed, many similarities between domestic cats and lions, but while the former is a solitary animal, lions are sociable, hence the size of the pride depicted here.

SAVANNA SIESTA
John Seerey-Lester

AFRICAN ELEPHANTS
Donald Grant

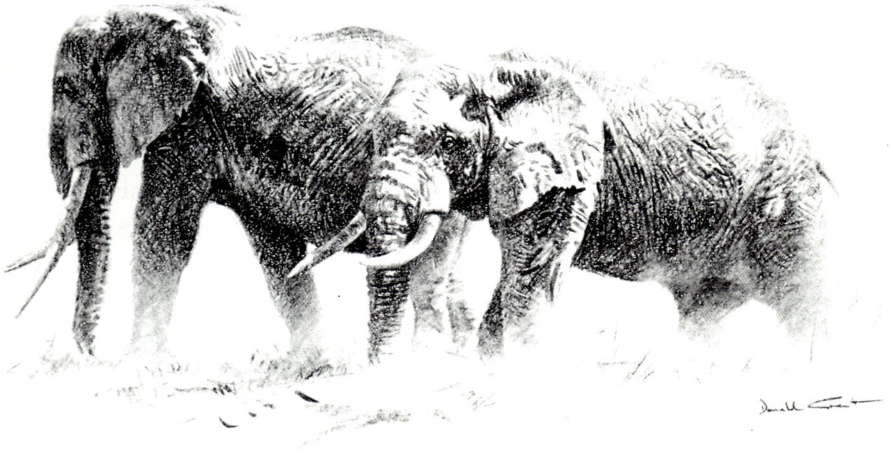

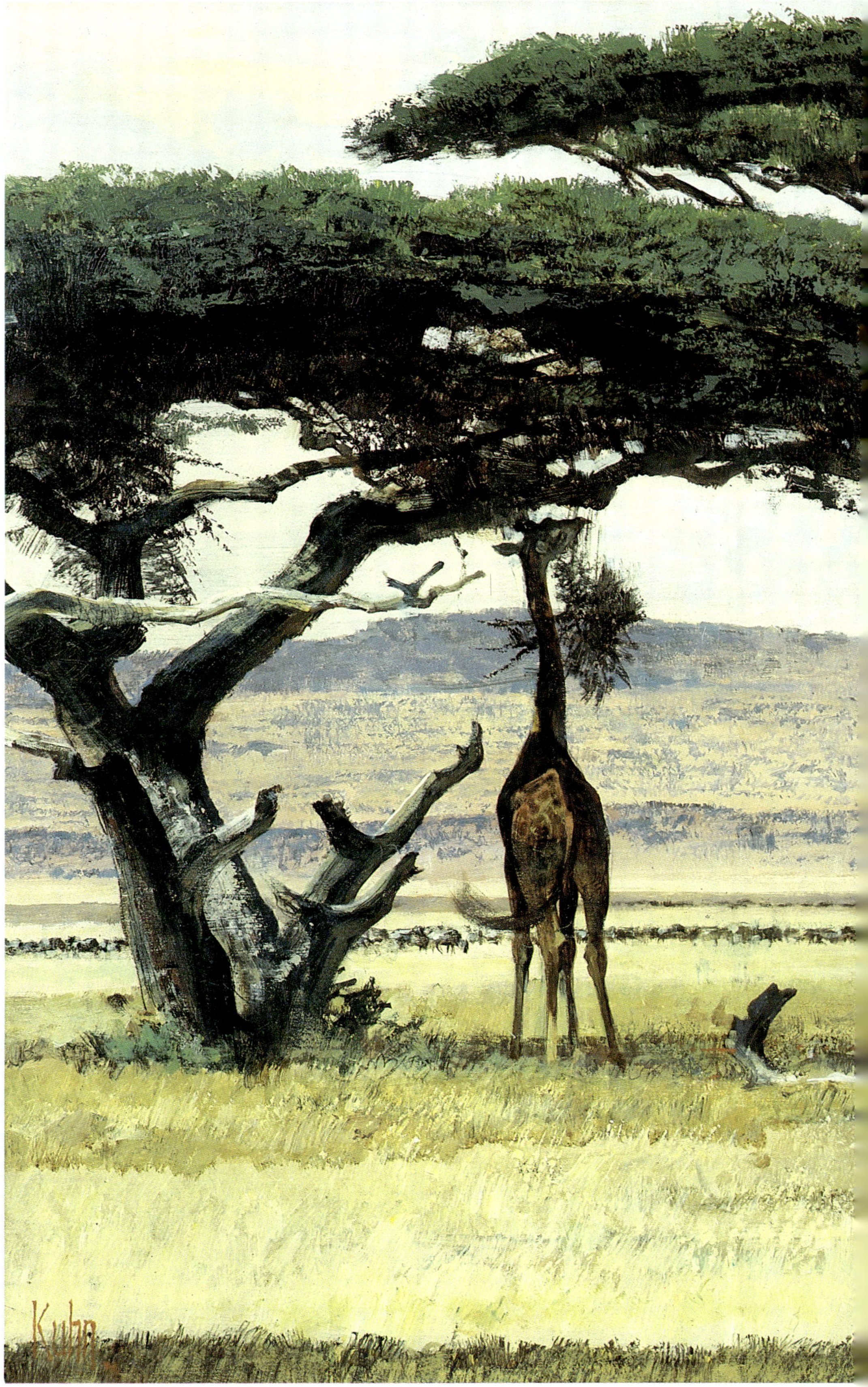

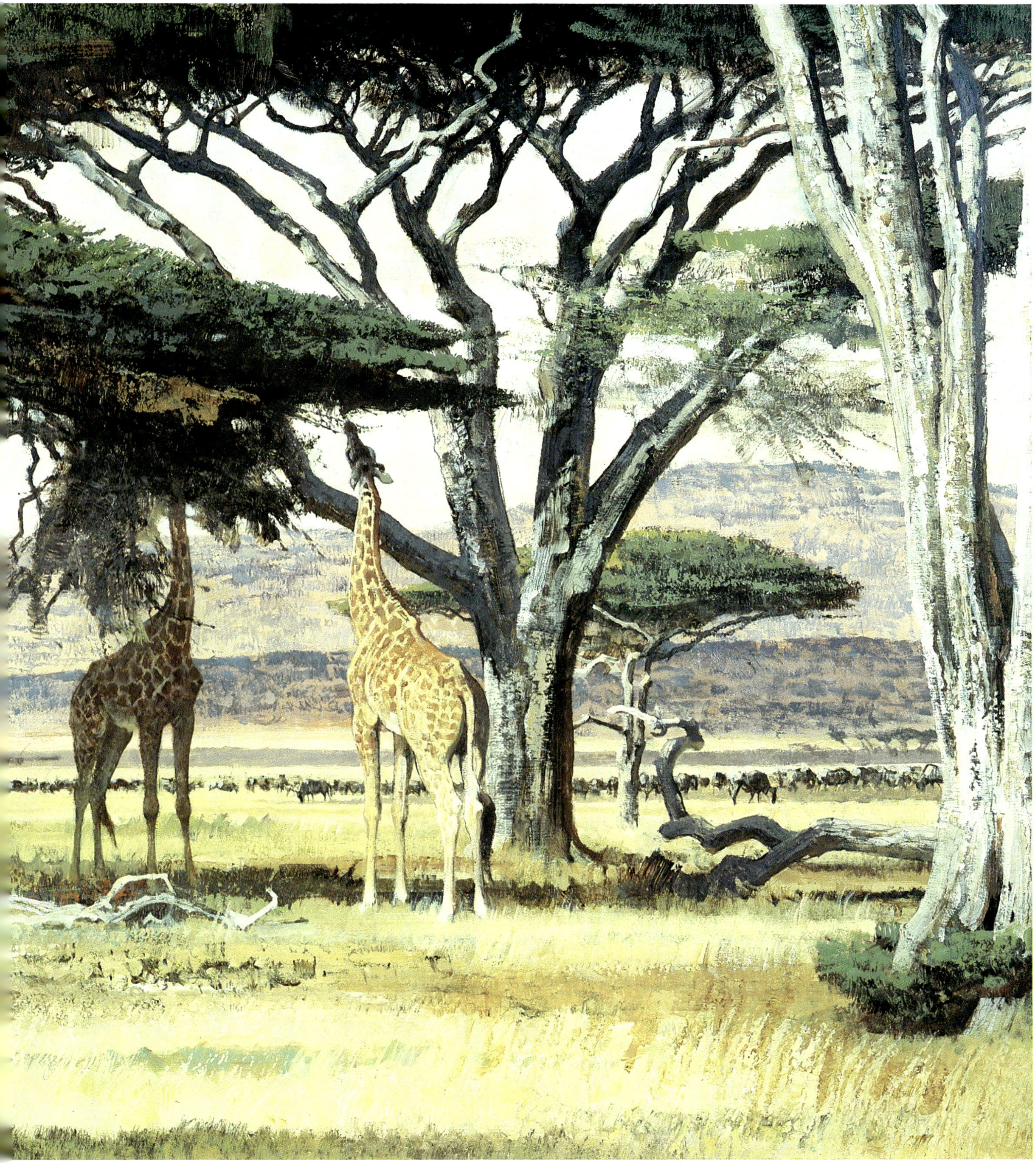

For many, Bob Kuhn is the most accomplished of African wildlife artists, his broad brush strokes and ability to capture movement setting him apart from the more formal, more detailed painters. But here (*left*), with this Serengeti scene of giraffes browsing acacia in the heat of the day, he has produced a painting of great calm. Kuhn was born in Buffalo, New York, in 1920, not making his first visit to Africa (on a hunting safari) until 1956. According to Tom Davis, writing in *The Art of Bob Kuhn*, "nothing prepared Kuhn for Africa. The sheer variety and abundance of animals was staggering . . . the landscape, too, in its shapes, colours and textures, shimmering vistas, and infinite combinations, enthralled him." Not surprisingly, Kuhn has been a regular visitor since then, with safaris that have taken him to most of the great wildlife areas in both eastern and southern Africa. Kuhn remained a professional illustrator until 1969, before finally becoming a full-time painter of wildlife. Many of his most successful paintings have an African theme.

"EDEN"
Bob Kuhn

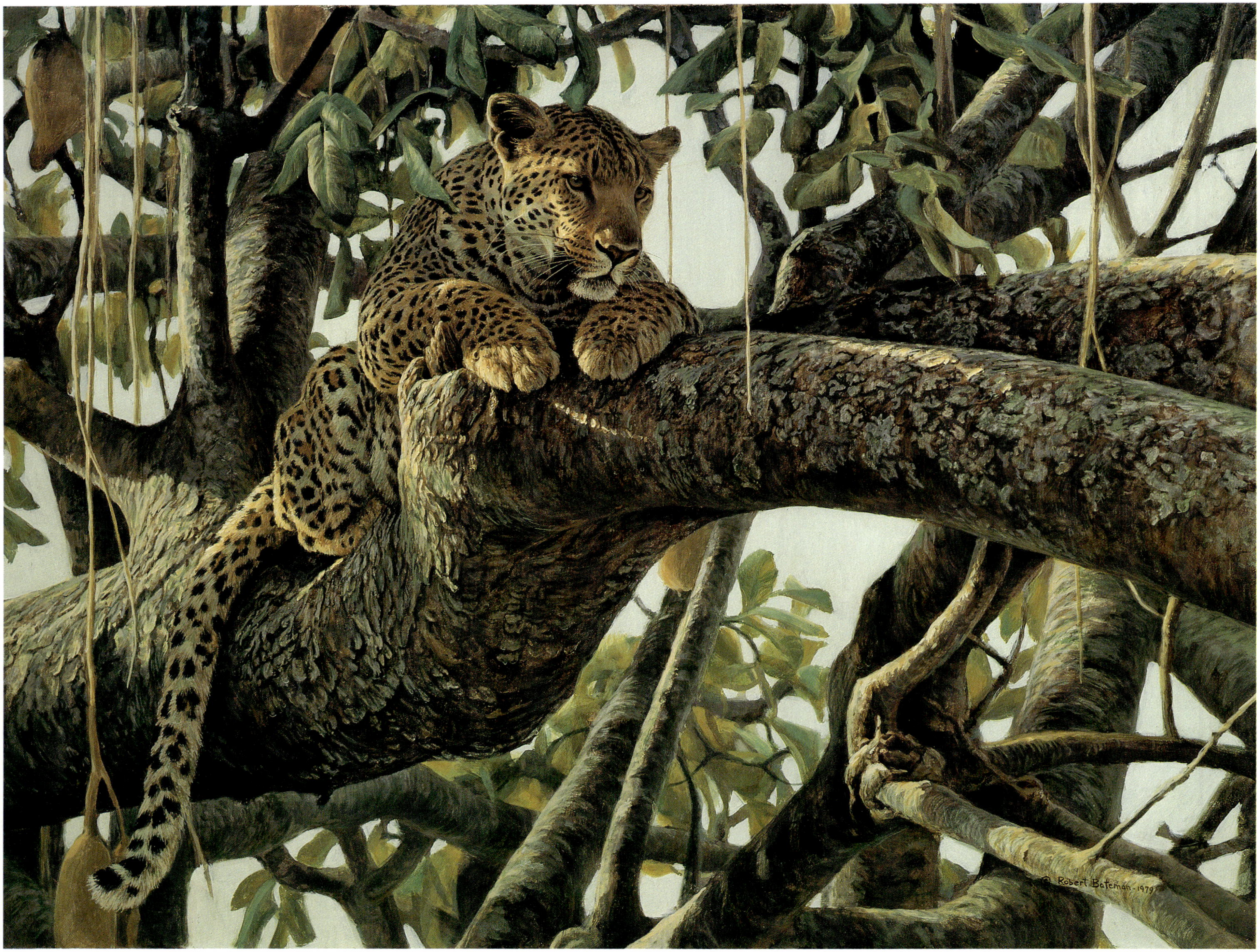

Leopards (*above*) do not like lions, and do their very best to avoid them. If this "Leopard in a Sausage Tree" looks a little put out, it is because he has just been chased up the tree by a lioness with a family of cubs. After showing proper unconcern, the leopard glided through the branches without effort or sound. He instantly blended with the convoluted limbs. The coolness of his attitude in his green, airy world reminded Bateman, in a strange way, of the atmosphere in a tropical café, complete with potted trees and an old ceiling fan . . . exotic and relaxed.

LEOPARD IN A SAUSAGE TREE
Robert Bateman

Africans call the baobab (*right*) the upside-down tree, and it looks just like that. Baobabs can hardly be called beautiful, but their very ugliness gives them real character. Robert Bateman is drawn to "sculptural forms in nature", of which this tree is a classic example. "The trunk of this baobab reminds me of a great castle or a piece of mountainous landscape. The textures are varied and interesting and reflect the events that have taken place in the life of the tree. One of the most common and dramatic events affecting baobabs is an elephant attack. Elephants like the taste of the bark. They hook their tusks under a slab and tear it off with their trunks. This accounts for the large vertical forms in this tree. Elephants sometimes will totally demolish one of these giants, and it collapses in utter ruin."

Bateman has used a little artistic licence with this large (5ft high) painting. He admits to having cropped most of the branches "so that the massiveness could be emphasized. This also has the effect of creating strong and interesting white negative background shapes." The two impala bucks were added to give the painting life, and also to give scale to the tree. Blot out the impala and the painting loses much of its impact, but with the impala in place it becomes as fine a study of a baobab as one can imagine.

BAOBAB TREE AND IMPALA
Robert Bateman

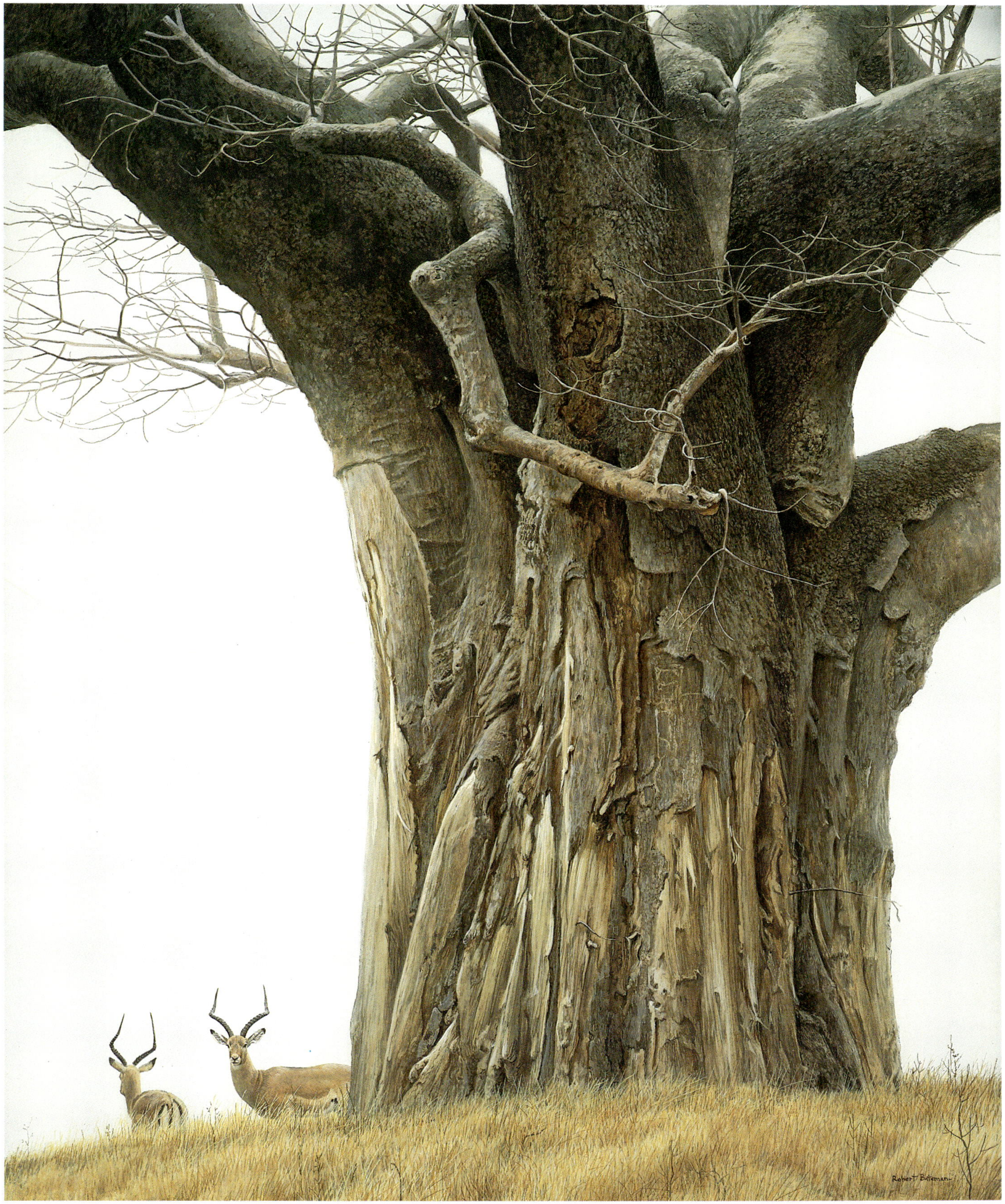

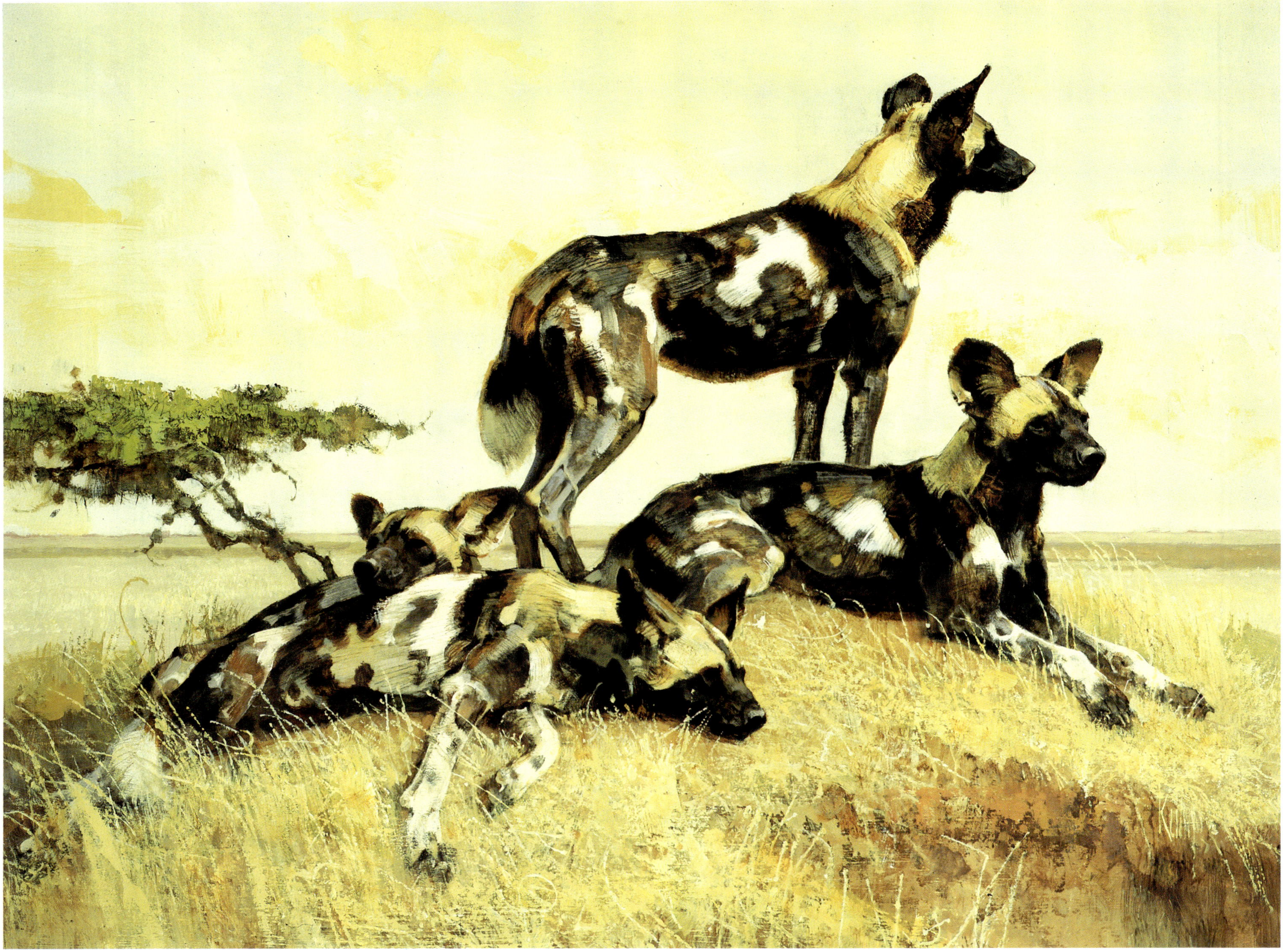

Hunting dogs have long been the most misunderstood of Africa's predators, and as a result are among its most endangered. In this acrylic, Bob Kuhn depicts a small pack in the late afternoon. Like lions, hunting dogs spend much of the day asleep, but they generally like to hunt during the last hour or so of daylight. Following a hunt is a memorable experience: the dogs will stick relentlessly to their chosen prey, before finally running it down by sheer perseverance and endurance. A kill I once watched in Kenya's Masai Mara was typical. The large pack of 22 dogs pulled down a young wildebeest: 20 minutes later just a skeleton and a few scraps of hide were left.

This painting was, so Bob Kuhn recalls, "the result of an unexpected photo opportunity – when you locate a bunch of dogs, it's usually an accident since there aren't many left and the country they range over is vast". Kuhn felt the painting turned out well, "but it took me a long time to sell, the dogs' unsavoury reputation having accompanied them to their penultimate destination on the wall of my New York gallery". Recent studies of hunting dogs have shown them in a new light, and some safari cognoscenti rate these attractively coloured animals as the most fascinating to watch and follow.

HUNTING DOGS RESTING
Bob Kuhn

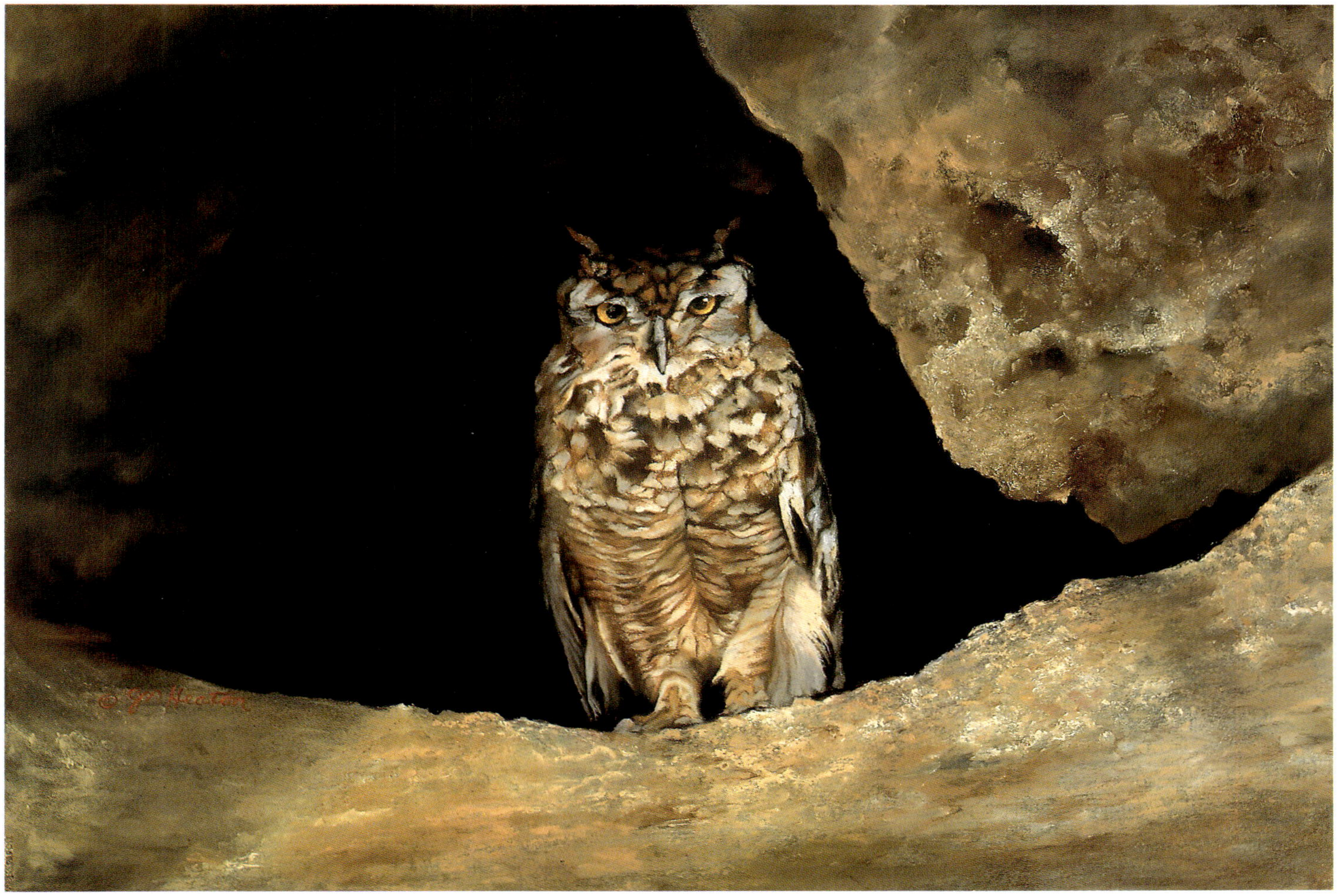

Africa is a great place for owls – my last Kenyan safari produced nine species. One of the commonest is the spotted eagle owl, a bird one not infrequently finds roosting during the day. Janet Heaton encountered this individual in the Ngorongoro Crater in Tanzania. She had followed a group of five lionesses into a rocky area in order to photograph them, and chanced upon a small cave. "Our curiosity was aroused by some movement, and slowly the female spotted eagle owl presented herself – first the fluffy ears and piercing eyes, and then the full body."

SPOTTED EAGLE OWL
Janet Heaton

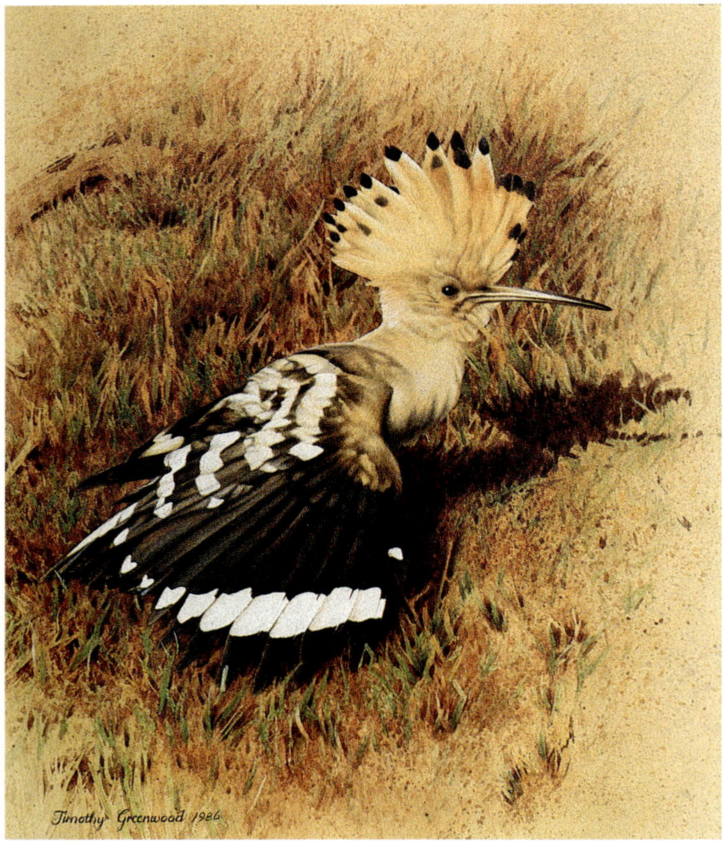

East Africa can offer what is arguably the finest birdwatching of anywhere in the world, yet so many safari-goers overlook the birds in their enthusiasm to see big game. However, the showy hoopoe (*above*) is one bird that few people ignore: Timothy Greenwood's delicate watercolour depicts a sunbathing European hoopoe. The European hoopoe is a sub-species of the widespread African hoopoe, and a common winter visitor to East Africa. European birds are generally much paler than the African residents, but their behaviour is just the same, spending much of their time foraging on the ground for insect larvae or perhaps the occasional lizard.

HOOPOE SUNBATHING
Timothy Greenwood

You have to look twice at this painting (*right*) to make sure that it is not a photograph. The sharpness of the animals, the out-of-focus background, suggest perhaps a Nikkon 400mm, f5.6 at 250th of a second. Photographic this painting may be, but this in no way lessens one's admiration for Combes' skill with his brush. The artist has the advantage over the photographer in that he can position his animals exactly as he wants them, and choose the lighting and the background. What is more, the artist can turn a mere portrait into a serious study. What is it that has caught the attention of this trio, and which they are staring at so intently? The flattened ears suggest that they are ill at ease, they have been disturbed while at rest, and are uncertain whether to flee. When this painting, a 2ft by 3ft oil, was exhibited in California, the catalogue described it as a "split-second tabloid of elegant tension" – one does want to know what happens next.

STUDY IN CONCENTRATION
Simon Combes

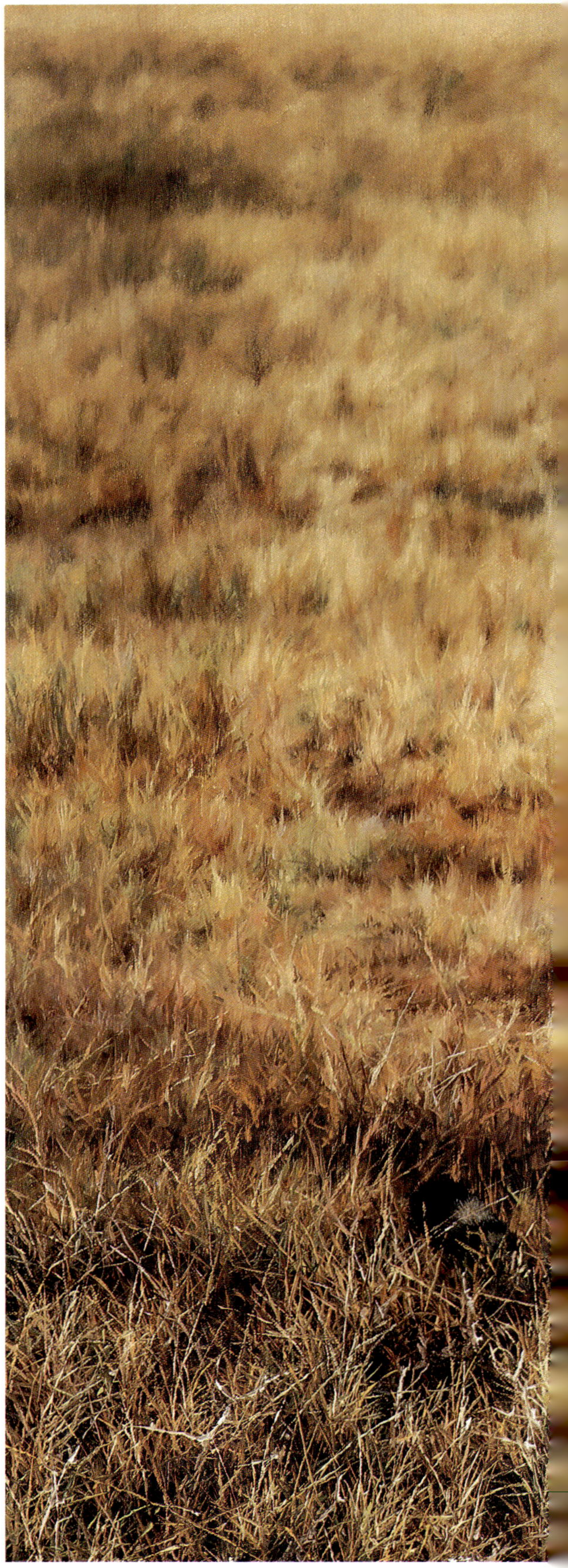

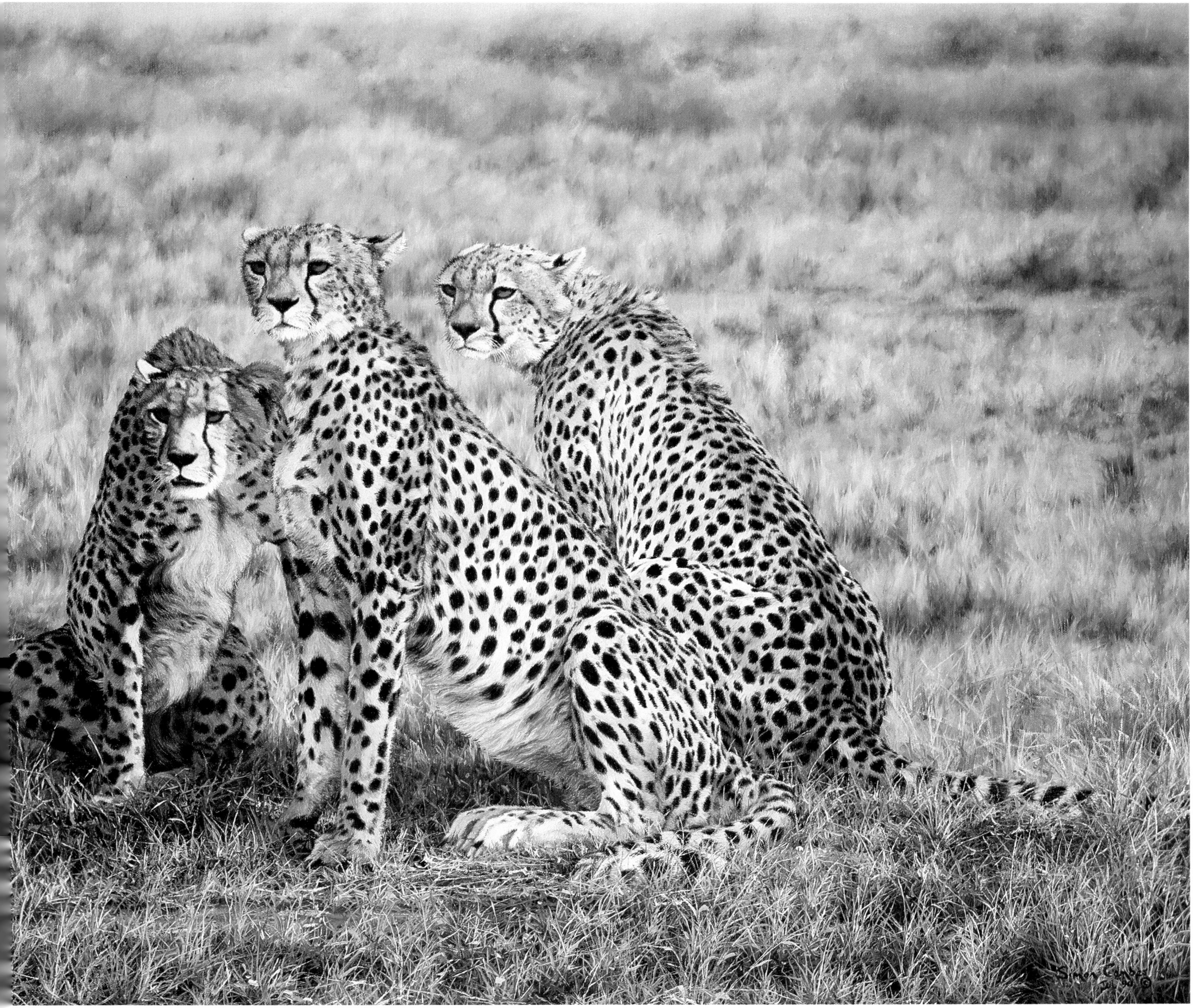

A tree on the banks of the Sabi River in South Africa's Kruger National Park provides the setting for this pastel. Leopards tend to spend a great deal of time in trees, especially in wooded areas, away from rocky outcrops or cliffs. Finding them can be extremely difficult, for unless the animal stands up and moves, as this individual is doing, it can be almost invisible. One suspects that for every leopard you see in a tree, you have driven past three or four more. However, they often forget about their tail, and it is usually the dangling tail that reveals its owner.

Leopards are the most successful and adaptable of Africa's big cats, and partly as a result of this they are also the hardest to find. You can spend weeks in the bush without gaining as much as a glimpse, even though you may hear their deep, rasping call, like a two-man saw biting into the wood, at night.

LEOPARD IN A TREE
Dino Paravano

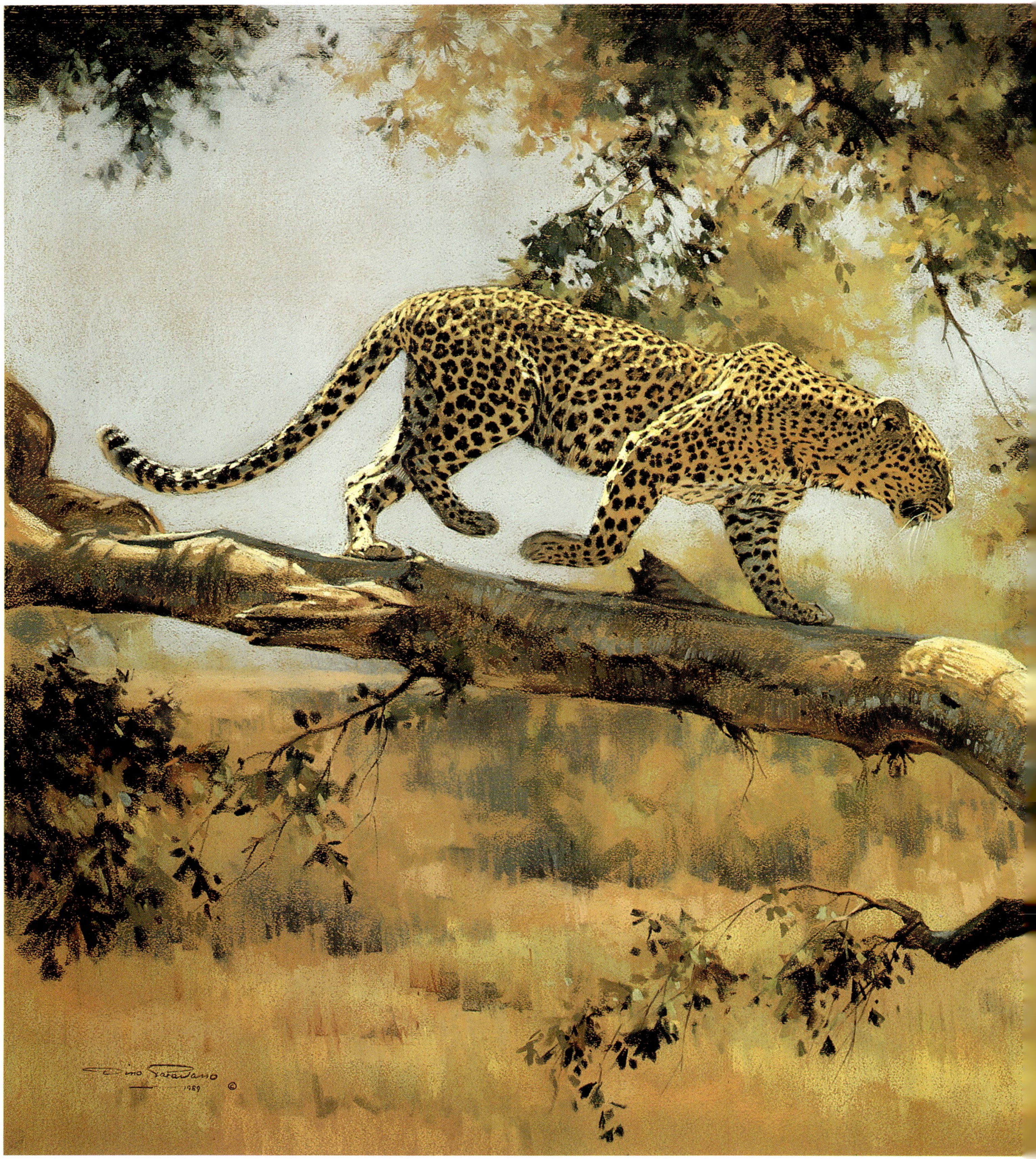

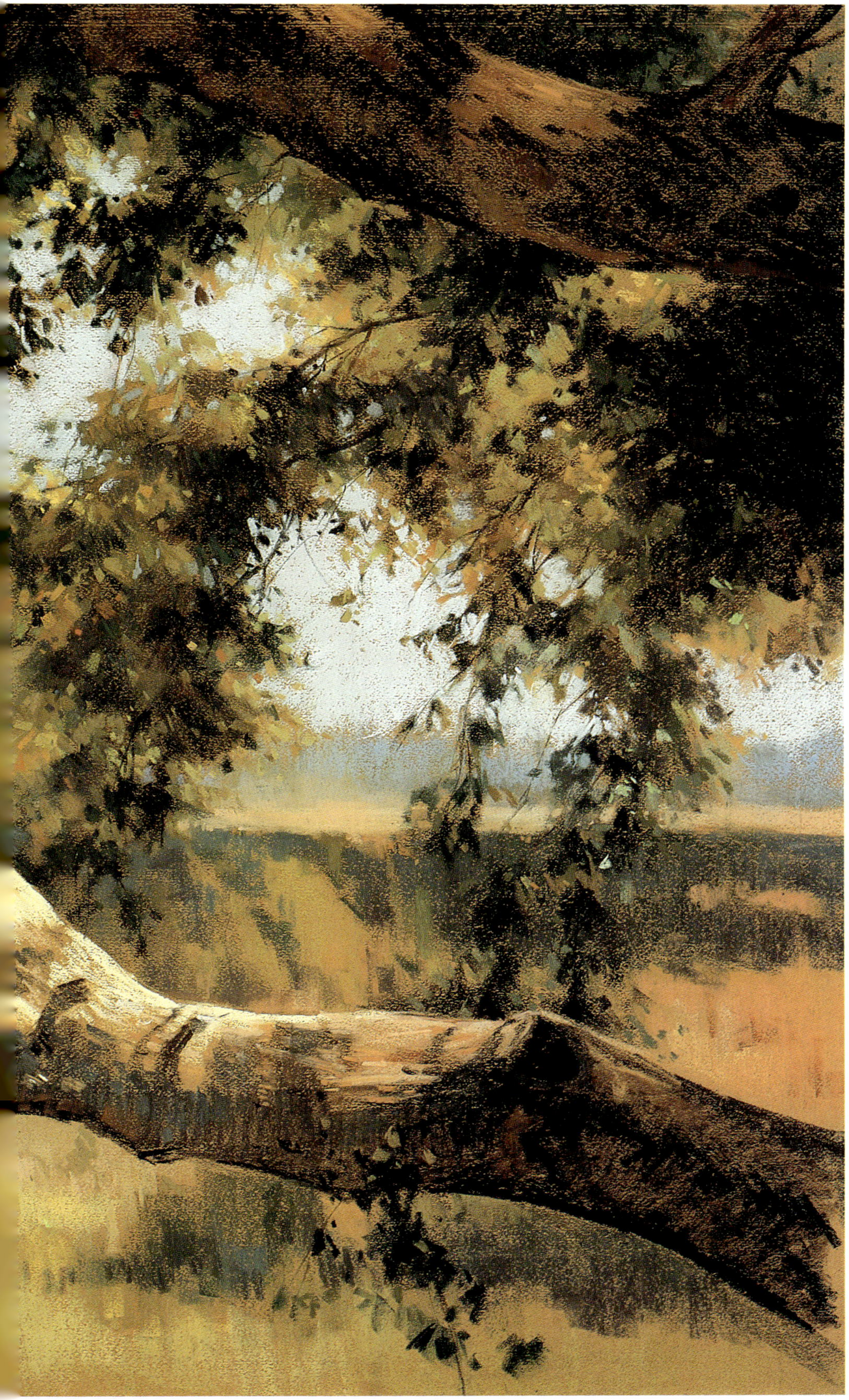

WHITE-THROATED ROBINS
Ingrid Weiersbye

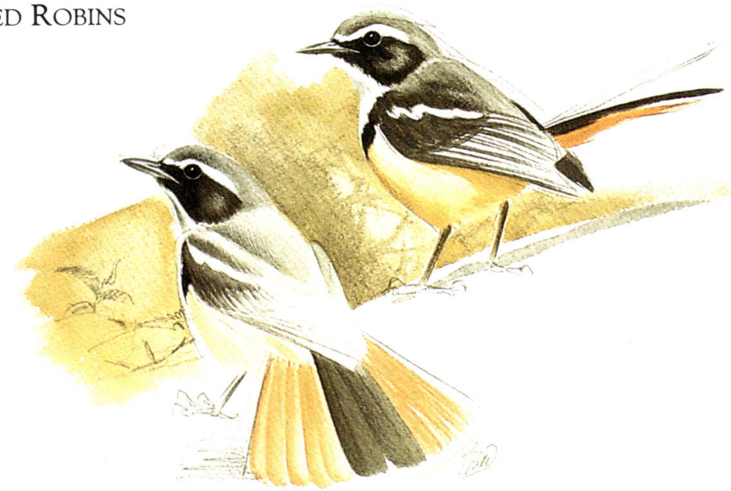

Impala are the commonest of the savanna antelope, and are invariably found in small groups, as they are very social. During the dry season the groups join together, forming sizeable herds. Though they can survive for long periods on dew, they are heavily dependent on water, and here Dino Paravano has portrayed two old does and three younger animals coming down to the water hole to drink. The contrast between the light and shadow, and the golden quality of the sunlight, suggests that this is a late afternoon scene.

While the youngsters drink, the two old does watch warily, for they are specially vulnerable to predators while at the water hole. It is interesting to note that impala are not renowned for their sense of smell, which appears to be poorly developed, but their eyesight is exceptionally sharp. Their chief defence against predators is flight, for they are very fast, and are among the champion jumpers of the animal world, able to leap 10ft high, or cover 30ft, with consummate ease. Such abilities are important for survival, as they are the favourite prey of leopards, cheetahs and hunting dogs.

IMPALA IN LATE AFTERNOON
Dino Paravano

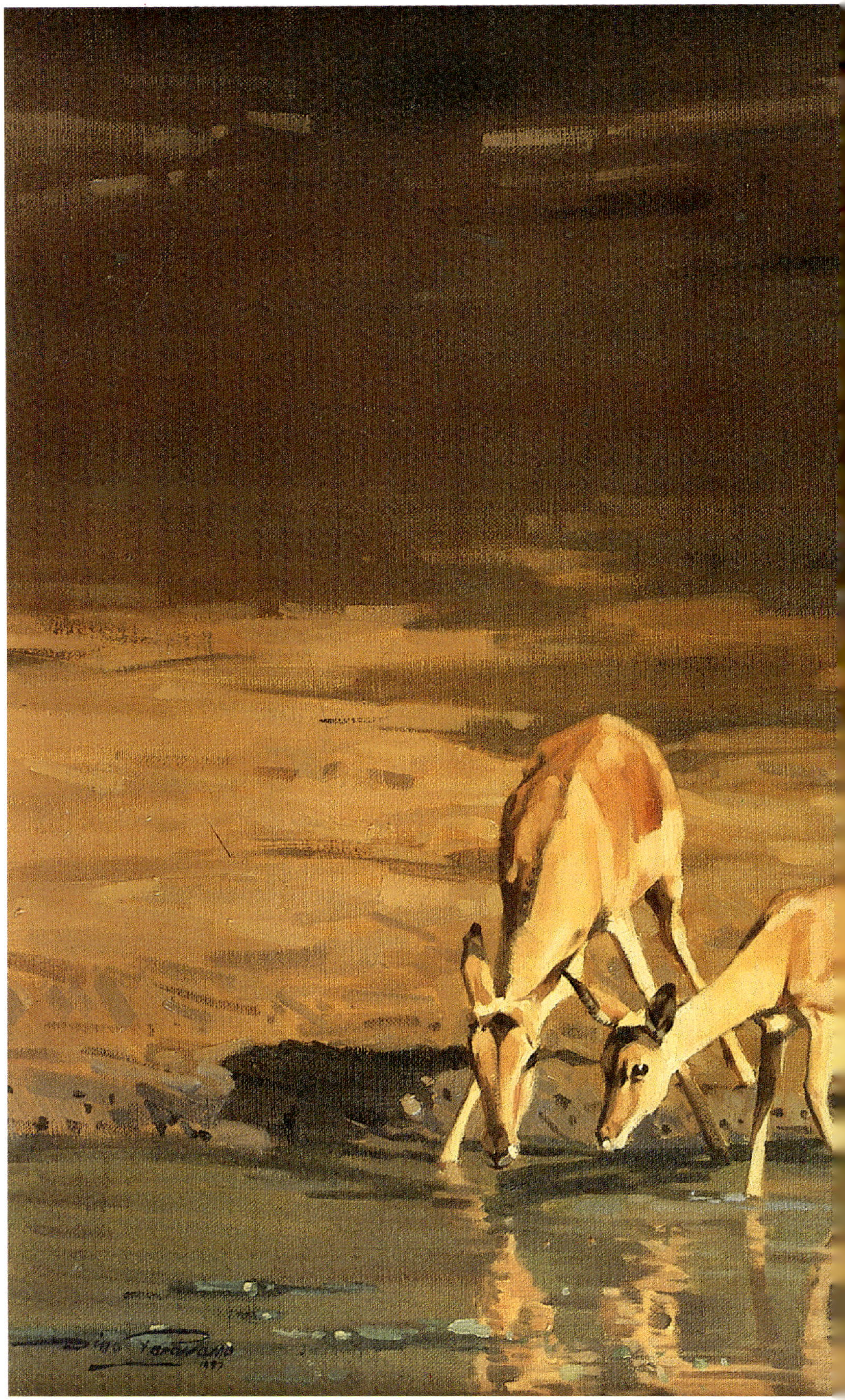

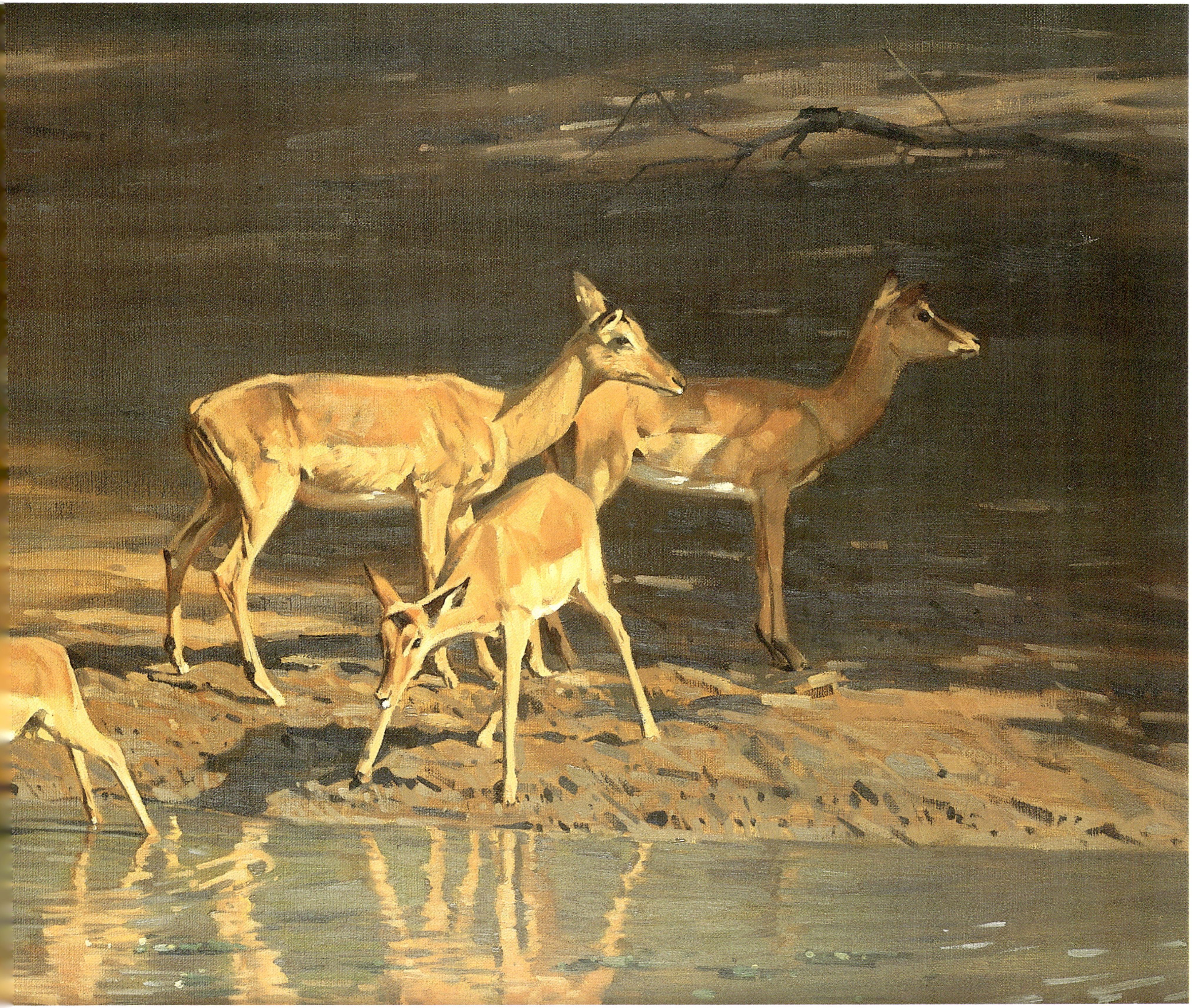

34

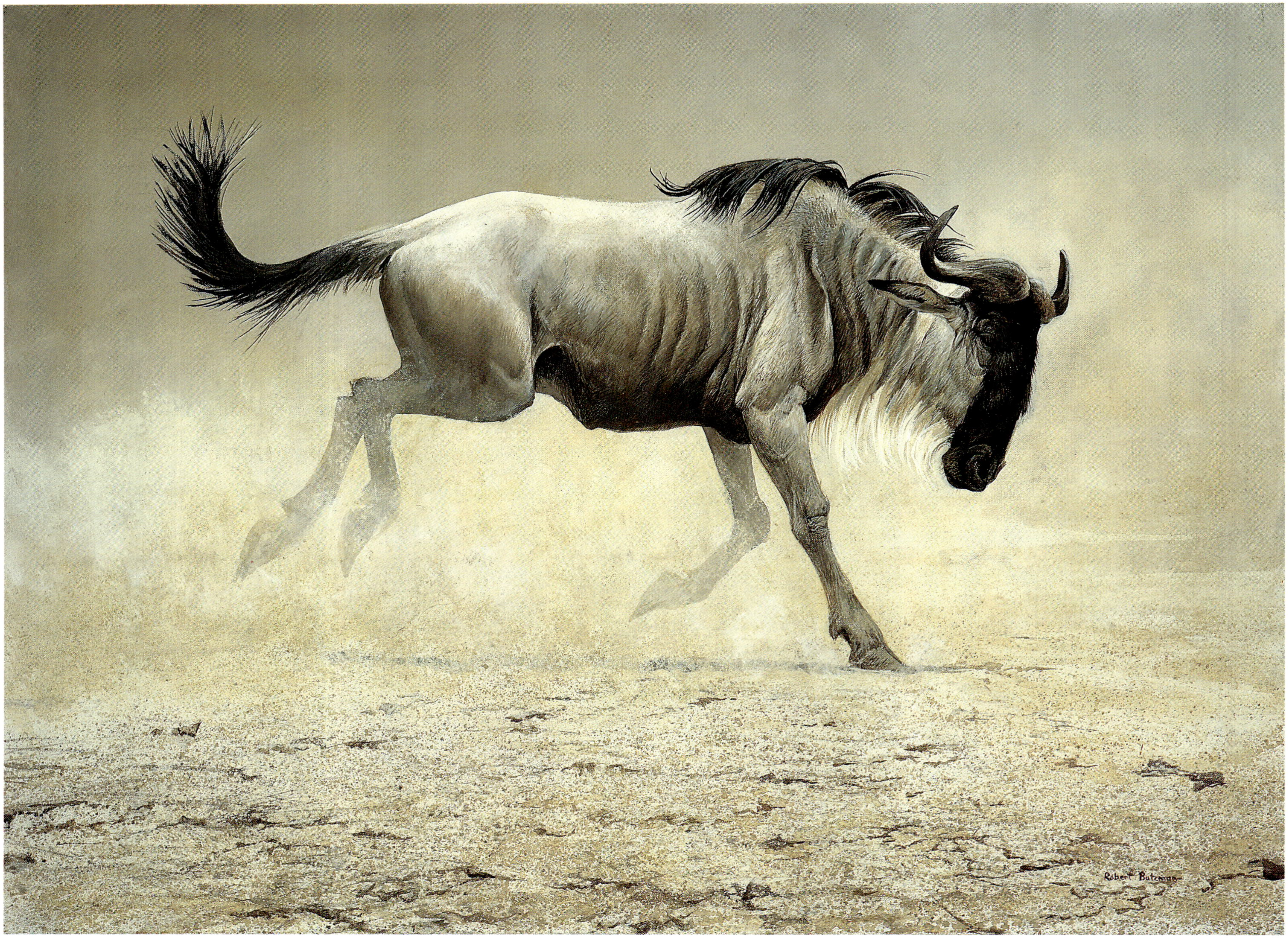

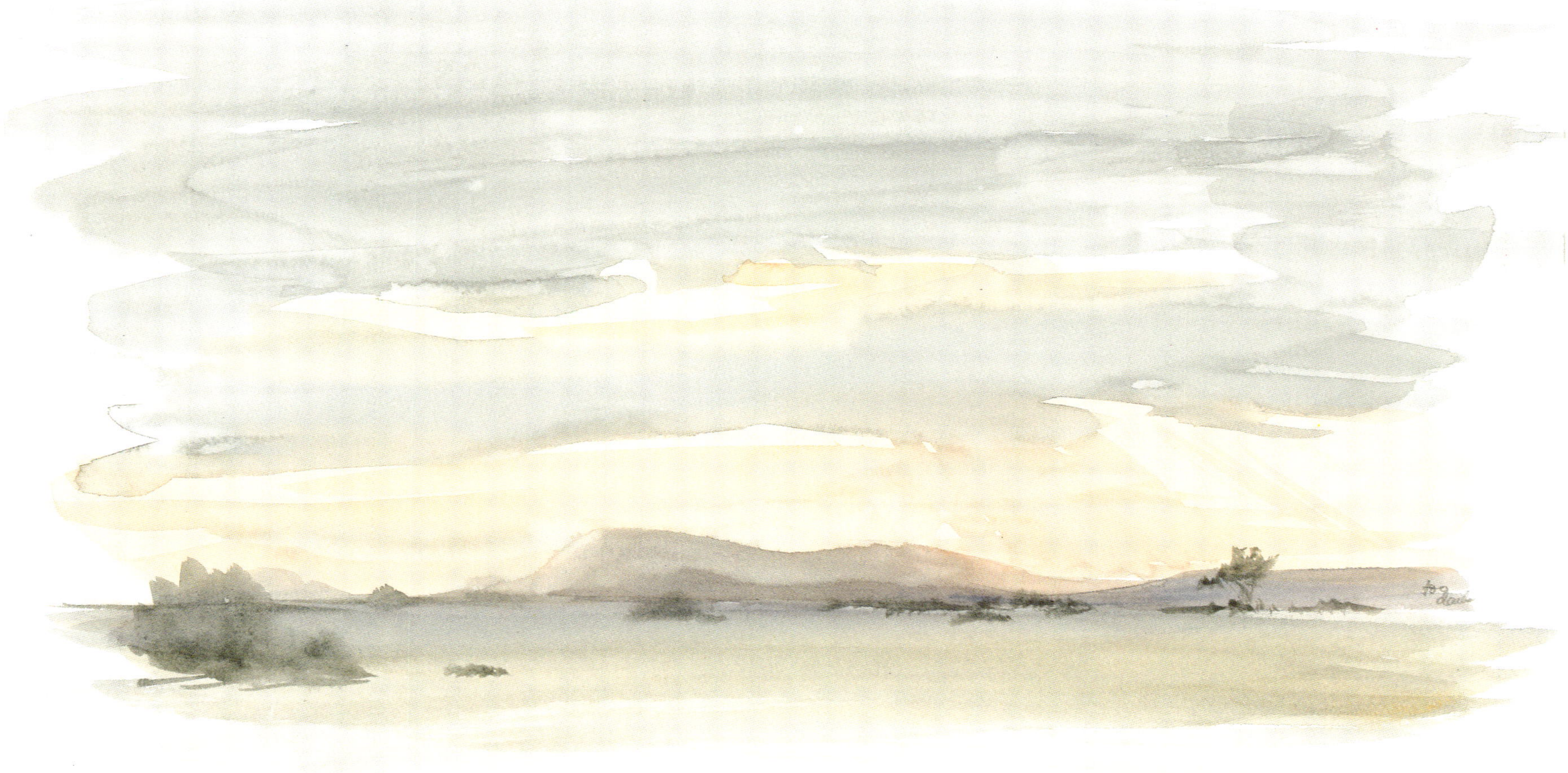

AMBOSELI
Rena Fennesey

Wildebeest (*left*), or brindled gnus, are the most extraordinary animals. Like the camel, they appear to have been designed by a committee, for not all the parts seem to match. Heavily built and almost ox-like at the front, their rear-quarters are slender and quite disproportionate. Their behaviour can be as unexpected as their looks. As Robert Bateman explains, "their rather freaky appearance is augmented by the fact that they will suddenly break into unexplained gambolling, almost like a bucking bronco".

WILDEBEEST
Robert Bateman

Simon Combes (*overleaf*) painted this sequel to his picture "The Migration" despite having vowed never to paint another wildebeest; for several thousand of them appear in the latter, and for months he was painting wildebeest in his sleep. In this enthralling landscape, one can almost hear the explosive snorting of the excited animals as they plunge down to the Mara River. I like Simon Combes' own explanation of this powerful painting: "I attempted to create a contrast between the struggling, tension-packed chaos on the left bank and the peaceful greenness of new pastures on the right. The inclusion of a stark, dead tree, vultures, marabou storks, swirling dust and the ominous interest of two hungry lions hopefully emphasised the frantic atmosphere on the side of those waiting to cross."

THE CROSSING
Simon Combes

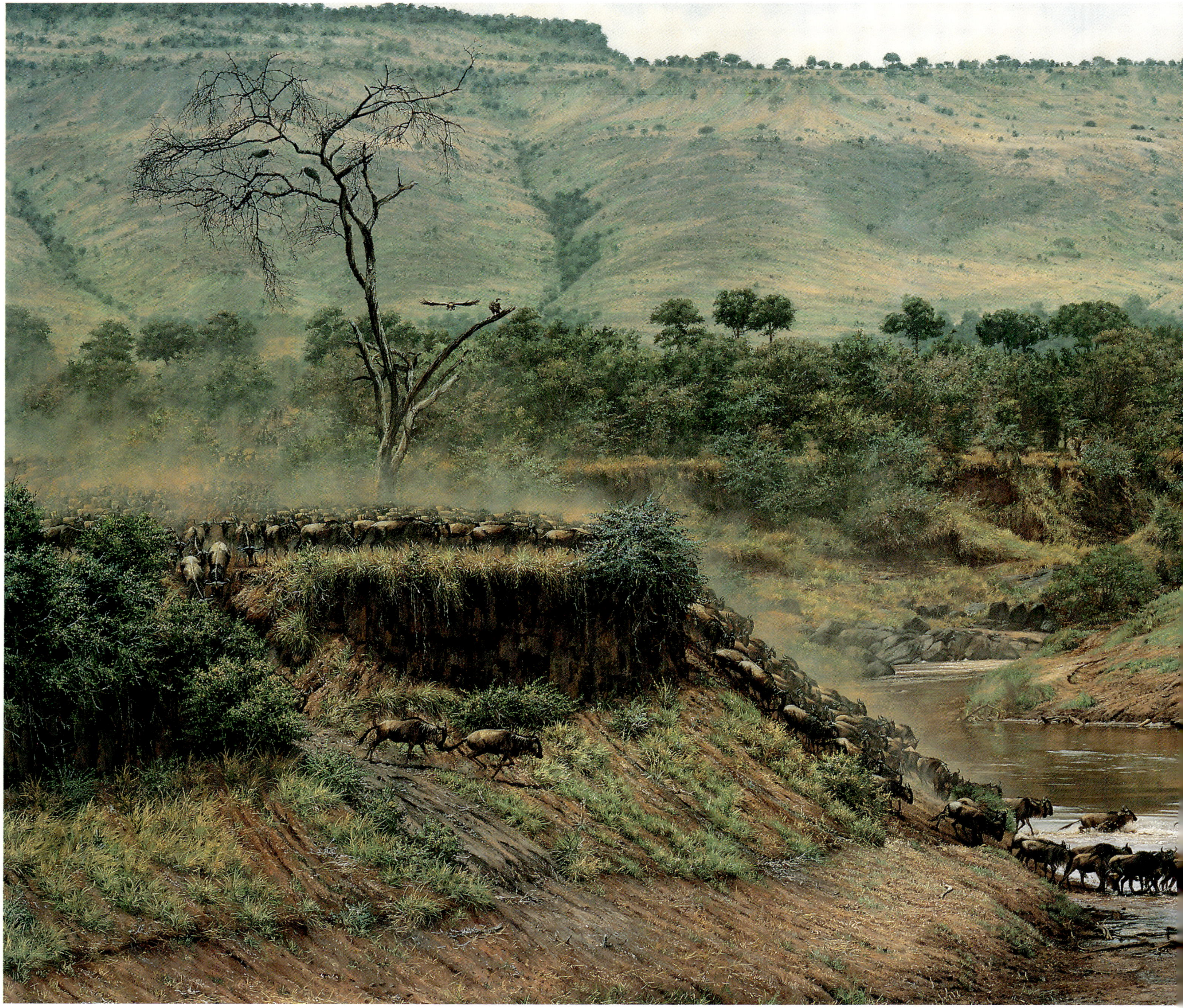

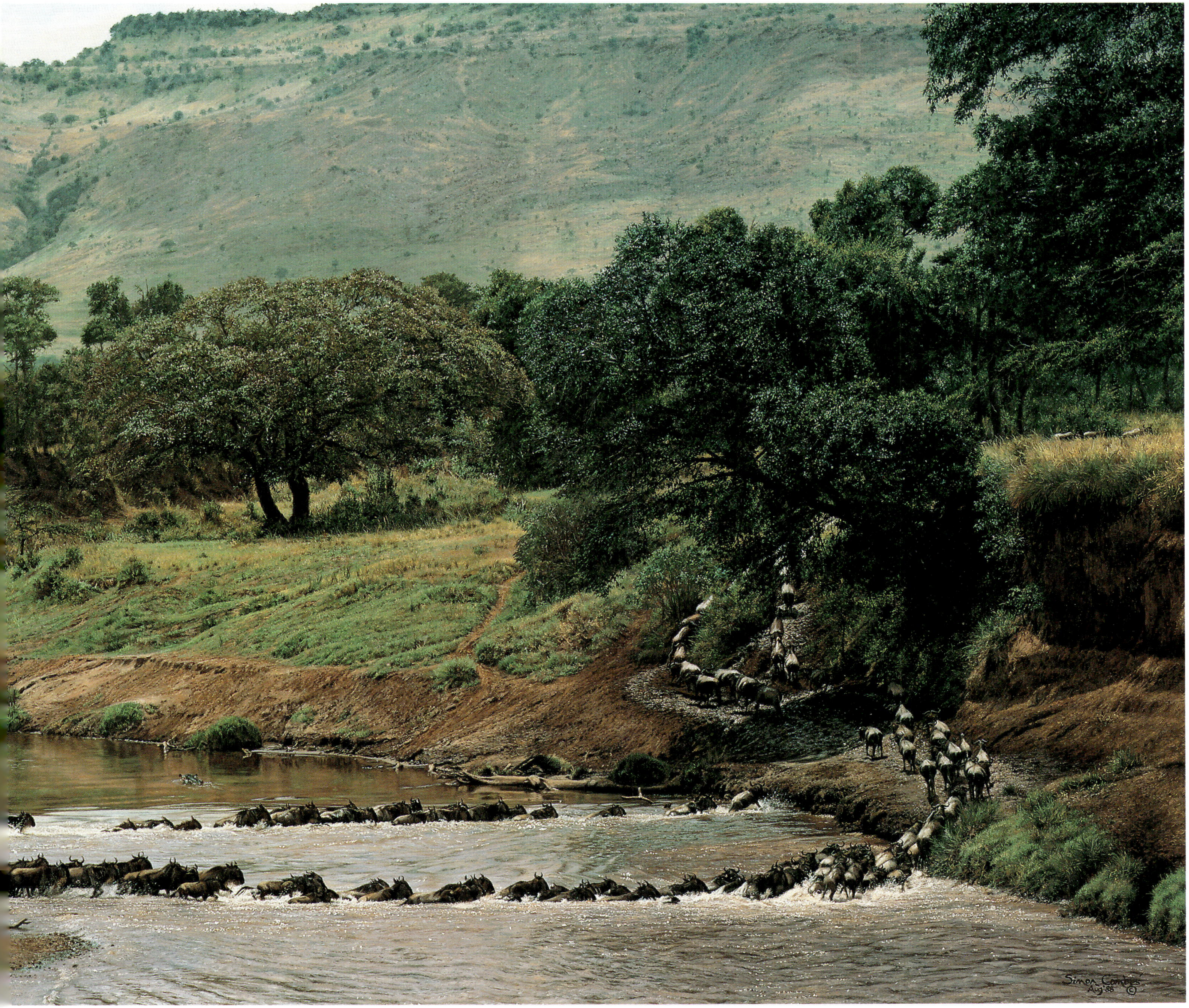

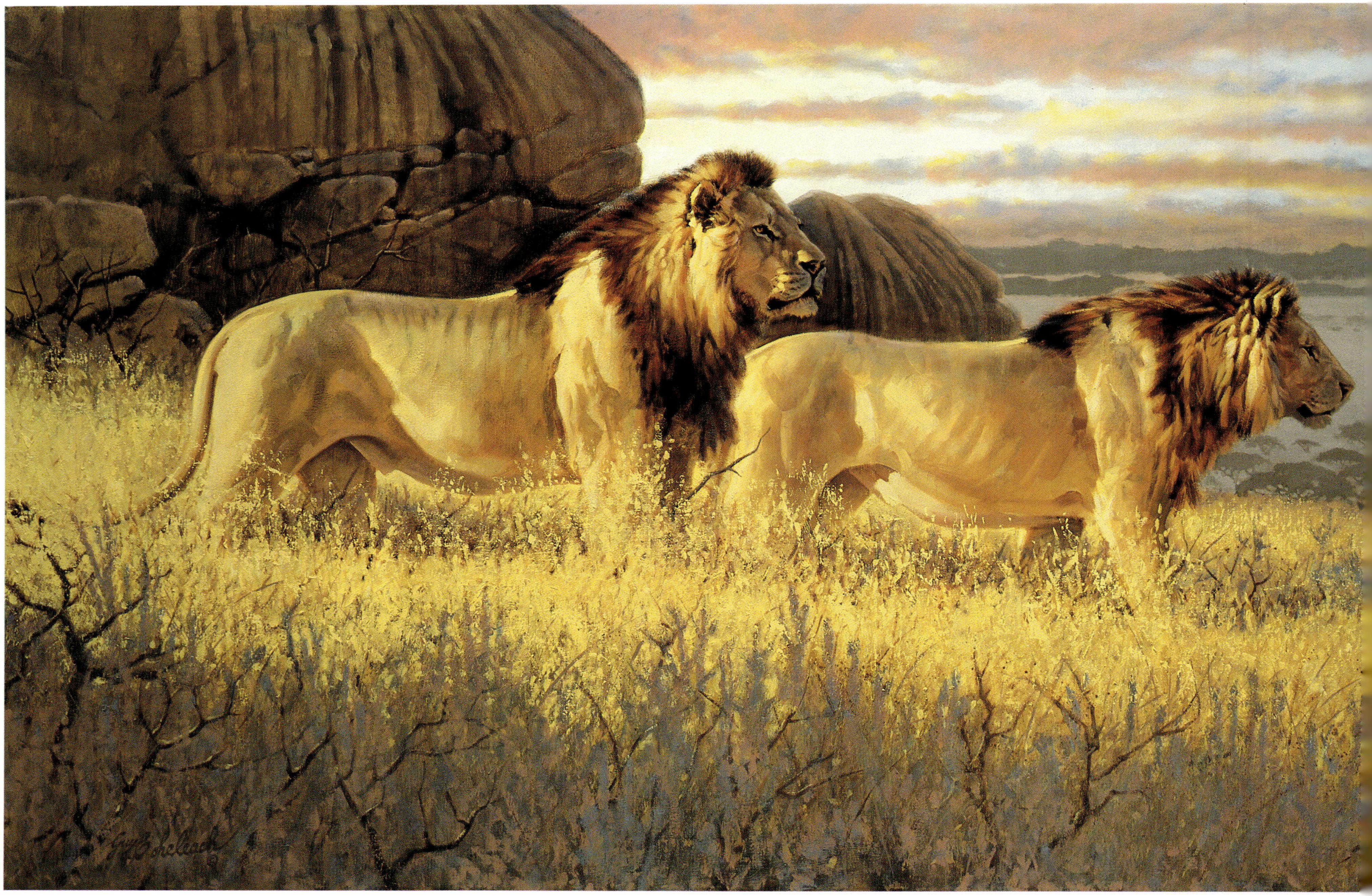

Guy Coheleach made his reputation painting the birds of North America, but his versatility and sheer ability have established him as one of the best known of African wildlife artists. Coheleach admits that "I love painting lions – hell, I love lions! – and particularly black-maned lions. A dark mane adds so much in the way of contrast and drama." This fine study of two black-maned lions proves his point.

Two Lions
Guy Coheleach

One evening in Amboseli Park in Kenya, Robert Bateman saw a big herd of wildebeest drawing together for the night. He was impressed by the mellowness of the mood and by the light and colour – a kind of liquid gold over everything just before the sun set.

Wildebeest tend to be active throughout the day and night, and only in the middle of hot days will they seek shade and rest.

Wildebeest at Sunset
Robert Bateman

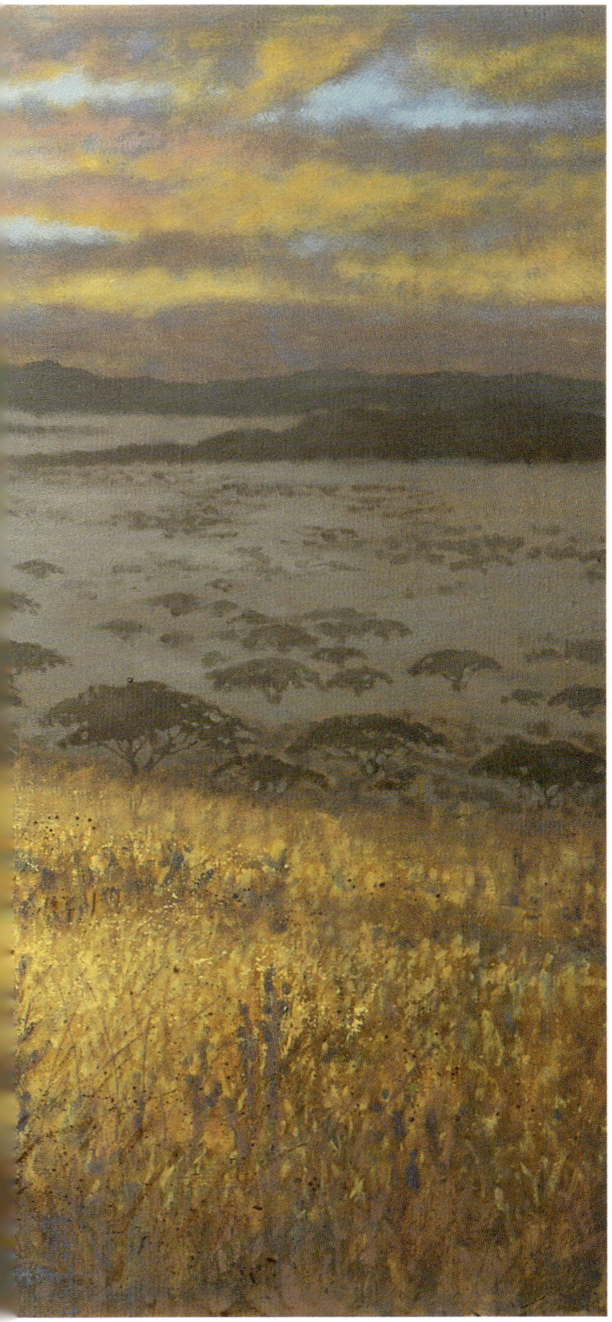

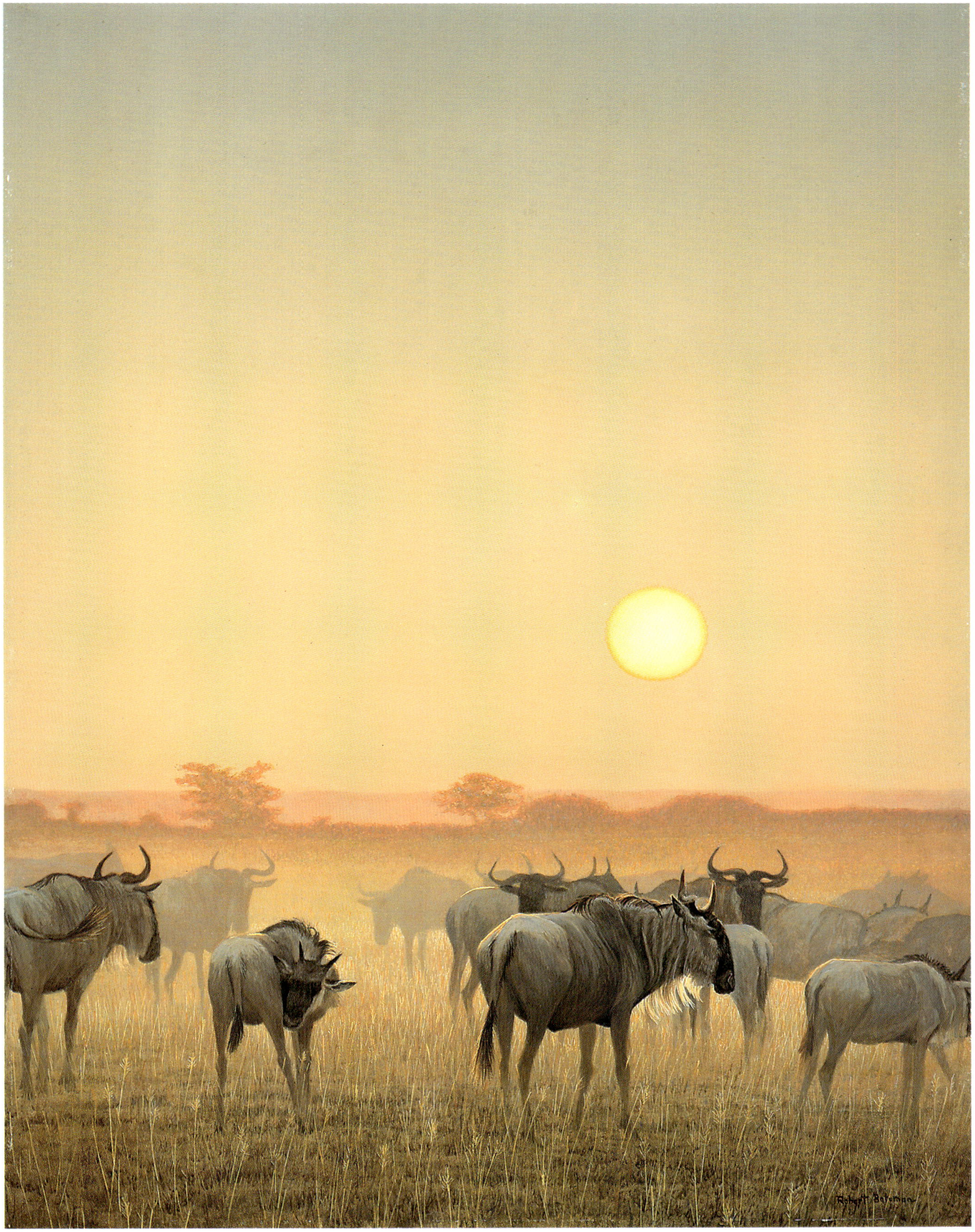

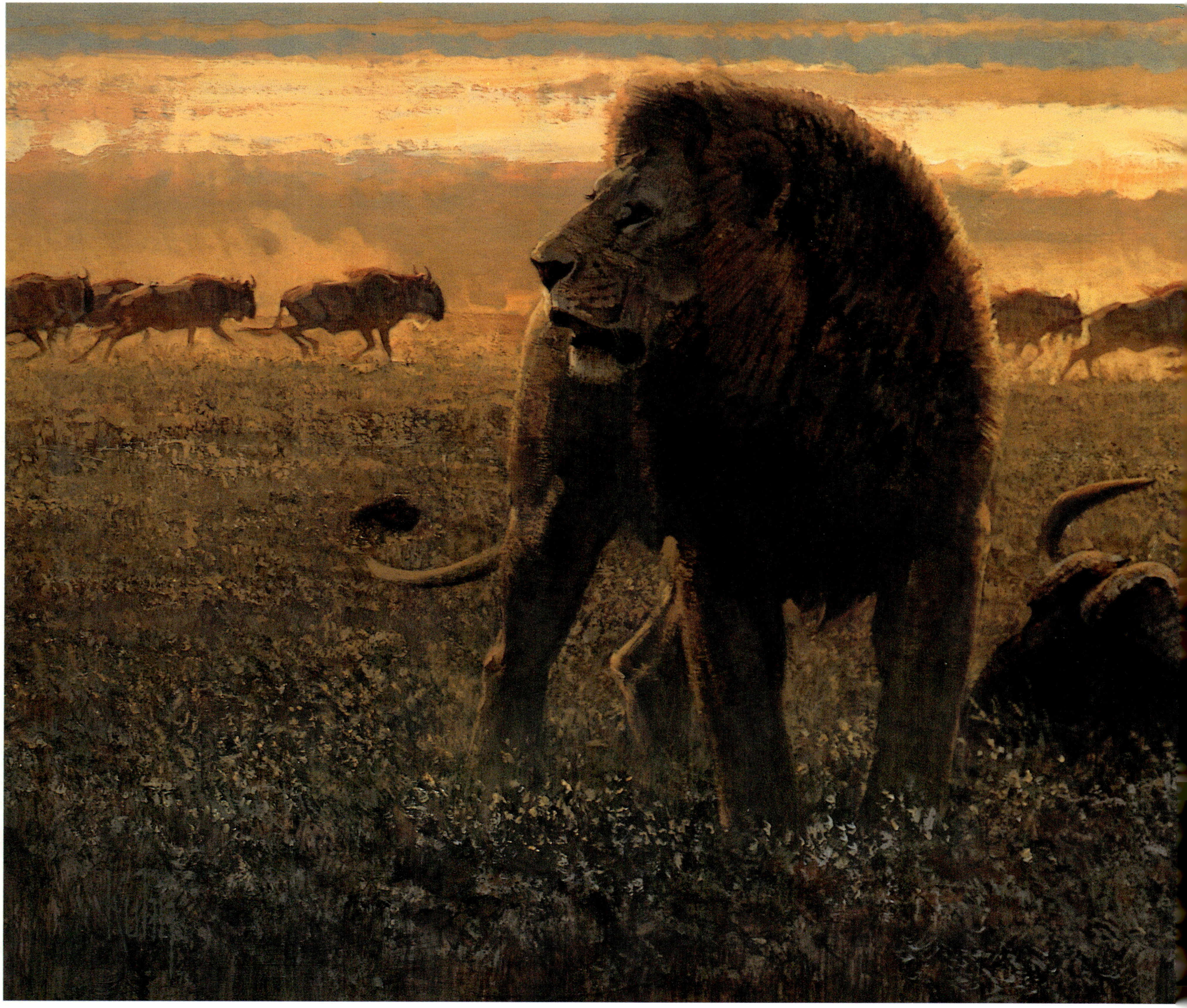

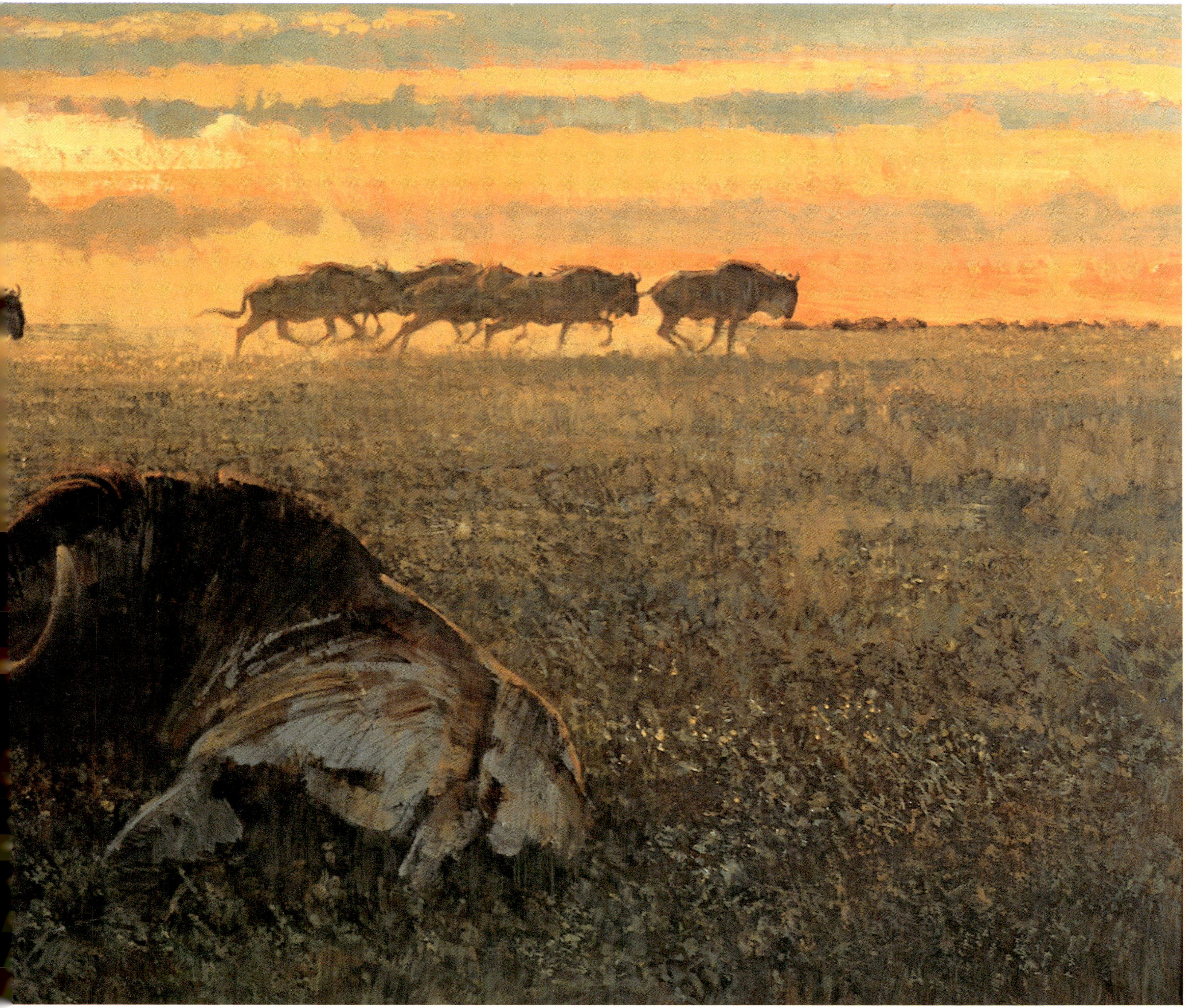

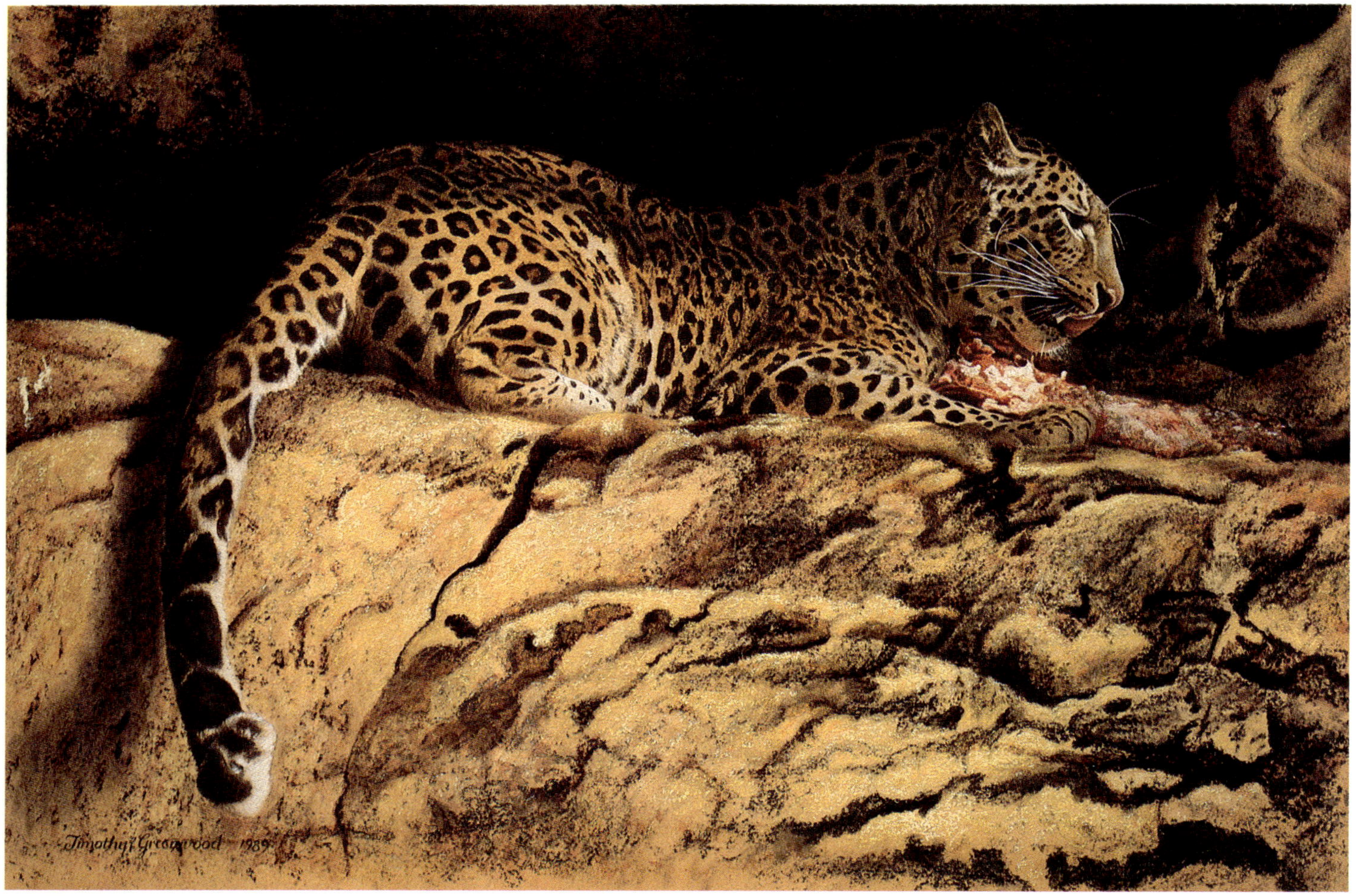

There are a number of artists who have painted African wildlife with rare skill and touch, but for various reasons their work has never become well known. Timothy Greenwood fits into this category. It would be difficult to find a better study of a feeding leopard than this, drawn in crayon and watercolour on coloured paper. Greenwood has been a professional wildlife artist since leaving a London art school in 1986. A passionate traveller, his first love was India and Pakistan, before finally coming to Kenya in 1985. On his first safari leopards totally eluded him, though he had seen them on several occasions in India. The Asian race of the leopard is very similar to its African cousin, although it tends to have larger spots.

LEOPARD ON A ROCK
Timothy Greenwood

Death (*previous page*) may be the only certainty of life, but for a wildebeest the end is likely to be a violent one. Some wildebeest may die of accidents or disease, but the great majority will be killed by predators; none die of old age. Bob Kuhn comments: "The scene portrays two vital aspects of the wild. First, the inevitability of death, and second, the assurance that life will go on. While most wild creatures meet a violent end, including the predators themselves, there are very few neurotics among them. Only man agonizes over these things."

Bob Kuhn admits to an admiration for the work of Wilhelm Kuhnert, and there is a hint of Kuhnert in this moody painting. However, Kuhn points out that as Kuhnert grew older, he developed mannerisms. "One of them was to give lions jowls that drooped forever. Lord knows they have droopy jowls, but there's a limit. . . However, Kuhnert knew how to compose a picture, and he painted with verve and lovely, fresh colours. He truly captured the pulse of Africa." The same can be said of Kuhn's own work.

LION WITH WILDEBEEST
Bob Kuhn

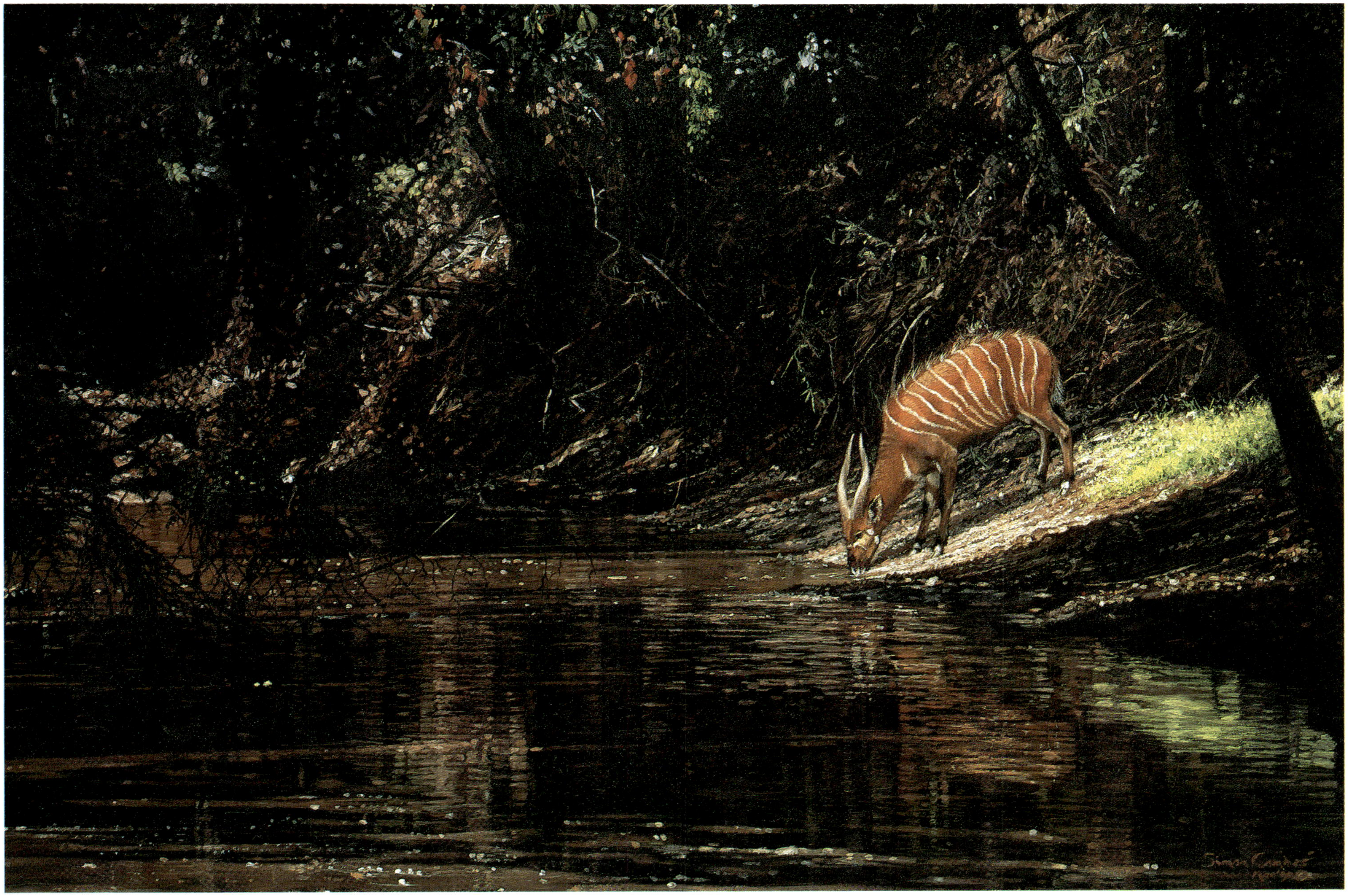

Bongo are the most elusive of African antelope: chiefly nocturnal, they are hard to see due not only to their shyness, but also their liking for dense, impenetrable cover. They are animals of the rainforests of Central and West Africa, occurring in East Africa only in montane areas such as the Aberdares, the setting for this study by Simon Combes. A piercing shaft of sunlight illuminates this old male as he comes down to the water to drink, his bright chestnut-red coat glowing against the darkness of the forest.

This is one of Simon Combes' most successful antelope studies: the animal is small in ratio to the size of the painting, but the skilful use of light ensures that one's eye is drawn straight to the bongo, before slowly absorbing the rest of the picture. An economy of brushwork captures the gloom of the bongo's surroundings.

THE RARE AND BEAUTIFUL BONGO
Simon Combes

Africa is not only blood and thunder, as this delightfully tranquil oil reminds us. The painting captures no more than a fraction of the scene, but Ghaui's words fill in much of the remainder: "The setting is a sand river in Ruaha National Park. From my observation point I can see a huge old tamarind tree that is alive with baboons feeding on its pods. Beneath, on the clean white sand, the younger generation are at play – leaping up into the creepers, swinging and landing on the more serious elders of the group, then escaping just in time.

"Impala are also feeding – picking up the pods that drop down onto the river bed. And all this activity caught by the morning light – its shafts cutting through the gentle haze of mist and dust."

Cooling Off – Impala and Baboon
Michael Ghaui

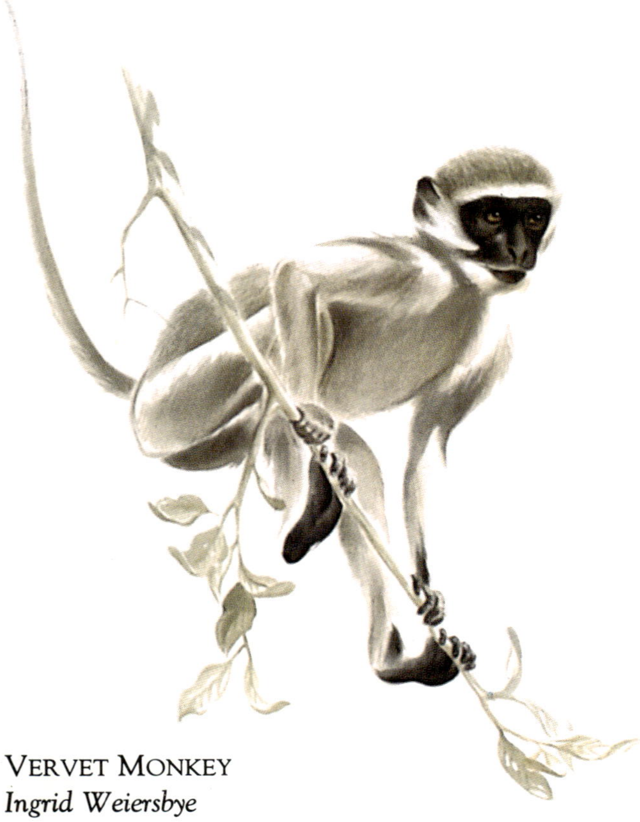

Vervet Monkey
Ingrid Weiersbye

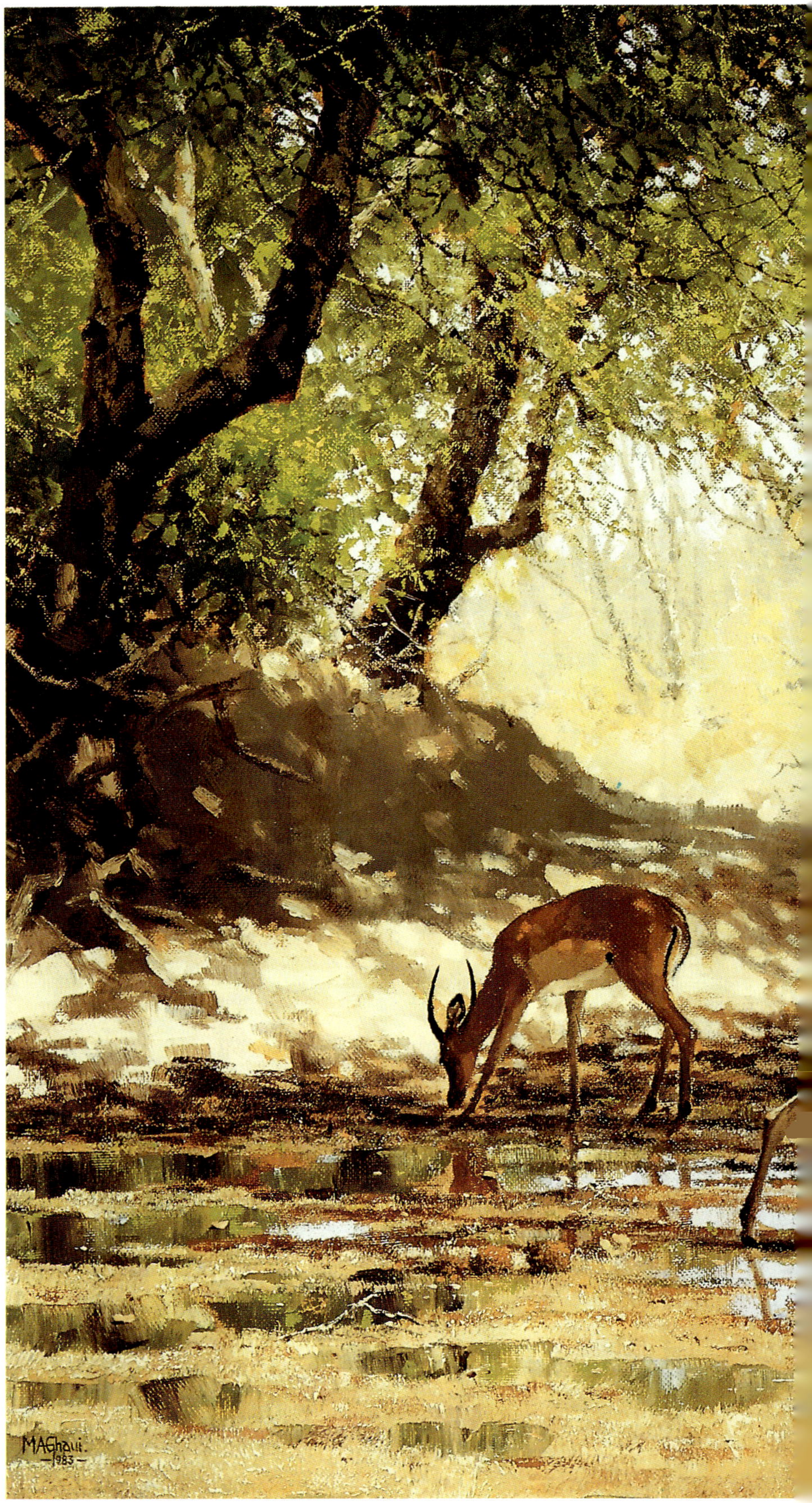

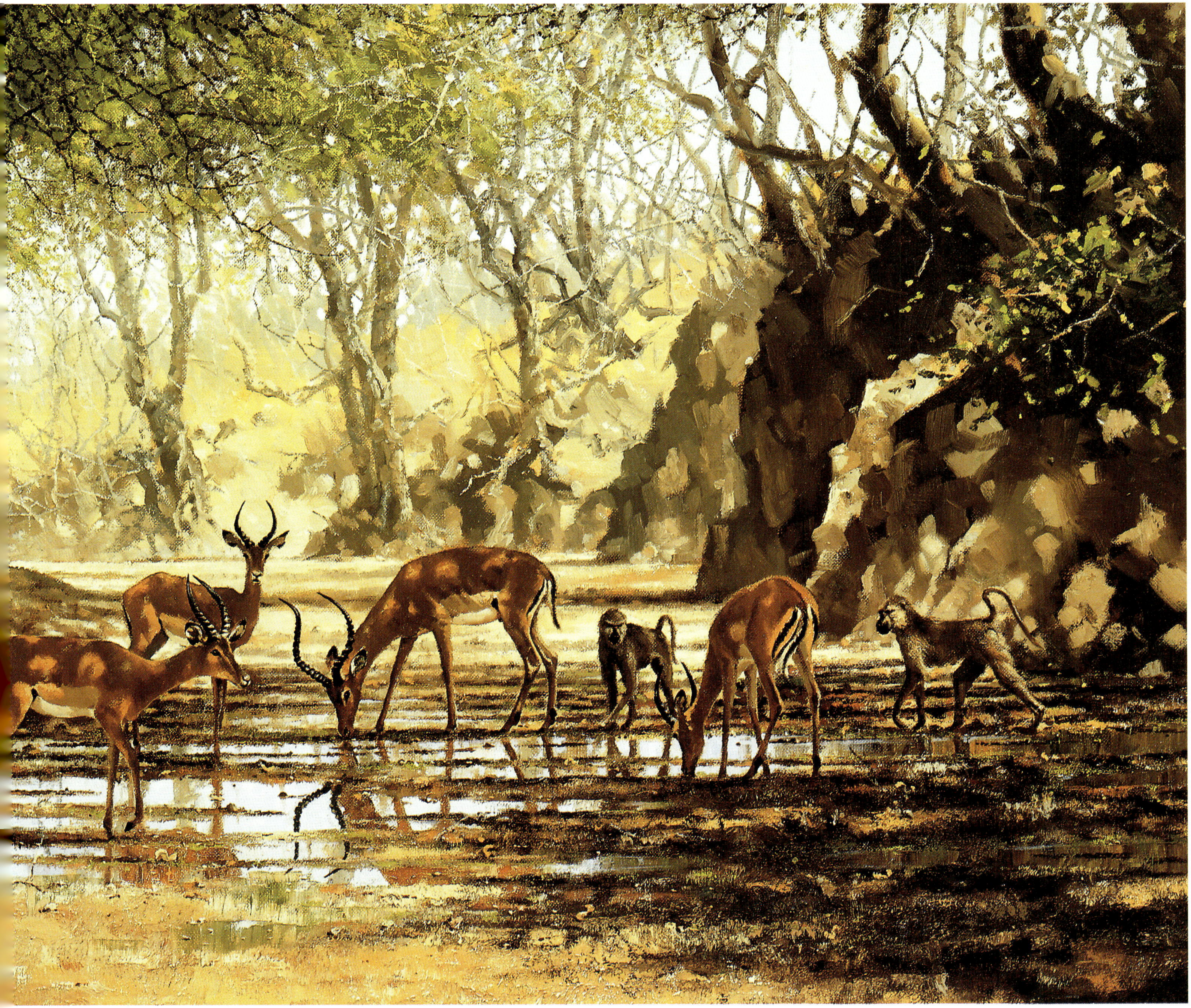

An old bull, disturbed at his favourite water hole, makes a fine subject for Michael Ghaui. "He lifts his head indignantly, flicks his tail and paws the dirt – a snort before he moves off. In this case he crashed off through the bush with his head held high. I have learnt to respect those warning signs, as on other occasions a charge has been imminent."

Unmolested, a buffalo bull is no more dangerous than a Hereford or Aberdeen Angus. But when threatened or wounded, a buffalo is a very serious adversary for the hunter. Wounded buffaloes are reputed to be extraordinarily cunning, and will double back and wait for the hunter, before making an explosive charge at close-range. The great boss of horn is strong enough to turn a bullet from a high-velocity rifle, so stopping a charging buff is far more difficult than halting a lion.

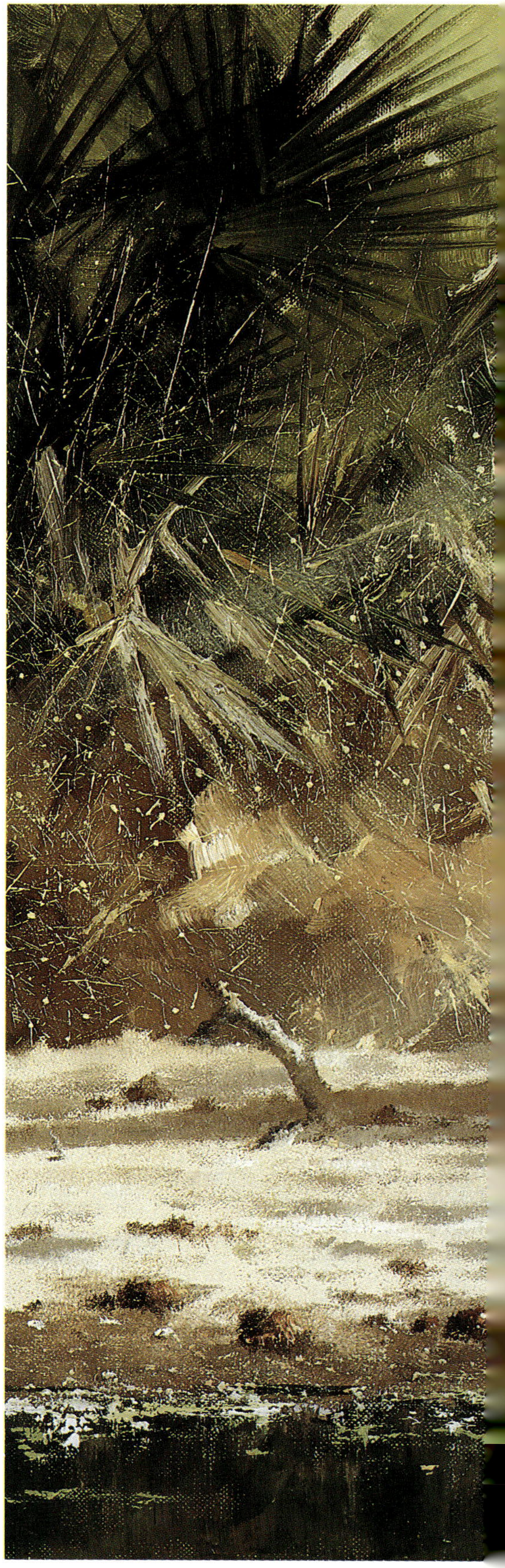

MEAN BUFF
Michael Ghaui

TWO OLD BUFFALO BULLS
Donald Grant

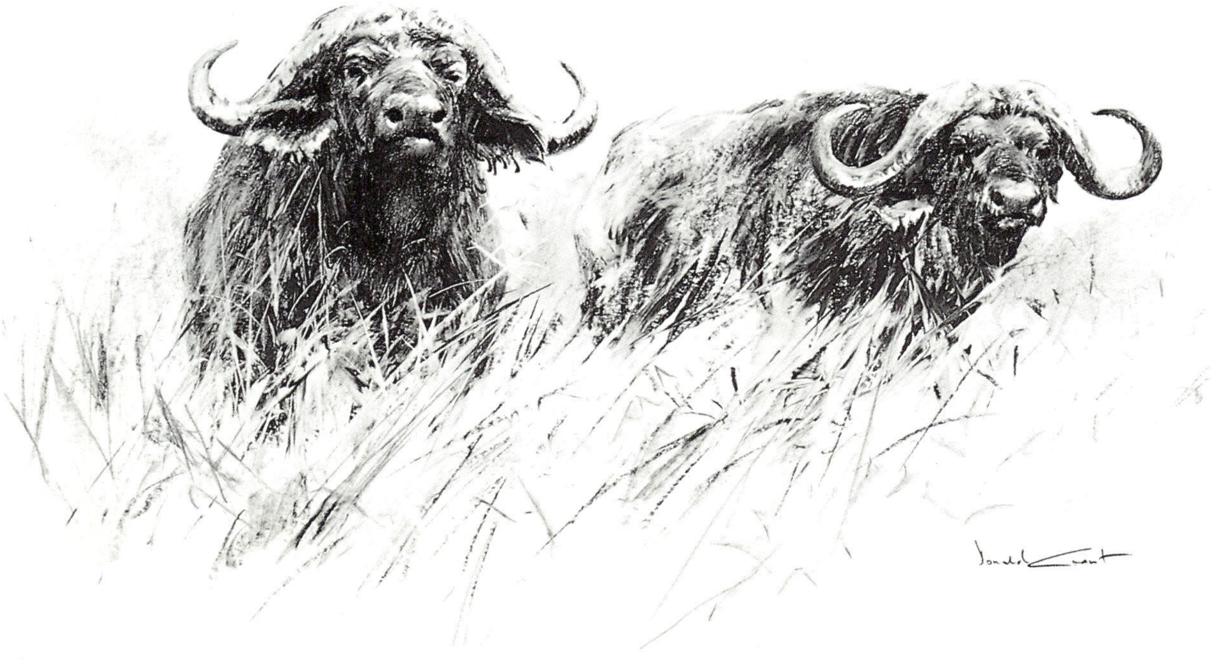

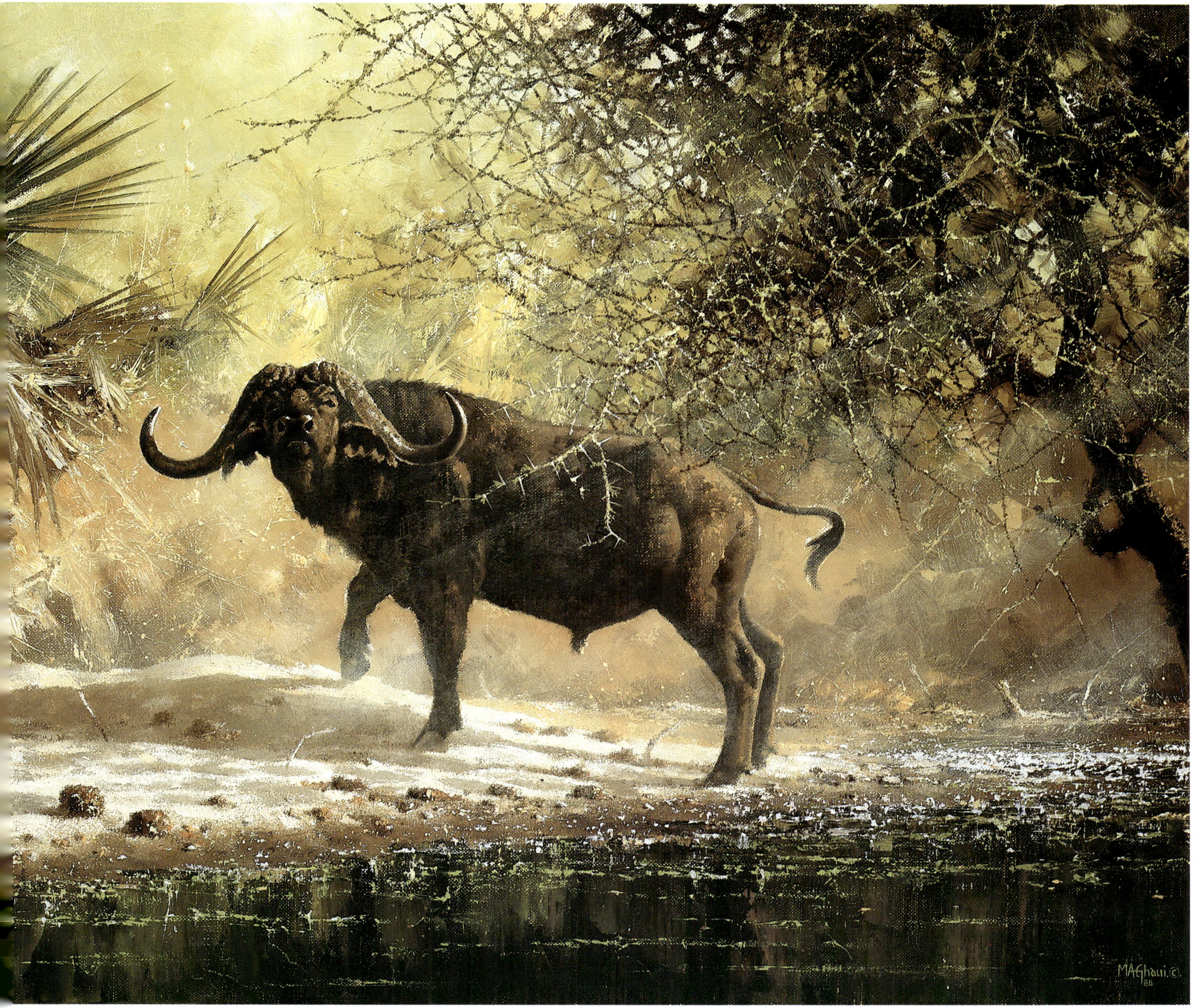

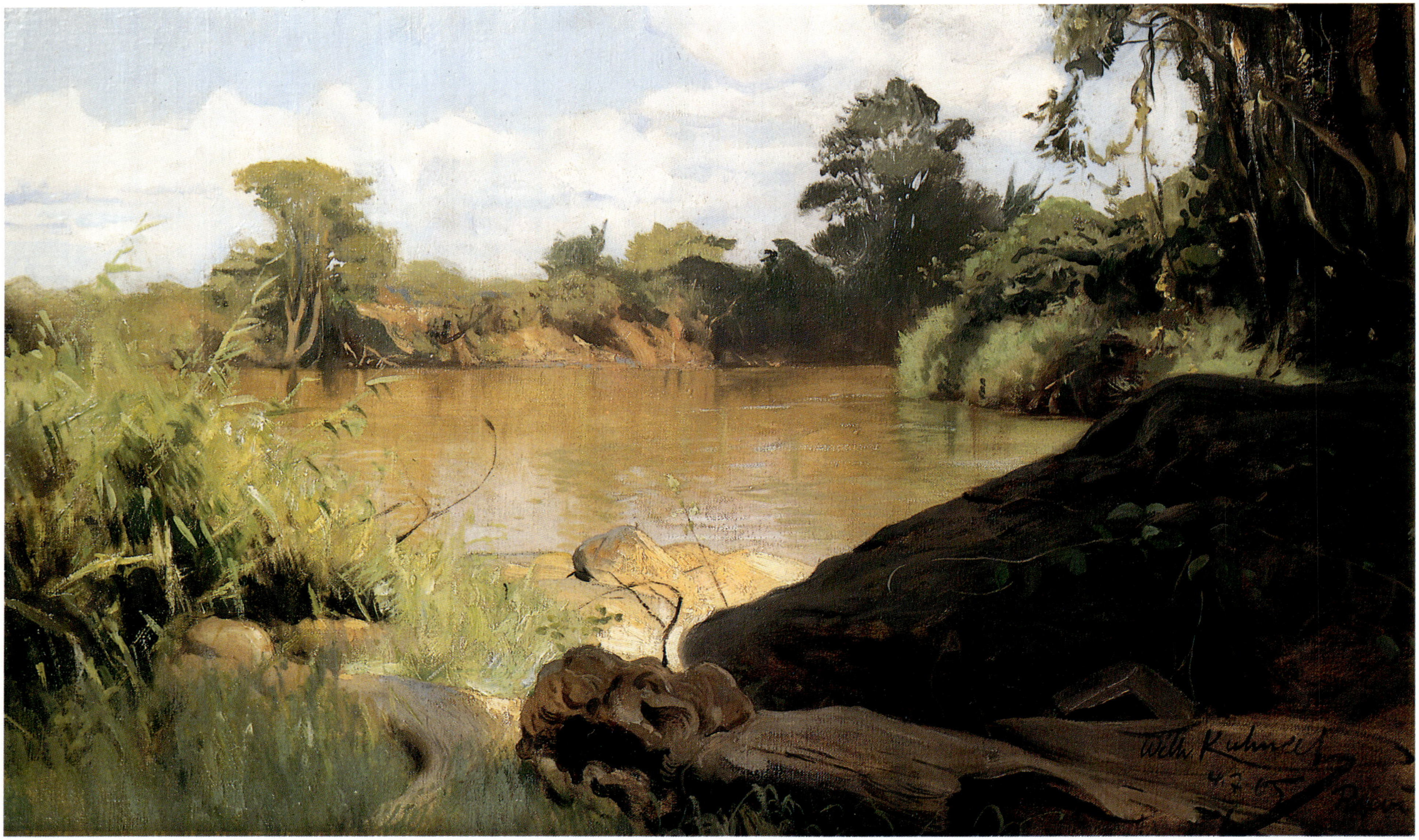

With this simple landscape, Wilhelm Kuhnert conjures up an image of Africa. If you have never been in the bush, then this is a picture you can dismiss, pass over. But for those who have been on safari, this is the most evocative of landscapes. Look at it for long enough and you can hear the cooing of unseen doves, the rasp of cicadas, and you can expect to glimpse the flash of a malachite kingfisher. It is the sort of river where you are certain to encounter hippos, and possibly crocodiles, too. Above all, it is a testimonial of the ability of Kuhnert to portray Africa with the mastery of his brush.

AFRICAN RIVER
Wilhelm Kuhnert

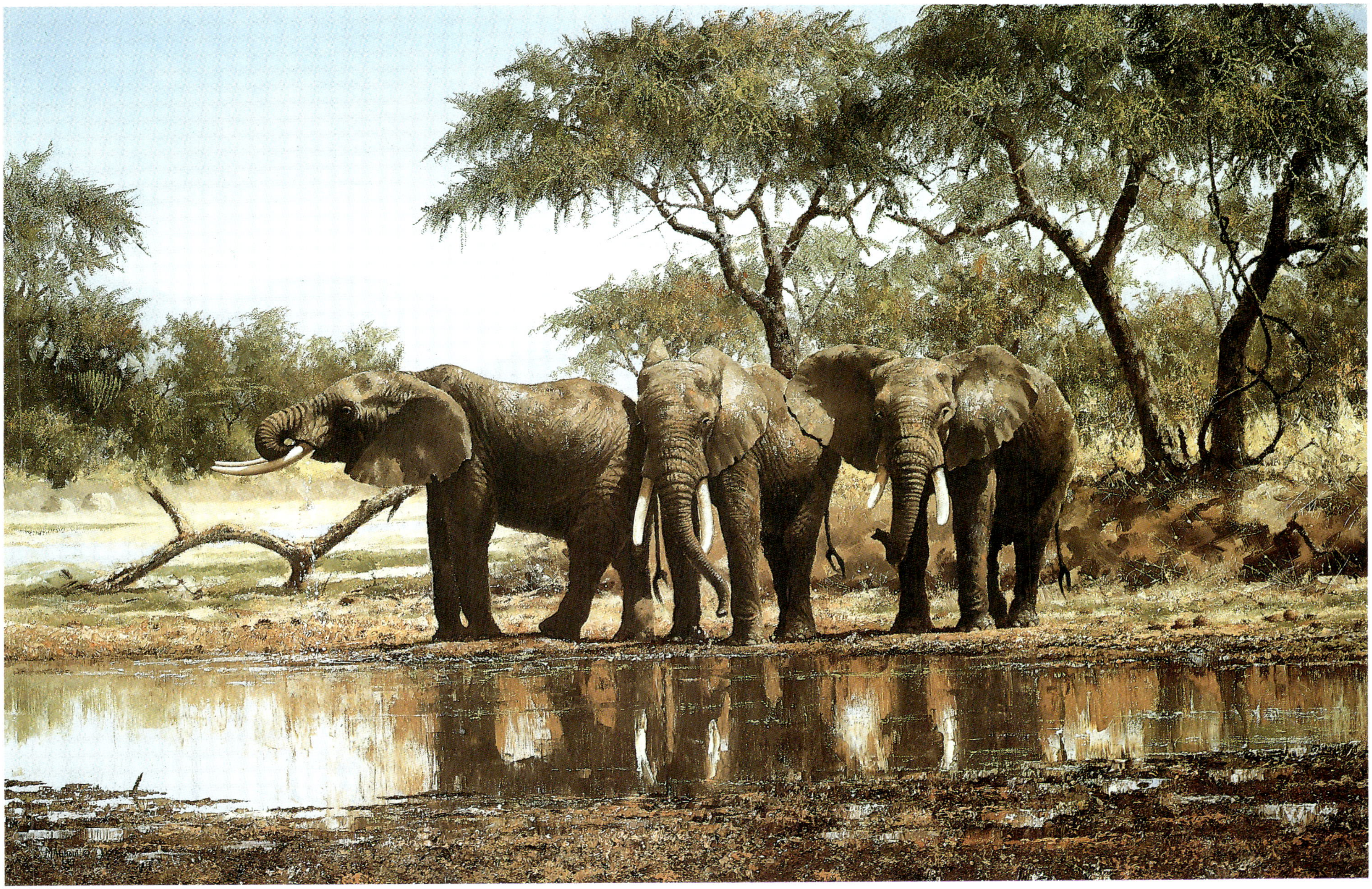

An elephant's life revolves around water, for it needs to drink at least 40 gallons a day, while wallowing is a favourite pastime. Here, Michael Ghaui depicts a trio of bulls at a seepage area in the Ruaha River course. The water here has a very pungent, sulphurous smell, and most animals prefer to drink from the mainflow of the river, using this area purely as a salt lick and wallow. One of the bulls has taken a trunkful to his mouth, either to taste the minerals or perhaps get a better scent of those that have been to the wallow before him.

These young bulls are carrying reasonable ivory, but genuine big tuskers are now creatures of the past, shot-out by poachers. What is more, a century of selective shooting of the bulls carrying the heaviest ivory means that the genetic stock which produces long tusks no longer exists. Like people, elephants are right- or left-handed, and their favoured tusk works harder than the other. Here the bull on the right clearly has one tusk shorter than the other.

THE TASTE OF MUD
Michael Ghaui

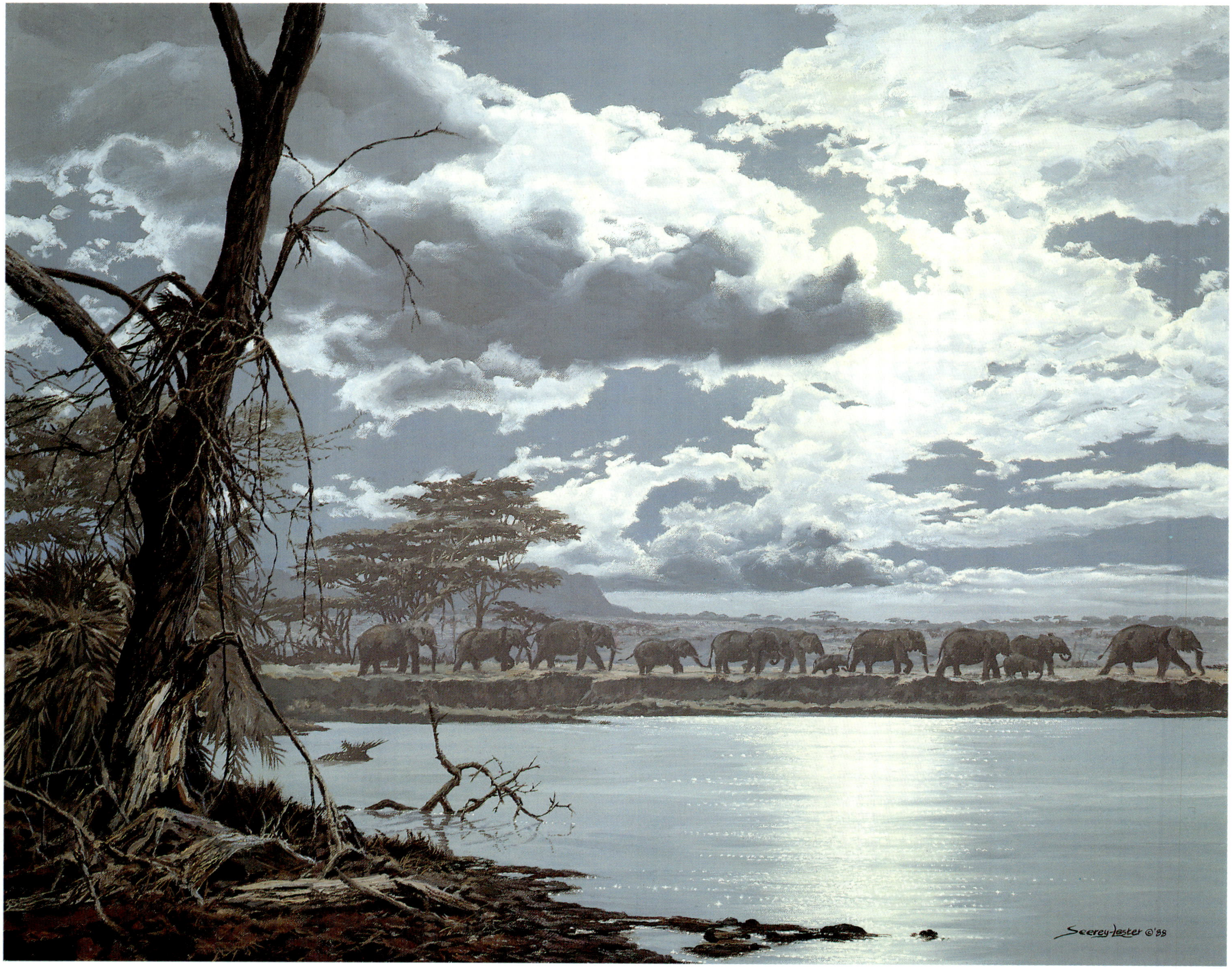
Seerey-Lester ©'88

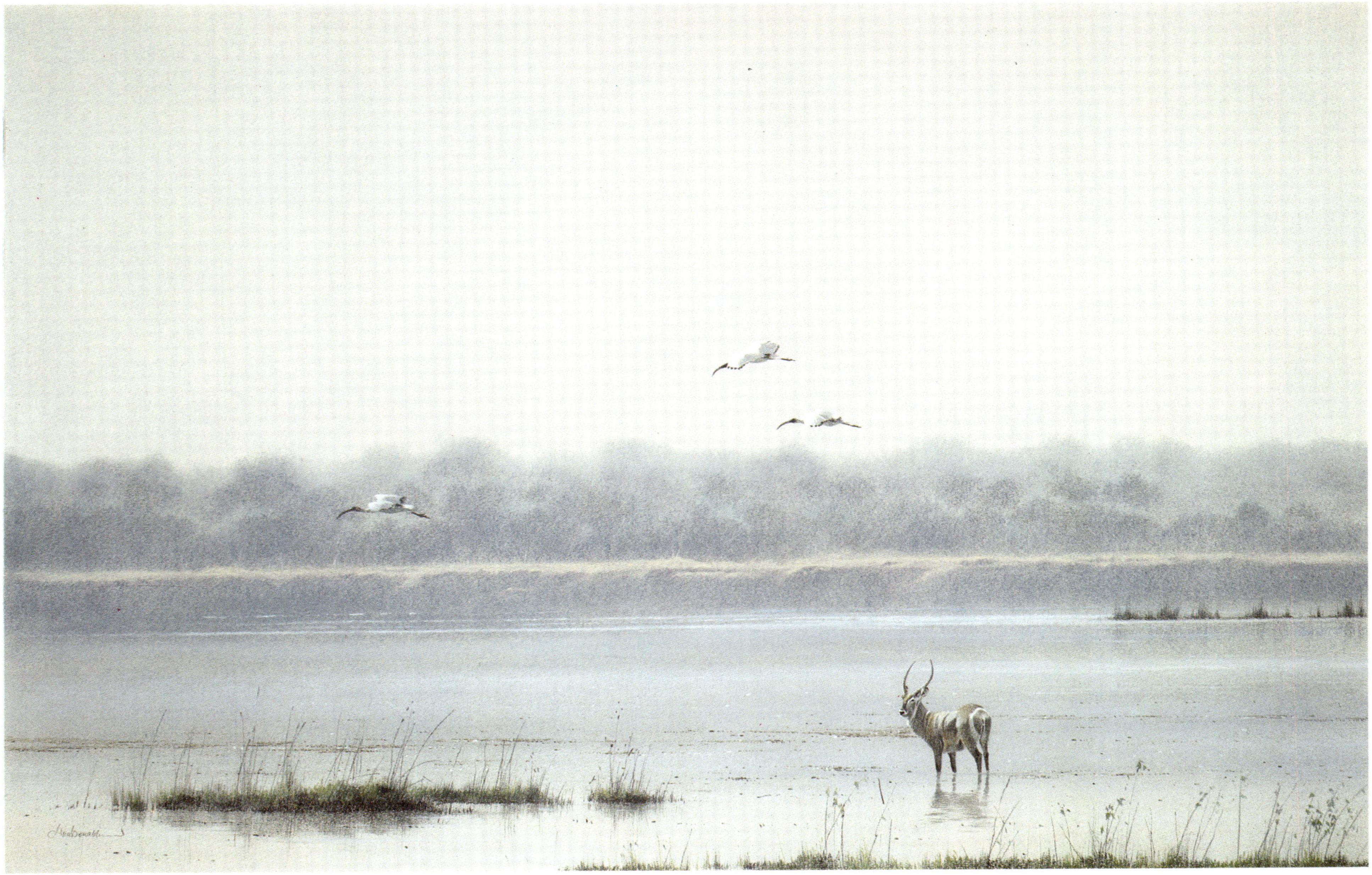

Seerey-Lester was inspired to paint this picture (*left*) by one of his first encounters with wild elephants while camping in Samburu in northern Kenya. He discovered that his tent had been erected on an elephant path and that each night a herd would walk through the clearing where his tent was pitched. Not used to sharing his camping grounds with such large creatures, he found it difficult to fall asleep. It was during one of these evenings that he was introduced to the brilliance of the African nights "and the illuminating magic of the African moon".

NIGHT MOVES – AFRICAN ELEPHANT
John Seerey-Lester

This painting, of Mana Pools in Zimbabwe, is one of the simplest in the book: water, sky and just a hint of bush, with a lone waterbuck and a trio of sacred ibises. It makes an effective composition, and one that is characteristic of the work of Kim Donaldson.

For Donaldson, who was brought up in what was then Southern Rhodesia, "there is something of old Africa in the Zambezi valley that is a mixture of peace and violence. . . This painting is a view across the river from the Zimbabwe side, and attempts to capture the tranquillity of the area."

WATERBUCK – MANA POOLS
Kim Donaldson

Both these paintings have the same powerful feel about them, and are instantly recognisable as the work of Bob Kuhn. Kuhn uses a camera when on safari. When he was painting "Buffalo Moving Out" (*below*) he projected the shape of the dominant animal onto the painting. Though the buffalo looked good on the slide, it failed to do so in the painting. "All sorts of unworkable distortion, that a long camera lens invariably produces, made the image unusable. In the end I did what I usually do, making the adjustments in proportion to my eye, not the cold thoughtless eye of the camera."

BUFFALO MOVING OUT
Bob Kuhn

In "Rhino Flushing Cattle Egrets" (*right*), the splashing water and the delicate white cattle egrets add atmosphere and movement to the painting. Black rhino have a reputation for being both dangerous and unpredictable, both of which are only partially true. Being short-sighted, a rhino will often blunder in one direction, when it is liable to toss or trample anything that gets in its way. Left on its own, it is a peaceful animal: most fights between rhinos have been found to be females warding off amorous males.

RHINO FLUSHING CATTLE EGRETS
Bob Kuhn

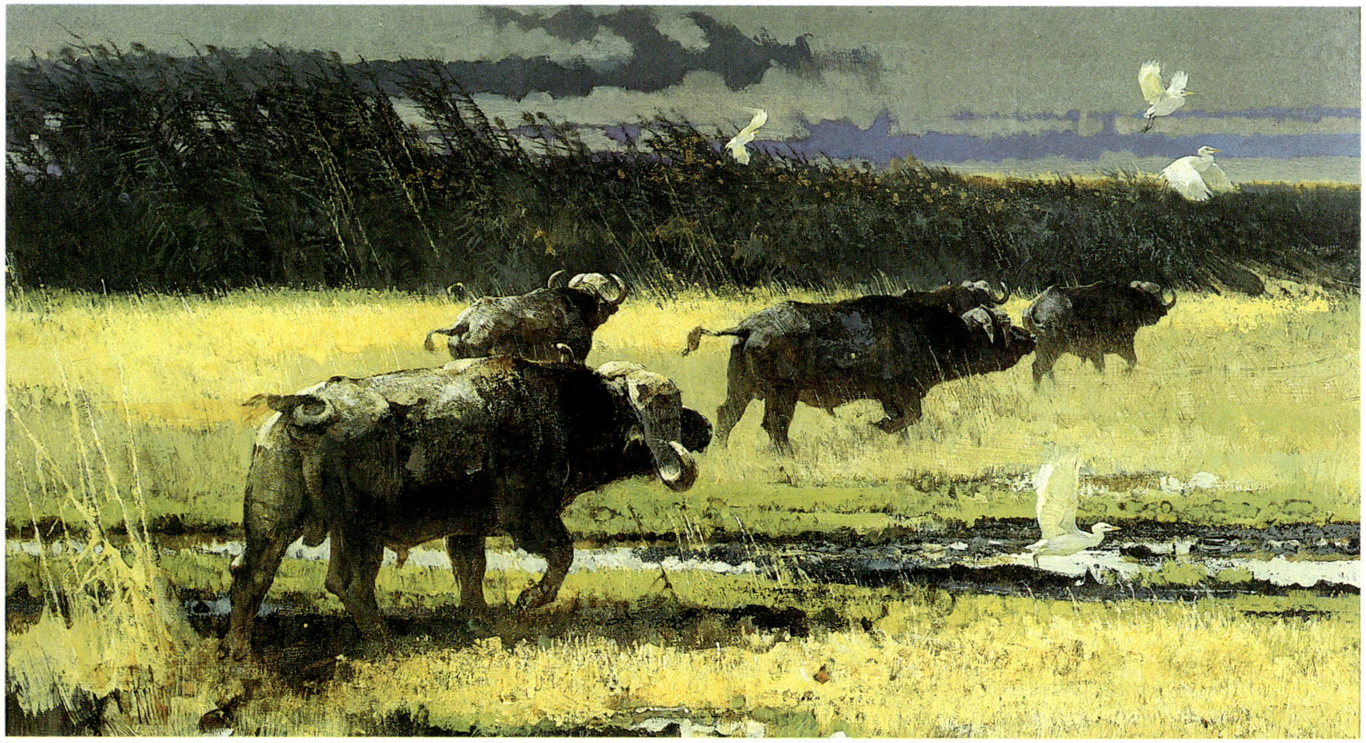

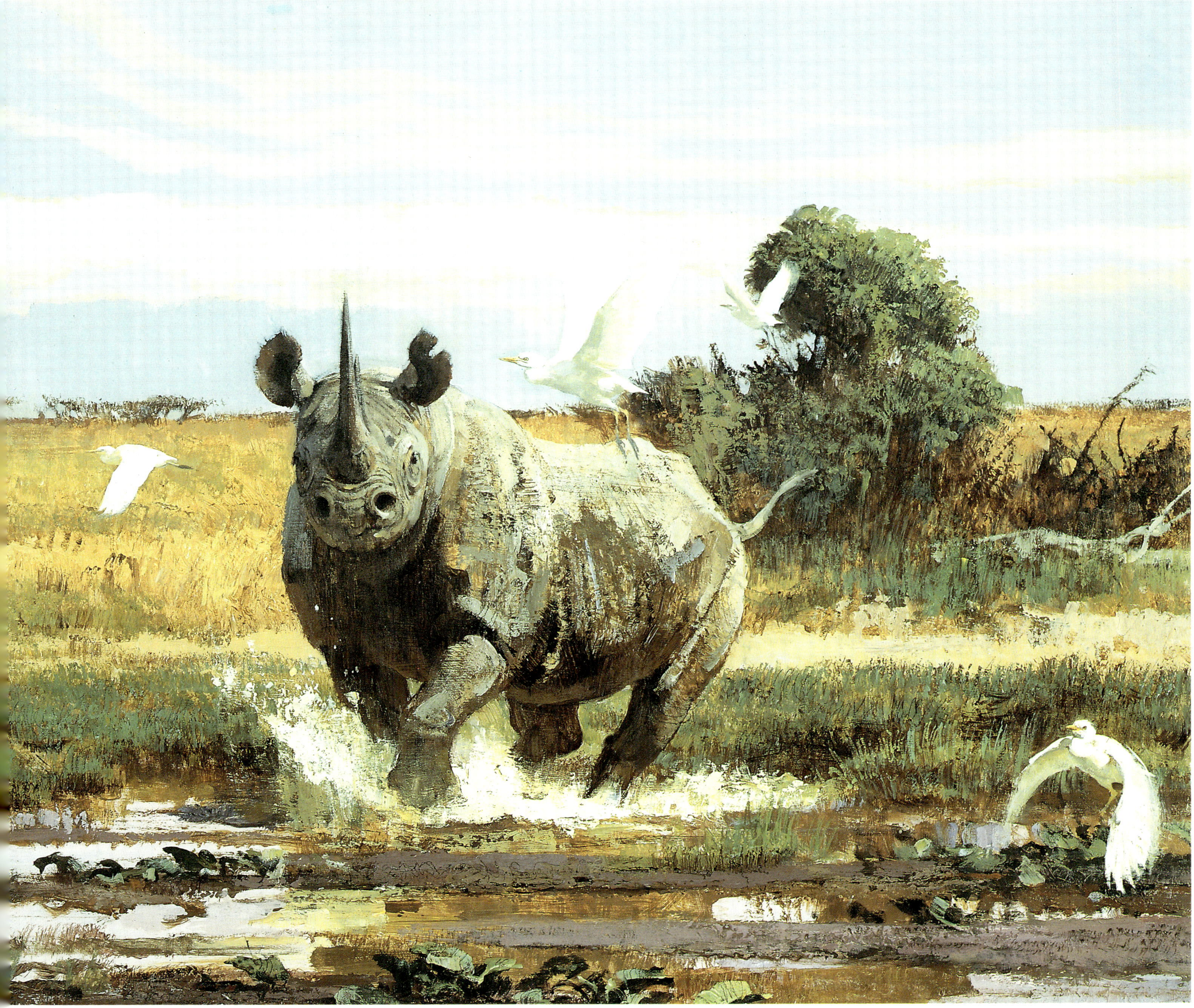

Giraffes can survive for considerable periods without drinking. They will drink whenever they get the chance, but actually getting down to the water is a problem for an animal that is rather more than 16ft tall, and requires the giraffe to perform a series of seemingly awkward movements in order to spread its forelegs as wide apart as possible. Dino Paravano painted this oil from a scene he saw in stony terrain in Namibia, and admits to always being amused at the antics a giraffe has to go through in order to reach the water.

GIRAFFES DRINKING
Dino Paravano

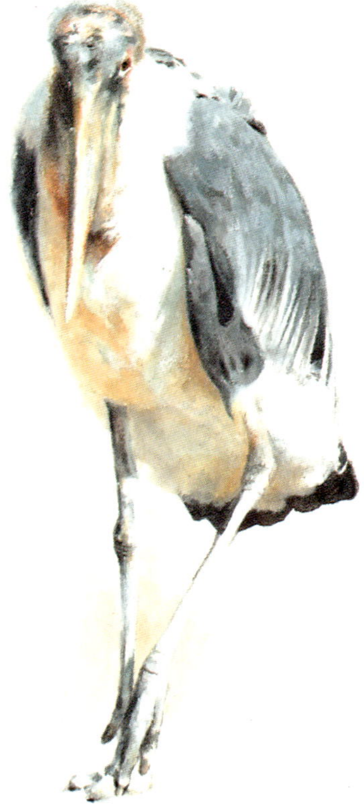

MARABOU STORK
Mandy Shepherd

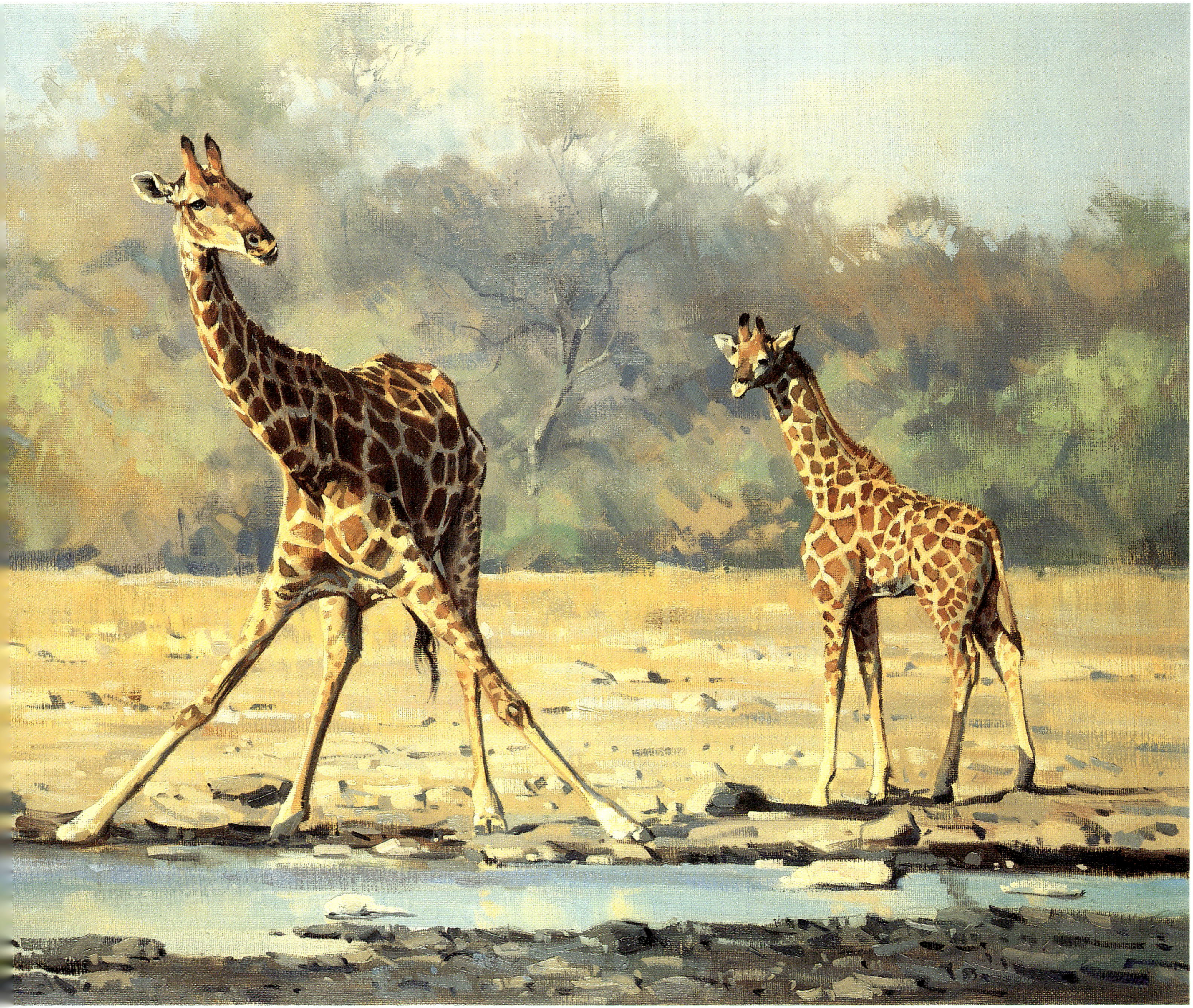

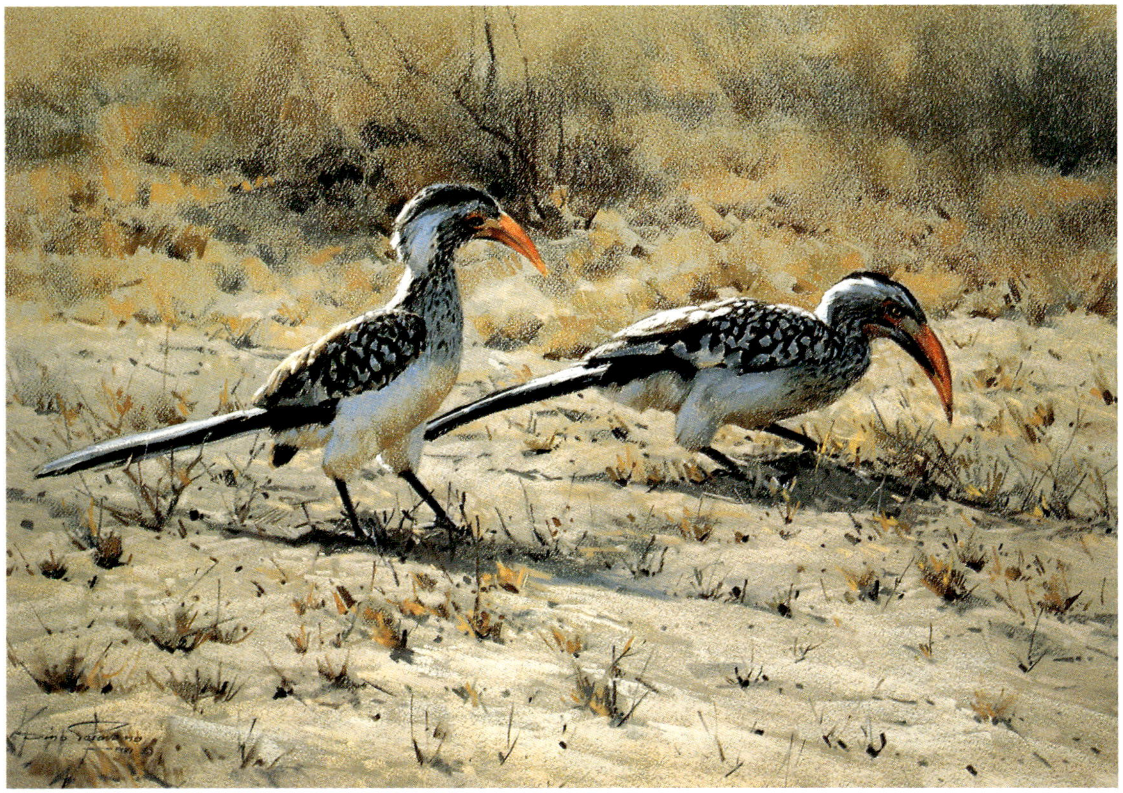

Of Africa's 23 species of hornbills, the red-billed (*above*) is the commonest, the most widespread, ranging from Senegal in the west to the Transvaal in the south. It is a bird of open savanna, woodland and thorn scrub, and particularly favours heavily grazed areas. Entertaining, noisy birds, they frequently venture into safari camps, where they hop around the tents, prospecting for beetles and grasshoppers. Like nearly all the hornbills, the female seals herself inside her nest chamber before she starts to lay: she remains there until the young birds fledge. Here Dino Paravano shows a pair of red-billed hornbills foraging together.

RED-BILLED HORNBILLS
Dino Paravano

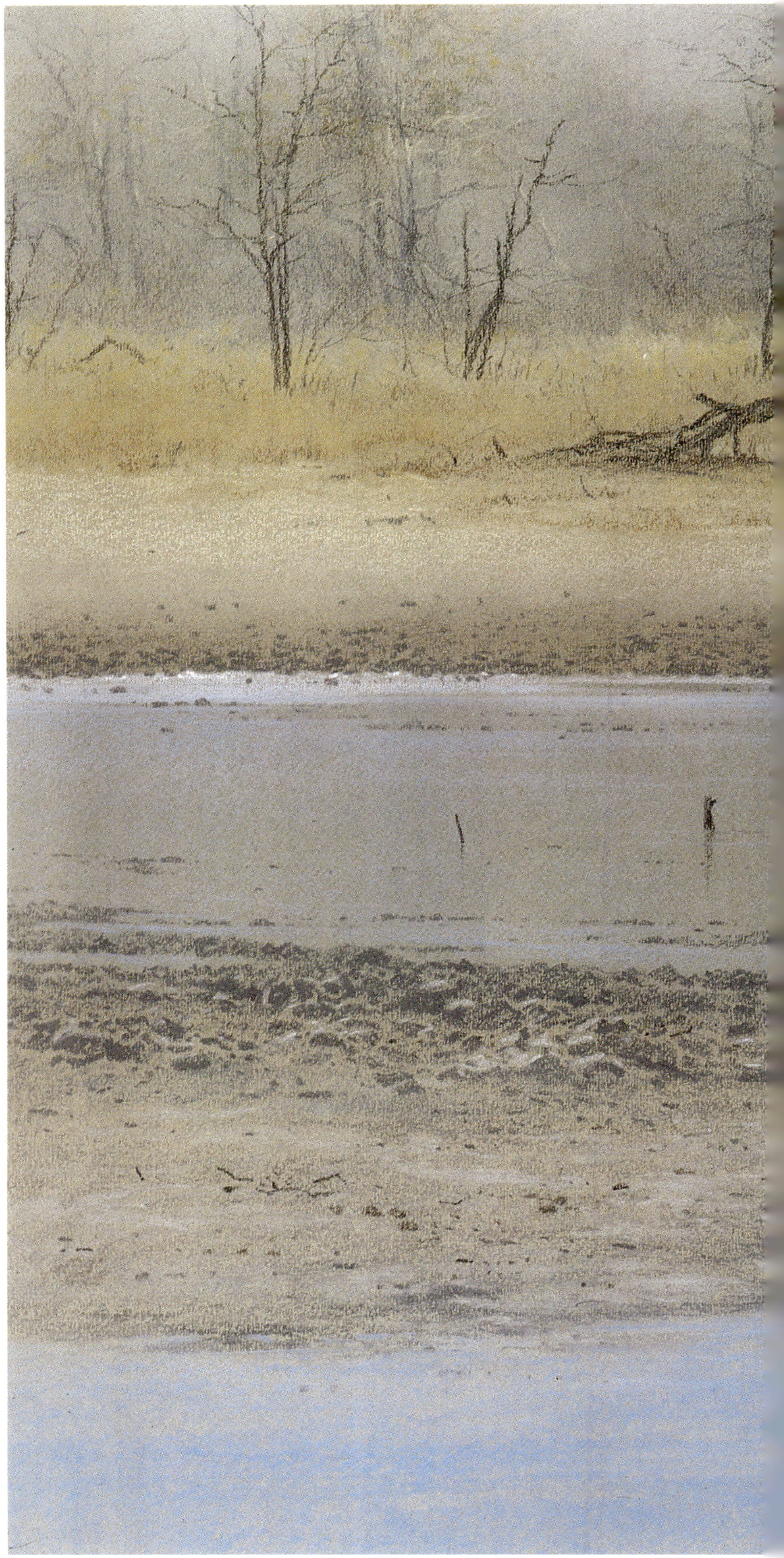

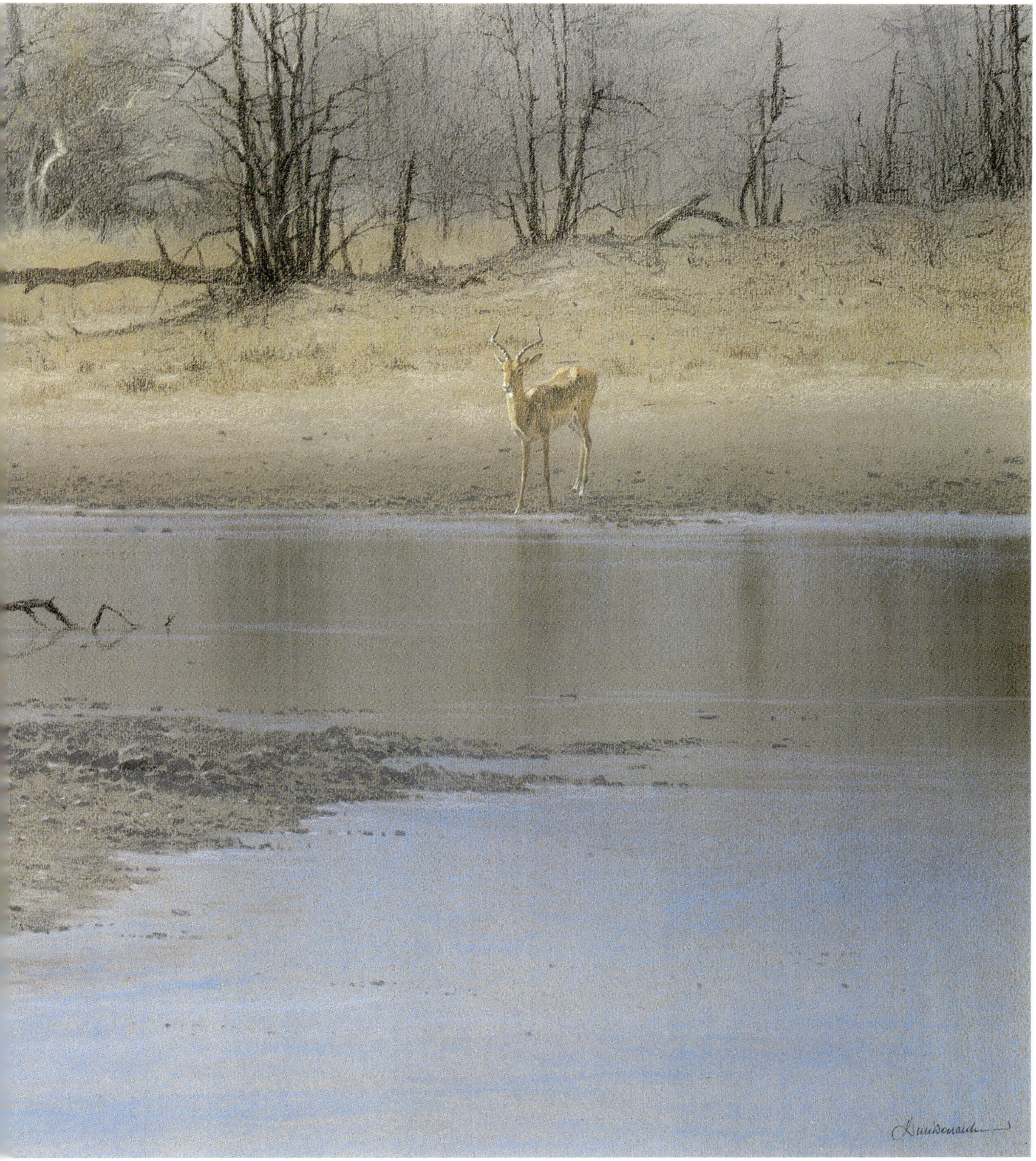

Kim Donaldson's work (*left*) is characterized by expansive landscapes in which the animal, or animals, are often a small feature. Here, the solitary impala buck sets off a delicate pastel of a water hole in Zimbabwe's Hwange National Park. Donaldson's skill comes from the clever use of lighting, and the soft reflections in the water, producing a finished work which is delightfully evocative.

IMPALA – HWANGE WATER HOLE
Kim Donaldson

58

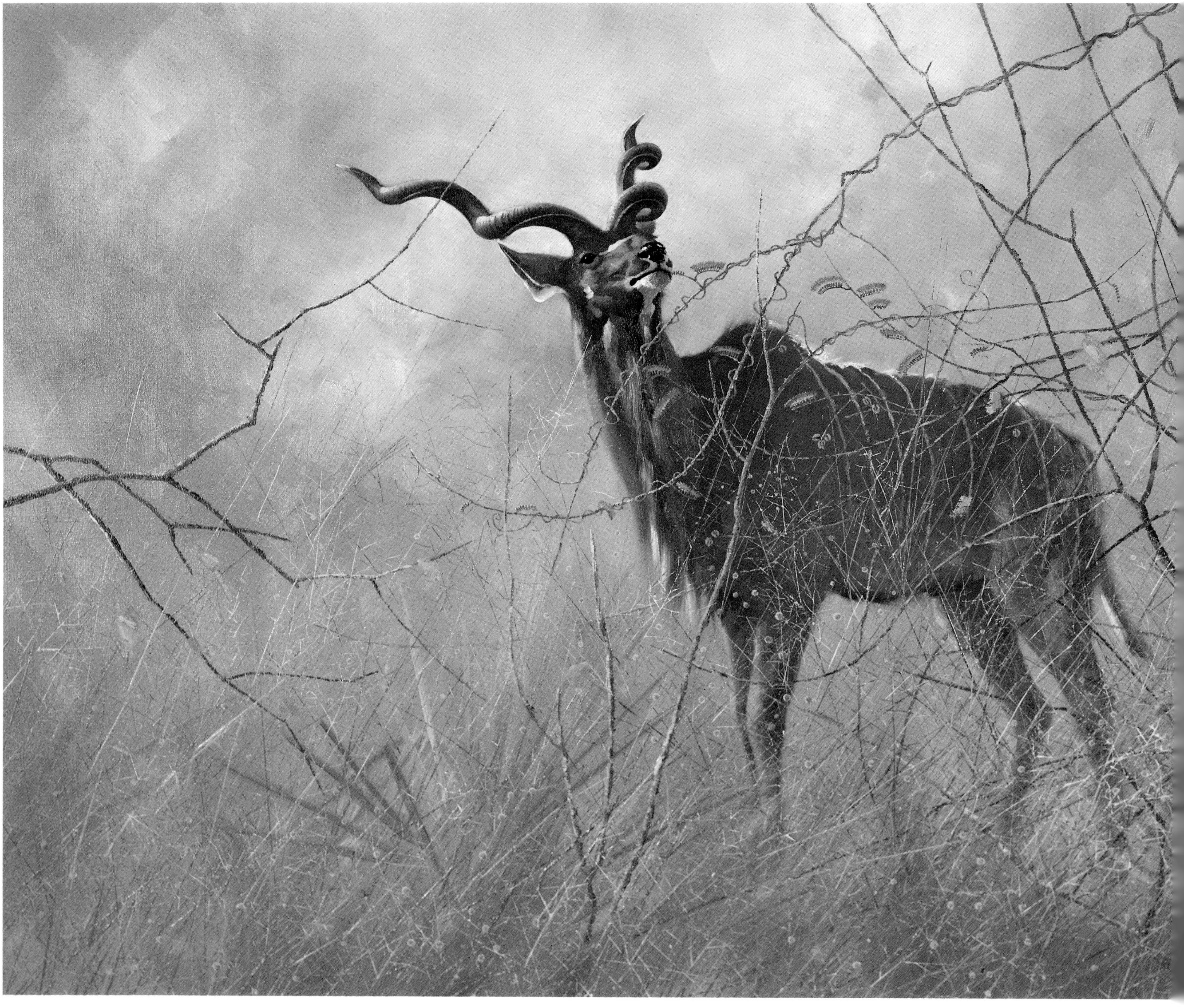

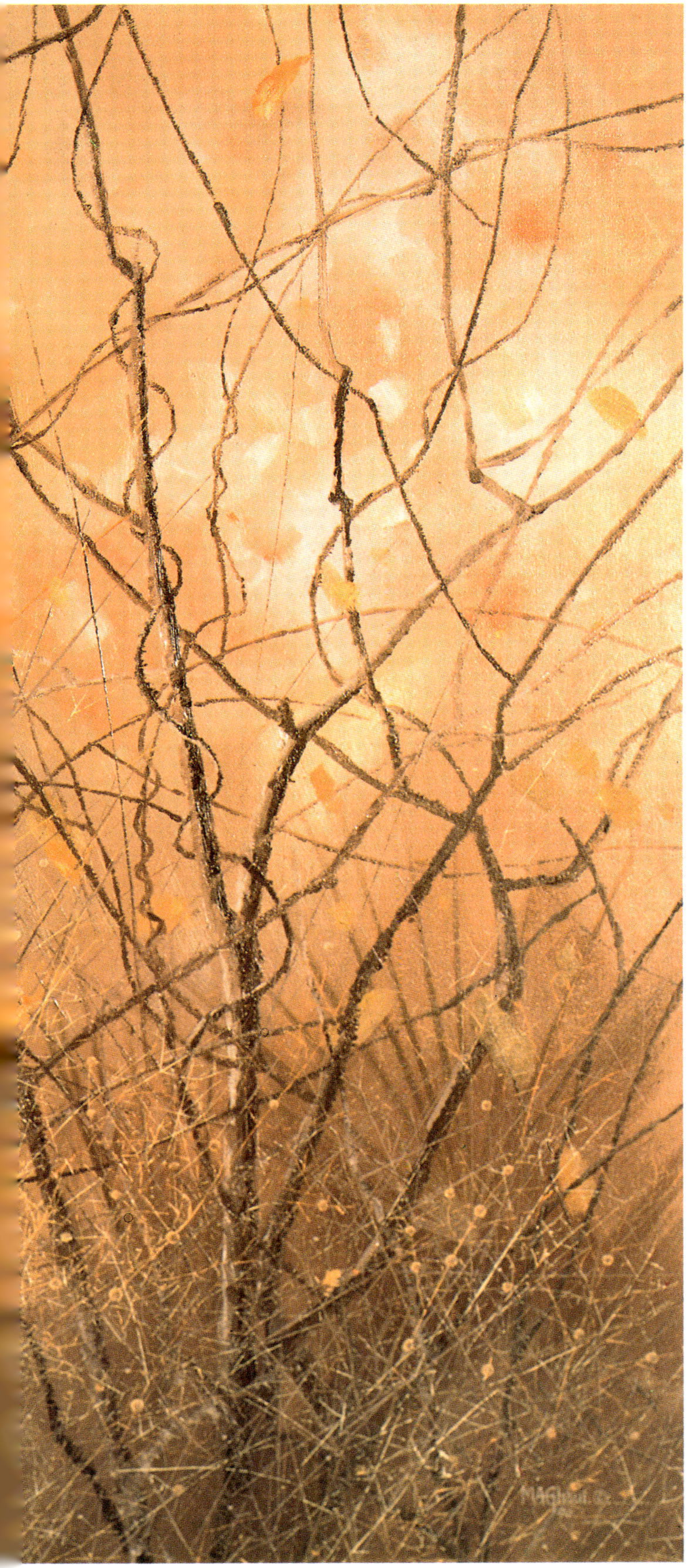

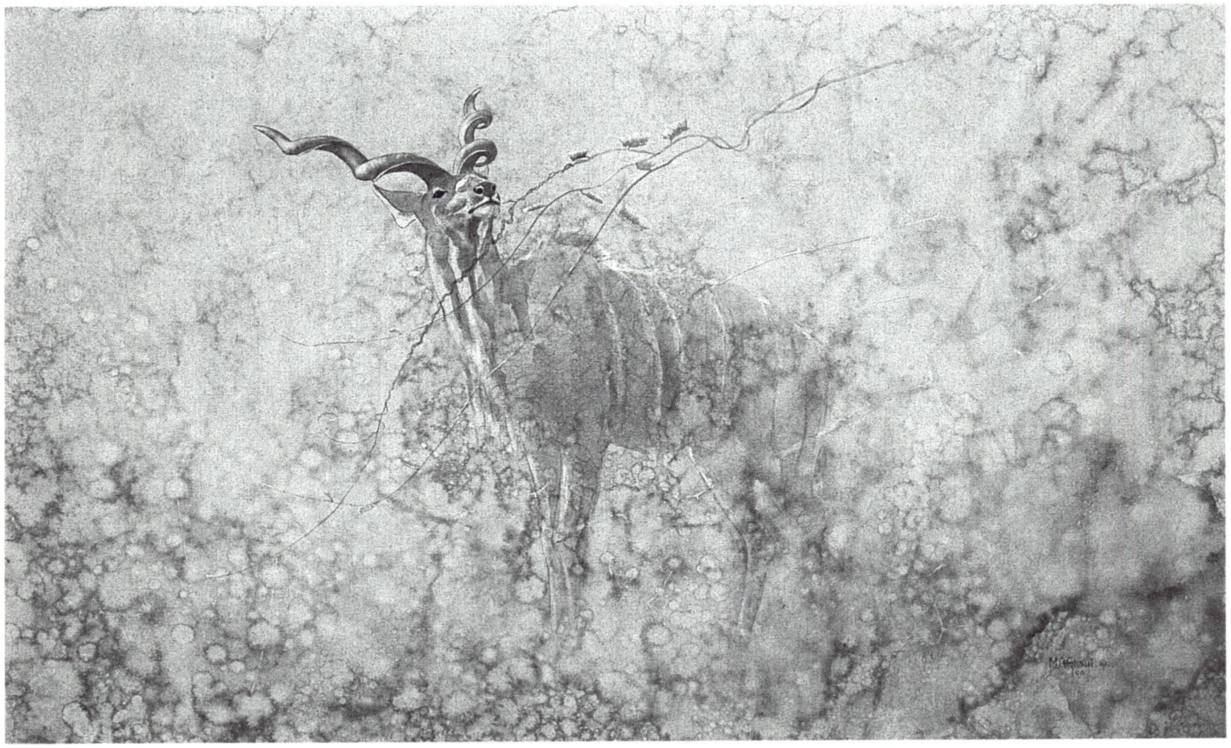

Ghaui found this magnificent bull kudu early one morning, browsing on toothbrush flowers. "The sun was coming up behind him, and the effect of backlighting on the flowers was enhanced by the shaded grey of his body. The background of this painting is fairly abstract in an attempt to create an ethereal atmosphere, as this bull seemed to float, quite literally, from one bush to another, nipping at all the new buds."

Greater kudu can be found throughout much of eastern and southern Africa, their range sometimes overlapping with the smaller, more graceful, lesser kudu. In some parts of Africa kudu are prized by hunters, making them particularly wary and difficult to approach.

BROWSING BULL – GREATER KUDU
Michael Ghaui

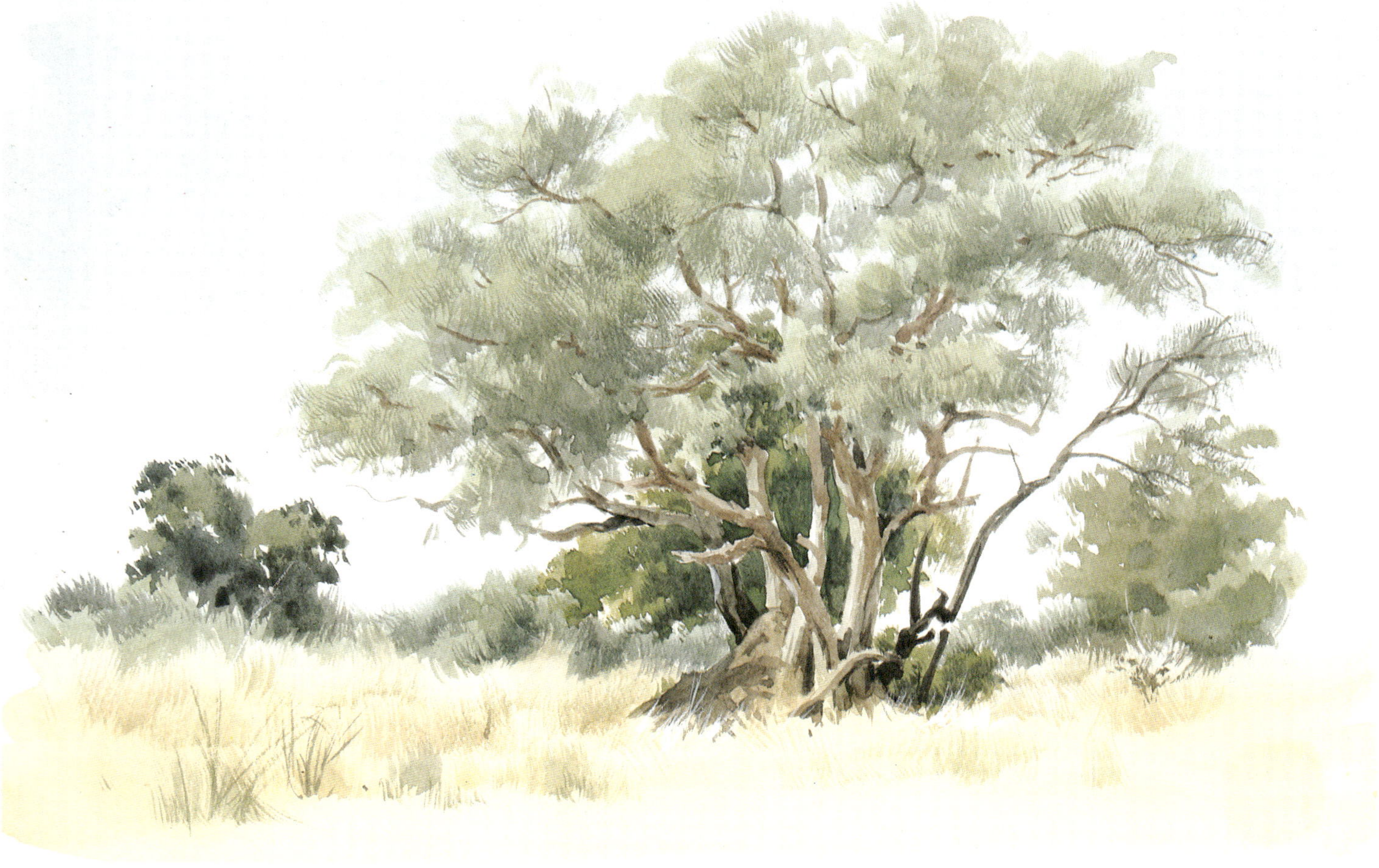

COMBRETUM
Rena Fennessey

Watching a lioness with her cubs can be entertaining, for lion cubs enjoy a rough-and-tumble, and take considerable liberties with their seniors. Dino Paravano had spent four days in South Africa's Mala Mala game reserve, looking unsuccessfully for lions, when he was contacted by radio and told that two lion cubs had been spotted in a river bed a few miles away. He drove over and found the cubs in a boisterous mood. He was able to watch them for some time, before a sudden call from the lioness drew them away. He then tracked them in the sand, and soon caught up with them greeting their mother, "jumping all over her, biting her playfully and altogether making nuisances of themselves". The resulting painting speaks for itself.

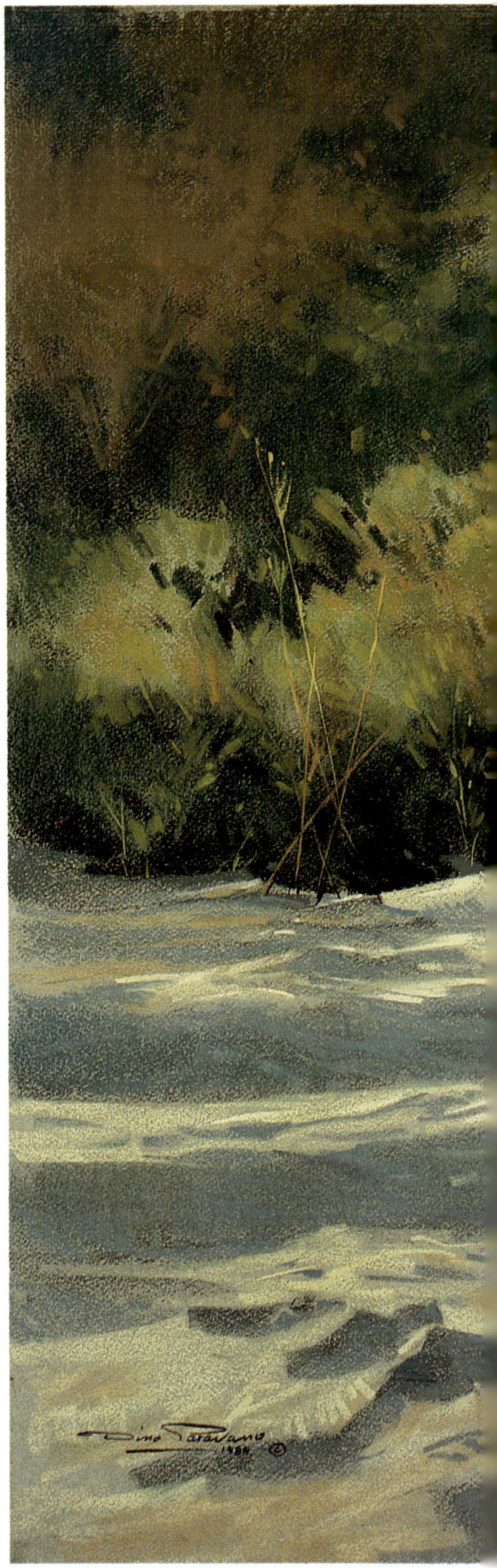

LIONESS AND CUBS ON THE RUN
Dino Paravano

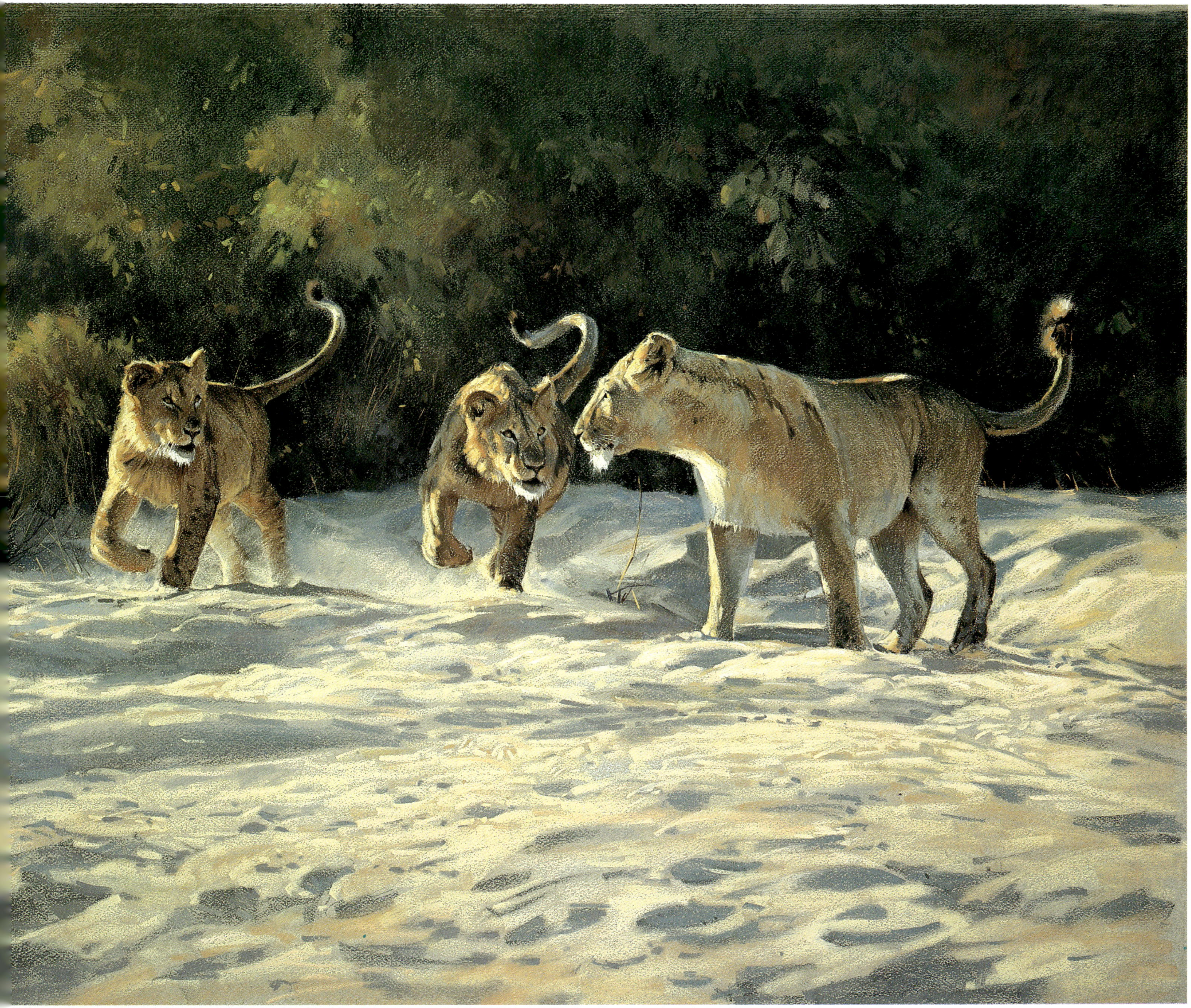

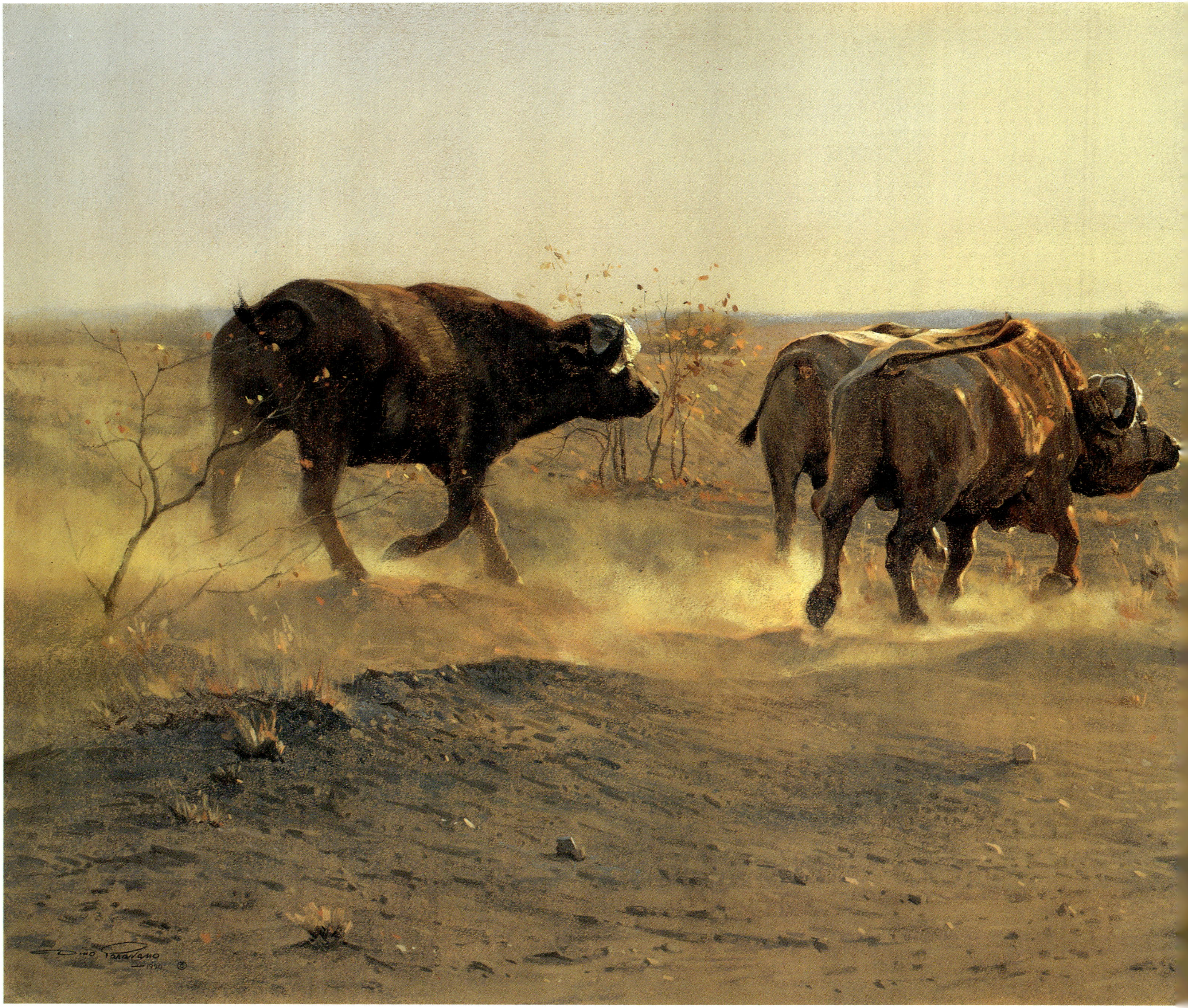
Dino Paravano
©

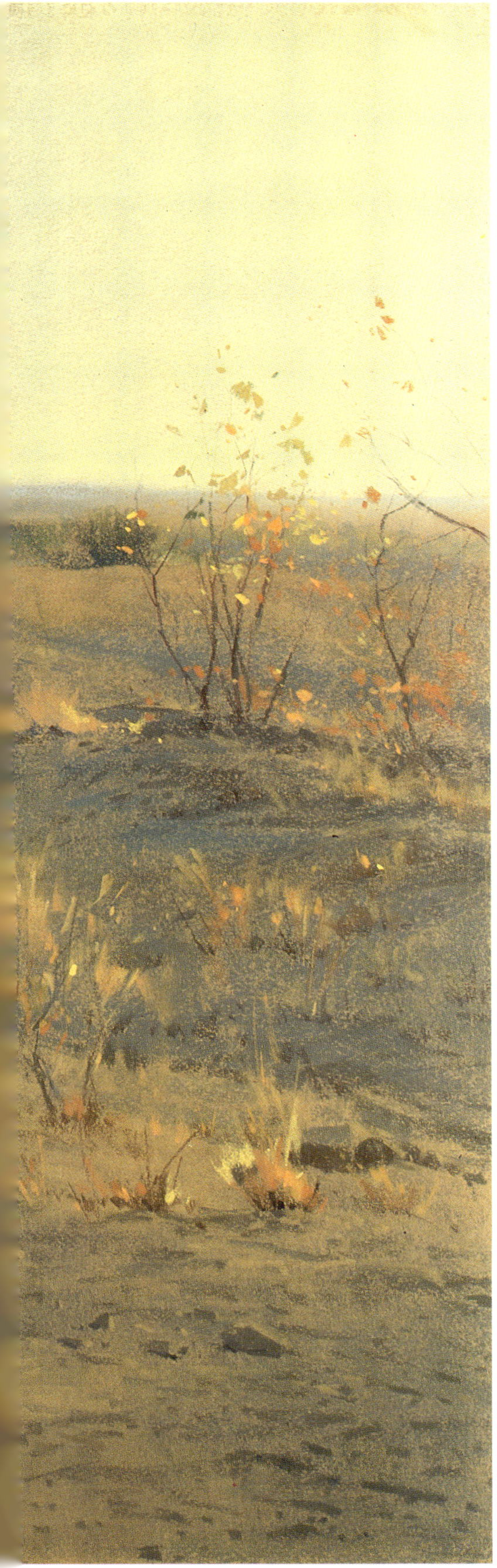

Running buffalo (*left*) create a powerful image: these animals, at Letaba in the Kruger National Park, are simply drawn, with no unnecessary detail. What makes this pastel so successful is Paravano's skilful painting of the red dust, churned up by their hooves, and lit by the low sun. Compare this painting with Bob Kuhn's study of running buffalo, shown on page 52. Both have a similar theme, even a similar composition, but there the similarities end.

BUFFALO ON THE MOVE
Dino Paravano

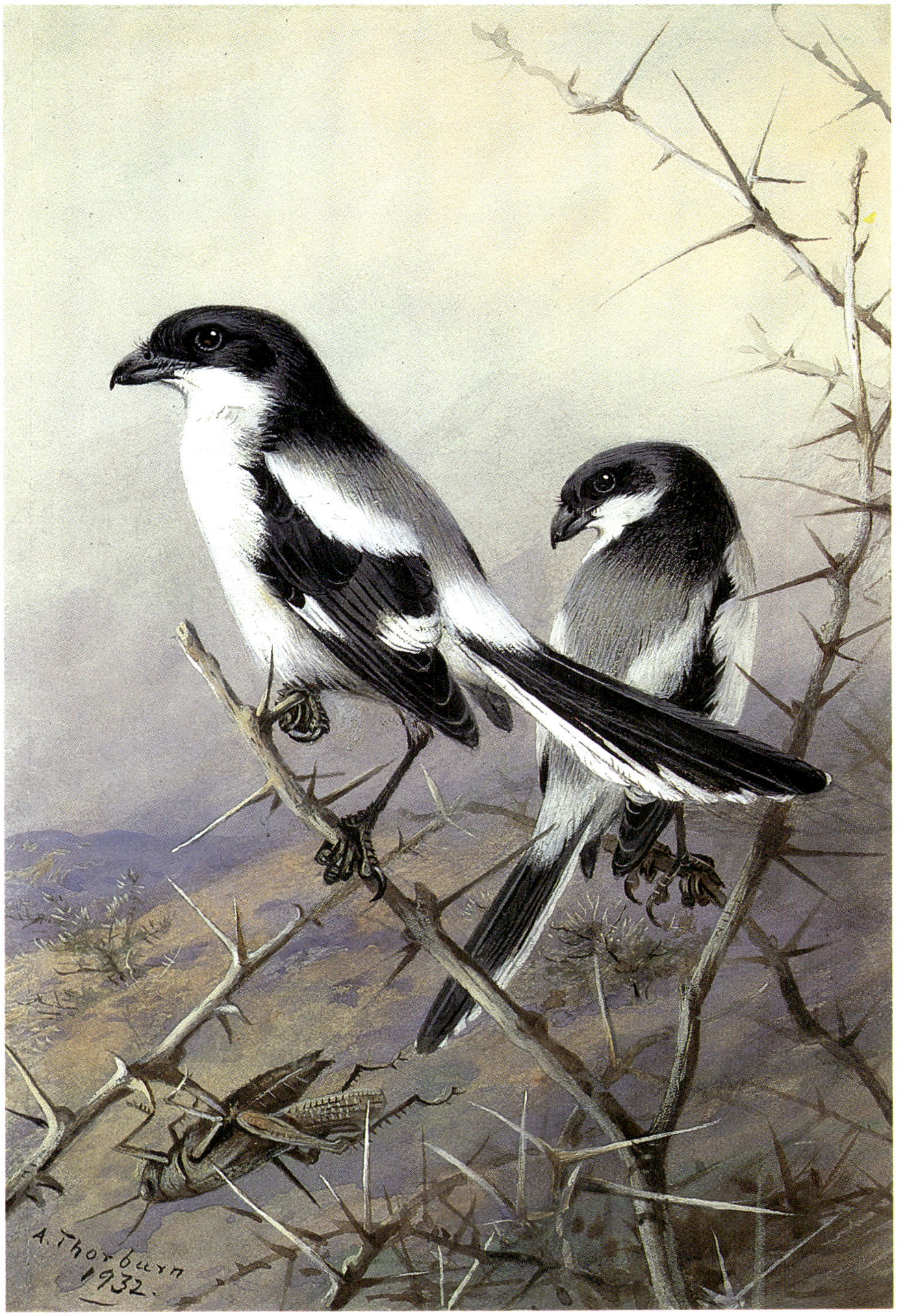

Africa can boast a bewildering number and variety of shrikes: shown here are a pair of Somali fiscals (*right*), painted by Archibald Thorburn. In East Africa 13 species of shrikes occur, of which the common fiscal is the most widespread. But there are several species which closely resemble the fiscal, and some care is needed to identify them. The Somali fiscal is a bird of the thorn bush of Somalia, eastern Ethiopia and northern Kenya: It looks like the more widespread Taita fiscal, from which it can be identified by the broad white tips to the secondaries, so that in flight it appears to have black and white wings.

Archibald Thorburn (1860–1925) is remembered as one of Britain's greatest bird artists, illustrating numerous books, and influencing many of today's most successful artists. Apart from one trip to Norway, he never travelled outside the British Isles, but he did execute a masterful series of plates for *The Birds of British Somaliland* (1937), of which this is one.

SOMALI FISCAL SHRIKES
Archibald Thorburn

The stark simplicity of this Kim Donaldson pastel of gemsbok, lala palms and dunes is strikingly effective. The setting is Namibia, which can not only boast the world's highest sand dunes, but also its oldest desert. The Namib desert is home to a wide variety of creatures, all of which have adapted to withstand the rigours of living in a hostile environment. Gemsbok are surprisingly common in parts of the Namib, and it is difficult to believe that such a large antelope (4ft at the shoulder, and weighing around 450lb) can find enough food to survive in these harsh surroundings.

Gemsbok, a close relation of the East African beisa oryx, feed mainly on grasses, but they also eat fruits (with a particular fondness for wild melons and cucumbers) which provide sufficient moisture to sustain them during long periods of drought. They are necessarily nomadic, seeking out areas of desert where past rainstorms have brought on the vegetation.

GEMSBOK – NAMIB DUNES
Kim Donaldson

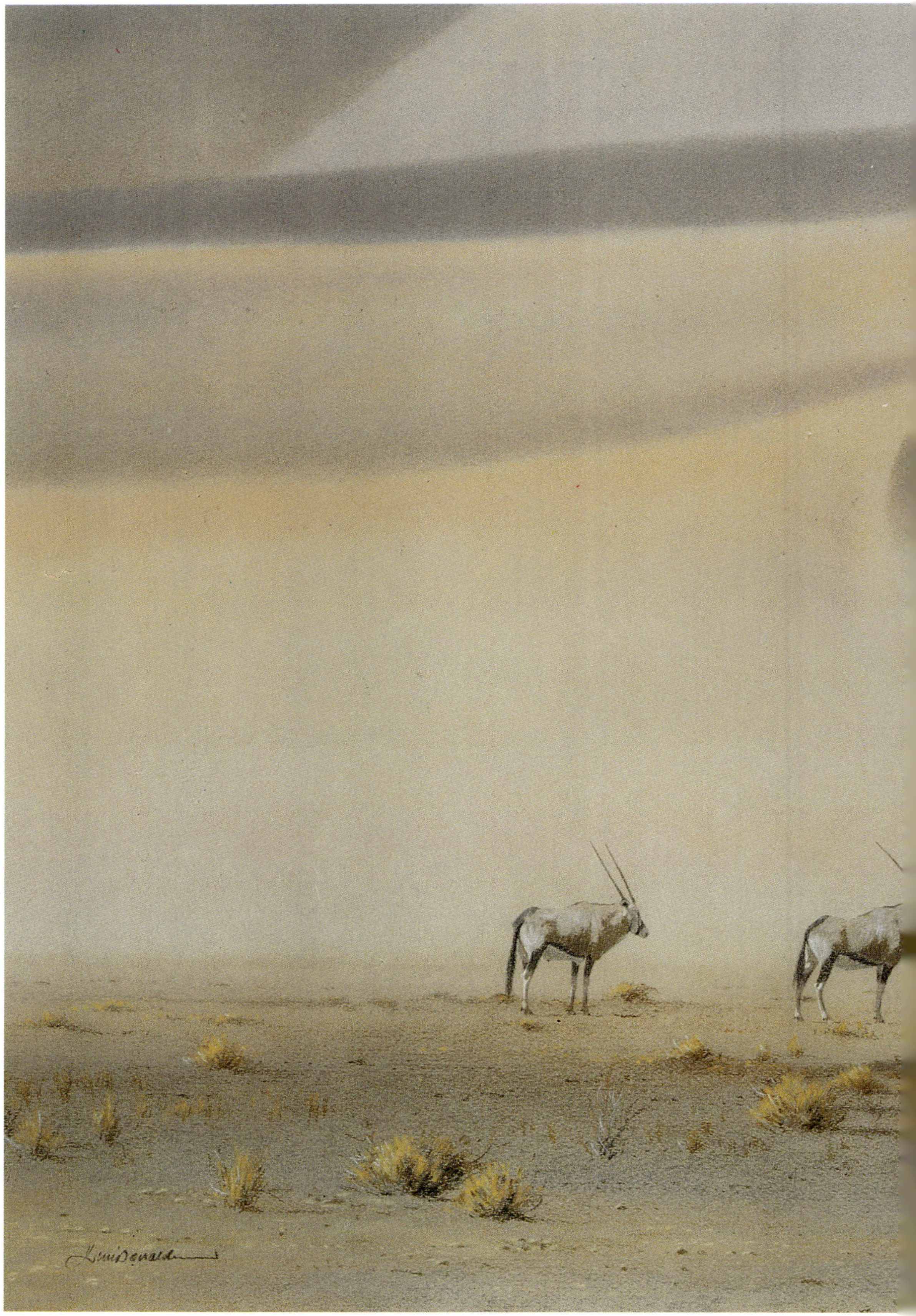

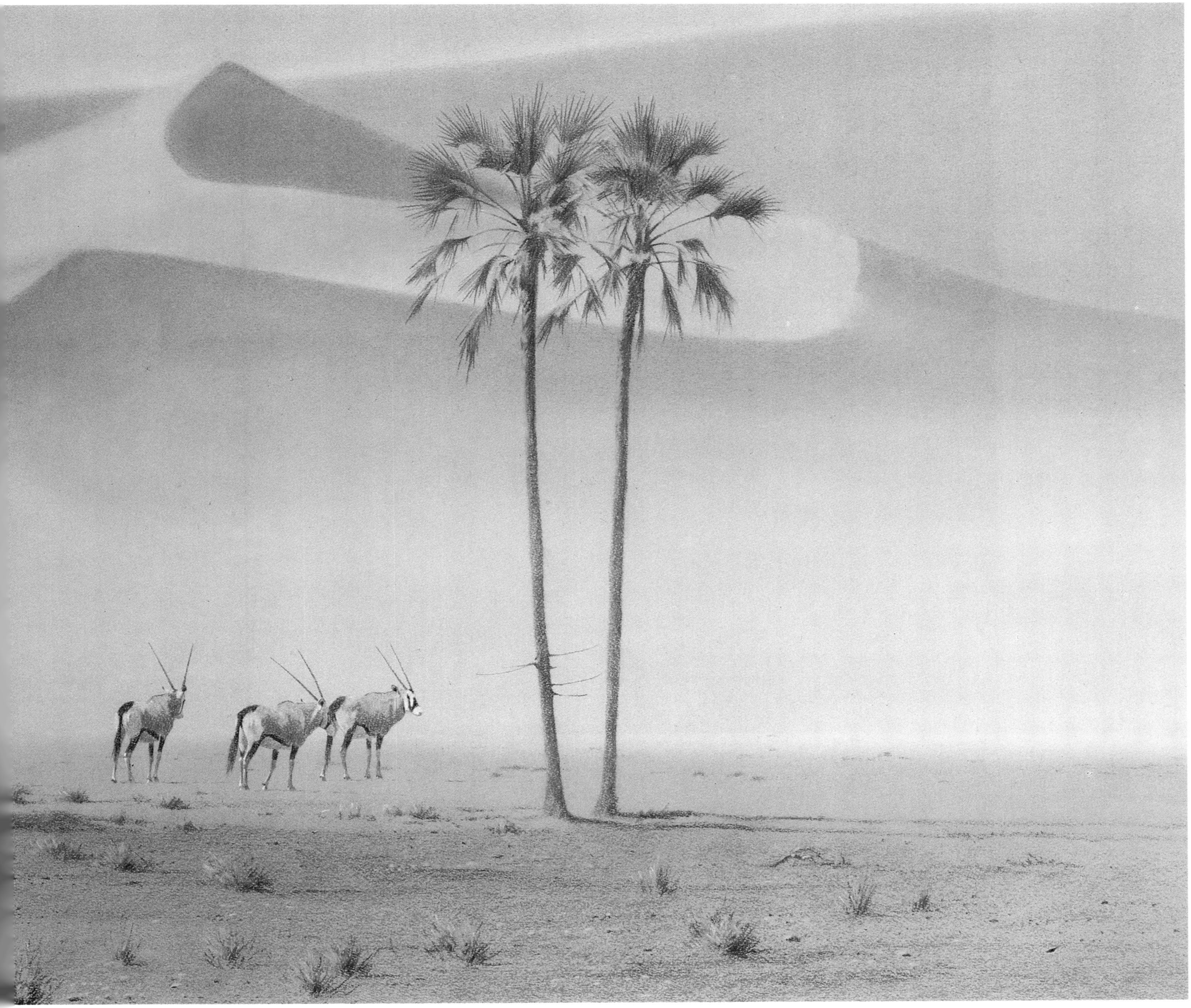

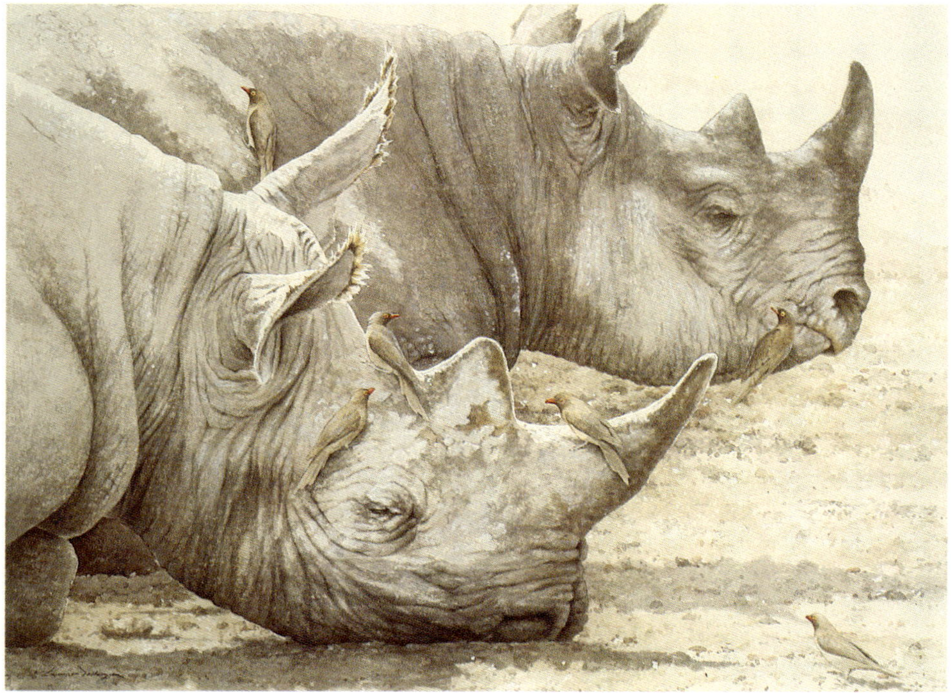

Swedish artist Gunnar Pettersson's watercolour shows a pair of black rhino with their attendant red-billed oxpeckers. The oxpeckers climb about on their hosts in search of ticks and other parasites, using their tail as a prop. They perform a useful service for the animals, and will also warn them of the approach of danger, but they not infrequently inflict minor wounds on their hosts. This is chiefly because ticks tend to congregate around eyes, ears and nostrils, where the skin is soft and easily damaged by the oxpecker's stabbing beak.

RHINO AND OXPECKERS
Gunar Pettersson

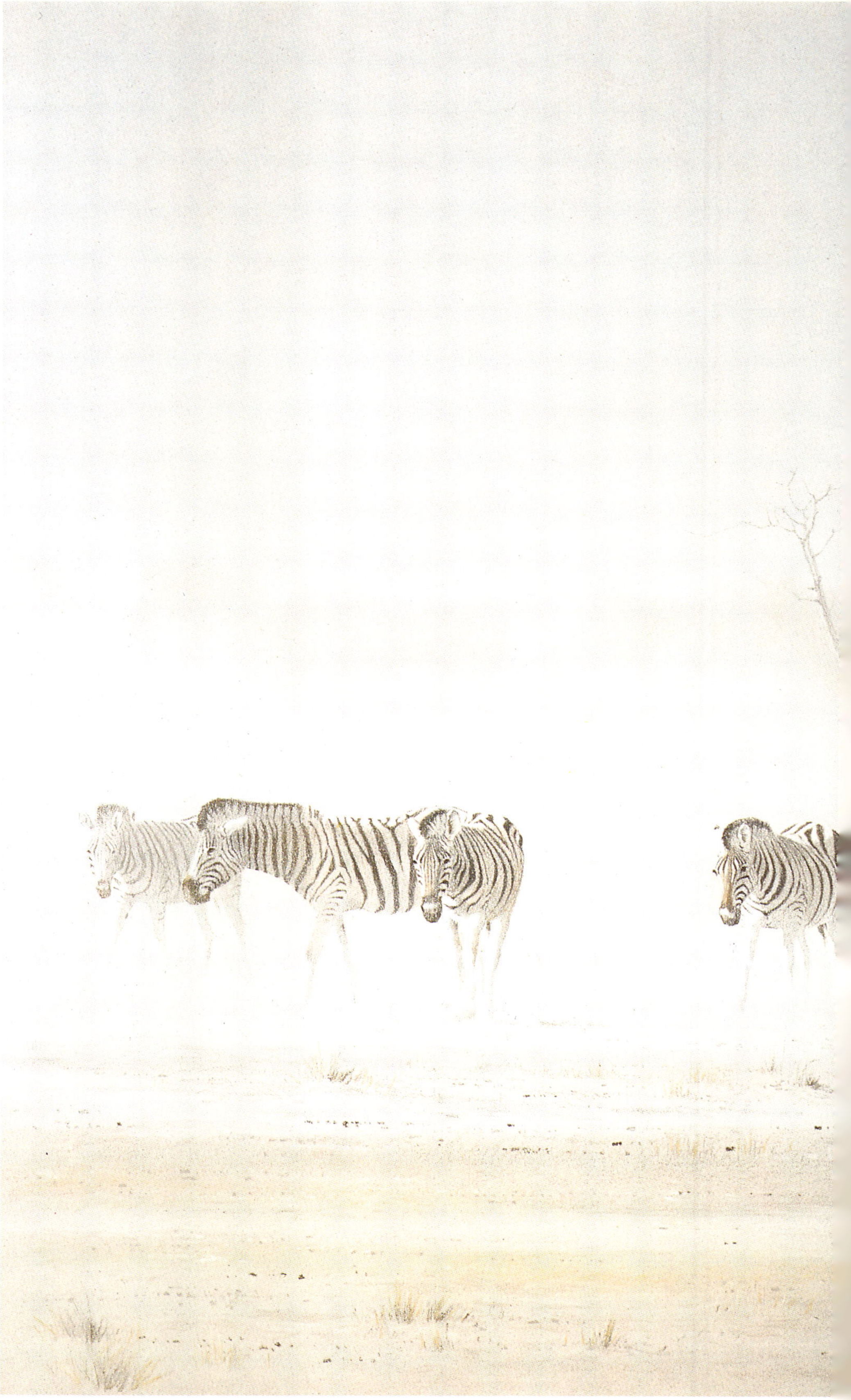

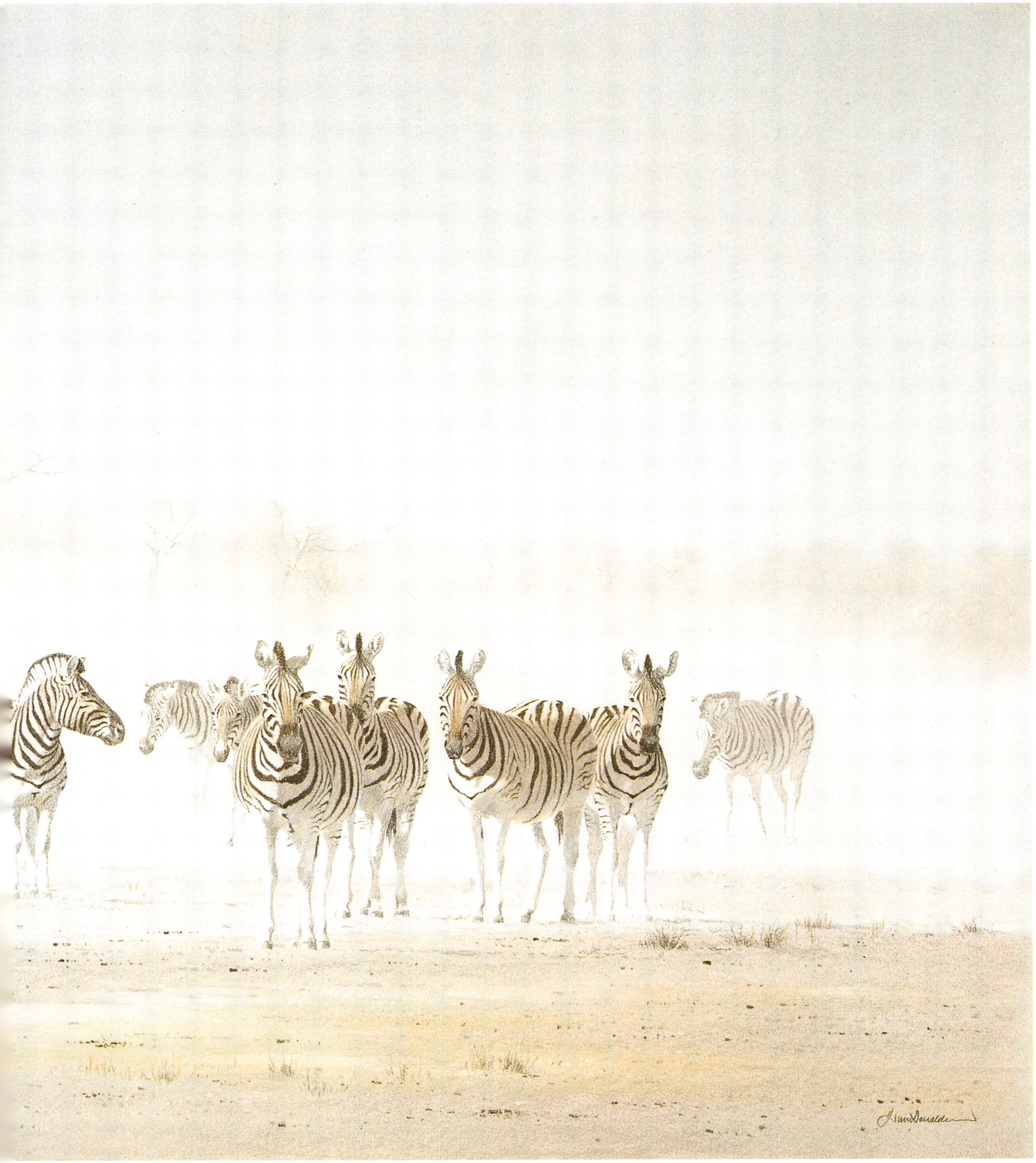

Chapman's zebra (*left*), in the Etosha Pan National Park in Northern Namibia. The dust and monochromatic colours of the dry surroundings make a strong contrast to the colourful grasslands and wooded areas normally associated with African game. This park with its parched landscape and short grass allows the viewer to see the game better and artistically provides a more suitable view. Zebra cope well with the Etosha climate and spare foliage but are reliant on water. They are nervous at waterholes and frequently gallop off at the slightest sign of danger, real or imaginary. In the protected environment of Etosha Pan, their only source of danger is from lions. However, nature has provided them with a deadly kick and the ability to run rather fast, so they are not necessarily an easy meal for a lion.

Chapman's zebras are identified by their ground colour of buffy cream, and their dark stripes alternating with pale shadow stripes. Their legs are almost unmarked. Contrast these animals with Michael Ghaui's Grant's zebras, shown on page 19.

ZEBRA OF ETOSHA
Kim Donaldson

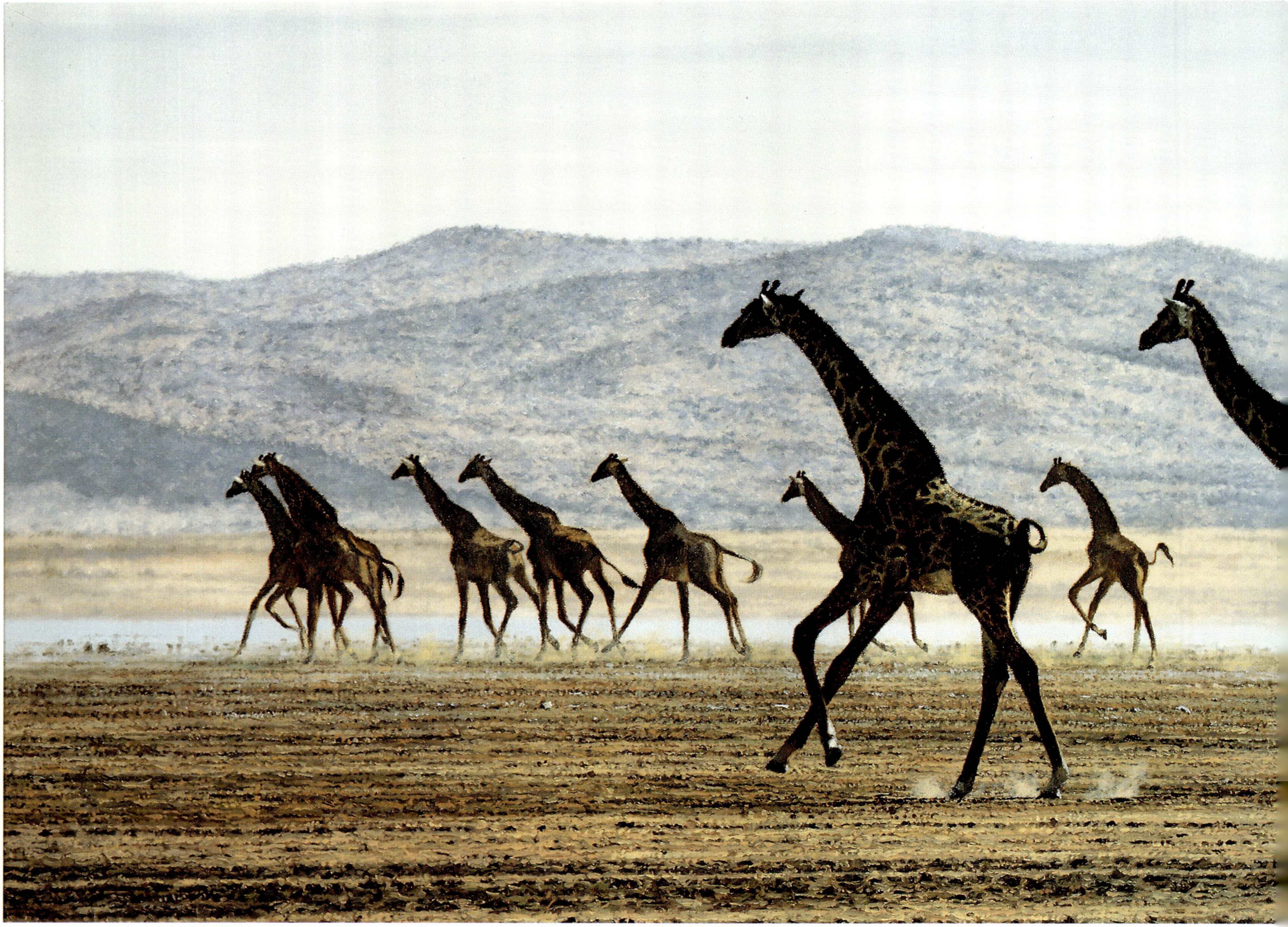

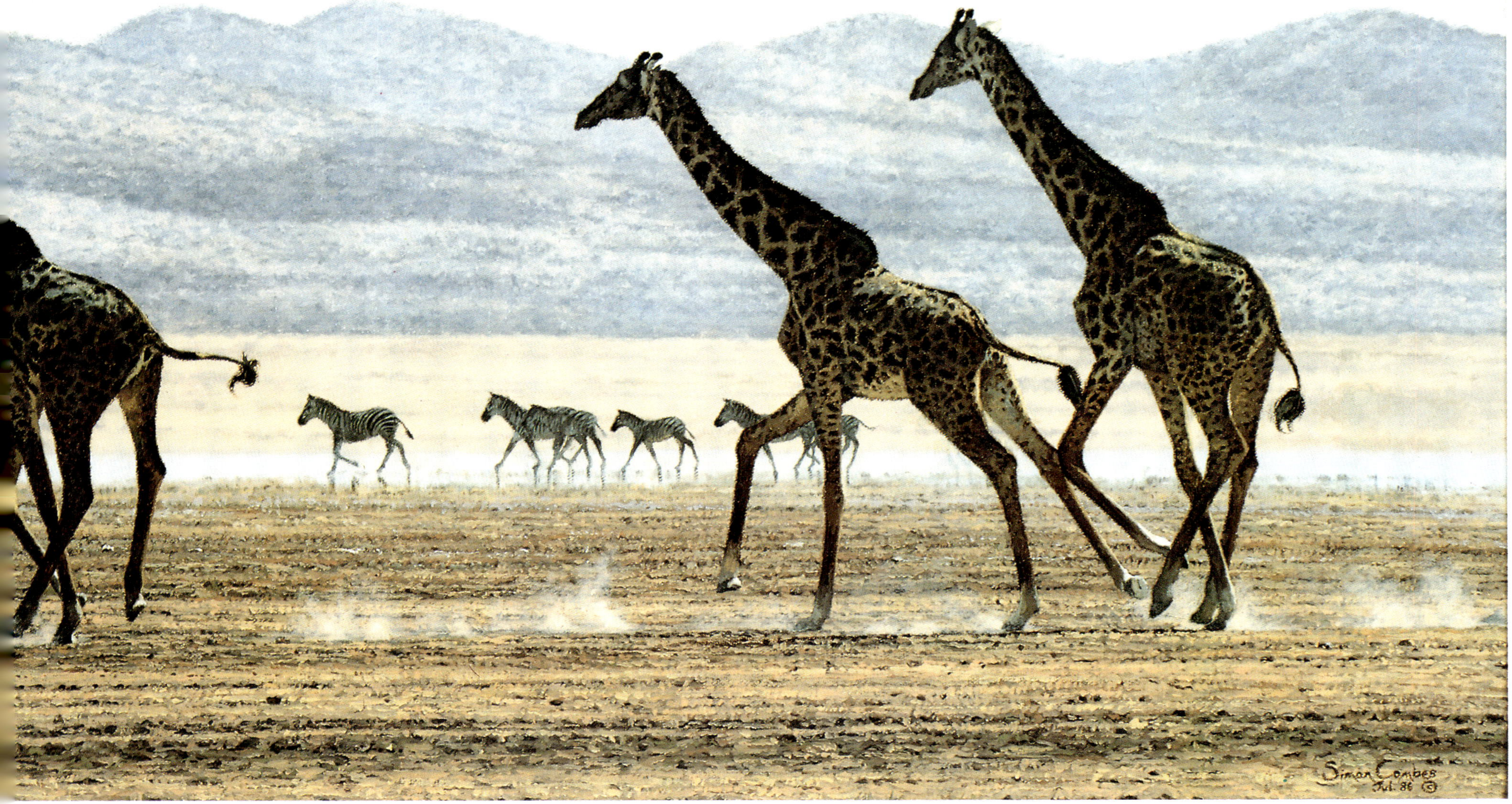
Simon Combes

70 Artists (*previous page*) have the advantage over photographers in that they can choose their light, and determine how it affects their subject. Look at the pictures in this book and you will discover that the great majority portray scenes in either the early morning or the late afternoon. In Africa, the harsh light of midday casts hard shadows, while the overhead sun ensures that landscapes lose their texture and form. In addition, distant mirages create the illusion of legless animals, paddling through shimmering lakes. Here, with *The Mirage*, Simon Combes attempts what most other artists would never dream of tackling, a midday scene.

"I approached the subject with some apprehension and shied away from overdoing the effect. Similar to an incredible sunset, I felt the viewer might be disbelieving if I painted the mirage as I actually saw it." The cantering giraffes are well handled. I like the puffs of dust, kicked up by the giraffes' hooves, which add to the feeling of movement. Difficult subject it might be, but it does succeed, whereas any photographs of the same scene would probably have been consigned to the bin.

THE MIRAGE
Simon Combes

Dust is impossible to escape in Africa: it is always with you, except during the rains when it turns to mud. Here Bob Kuhn shows a buffalo (*right*) settling down for a good dustbath. There is an air of contentment on the old bull's face as he slowly lowers himself to the ground, clouds of dust already blowing yellow in the afternoon sun.

Kuhn comments that "I am at the point where I can draw buffalo almost reflexively. But my batting average is terrible, for only a few eventually become paintings. I'll keep whacking away though, because you learn from the bad ones, too."

DUSTBATH
Bob Kuhn

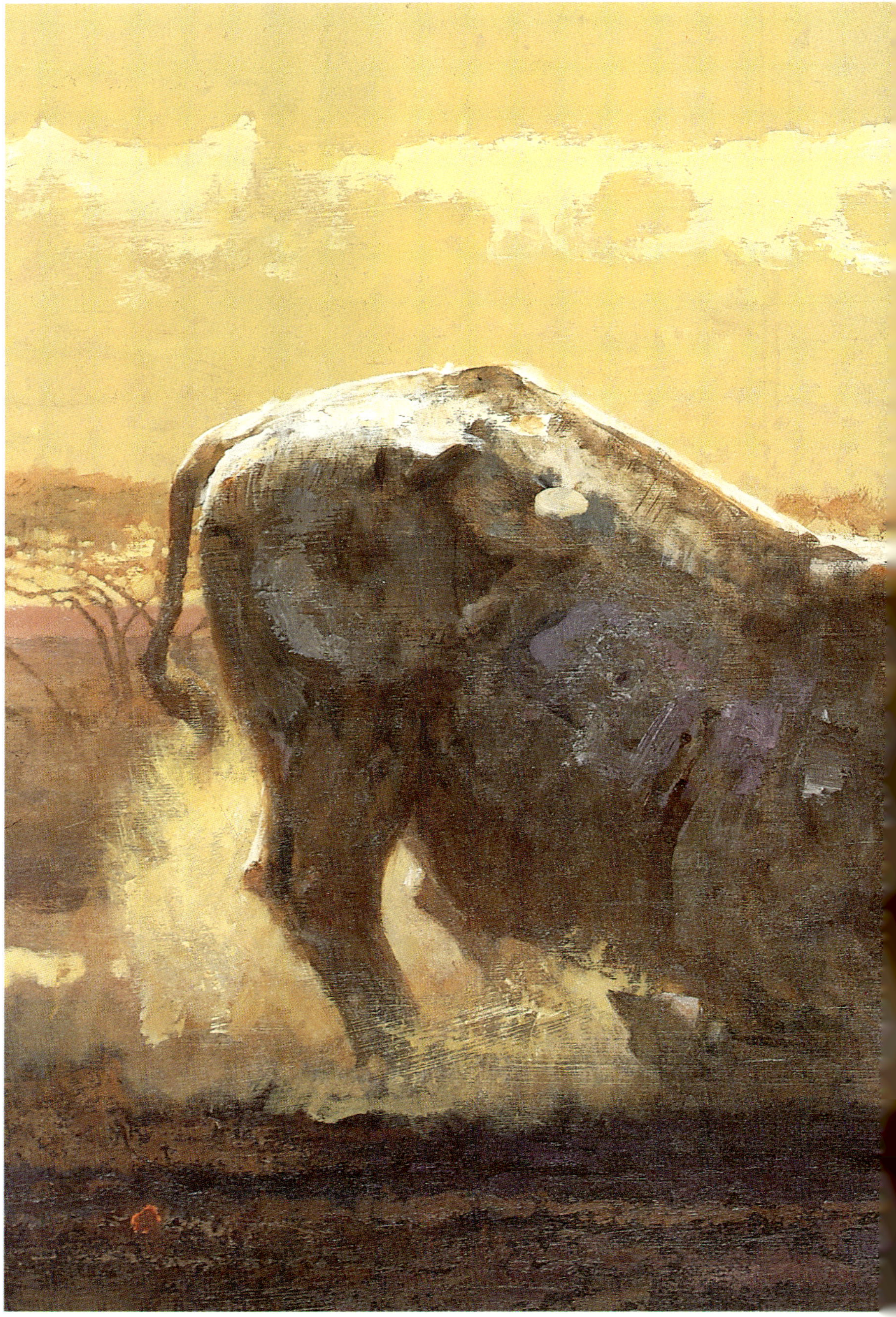

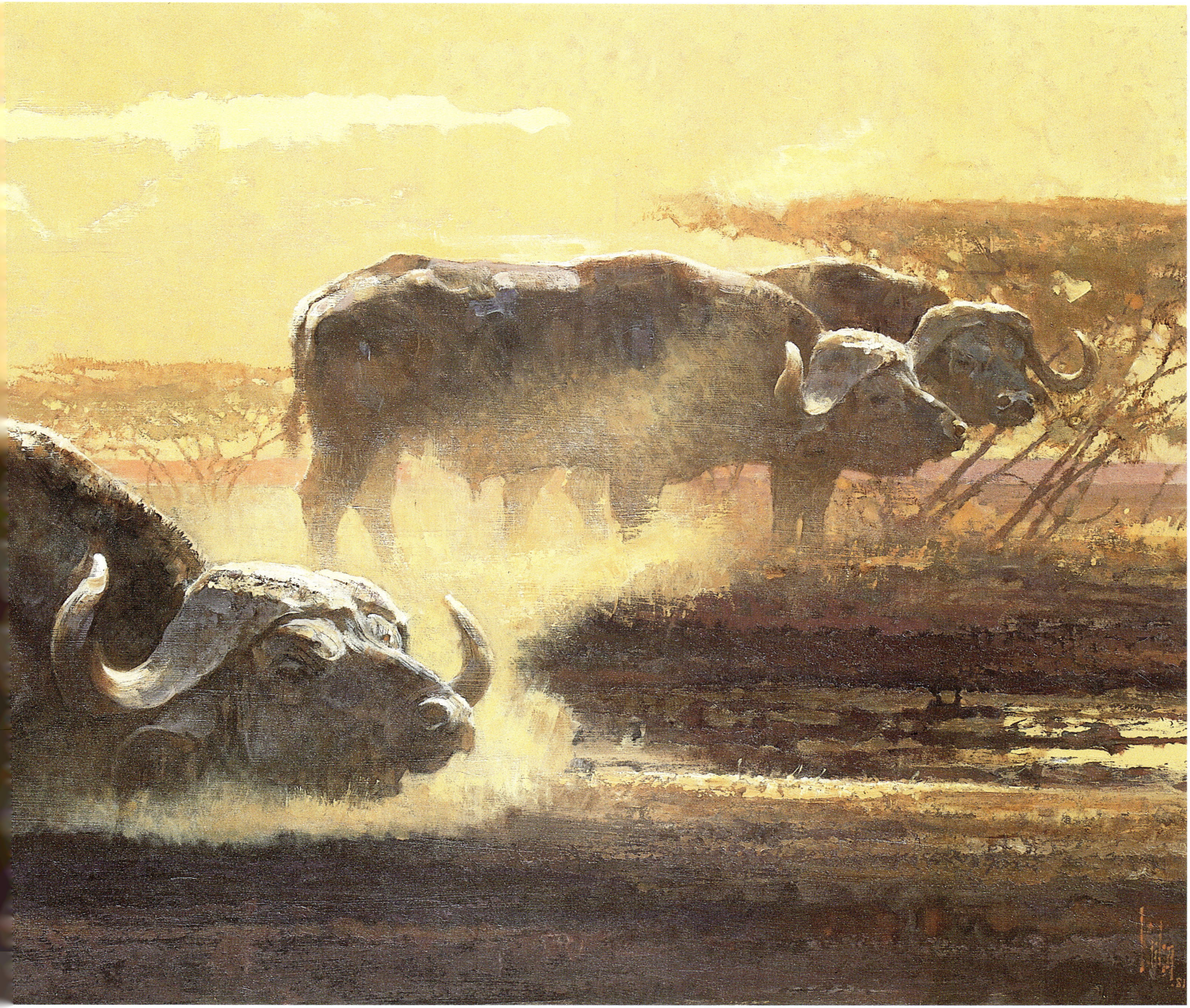

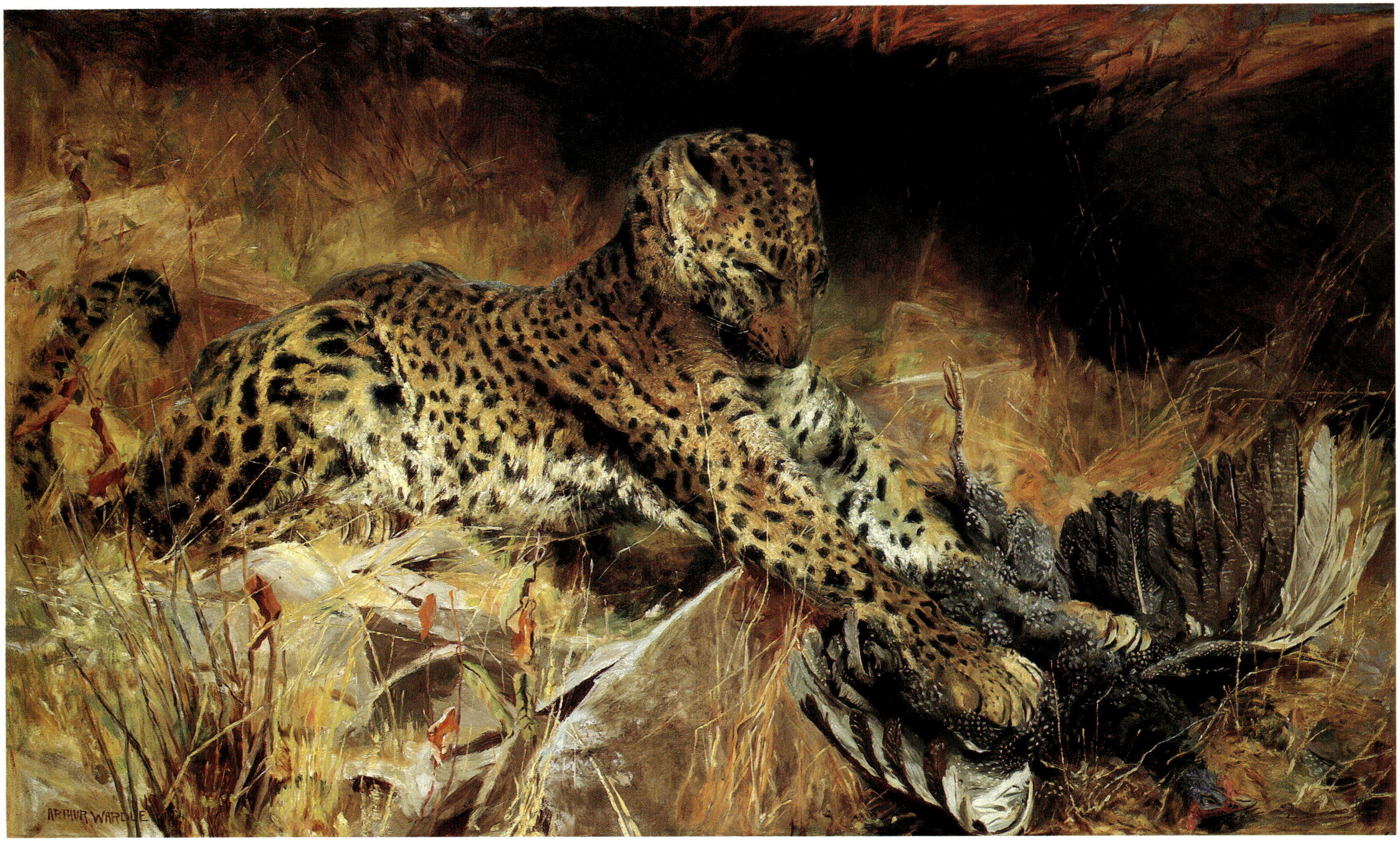

Considering how good they are to eat, guineafowl are surprisingly common in the African bush where they are preyed upon by even the most powerful of predators, including leopards. Arthur Wardle (1864–1949) was an English artist who worked in oils, watercolours and pastel, specializing in painting domestic and wild animals, as well as sporting scenes, but is best known for his paintings of big game and sporting dogs. Several of his leopard paintings were exhibited at the Royal Academy between 1905 and 1938.

LEOPARD AND GUINEAFOWL
Arthur Wardle

This Thorburn study is of a chestnut-breasted buzzard, *Buteo rufofuscus archeri*, now called the Somali buzzard and generally regarded as a race of the widespread augur buzzard. Though Thorburn may never have visited Somalia, he knew enough about birds to make life-like studies despite working from skins, and never having seen the bird alive. Thorburn invariably worked in watercolour, and was never very successful with oil.

CHESTNUT-BREASTED BUZZARD
Archibald Thorburn

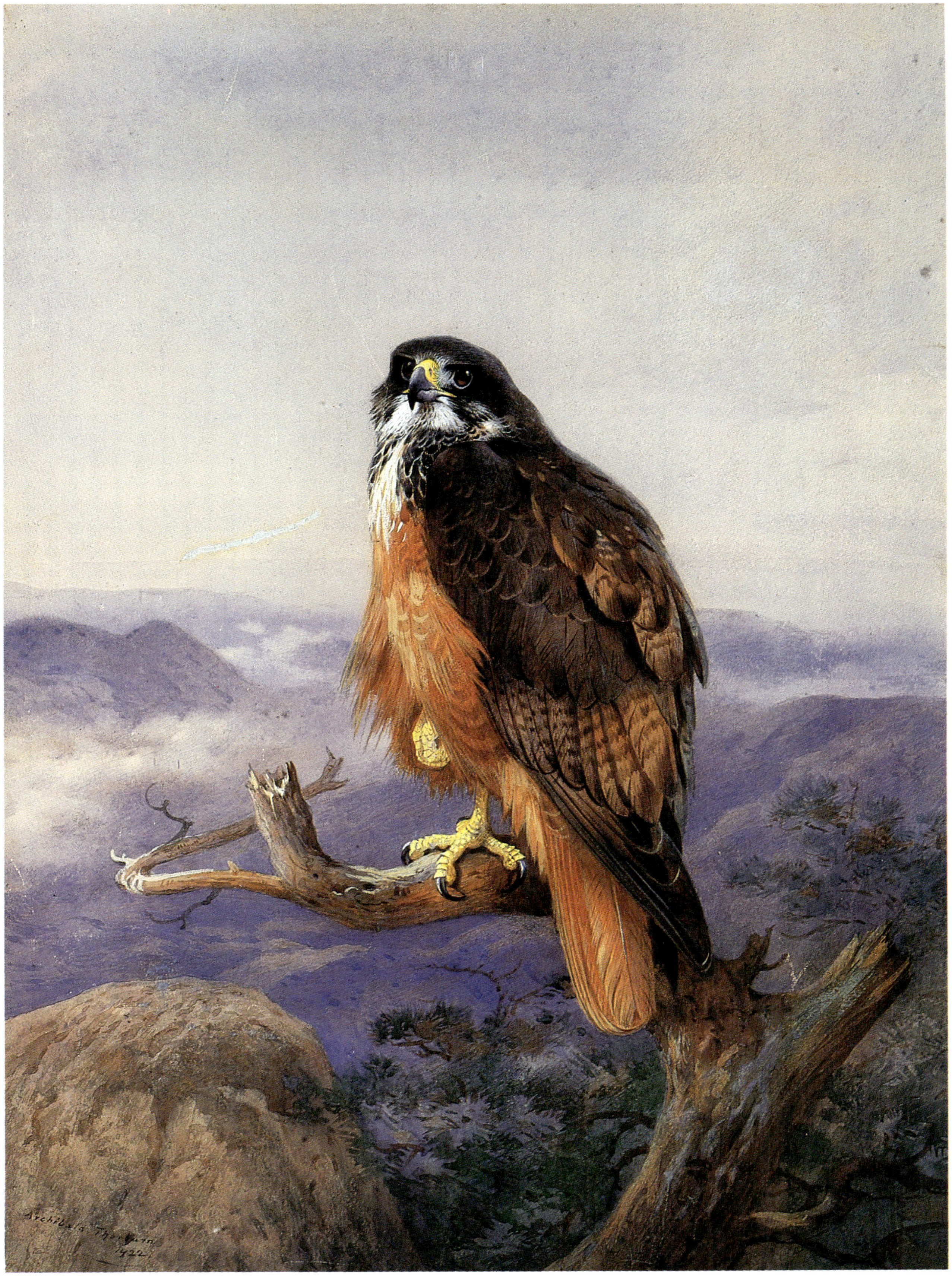

Wilhelm Kuhnert was one of the first artists to paint lions not only from life, but in their natural habitat, where his first-hand knowledge came from hunting them. He was a natural draughtsman, and here the converging lines of ridge and mountain draw the eye to the subject of the painting, the lion itself. Look at the picture closely and it is really very simple, and is unlikely to have taken Kuhnert long to complete. By placing the lion partly behind a rock, he has avoided painting the animal's back legs, with the resulting problems of perspective. No doubt he could have overcome such minor difficulties if he had wanted to, but there was no real reason to do so.

LION RESTING
Wilhelm Kuhnert

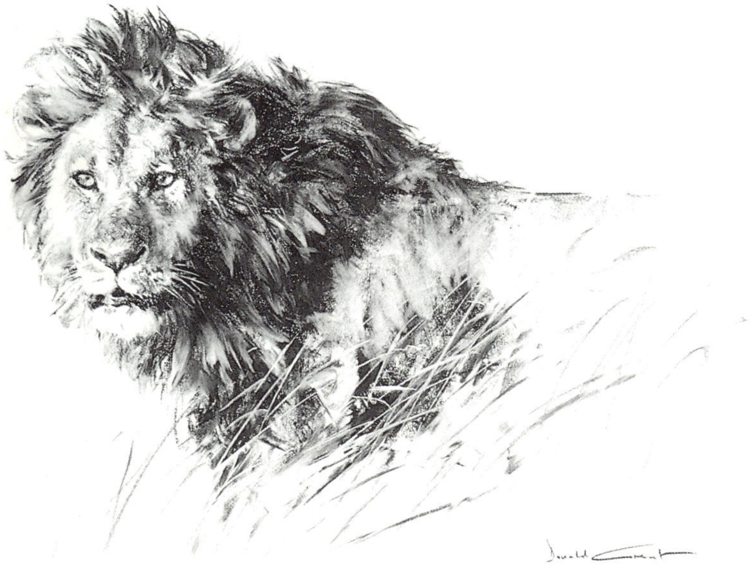

AFRICAN LION
Donald Grant

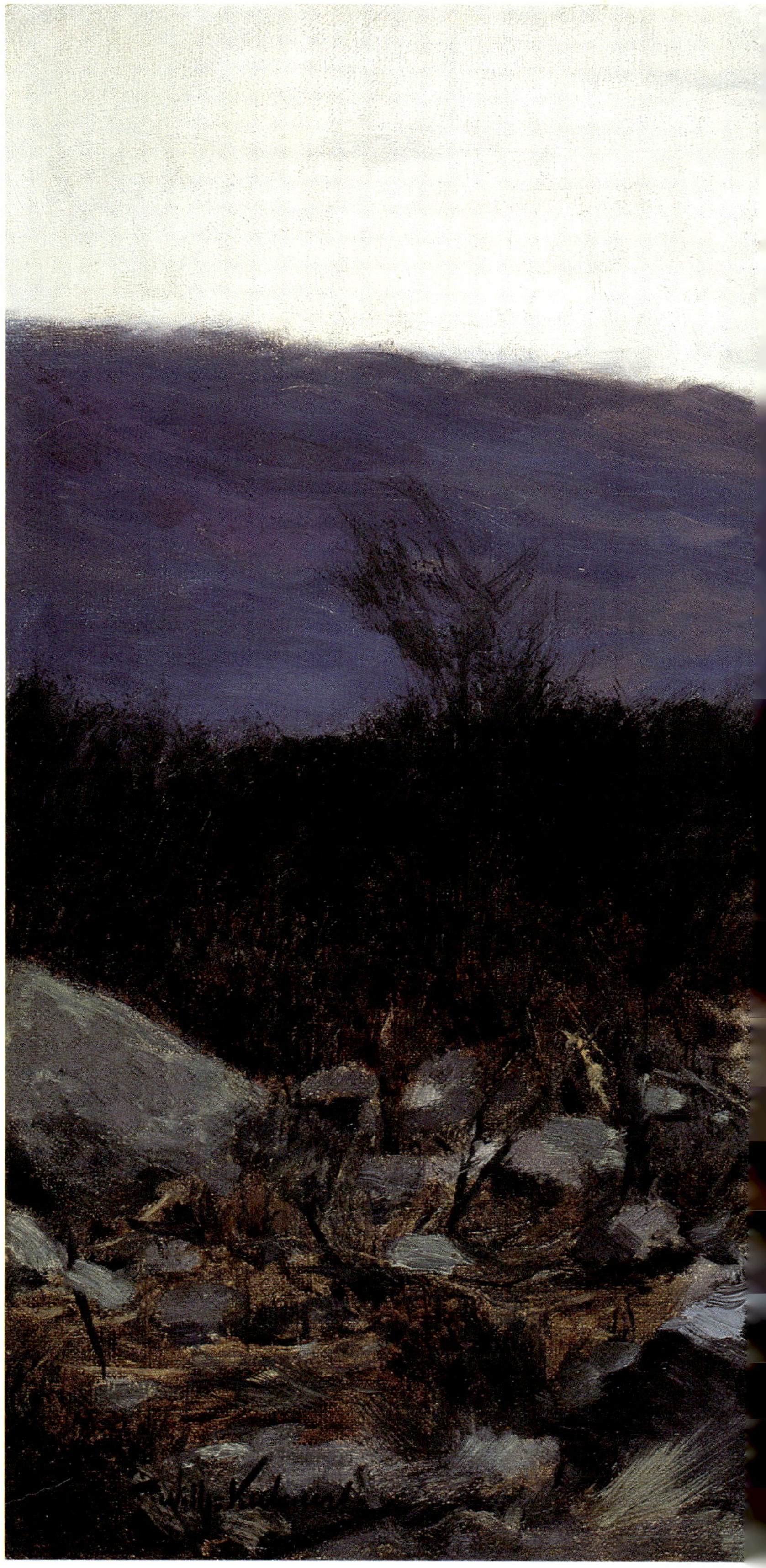

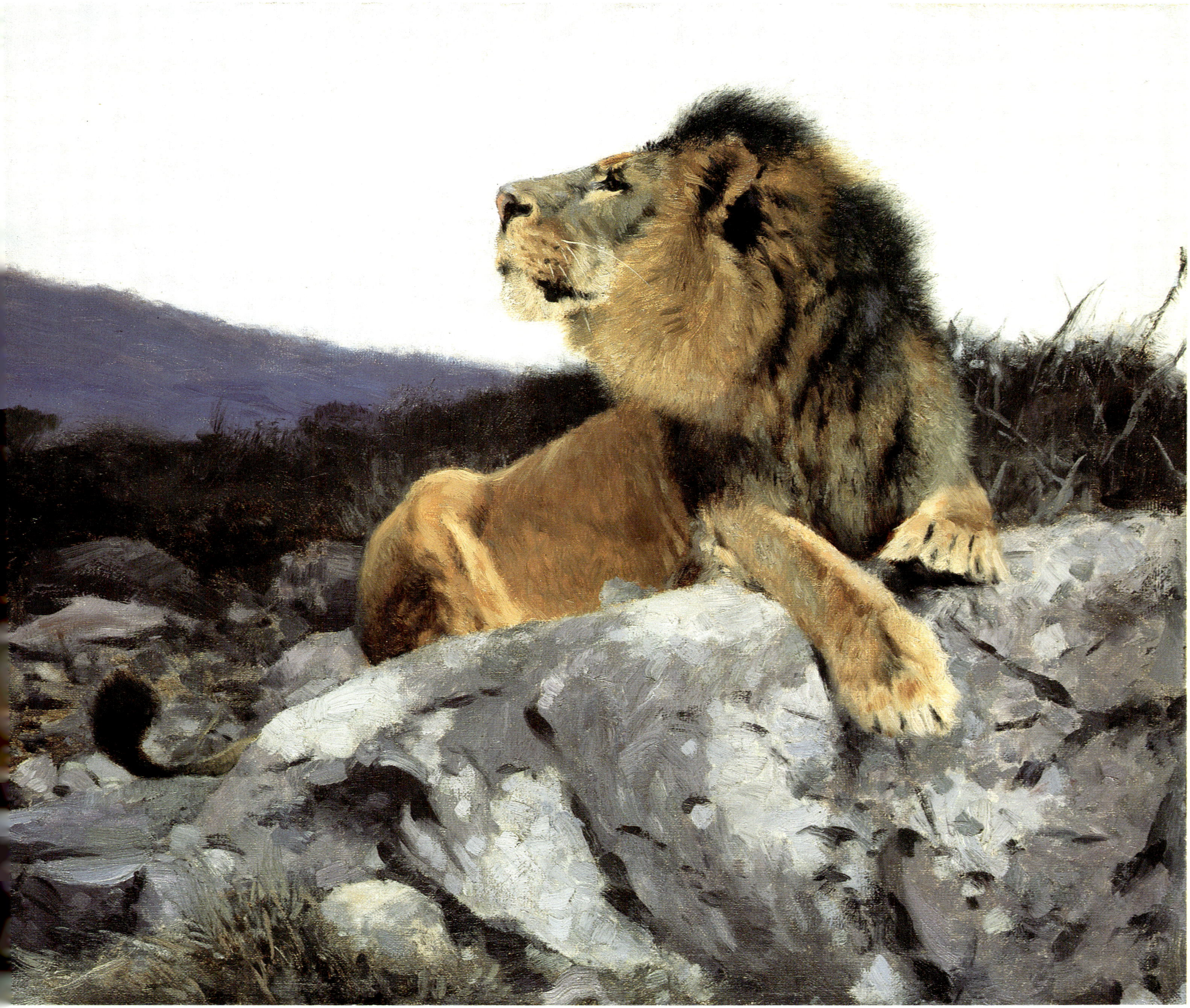

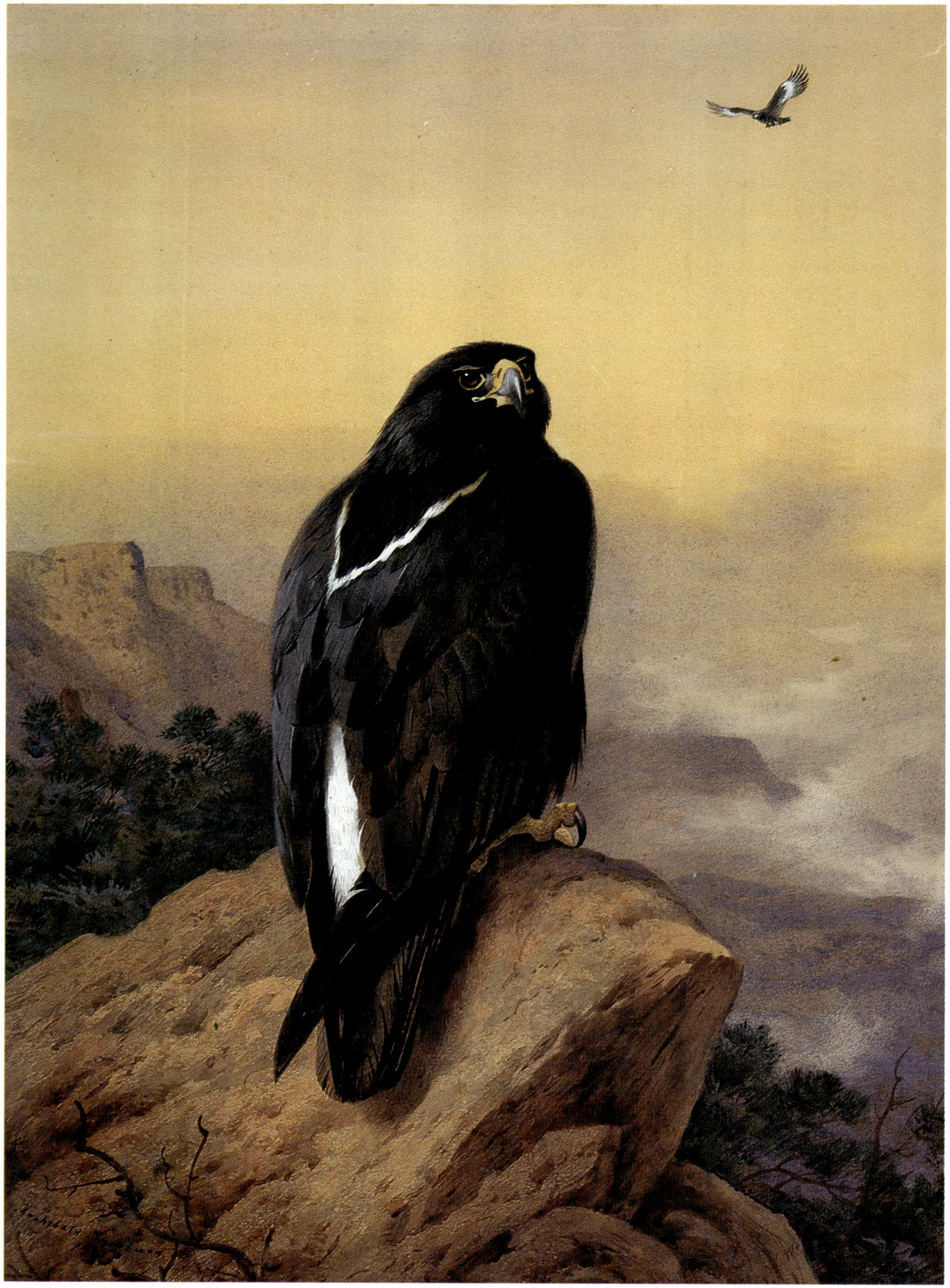

This is another study by Archibald Thorburn for *The Birds of British Somaliland*, and shows a Verreaux's eagle, one of the largest and most handsome of African eagles. Pleasing though the portrait is, it shows a striking resemblance to the chestnut-breasted buzzard on page 73. The pose is almost identical, the bird has the same regal expression, and even the landscape is little changed. Even so, this hardly detracts from the painting, which is every bit a classic Thorburn.

Today, Verreaux's eagle is more often known as the black eagle, a rather boring name for such an impressive bird. Jules Pierre Verreaux (1807–1873), after whom the bird is named, came from a well-known French family which ran a company supplying natural history specimens from a house in Paris. He made a number of expeditions to southern Africa, and this eagle is one of several birds and animals to bear his name.

VERREAUX'S EAGLE
Archibald Thorburn

DWARF MONGOOSES
Michael Ghaui

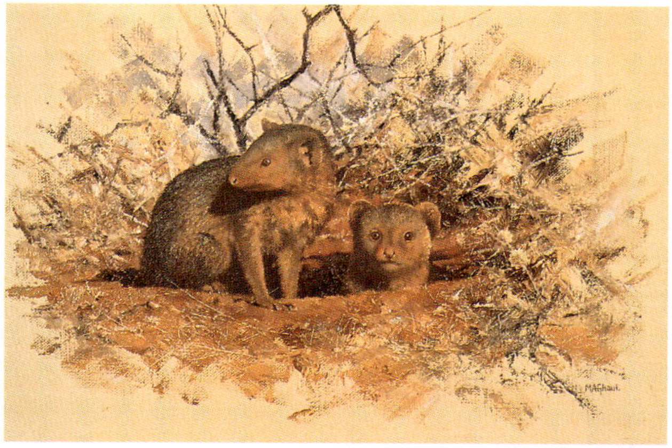

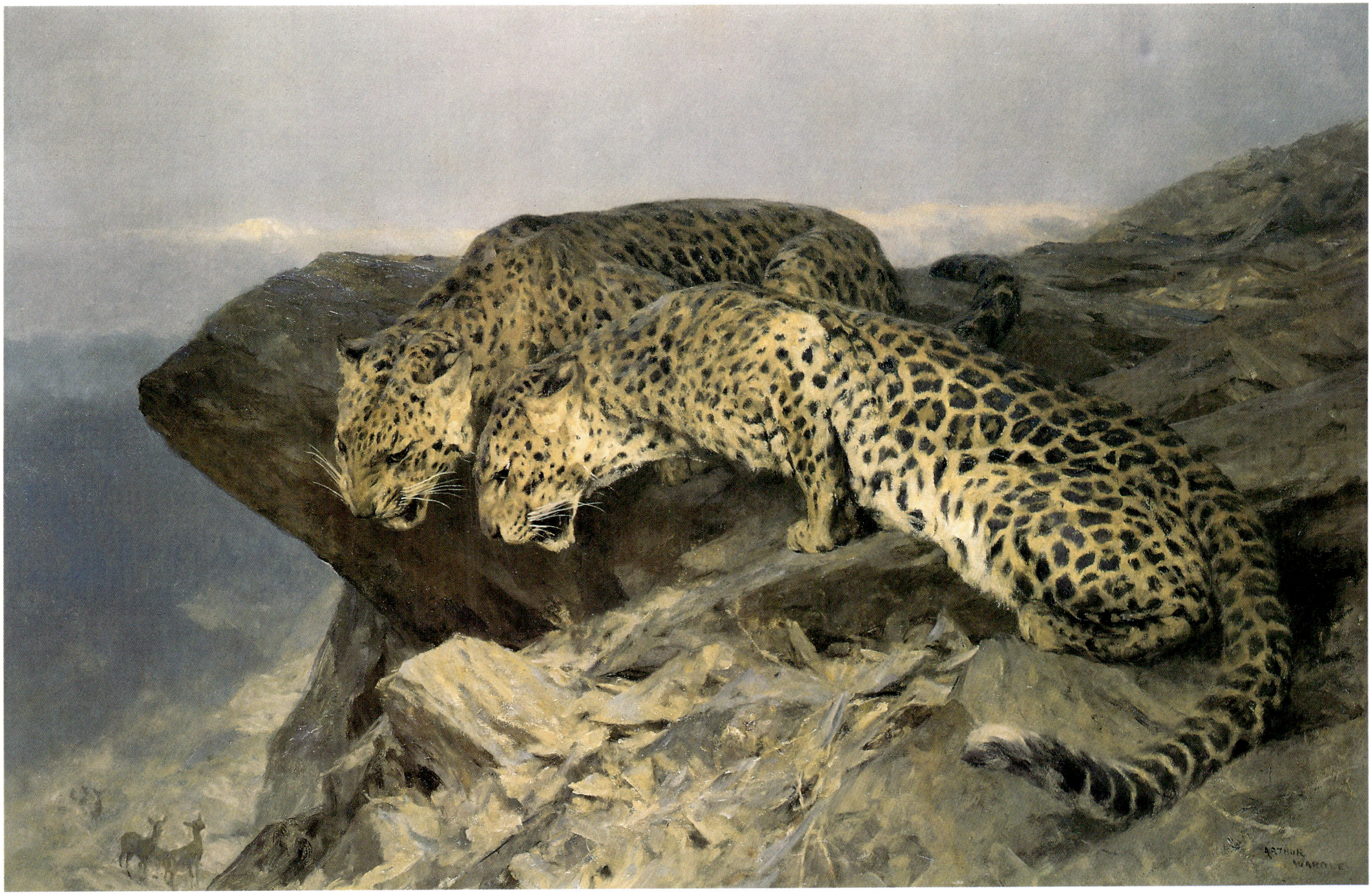

I have to admit that this oil, of a pair of leopards by Arthur Wardle, is not one I can take too seriously. The two animals appear to be engaged in conversation, possibly discussing which of the antelope below they should select for their supper. Leopards are the most solitary of animals, except during the mating season when both male and female live side by side, and hunt together. The female brings up her cubs alone, with no help from the male.

LEOPARD ROCK
Arthur Wardle

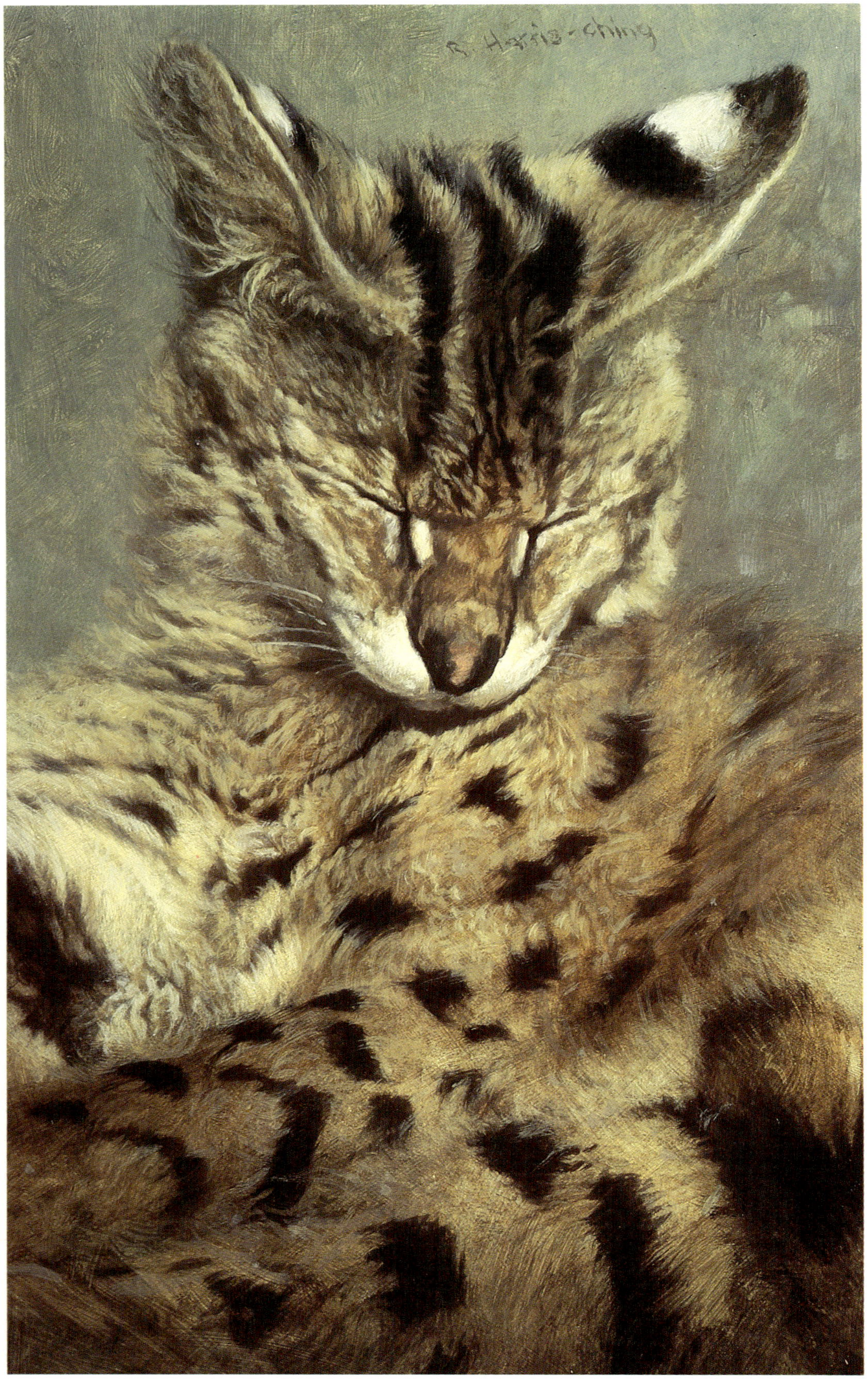

Shy, elusive and mainly nocturnal, servals can be as difficult to see as leopards. Their huge ears act like radar dishes, picking up the faintest sounds of movement from the hares, rodents and birds on which they prey. In the late evening, one sometimes sees a serval burst from the tall grass in a series of vertical leaps as it tries to spot its quarry. They are among the swiftest of all the cats, and can even catch birds on the wing, though Raymond Ching's dozing animal looks far too relaxed for such activities.

SERVAL
Raymond Ching

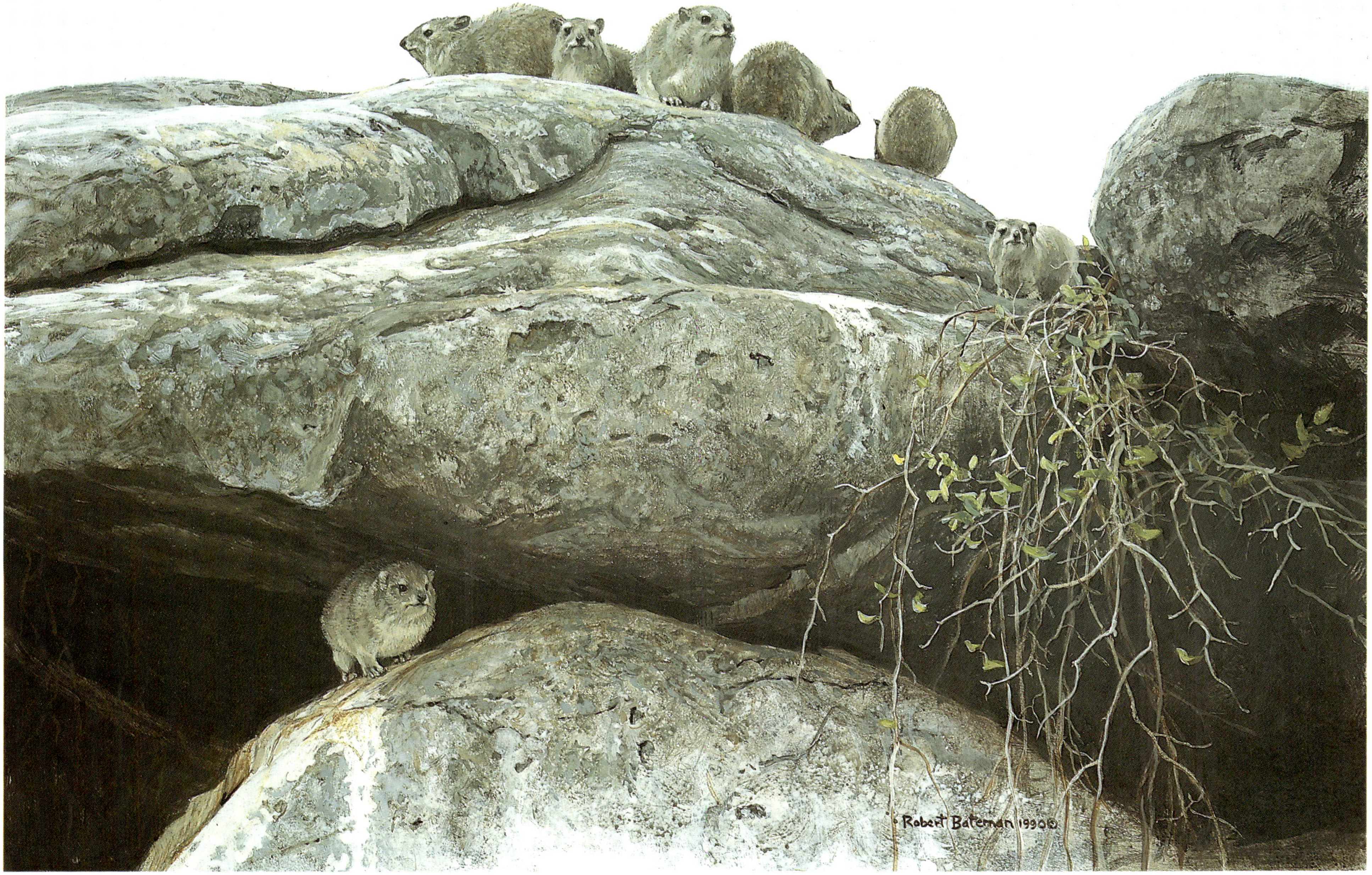

Rock hyrax are, so we are assured by zoologists, the closest living relations of the elephant. They are rarely painted by artists, which makes this oil by Robert Bateman all the more pleasing. Bateman explains that "when most people think of African wildlife, what usually comes to mind are the lions, elephants and antelopes – big inhabitants of the savanna or bush country that covers so much of the continent. But even within the savanna regions, there are very different habitats sheltering many other species. . ."

Hyrax share several anatomical similarities with elephants, and are common inhabitants of any rocky outcrop or kopje in the savannas. They live in colonies of up to 60 animals, made up of family units with a single adult male, females and young. They are fond of sunbathing, and are usually seen when warming themselves on top of a rock.

HYRAX
Robert Bateman

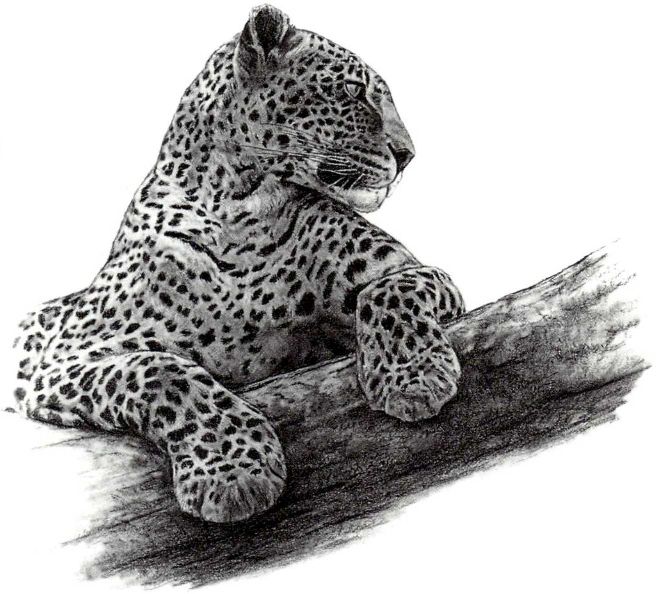

LEOPARD
Joseph C. Vance

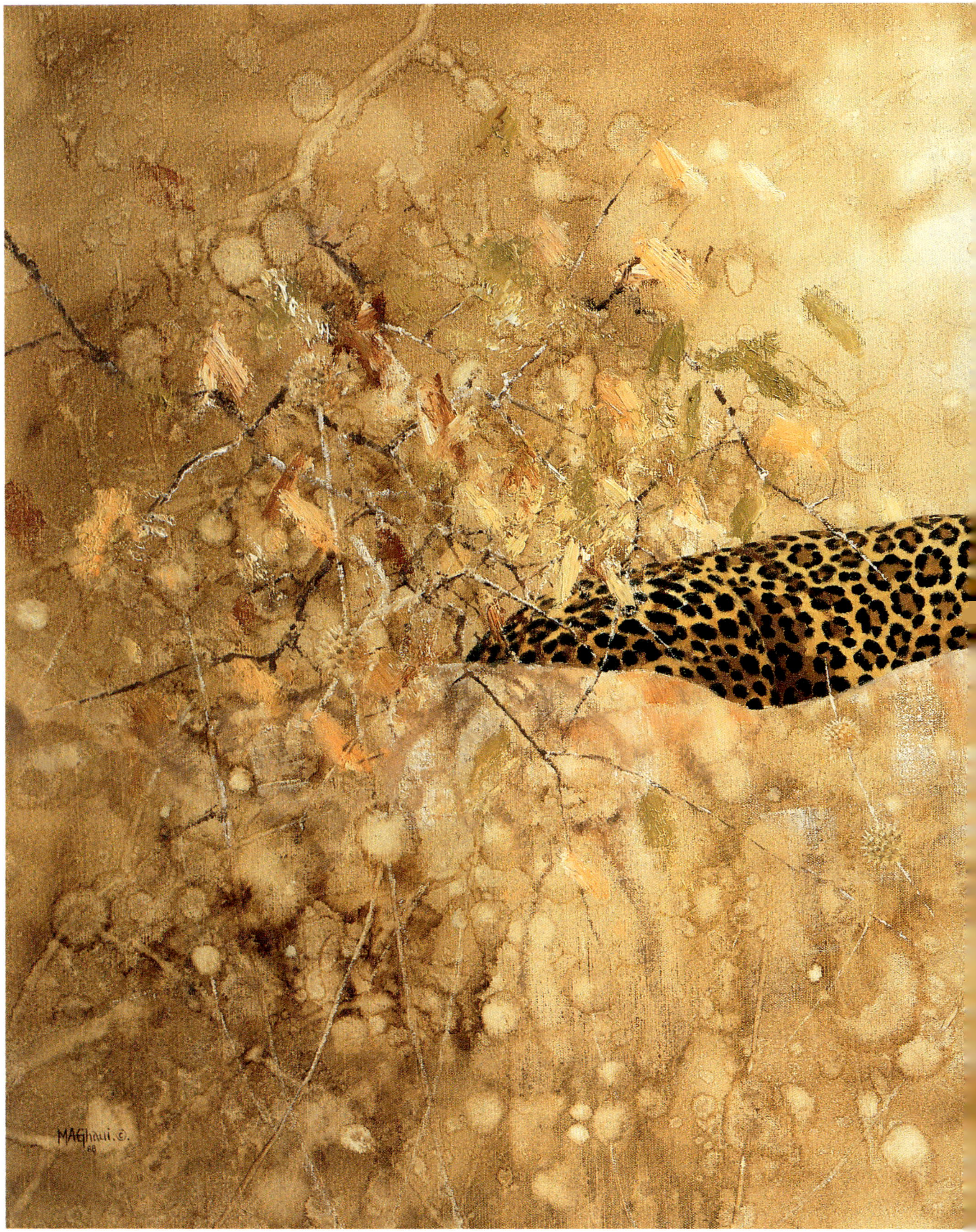

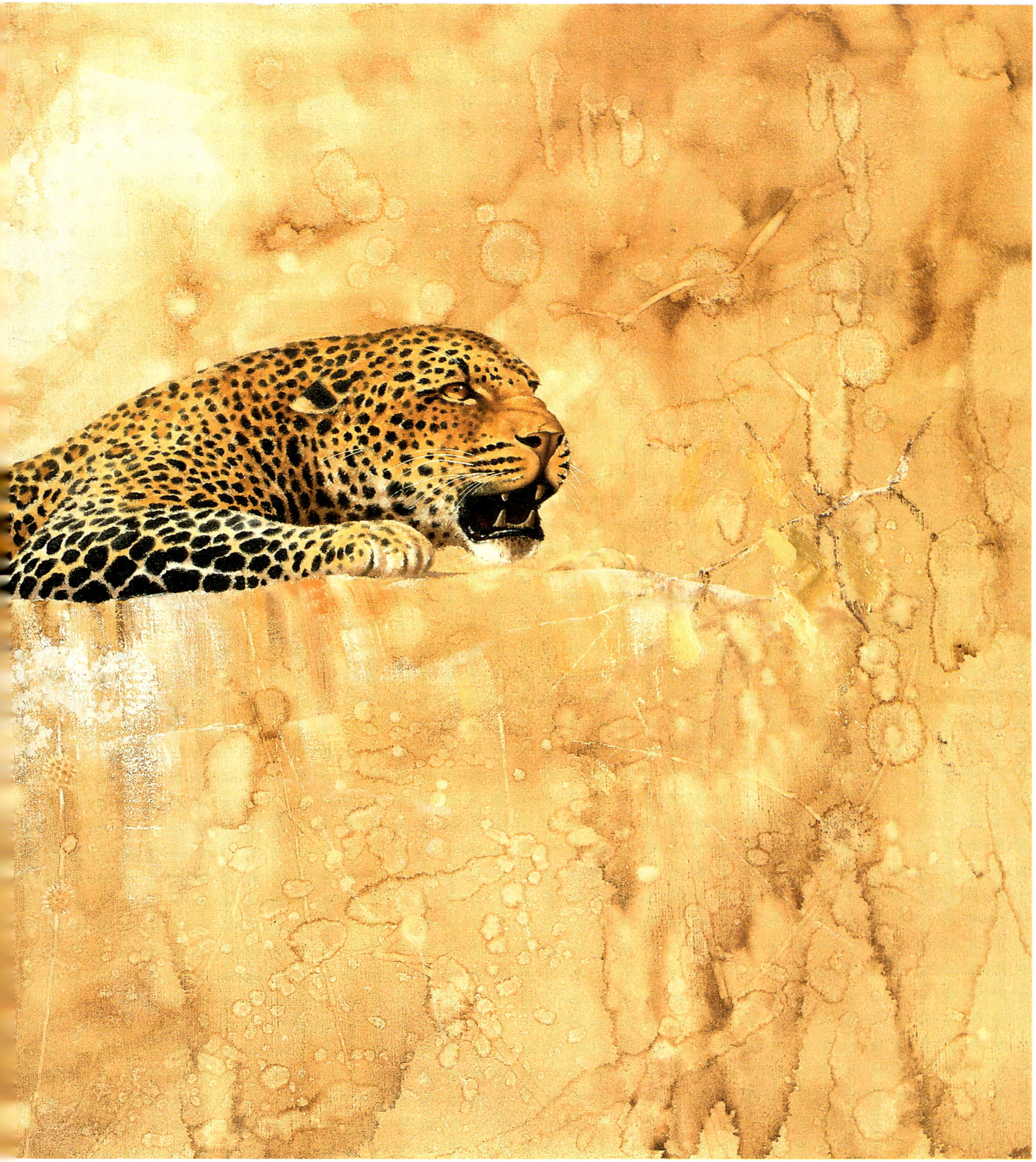

"This was the biggest leopard I had ever seen, probably over 200lb in weight. I found him basking on a ledge in the morning sun. The transition from a peaceful, prostrate form to a snarling, growling, bolt of lightning took a fraction of a second; a pause of uncertainty, a flick of the tail and then he was gone."

Michael Ghaui adds that he was not really in any danger, for it is unusual for a leopard to charge a human, unless it is wounded, cornered or protecting its young. "Normally they tend to be very shy and will slink away at the earliest opportunity." Like many artists, Ghaui enjoys painting leopards for the sake of the colour and pattern of their rosettes. Here he has kept the background and rock face very simple, emphasising the size, and the fury, of the leopard itself.

GROWLING LEOPARD
Michael Ghaui

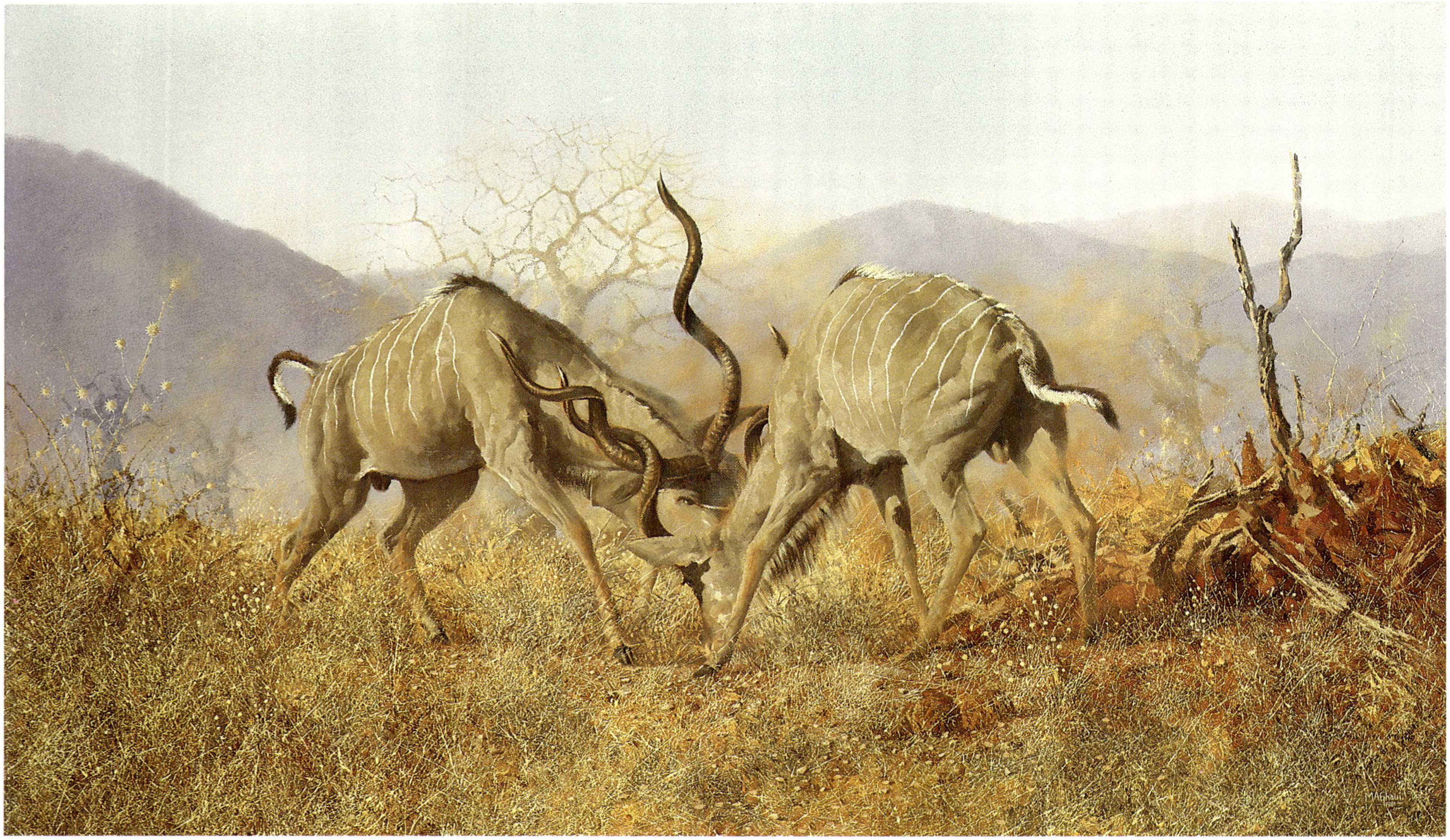

"We were driving along a track in the Ruaha National Park one morning when we noticed a group of dwarf moongooses peering out of a hole in an anthill. They were definitely watching something, and sure enough, on following the direction of their gaze, we noticed a beautiful bull greater kudu standing dead still in a thicket. Nothing seemed amiss, and after a while we decided to move on. Suddenly there was a commotion and another bull appeared from nowhere. Immediately a battle commenced. Heads down, muscles rippling, they clashed time and time again – often with their horns completely interlocking. They bulldozered each other up and down the path, totally oblivious to our presence.

"The battle continued for almost half an hour. Eventually, one bull decided he had had enough, and so with bloodied nose and a very sore head he disappeared over the horizon. It was at this point that the females of the herd came into view – obviously to admire the victor. It is on occasions such as this that you realize how nature works, with only the fittest being allowed to breed."

In common with many artists who have hunted in the past, Michael Ghaui has an excellent knowledge of his subject's anatomy, and this awareness is evident here: the rippling muscles are in the right places. The result is an exciting painting, full of action.

FIGHTING KUDU
Michael Ghaui

A kudu bull is a big animal – face to face with a man, the two pairs of eyes are on the same level. Here Michael Ghaui captures that fleeting moment when kudu and human make an unexpected encounter in the bush. The bull, with ears pricked forward, nostrils flared, looks directly at the intruder, assessing the degree of danger. Should it be instant flight or a more careful, considered withdrawal?

This is typical Ghaui, with the subject in sharp focus, the background impressionistic, unobtrusive. The composition gives priority to the kudu bull, and there are no unnecessary distractions to confuse the eye. The tone of the kudu's coat, broken up by the delicate white lines, makes surprisingly good camouflage in the animal's favoured woodland habitat. Here, though, Ghaui takes us so close to the bull that camouflage is forgotten – this is an animal waiting to leap off the canvas at the viewer.

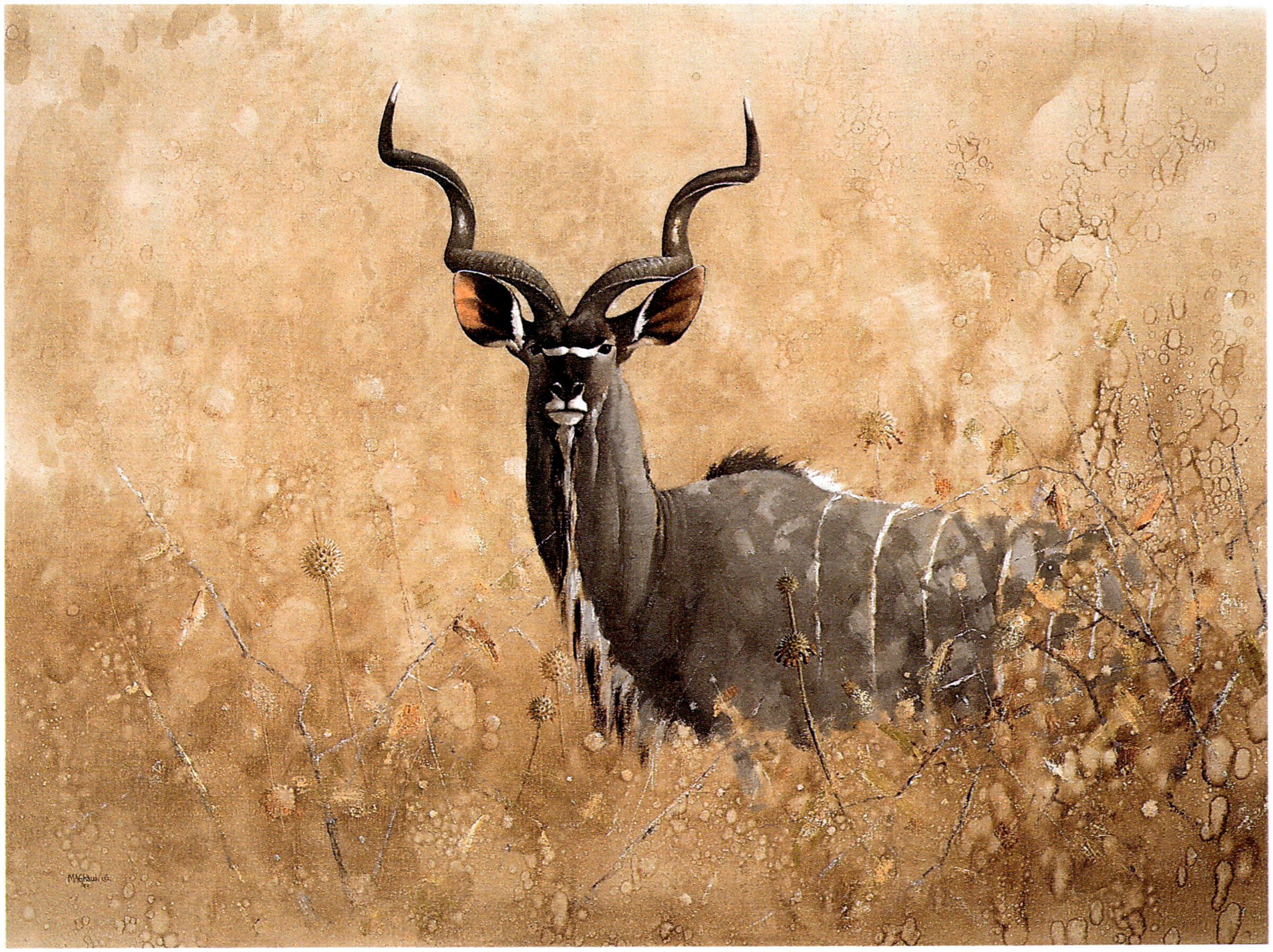

KUDU BULL
Michael Ghaui

To paint a landscape on as large a scale as this without any sky is a considerable achievement, but here Simon Combes succeeds. Skilled use of light and shade give this oil tremendous depth and feeling of space. The pair of black rhino are suitably dwarfed by the sheer scale of the Ngorongoro crater, one of the most famous of African wildlife sanctuaries.

A handful of black rhino still survive in Ngorongoro. Simon Combes points out that "their survival is somewhat tenuously ensured simply by the very geography of this awe-inspiring natural amphitheatre; a potential poacher would have to commit his dirty deed under the ever-watchful eyes of the game rangers who command an uninterrupted view of the whole crater floor from their positions two thousand feet up on the rim. Even these risks have not deterred some of the more daring killers who risk their lives to slay this rather sad, cumbersome animal which carries on its nose two horns worth more than their weight in gold. Most of the few remaining in East Africa have been translocated to special parks where they are protected by huge electric fences and heavily armed guards. It was therefore more poignant to paint two of Ngorongoro's last survivors against the vast, unprotective height of the crater wall as the sun creeps over the rim at dawn."

THE SURVIVORS
Simon Combes

ABOVE THE ATHI RIVER
Rena Fennessey

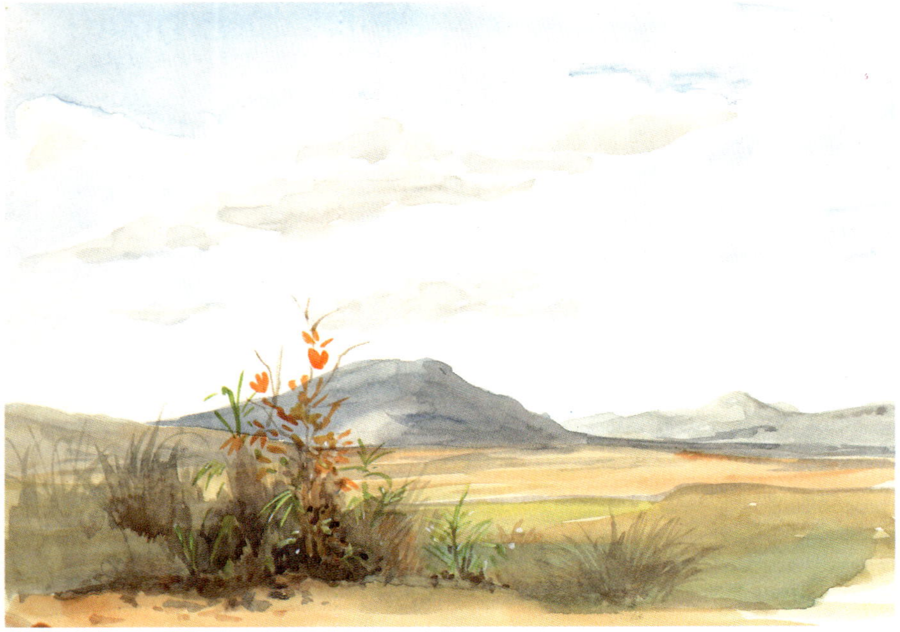

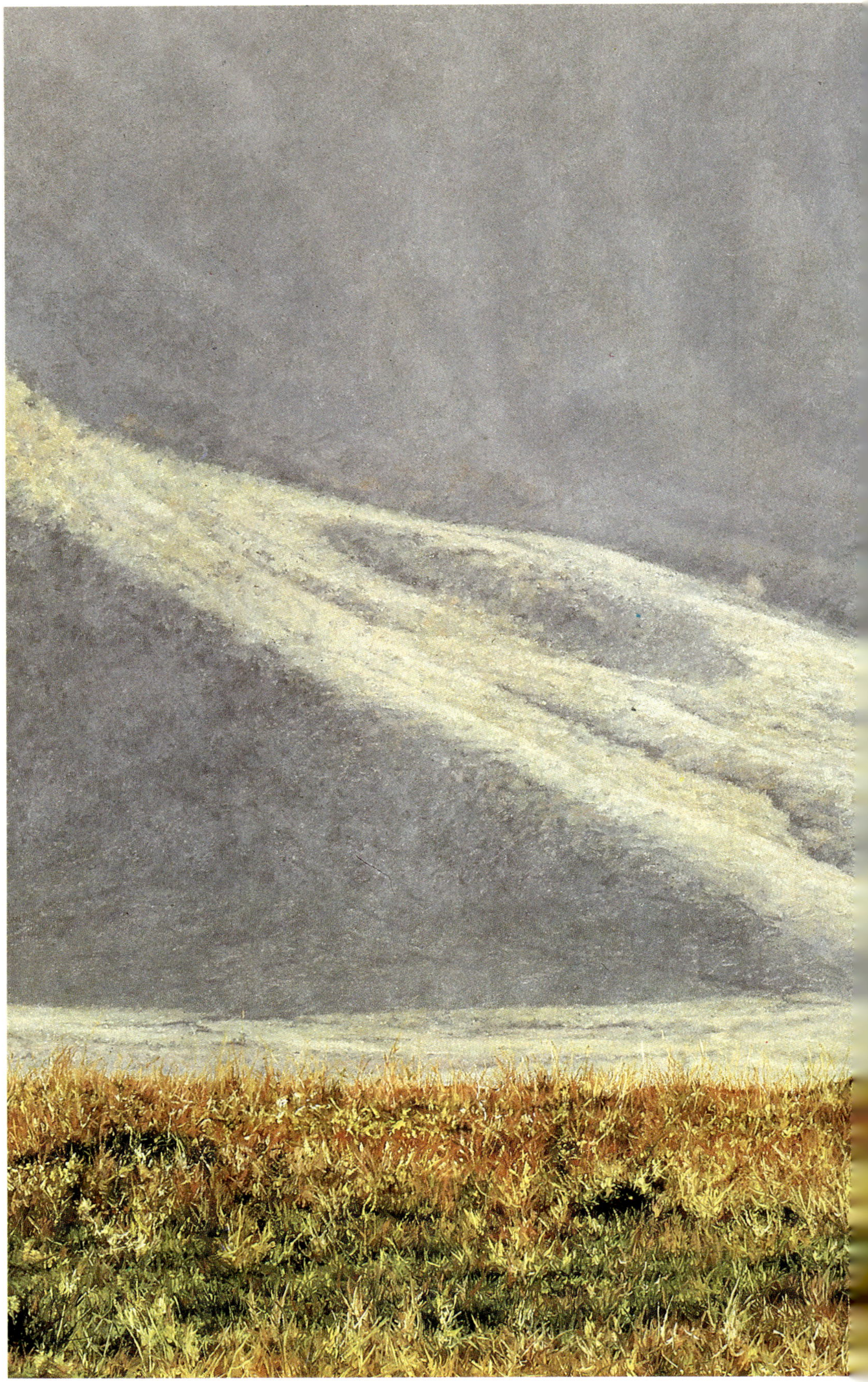

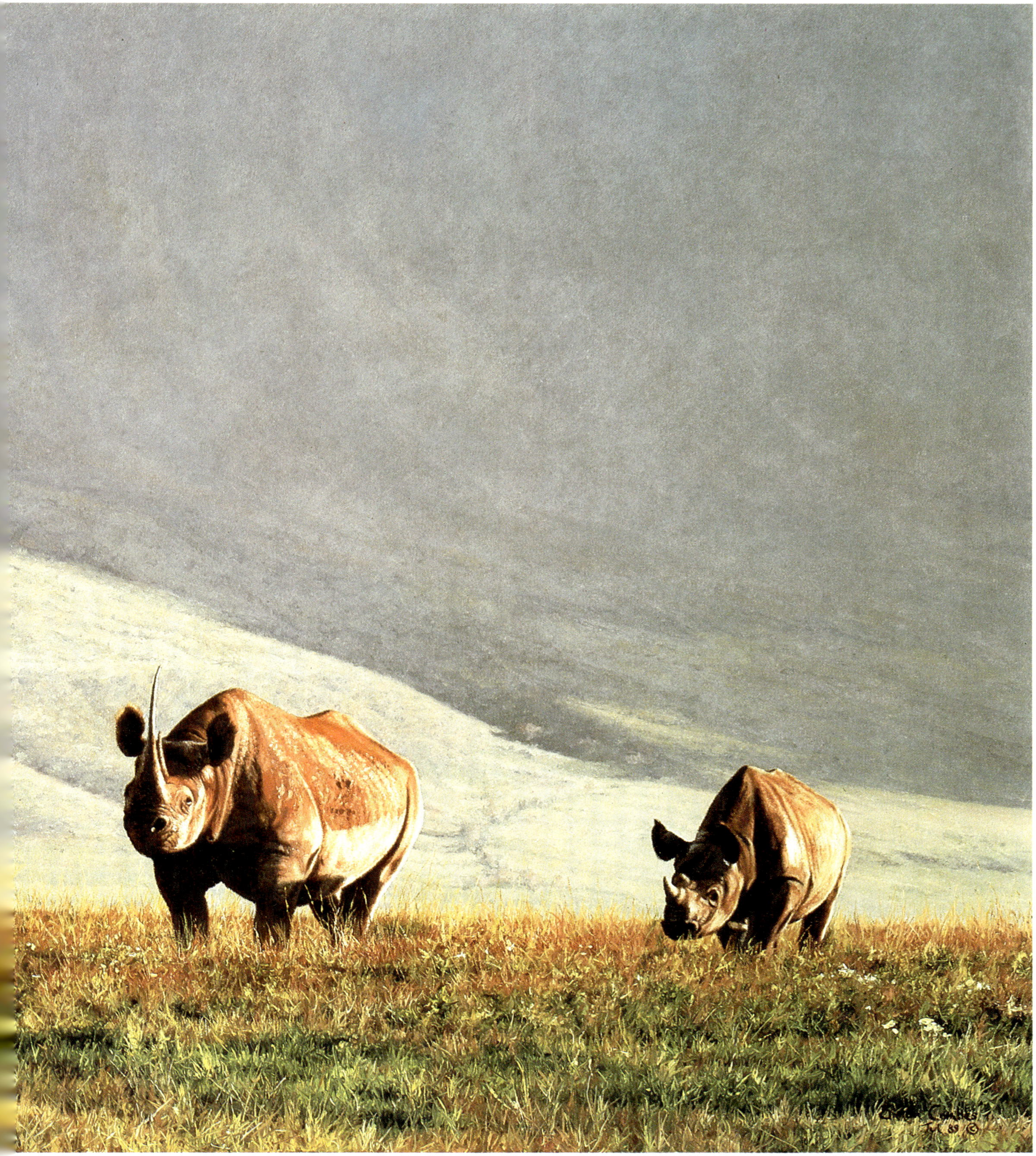

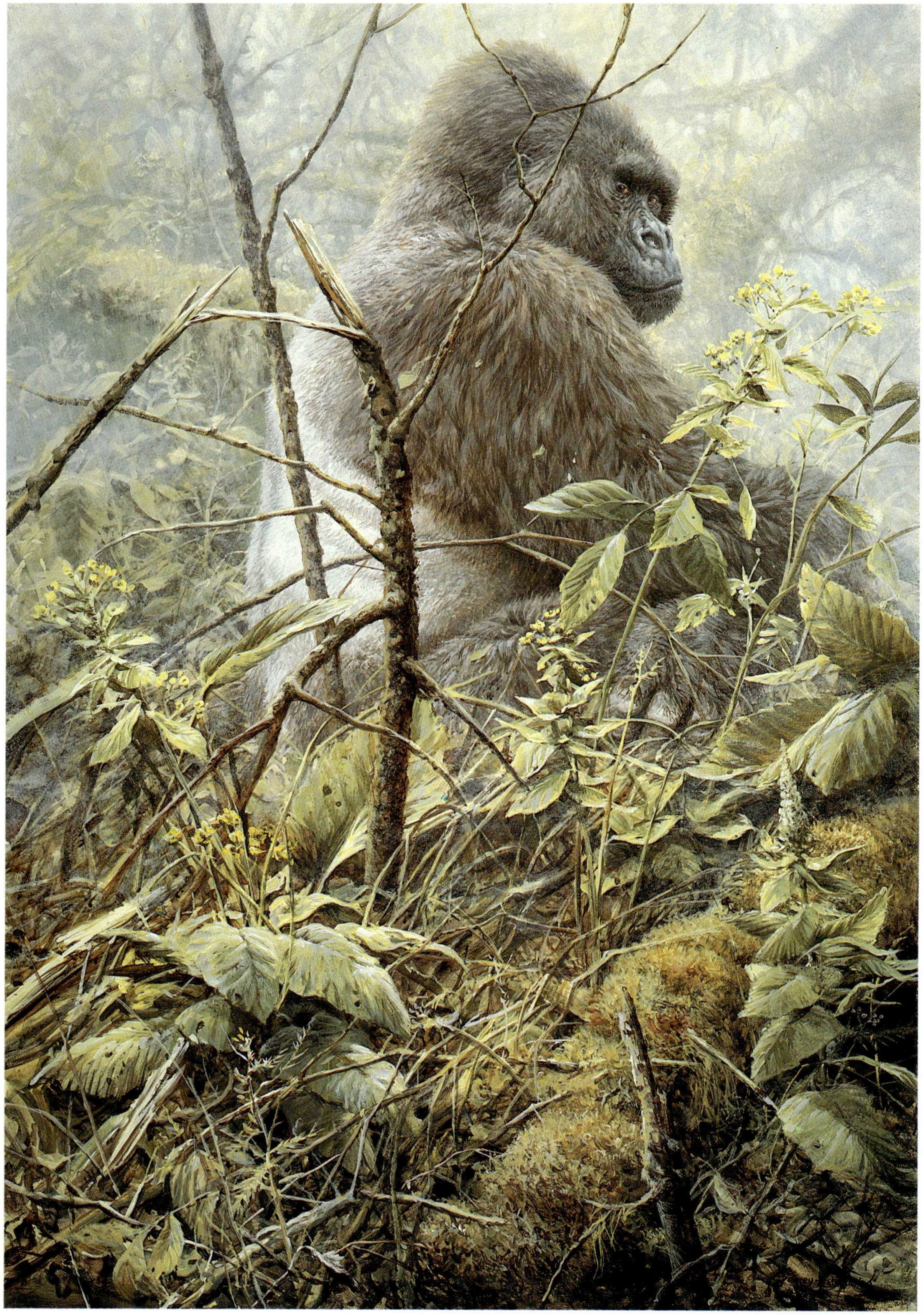

One of John Seerey-Lester's long-standing ambitions was to paint a gorilla, "maybe because the gorilla is, along with the chimpanzee, one of man's closest relatives. Or possibly I am fascinated by the gorilla's great strength. Perhaps it is its undoubted intelligence that appeals to me. It could also be the commanding presence exuded by this, the mightiest of the great apes."

Seerey-Lester chose to paint the largest and rarest of the three races of gorilla, the endangered mountain gorilla. "I selected a pose that would not be threatening, but instead one that I hoped would bring out the gorilla's quiet strength and composure. I wanted its human-like side-glance, which will follow the viewer wherever he stands to look at the painting, to serve as an unnerving reminder of just how close a relative the gorilla is to man." Perhaps when we consider man's inhumanity to man we should not be surprised that for years he has killed gorillas, though they may be our first cousins, and the most gentle of herbivores.

HIGH AND MIGHTY – GORILLA
John Seerey-Lester

Africa sustains a host of different species of monkey, but most are animals of the rainforests of West and Central Africa, seldom encountered by any except dedicated monkey enthusiasts.

Raymond Ching's portrait shows the strikingly handsome Diana monkey, which is found only in the dense, high forests of coastal West Africa. The Diana monkey has several close relations, such as the Mona monkey and L'Hoest's monkey, but neither species can boast the distinctive white beard of the Diana.

Raymond Ching is one of the most gifted of draughtsmen. Born in Wellington, New Zealand, in 1939, he did not start to paint wildlife until he came to live in England in the late sixties. His paintings of African wildlife are few: one longs to see more.

DIANA MONKEY
Raymond Ching

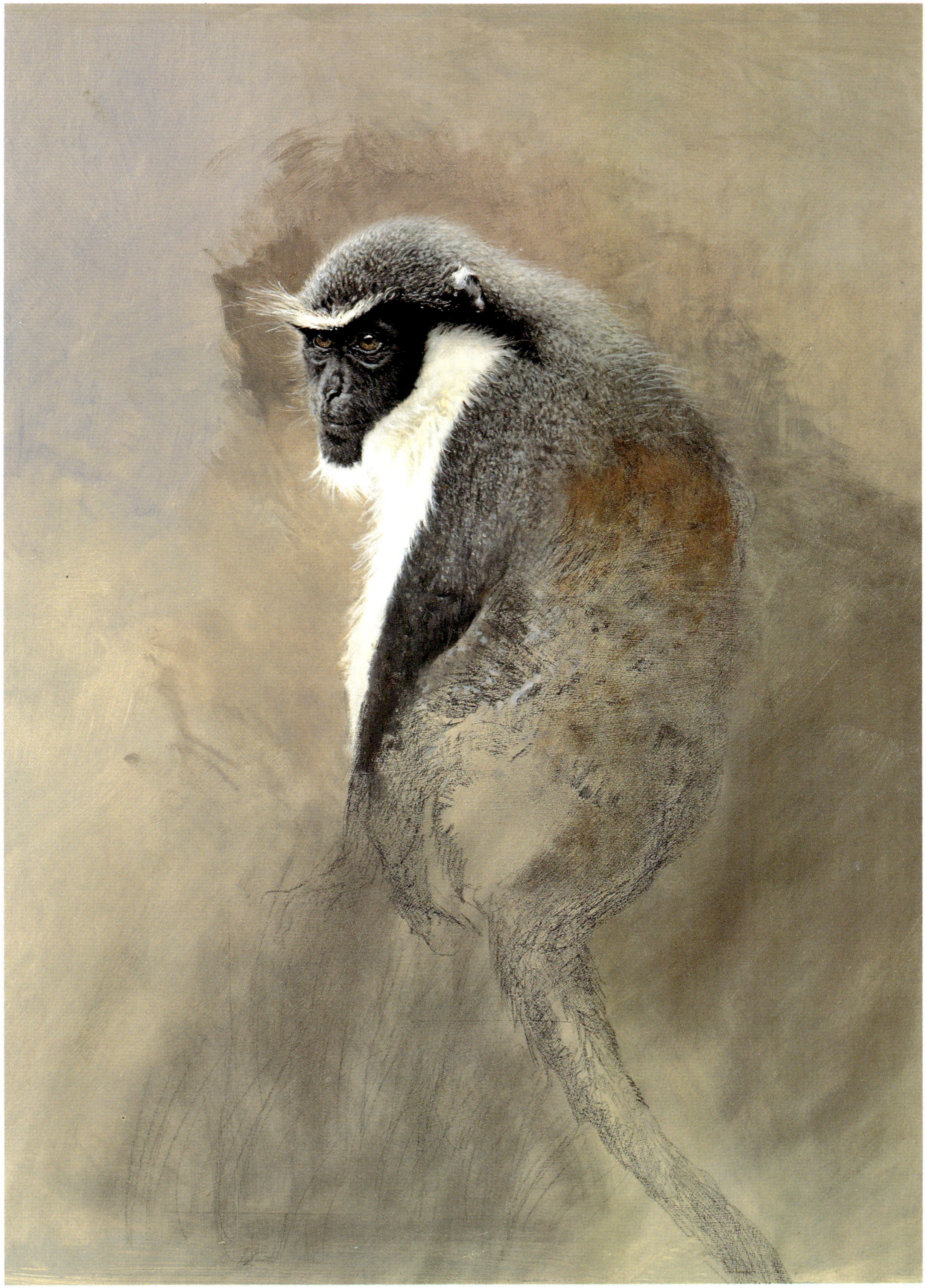

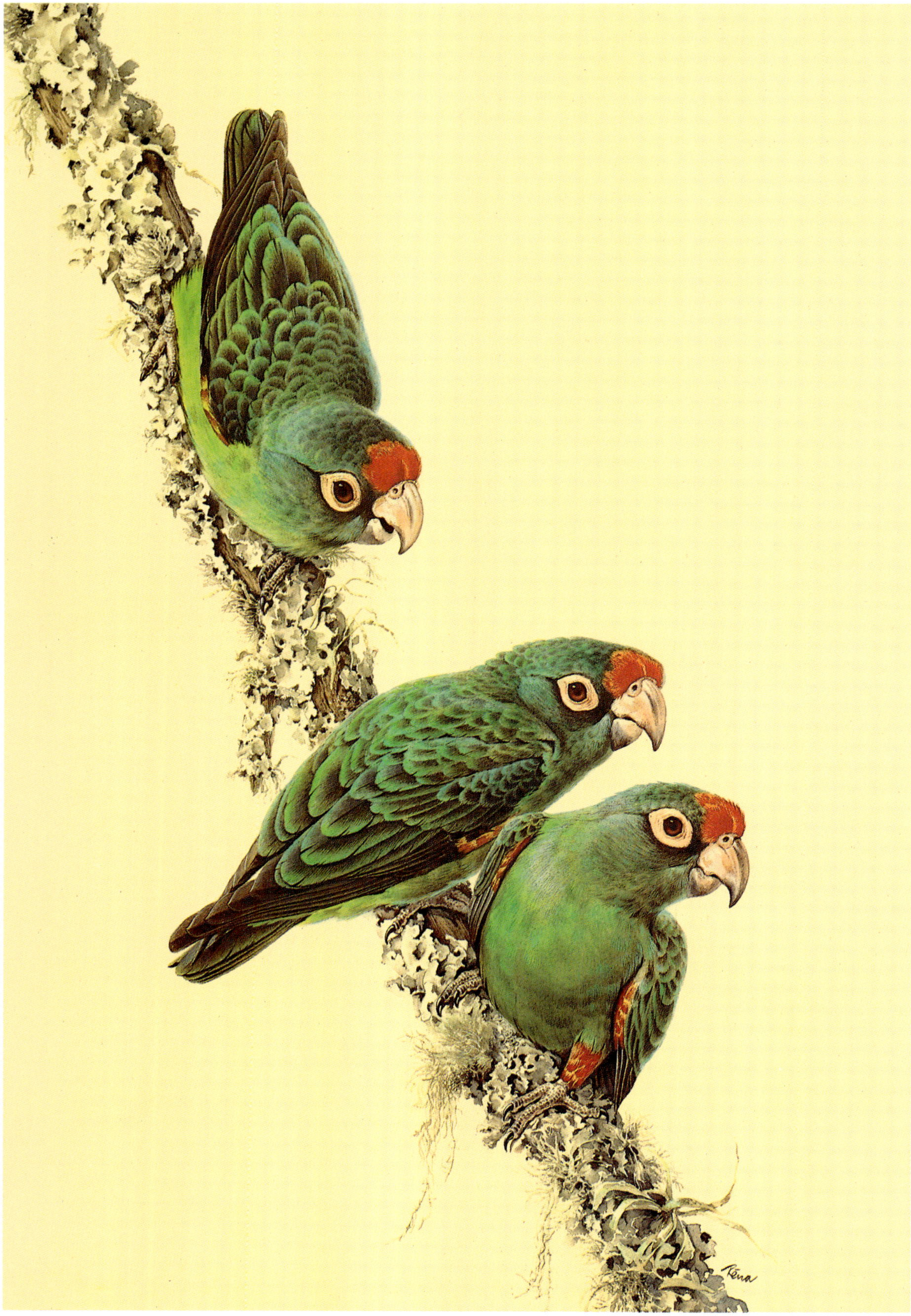

Africa has relatively few species of parrots – a mere 18, compared with 70 in Brazil. Fischer's lovebirds, illustrated here in a watercolour by Rena Fennessey, have a small, restricted range in north-west Tanzania, west to Rwanda and Burundi, but feral populations have become established in Kenya around Nairobi, Mombasa, Naivasha and Isiolo. Easily recognized by their green plumage, with orange–red face, red bill and broad ring of white skin around the eye, they are attractive birds, invariably found in pairs.

FISCHER'S LOVEBIRDS
Rena Fennessey

The grey parrot – portrayed here in another Rena Fennessey watercolour – is not only the largest African parrot, but is also the best known, as for many years huge numbers of wild-caught birds have been exported from West Africa to Europe and North America to supply the cage-bird trade. Despite heavy trapping, numbers remain high, and in some areas traditional roosts will attract up to 10,000 birds. The grey is a rainforest species, only found in the extreme west of Kenya.

AFRICAN GREY PARROTS
Rena Fennessey

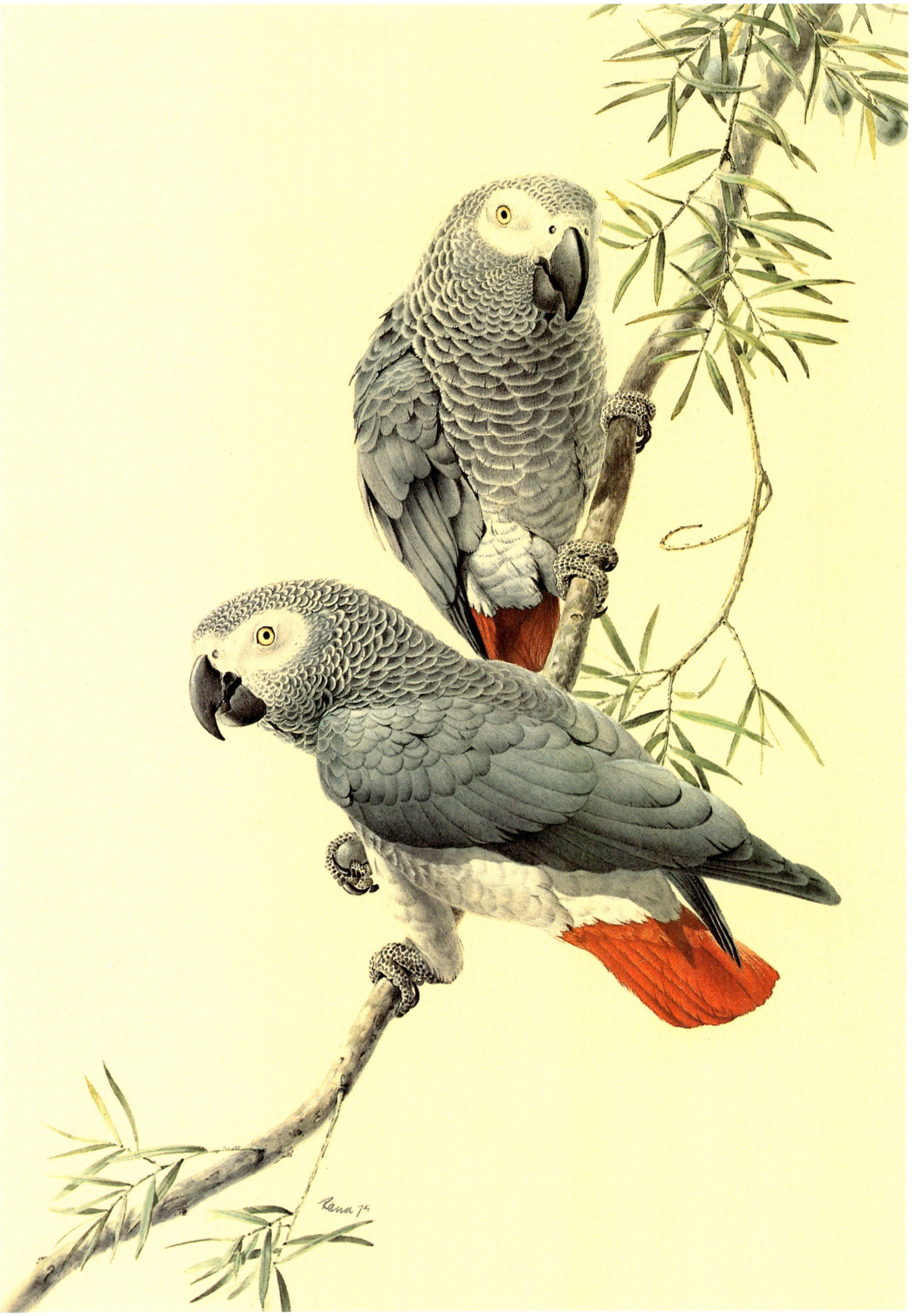

"Though they are considered large and ferocious, dark and menacing, gorillas have a gentle side, too," is how John Seerey-Lester explains his thinking behind "Mountain Cradle". "This painting was intended to show the placid side of the gorilla's nature, and to illustrate its close family ties. I focused on the expressions on the faces of this mother gorilla and her infant. I was especially struck by the young gorilla's expression as it stares out at the viewer with a look of childish curiosity, secure in the protective custody of its mother's arms. The mother, looking off into the distance at nothing in particular, has a look of contentment that shows a feeling of belonging."

The background is simple, and does no more than hint at the gorillas' mountain habitat. The cradle shape of the infant in its mother's arms is repeated in the tree branches above the mother's head and the branch in the foreground, emphasising the painting's clever composition.

MOUNTAIN CRADLE
John Seerey-Lester

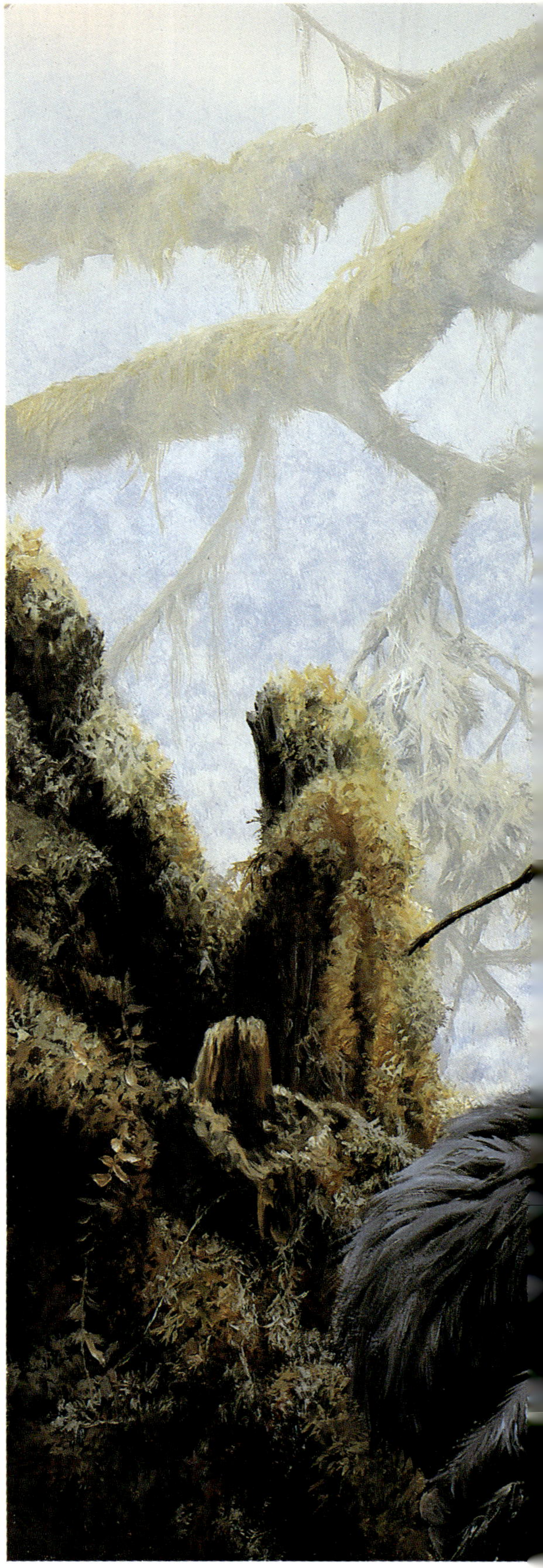

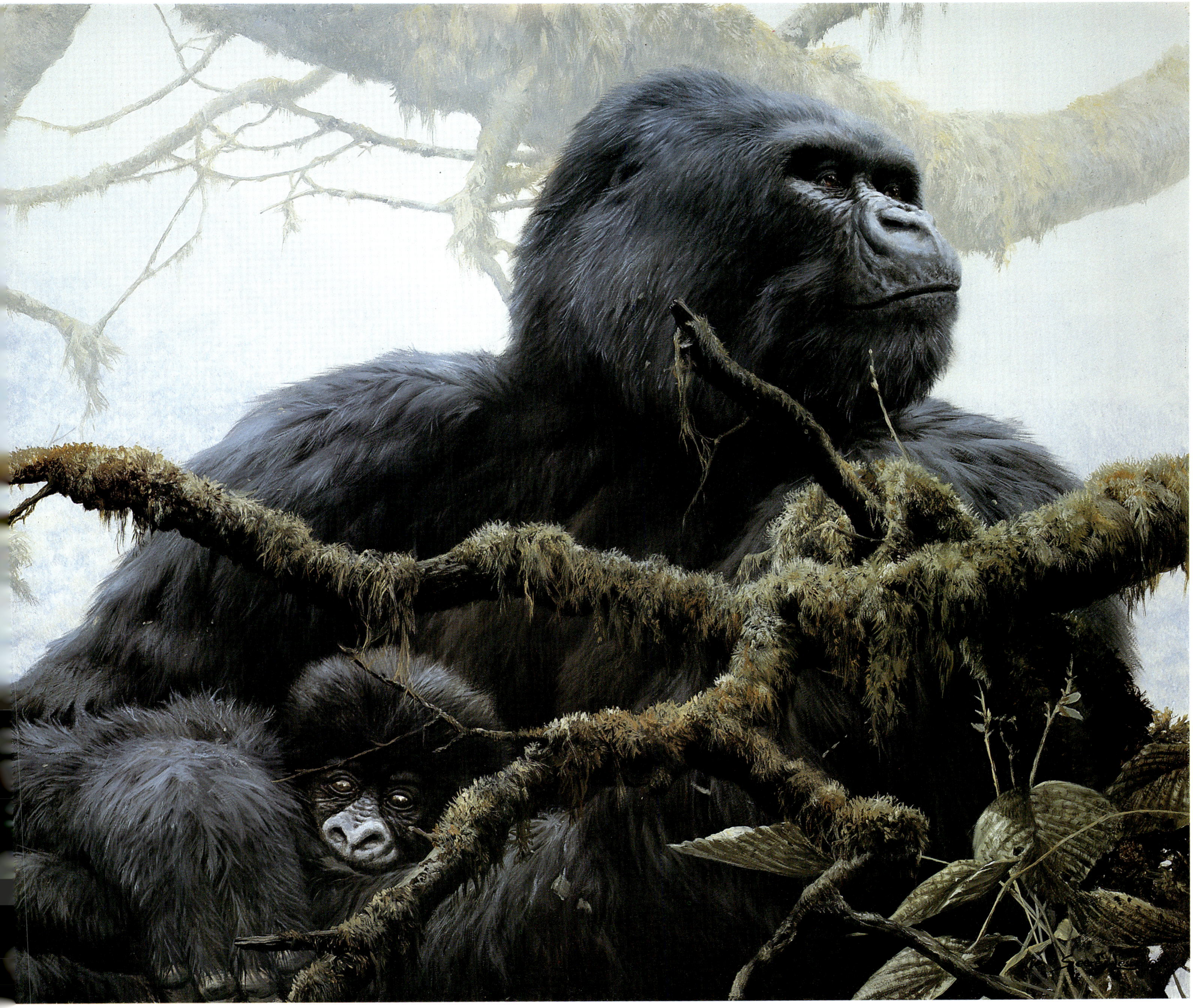

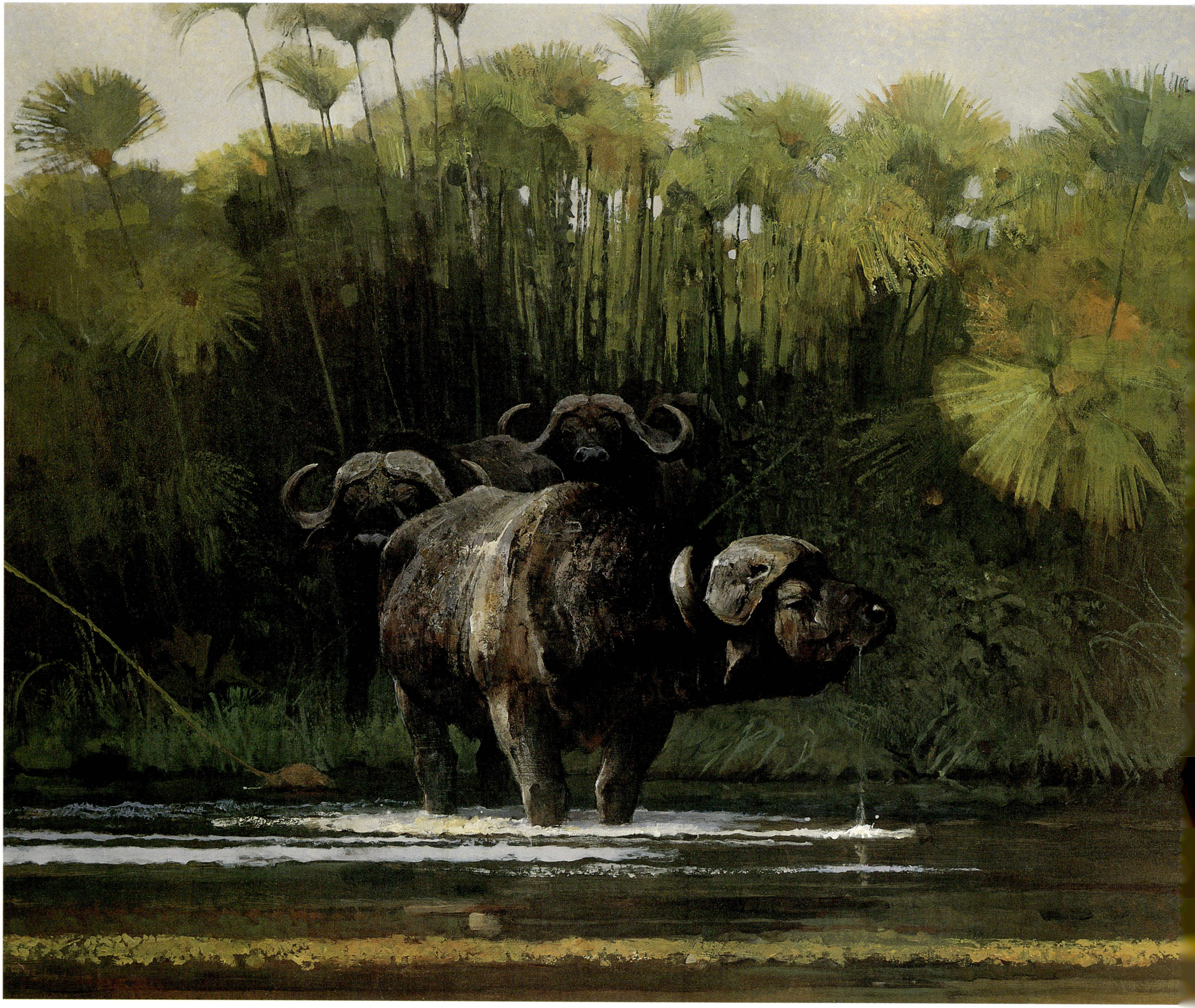

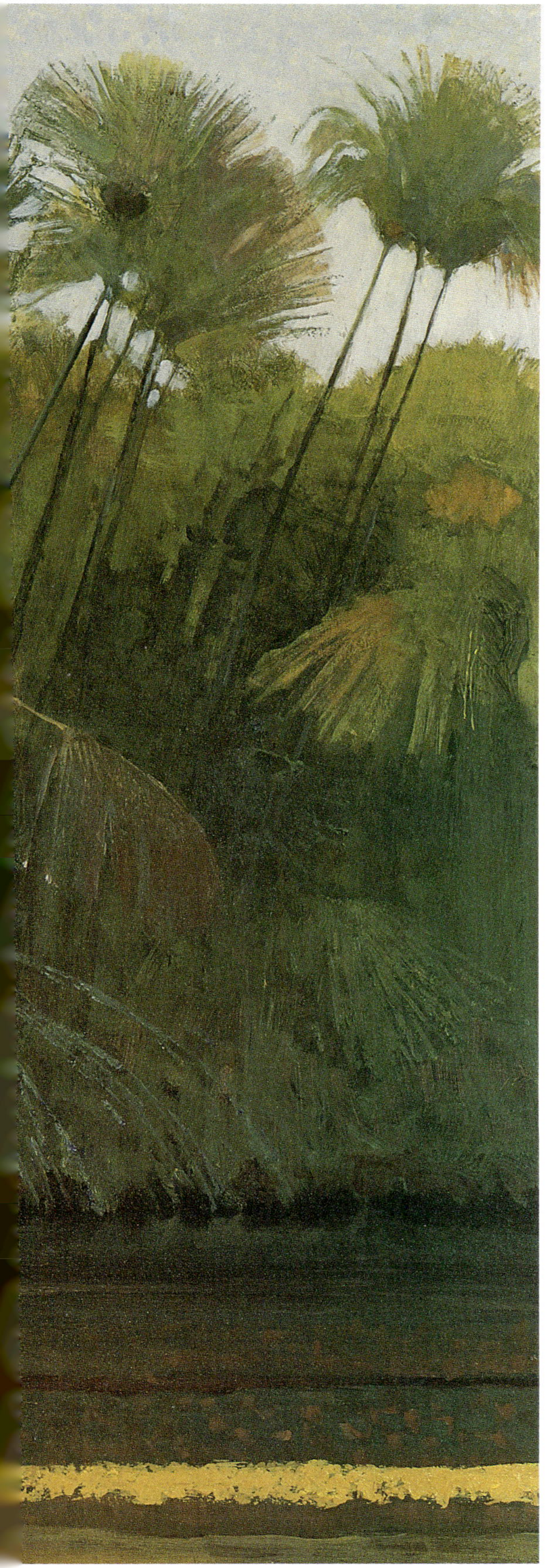

What is most remarkable about Bob Kuhn's buffalo paintings is how different each one is – none are simply variations on a theme, though differing backgrounds do help. Kuhn admits to a love for the "design motif that papyrus so richly provides. The plants line the edges of the watercourses in much of Africa, providing shade and a measure of security to water-orientated animals." He goes on to explain that although buffalo are a familiar sight on the dry plains, they can and do frequent water. "My choice of this setting was as much for its pictorial aspects as anything else."

BUFFALO BULLS EMERGING FROM PAPYRUS
Bob Kuhn

Buffalo are enthusiastic wallowers, and Tim Greenwood's highly detailed pencil drawing (*below*) of a bull after wallowing makes an intriguing contrast to the broad brush strokes of Bob Kuhn. Many artists use pencil for their sketches and preliminary work, but this is one of only two "finished" pencil drawings in the book, to remind us what an expressive medium pencil can be.

AFTER WALLOWING
Timothy Greenwood

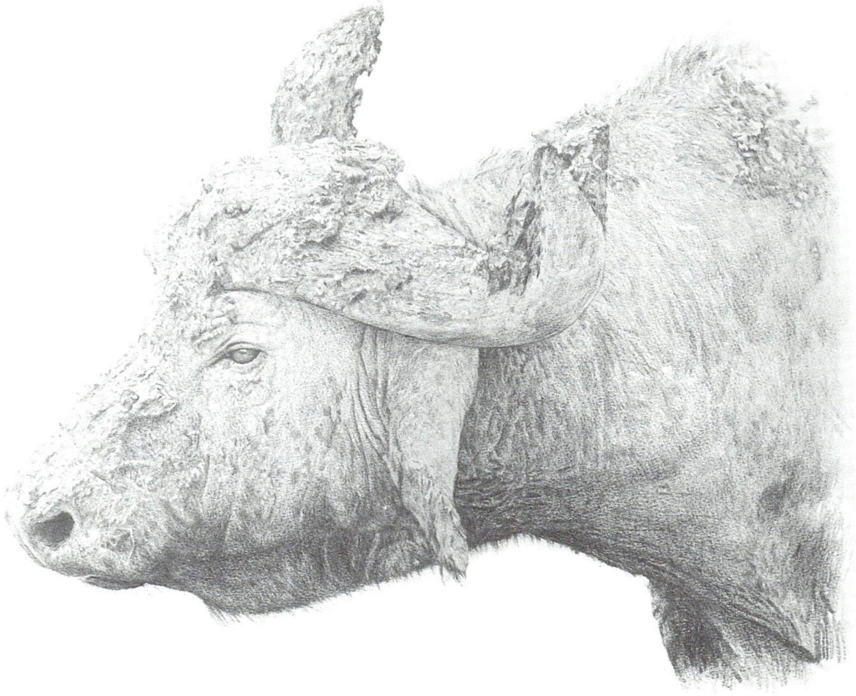

94 Short-sighted, bad-tempered, unpredictable: the black rhinoceros is all these things. It is also, in Robert Bateman's words, a prehistoric-looking beast. In this painting, Bateman has "tried to show him in his bold and rugged defiance". He has succeeded, too, though I believe that the picture might have benefited from a hint of background, without detracting from the impact of the animal itself.

It is a sobering thought that black rhinos were once found throughout sub-Saharan Africa, except where it was too dry, or too hot and humid. However, even in 1881 the famous hunter Selous was alarmed by the impact of hunting on the rhino population, and the sharp decline in numbers he had witnessed in South Africa where their range had already contracted severely; by the turn of this century we will be lucky if even a fragmented population remains.

CHARGING RHINO
Robert Bateman

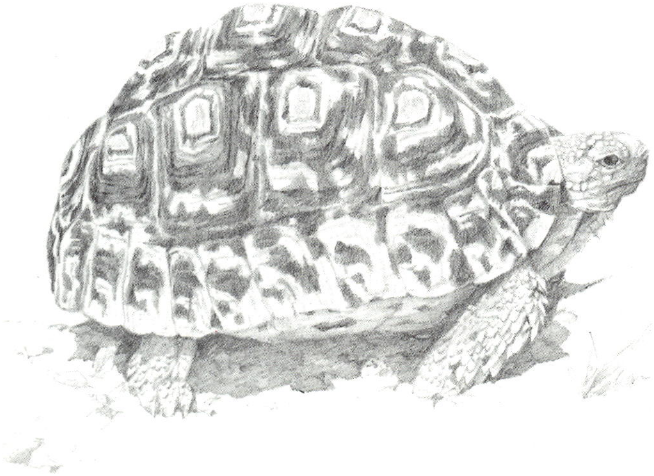

TORTOISE
Gunnar Pettersson

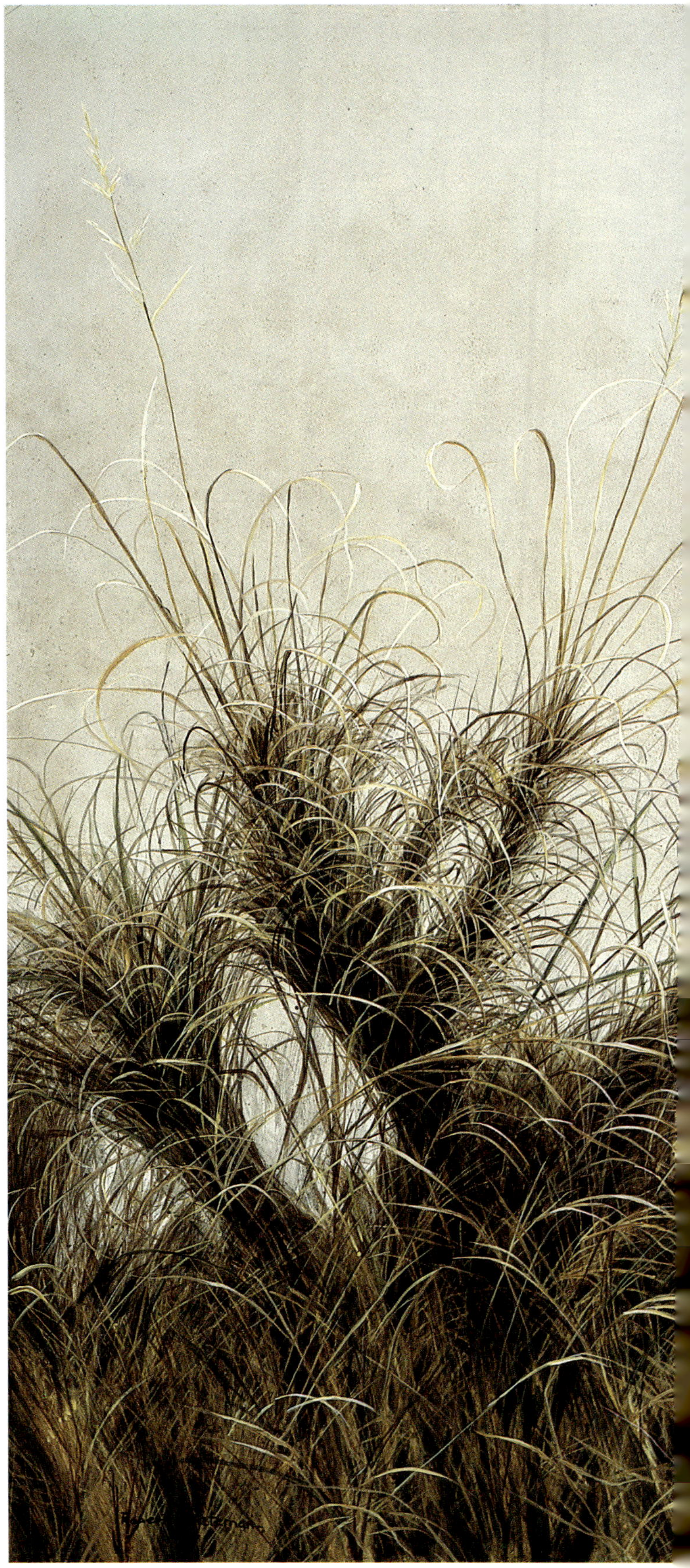

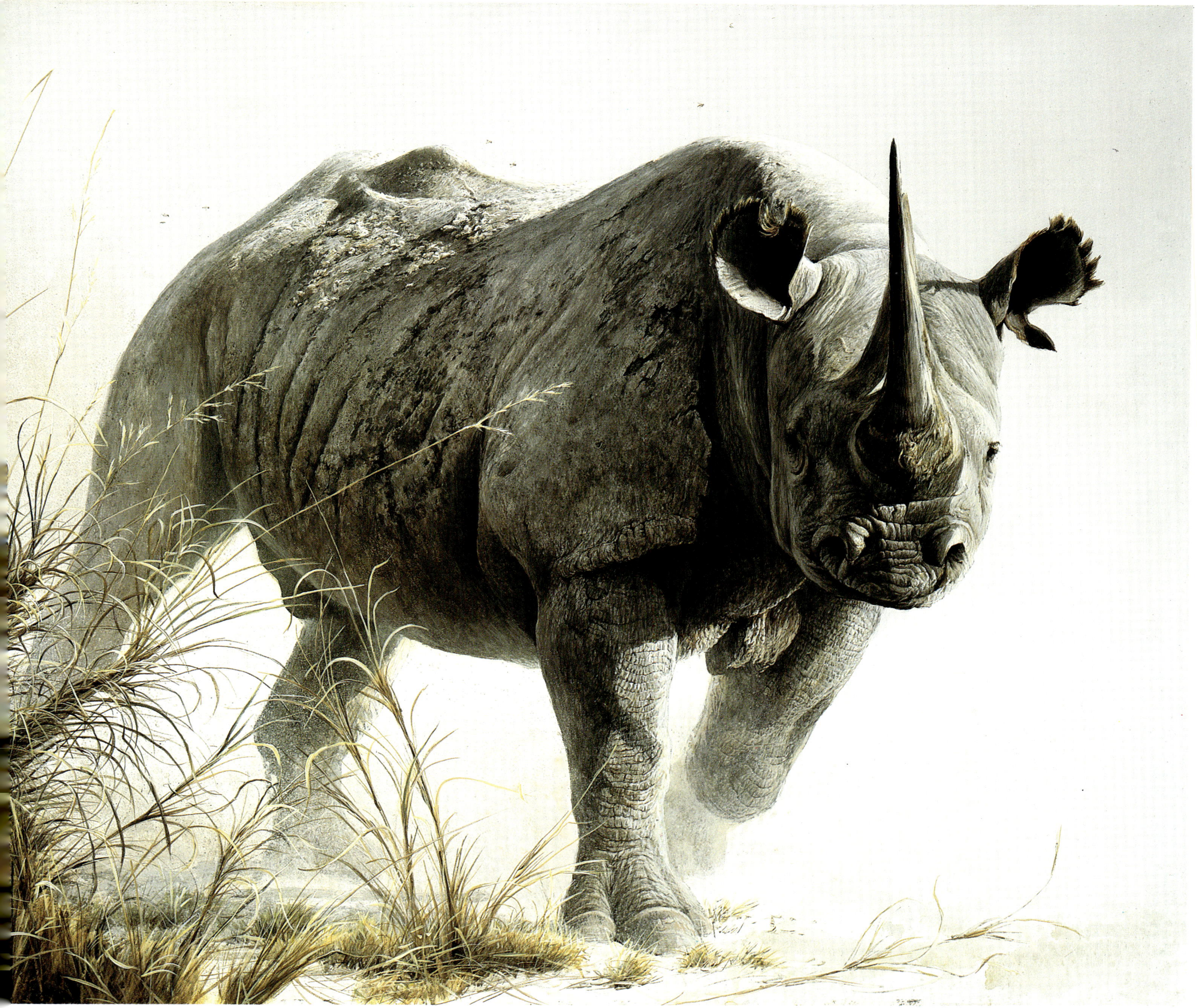

96

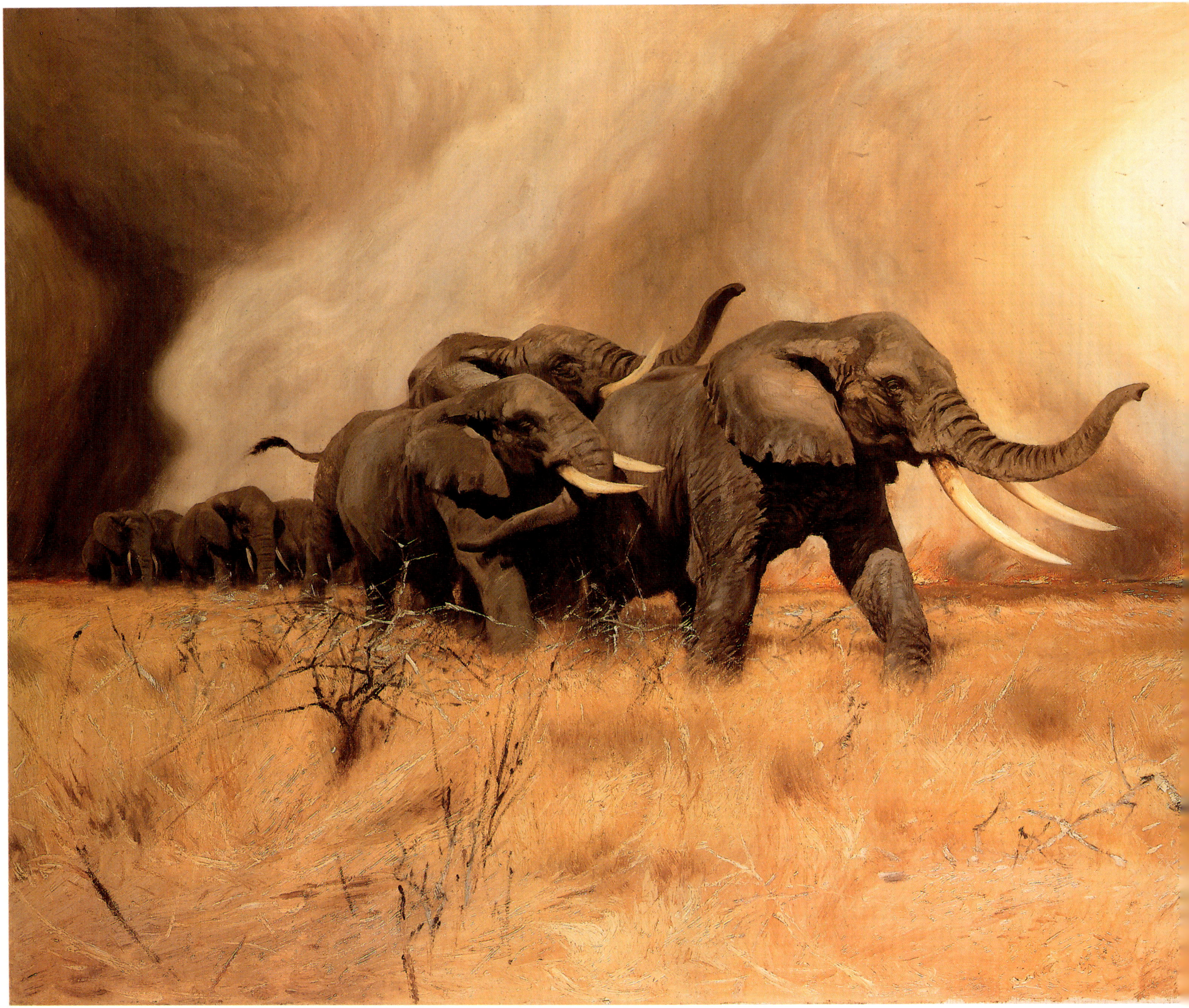

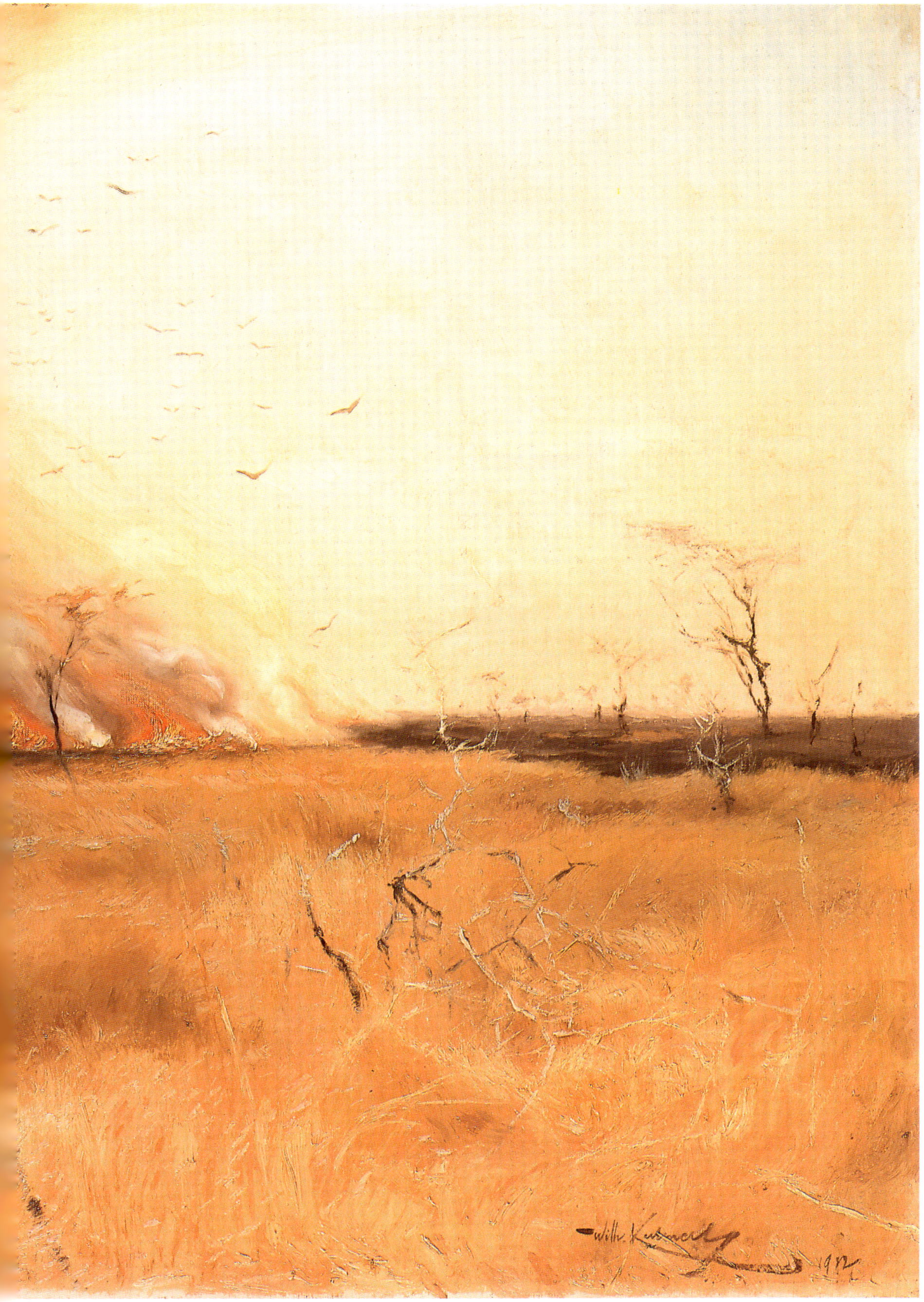

Fires are a natural feature of the bush, occurring regularly during the dry season. Most African trees are resistant to the flames, which usually pass quickly, burning off the old, dried grass. Note how the tremendous heat creates its own thermal, sucking up ash and loose debris that are later deposited over a huge area. Predatory birds, such as the ubiquitous black kite, are attracted to bushfires as scavengers are to the sight of vultures over a kill, and patrol the edges of the blaze, feasting upon flushed insects. Natural though fire may be, it can be dangerous for any animals that are trapped by it, and here Wilhelm Kuhnert shows a herd of elephants moving away, trunks raised in a quest for fresh, smokeless air.

BUSHFIRE
Wilhelm Kuhnert

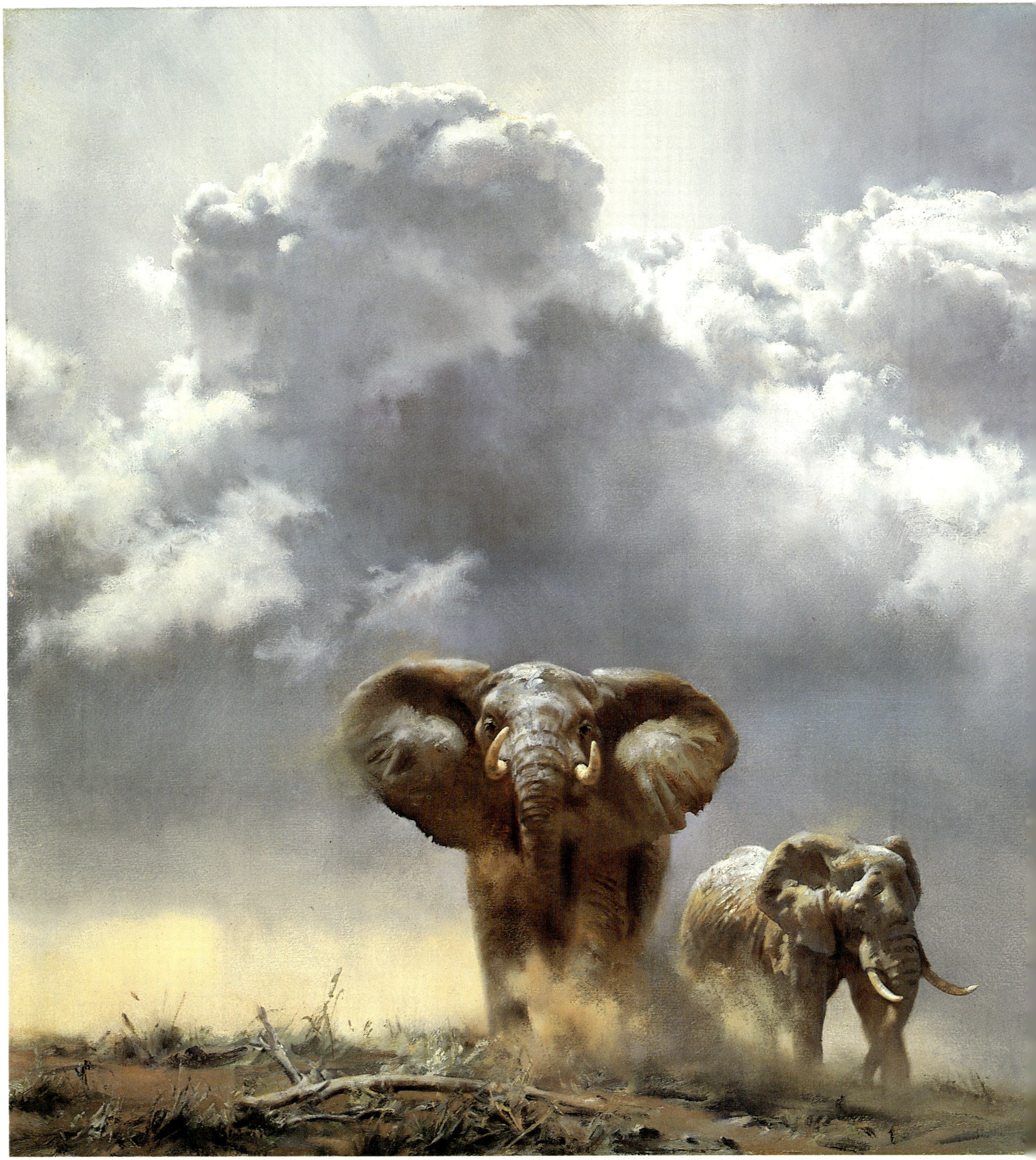

Forget the elephants, impressive though they are. This oil by Donald Grant is as much about skies as it is about jumbos, hence its title. "I have long been fascinated with skies, and clouds in particular. There was a period in the sixties when I painted little else. . . African cloudscapes can be spectacular and give added drama to a wildlife subject. The idea for 'African Rains' probably developed from witnessing many electrical storms followed by dazzling sunlight, here illuminating two wet elephants. The larger of the two, its huge ears extended, is demonstrating its powerful exuberance – probably a bluff and without serious intent. When an elephant means business, it is more likely to charge without warning except for a silent momentary rocking motion with head held high and ears at full stretch."

AFRICAN RAINS – ELEPHANTS
Donald Grant

RHINO
Donald Grant

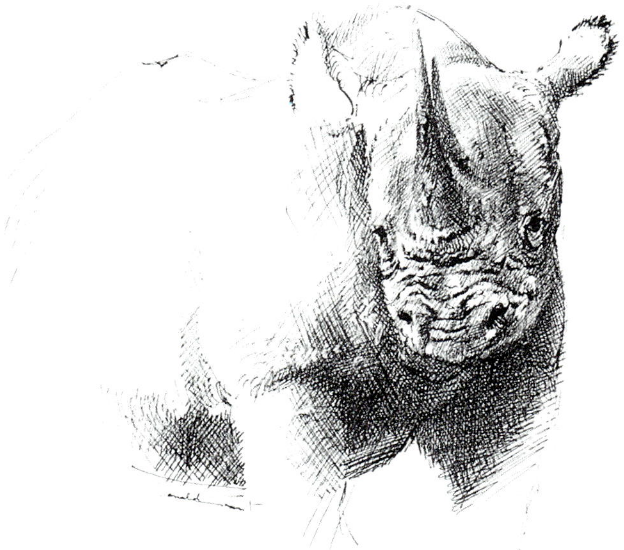

The rains are the lifeblood of Africa. Droughts which last months, or even years, are not unusual, but when the rains fall, the most barren landscape can be transformed within days, dormant seeds of forgotten flowers carpeting the savanna with colour. This is a brief but glorious time of plenty for the game, such as this fine Grant's gazelle buck, painted by Wilhelm Kuhnert. Pretty picture this may be, but Kuhnert certainly painted it from a scene he had witnessed during his extensive travels in East Africa.

Grant's gazelles are animals of the open plains, and in northern Kenya even occur in semi-desert. They can tolerate high temperatures, often remaining grazing in the middle of the day when most mammals have sought shade.

GRANT'S GAZELLE
Wilhelm Kuhnert

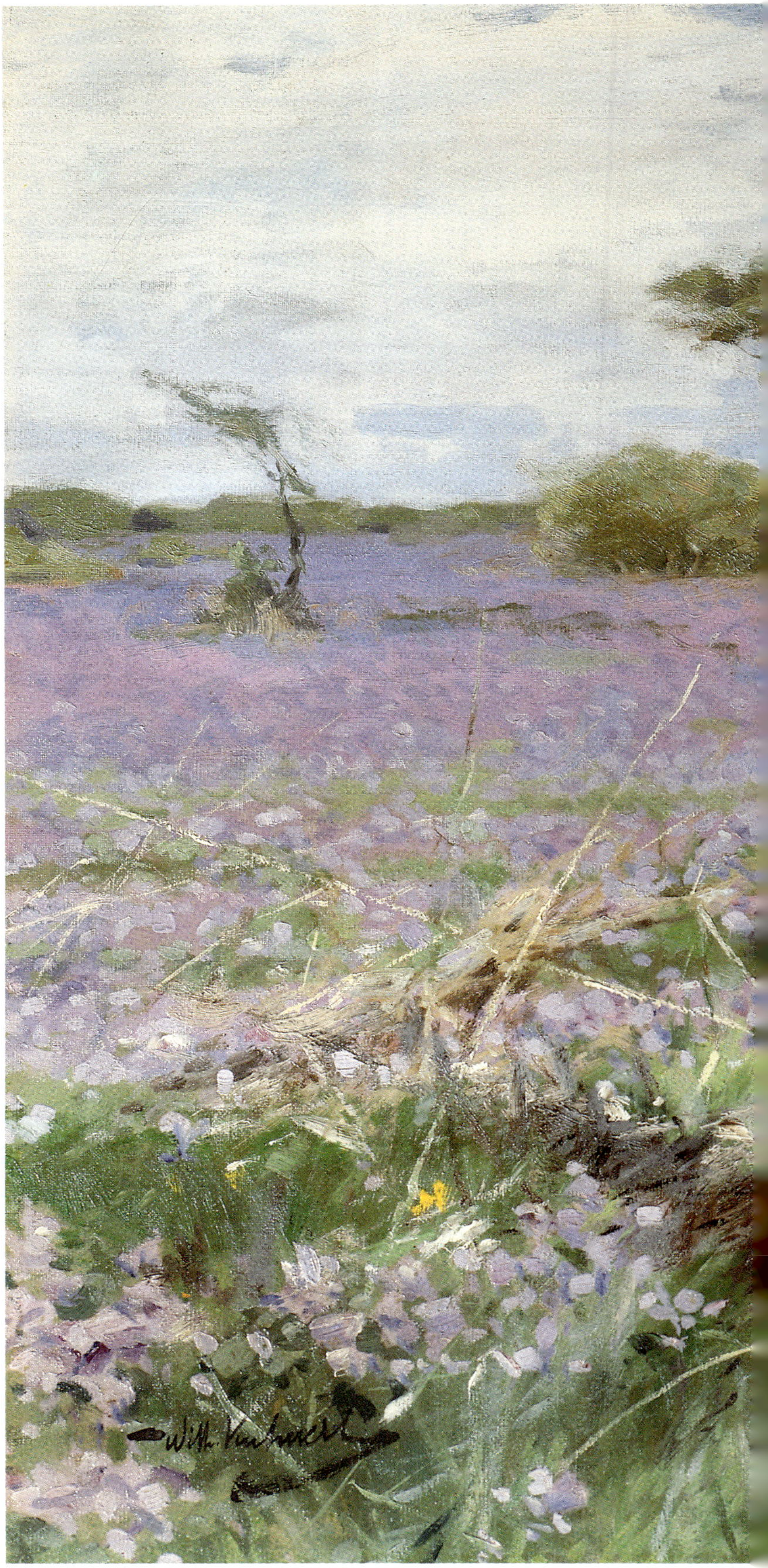

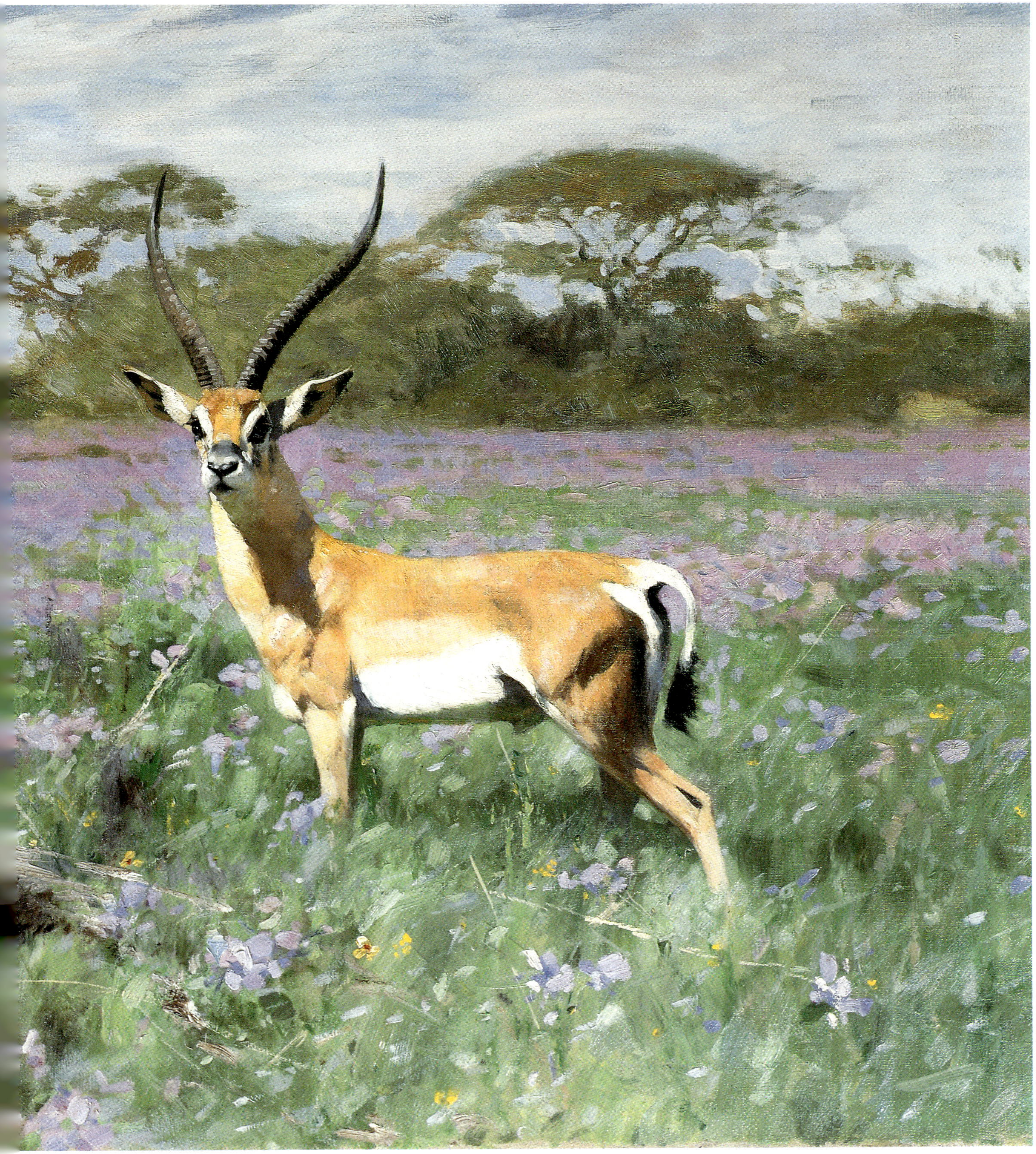

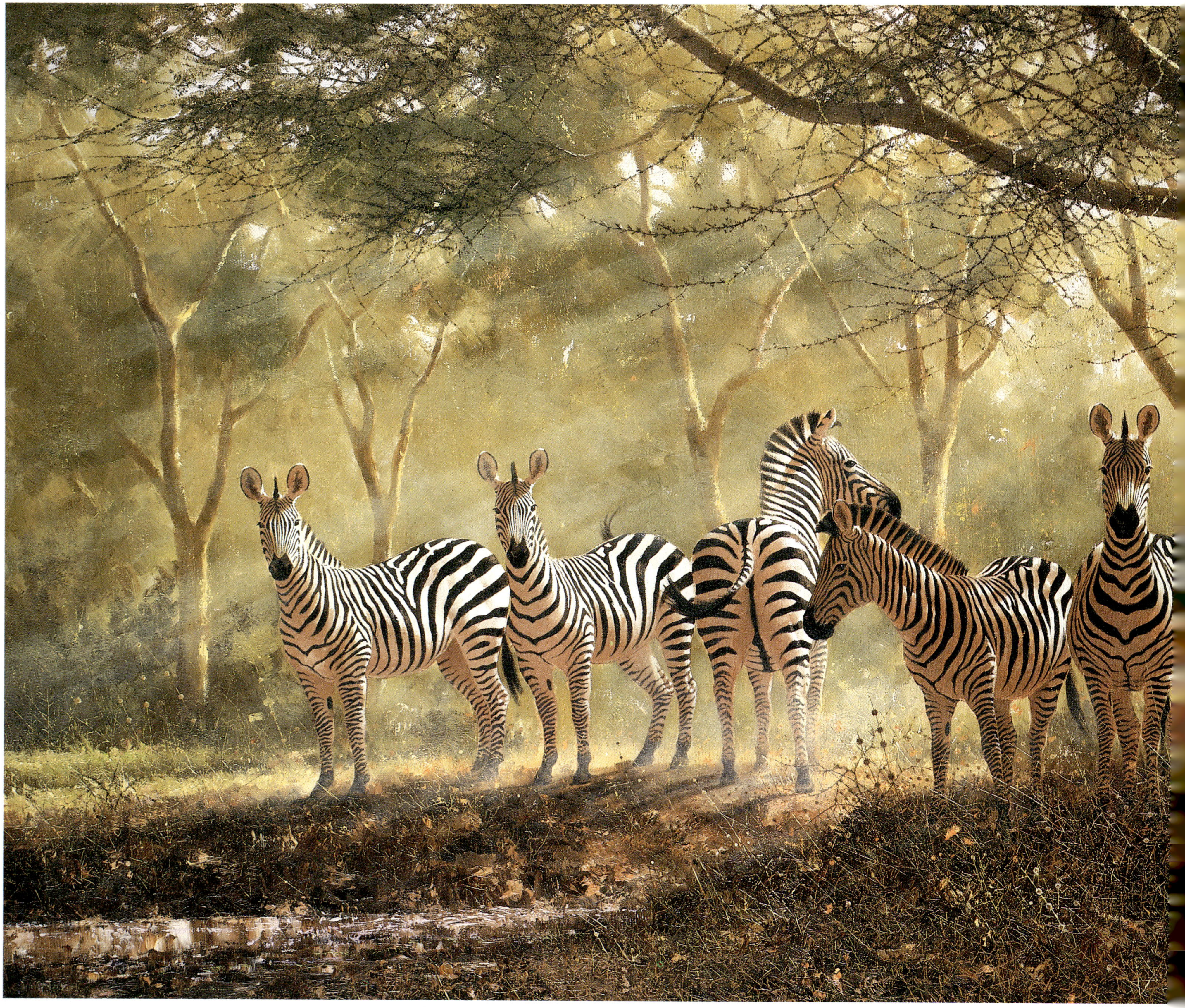

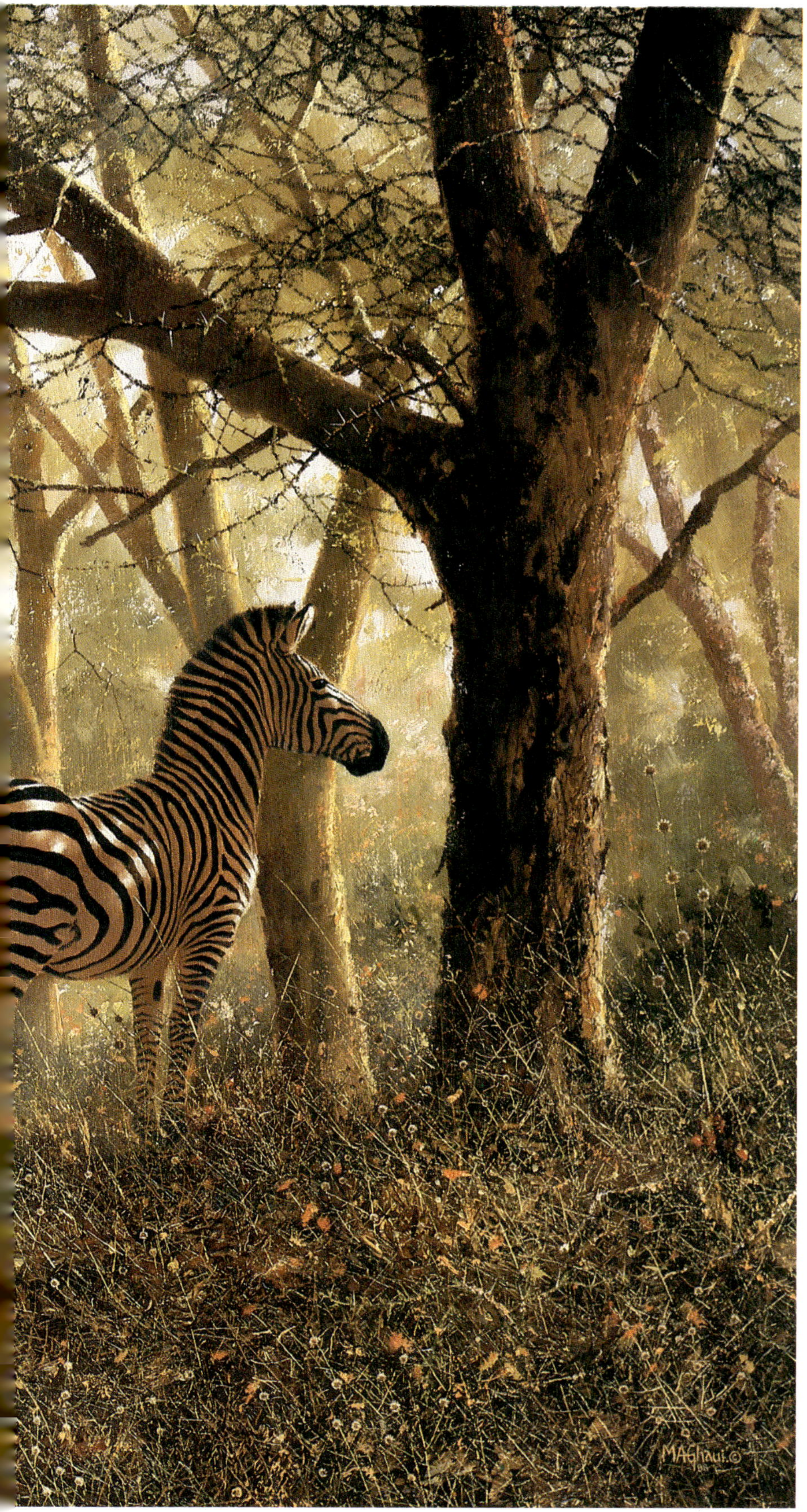

This is, for me, one of the most pleasing paintings in the book. Ghaui is fascinated by light, and "especially the effect created by shafts of sunlight shining through mist or dust". It is not the easiest subject to master on a canvas, but when successful it is most impressive.

The setting for this particular painting was close to the artist's home at Lake Naivasha. Ghaui found the stand of yellow thorn that he wanted, then proceeded to drive round and round in circles raising as much dust as possible. "It was a nice sunny morning and the effect was perfect – the shafts of light came streaming through, and all I had to do was imagine a group of zebra near a water hole." He adds that as he drove away, he noticed some bewildered spectators who had gathered to watch his unusual behaviour!

ZEBRA AND YELLOW THORN
Michael Ghaui

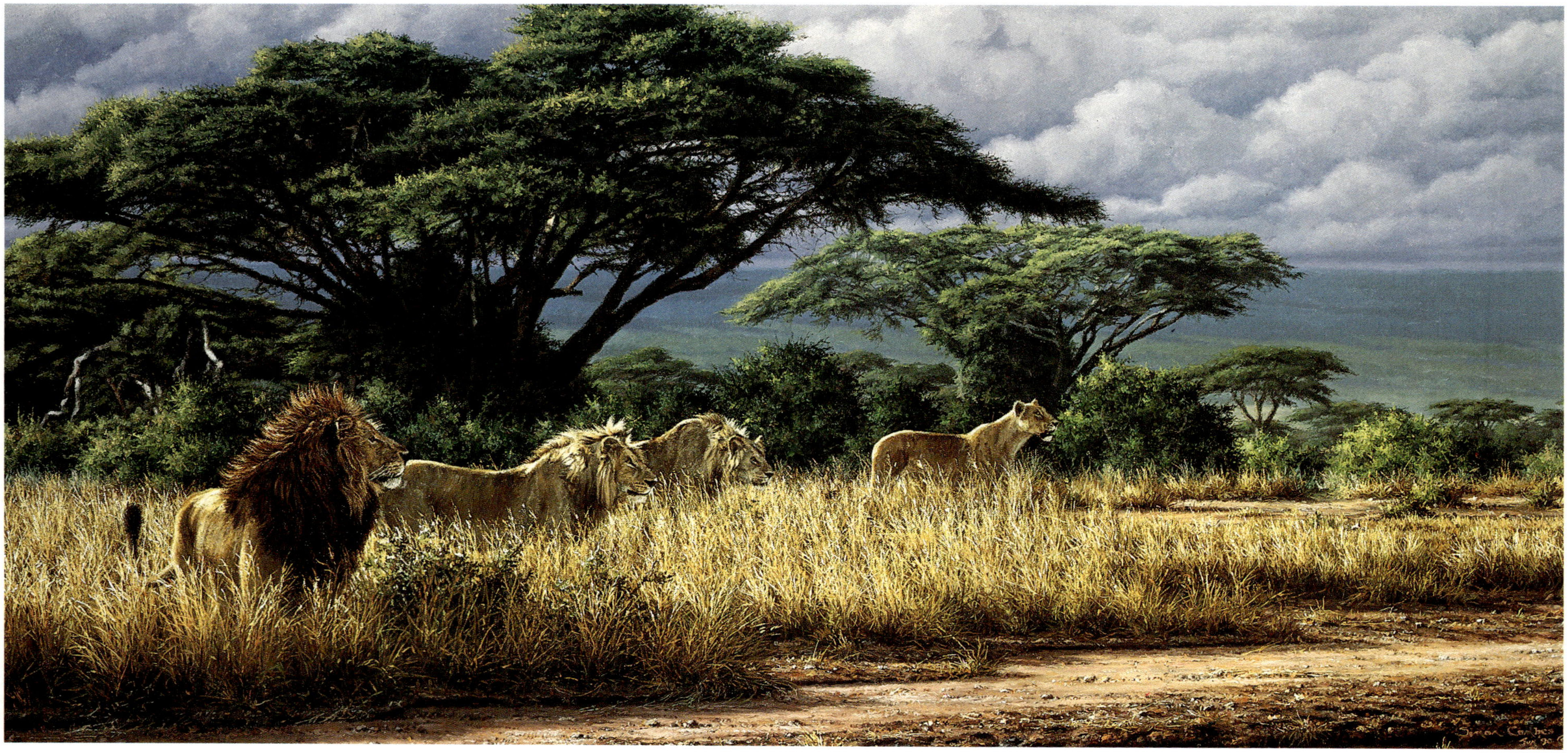

Few animals have a more uneasy relationship than lions and buffalo. Whereas lions prey readily on lone buffalo, a herd offers far too formidable opposition for even a pride of lions. Here Simon Combes has captured a surprise morning encounter at Amboseli, under a cloud-shrouded Kilimanjaro. The buffalo, plodding to their favourite water hole, have suddenly caught the scent of their age-old enemy. They have quickly grouped to face the cats, mature bulls and cows ranging cautiously forward, with the young animals behind. Snorting and foot-stamping, the milling herd are uncertain whether to flee or attack.

The lions, after a long night's hunting, are also hesistant. Most likely they will give way, melting back into the long grass, but if they stand their ground, the buffalo may well retreat, perhaps revealing a weak straggler that can be brought down.

In this two-part work, Combes has conjured up the majesty of Amboseli. We cannot see Kilimanjaro, though we know it is there, while the greenness of the trees, not to mention the heavy clouds overhead, remind the observer that this is the rainy season. It would be a fine painting without the animals, but the threatening power of the lions, contrasted with the bovine bulk of the buffalo, make it a memorable work. One wants to know what happened next. Lions do not like giving best to buffalo, but in a situation like this they may have little choice. I once encountered a young male lion, treed by a herd of around 300 buffalo. The arrival of my vehicle diverted the attention of the buffs, and the lion judged his moment nicely to leap to the ground and sprint away to safety.

STANDOFF
Simon Combes

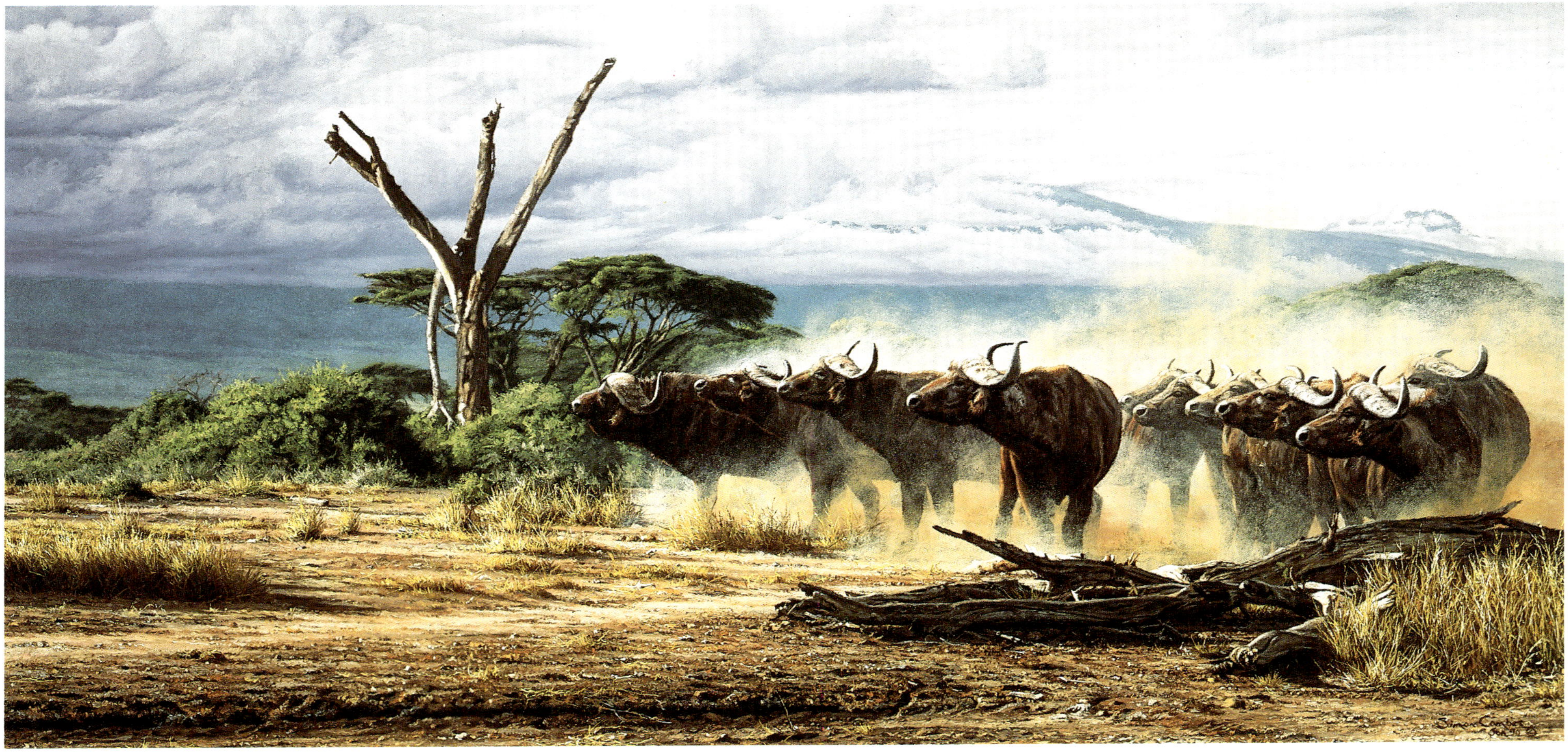

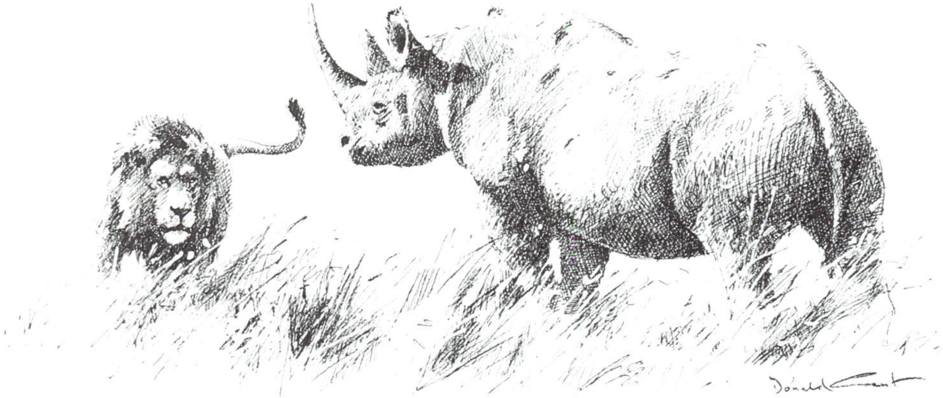

LION AND RHINO
Donald Grant

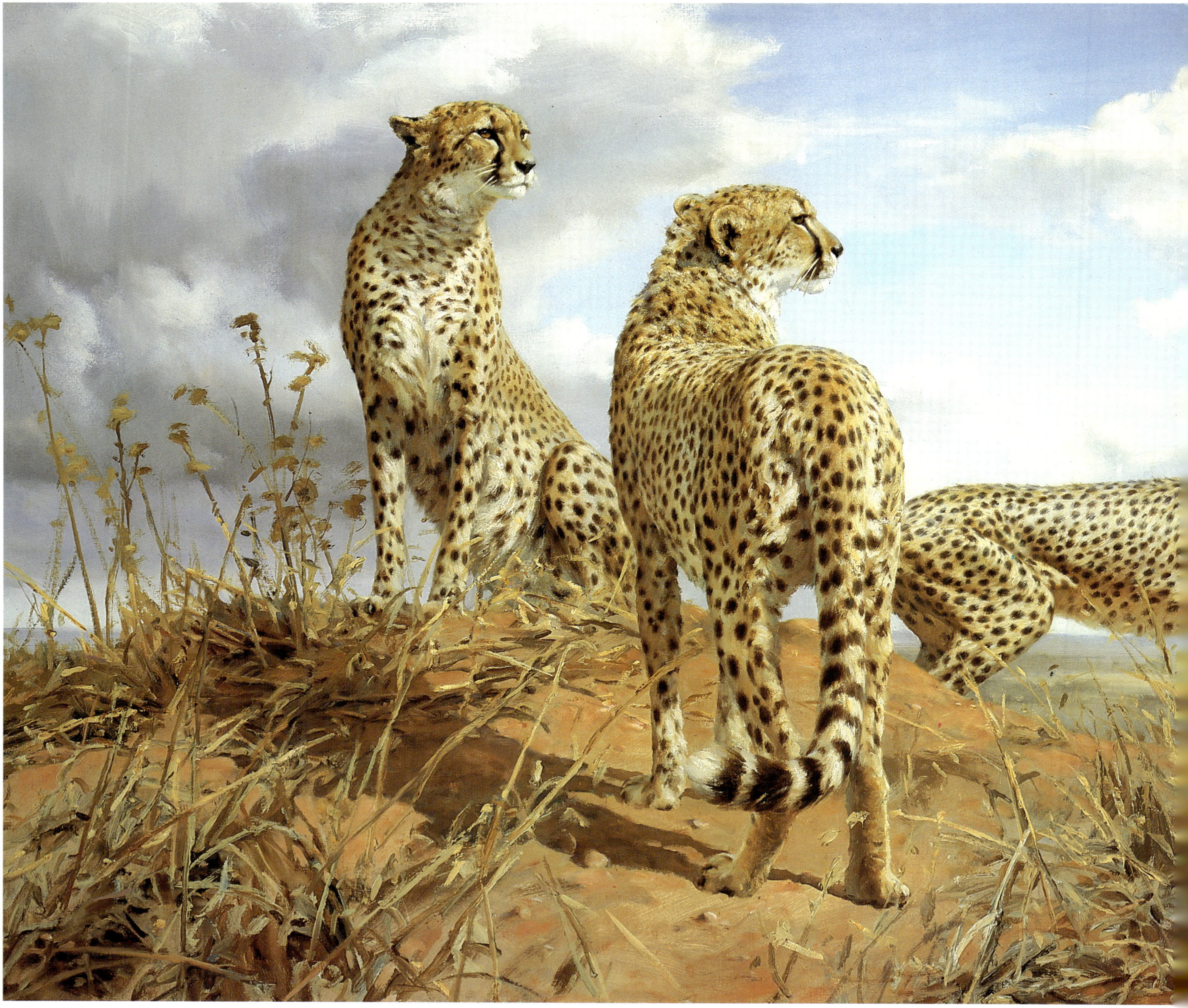

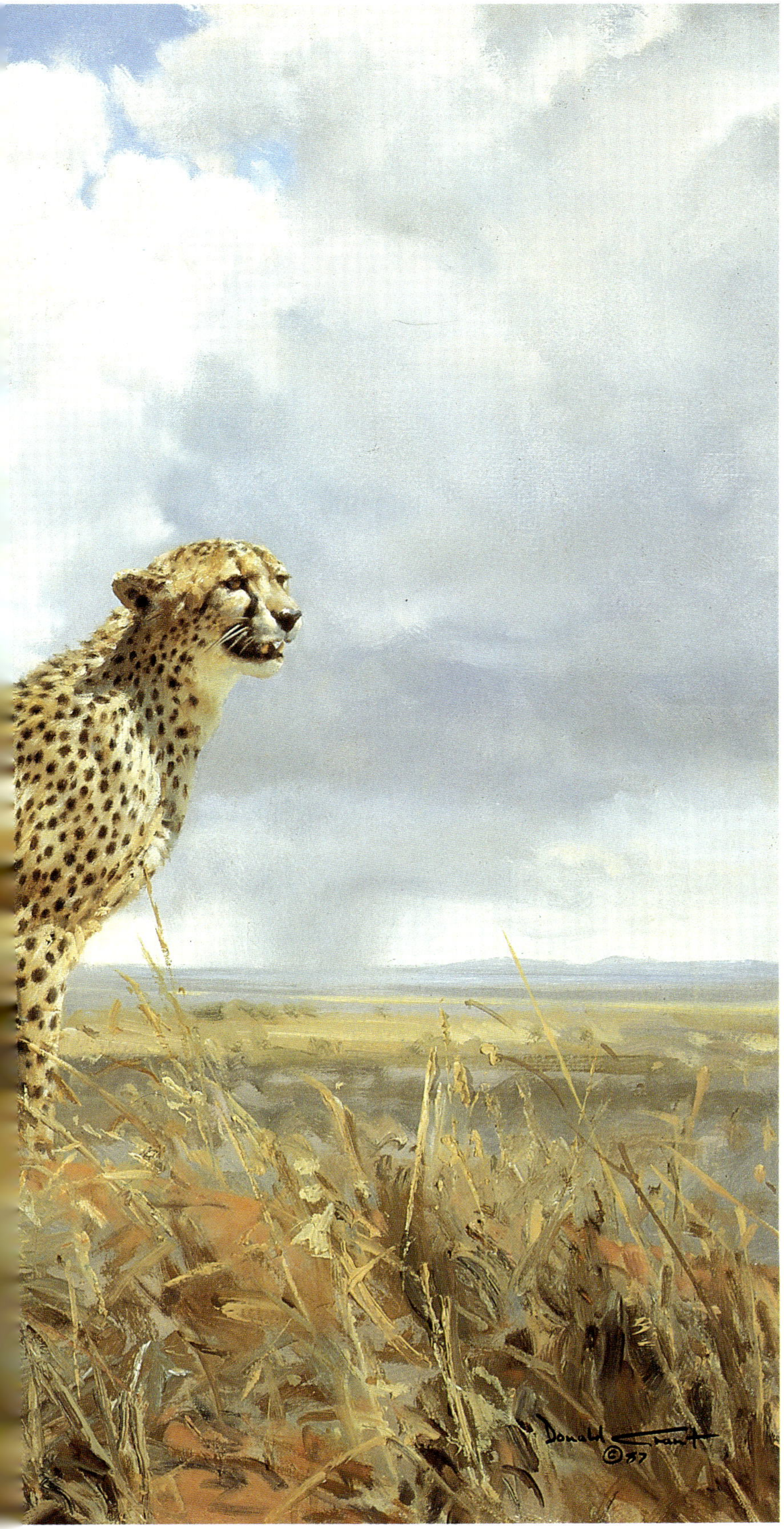

As Bob Kuhn is to buffaloes, so Donald Grant is to cheetahs. "I can categorically say that my favourite animal is the cheetah. I have certainly painted more of these long-legged, easy-going felines than any other animal, and maybe more than any other animal artist. Besides studying, drawing and photographing cheetahs in their natural habitat, I have made the acquaintance of many of these extremely likeable, friendly animals held in captivity around the world."

This oil shows three bachelor males, probably from the same litter. Though cheetahs often live singly, they are also found in small parties. Cheetahs are, sadly, the most threatened of the big cats, unable to tolerate changing conditions or disturbance. Lions are also a problem for cheetahs, as they will hunt and kill cheetah cubs whenever they get the chance. As a result, cub mortality is high, and even in protected areas and national parks cheetahs struggle to maintain their numbers.

CHEETAH TRIO
Donald Grant

HUNTING DOG STUDY
Donald Grant

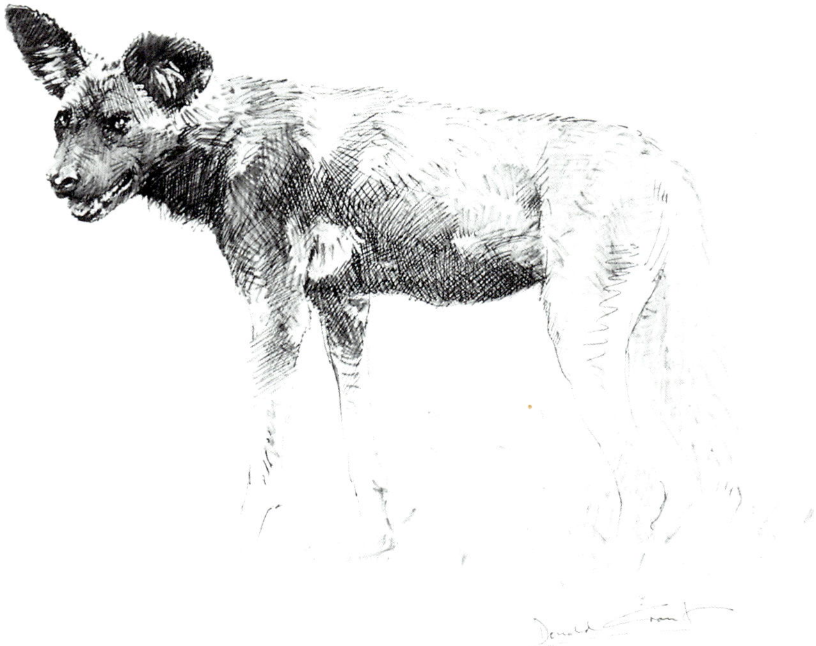

108

Watch a pack of hunting dogs for any length of time, and the dog owner is certain to recognize aspects of familiar behaviour, though the two are only distantly related. Simon Combes portrays a litter of hunting dog puppies outside their den. The setting is an old antbear hole, on the Serengeti plains. "I had followed the pack on many hunts watching with awe and some queasiness as they remorselessly ran down, dispatched and devoured their prey many miles from the den. After a long trek back, the pups would emerge and be fed on regurgitated meat by successive dogs – not just the mother.

"This is the rainy season on the plains, the grass is green and thousands of wildebeest provide ready food. My painting shows the pups huddled together for warmth after a recent shower."

HUNTING DOG PUPS
Simon Combes

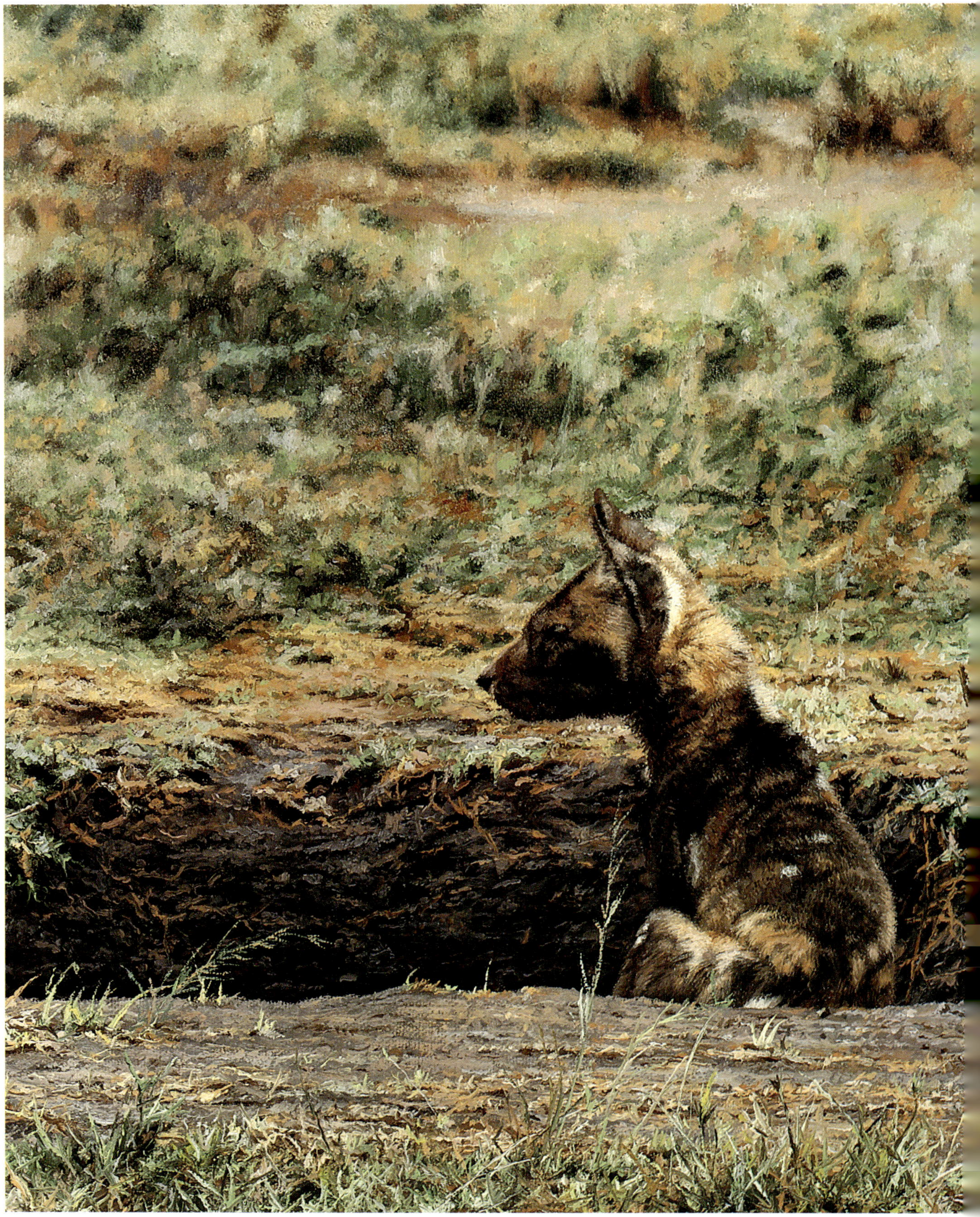

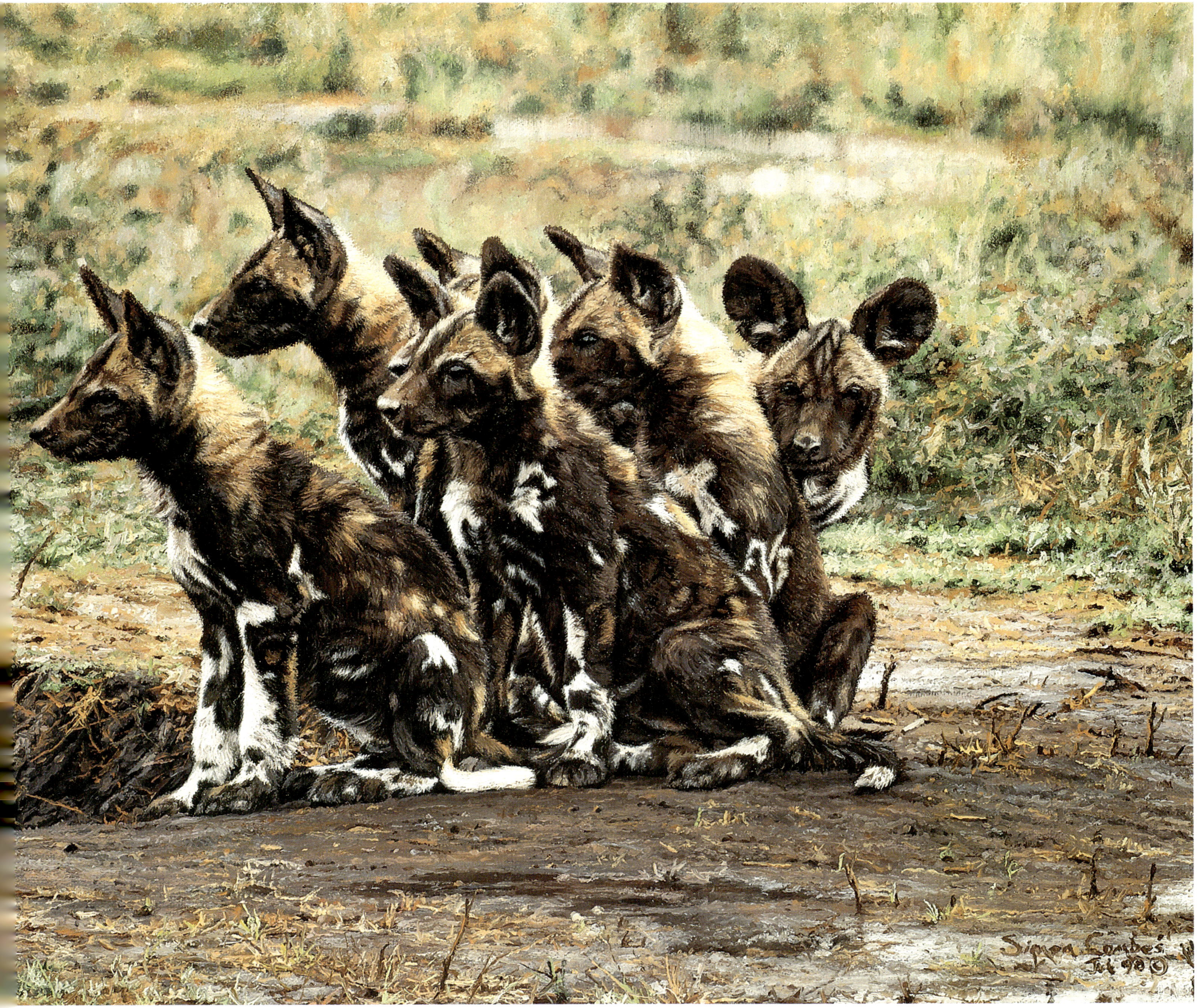

Beisa oryx are the East African equivalent of gemsbok: indeed, some authorities regard them as merely races of the same species. They are animals of dry open bush, often found many miles from water, and here Simon Combes shows them in a typical dry thornbush landscape, seeking respite from the heat of the day under an acacia.

Two races of beisa oryx occur in East Africa: these are typical of animals found from north of the Tana River to Eritrea. From the Tana River south to Tanzania, the fringe-eared oryx is found. They are a richer brown and have heavier horns, and a distinctive fringe or tassel on the ears.

ORYX
Simon Combes

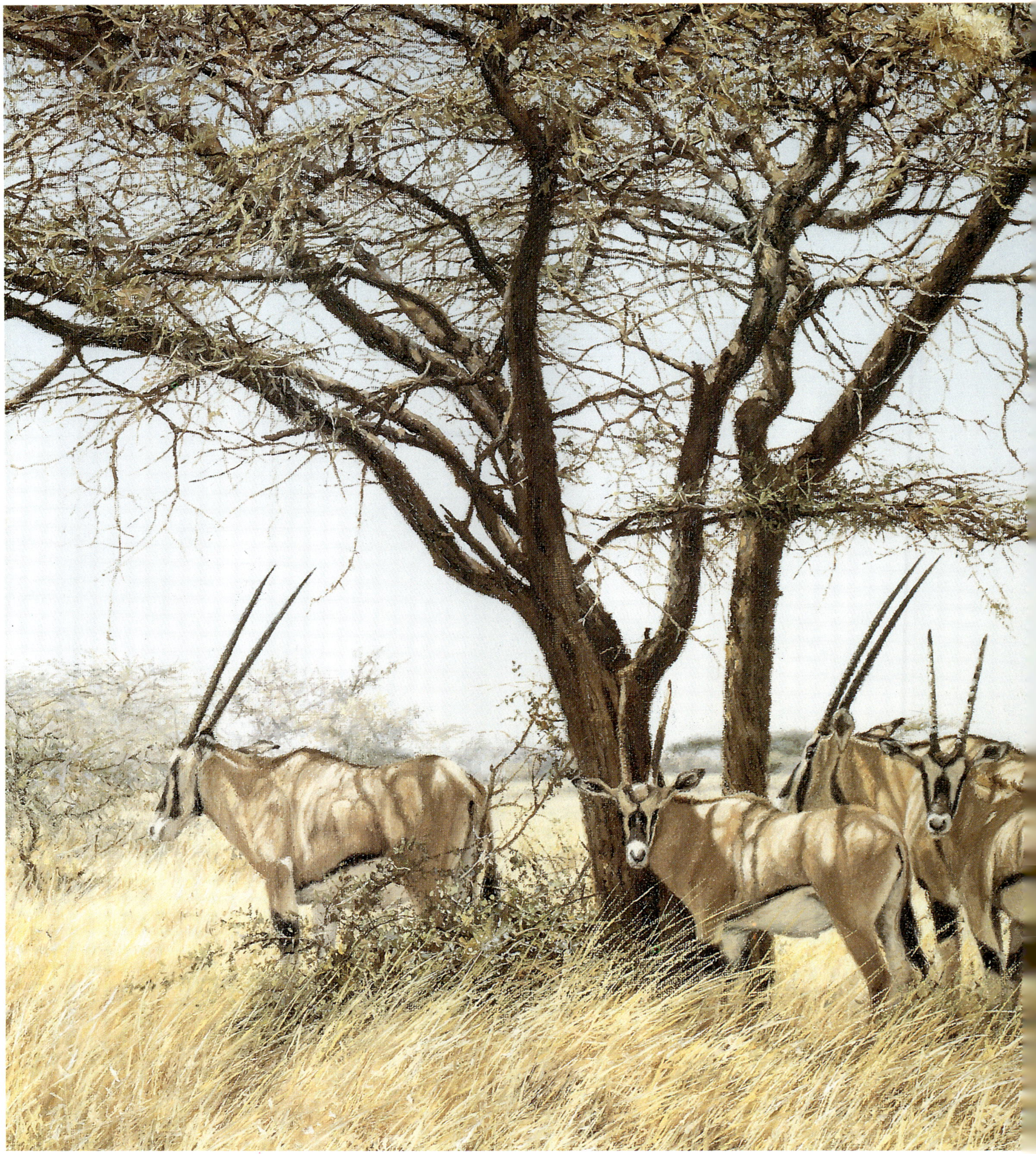

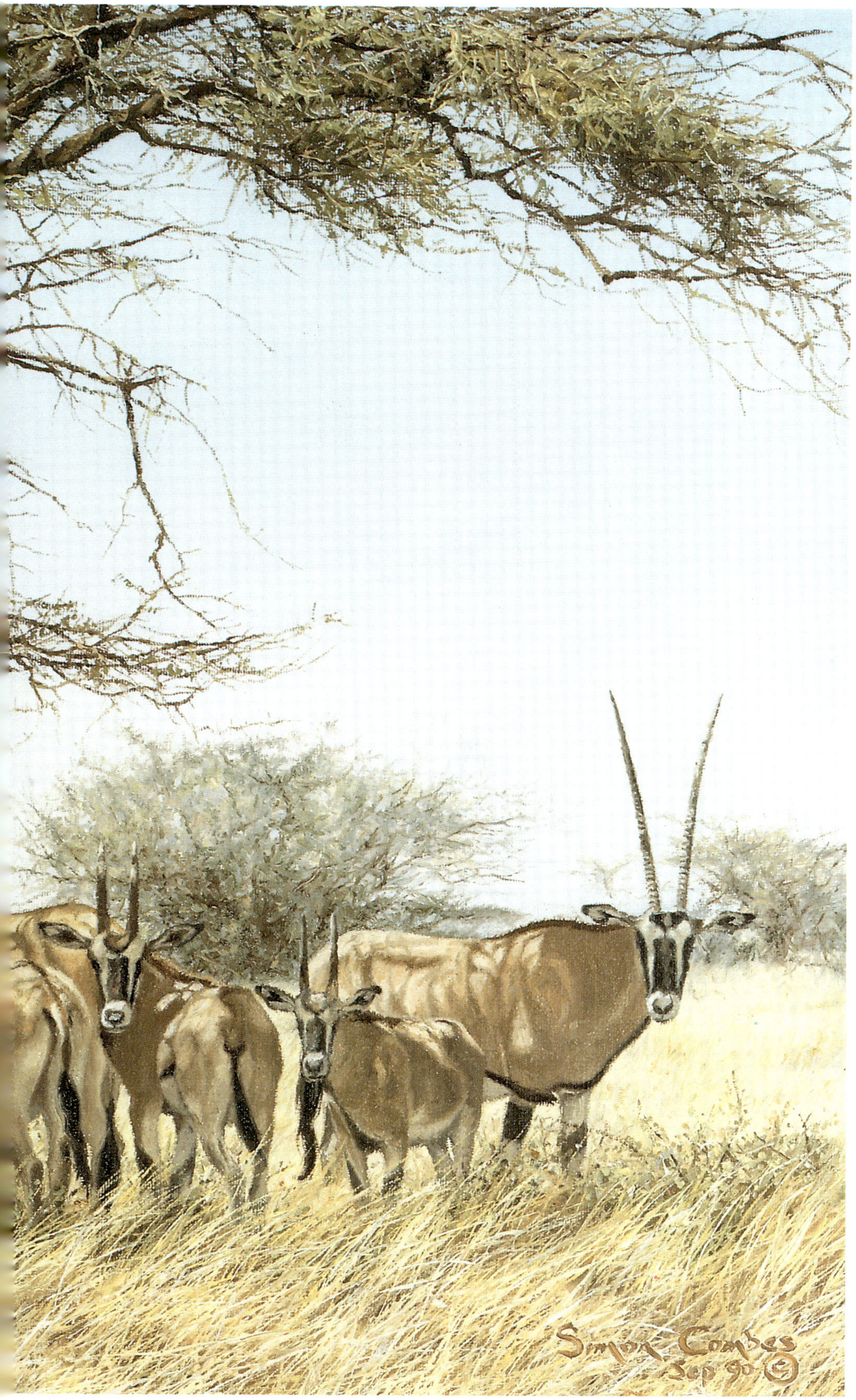

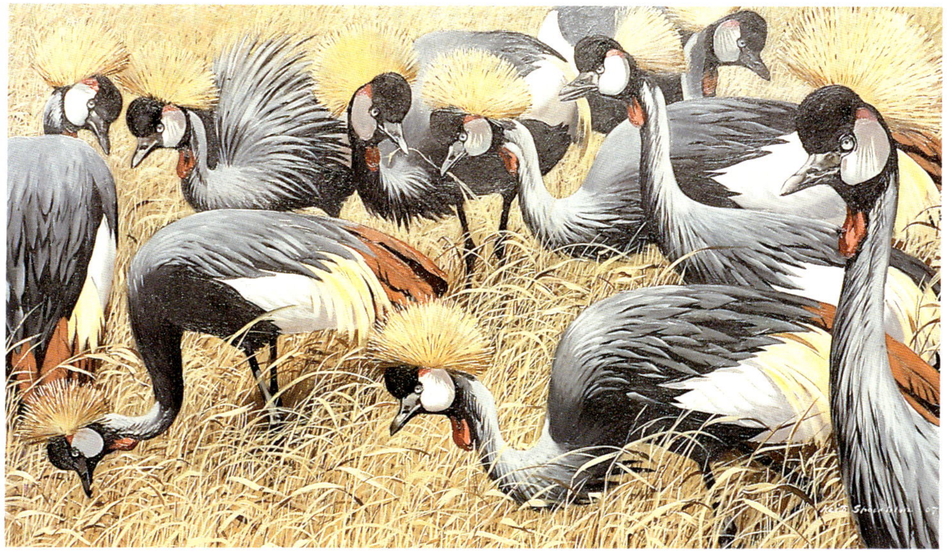

Keith Shackleton is best known for his magnificent paintings of Antarctica and its wildlife, but he has travelled widely in Africa. This oil of crowned cranes is a typical Shackleton: lively, with a strong sense of design. Crowned cranes are among the most improbable of birds, with their amazing mixture of colours, topped by that extraordinary crown. One expects such a bird to be rare, so it comes as a pleasing surprise to find that this is one of the most widespread of African birds, and one that is as happy in a ploughed field as the open plain. Two closely related species occur: here Keith Shackleton has painted the grey crowned crane, which is found from Kenya to the eastern Cape. The black crowned crane occurs sparsely in West Africa, but is more abundant in the Sudan and Ethiopia.

AFRICAN CROWNED CRANES
Keith Shackleton

112 Widely distributed on the savannas of eastern and southern Africa, the bat-eared fox (*below*) is a nocturnal hunter, feeding mainly on insects and small rodents. However, bat-ears are often to be seen during the day, basking in the sun at the entrance to their den. They are usually found in pairs, but it is common for several animals to share the same burrow, and when all are out, sunbathing together, they make a comical sight.

Though their enormous ears undoubtedly endow these foxes with exceptionally good hearing, their most important function is to help with heat-loss, a problem for an animal living in hot and dry conditions.

BAT-EARED FOX
Janet Heaton

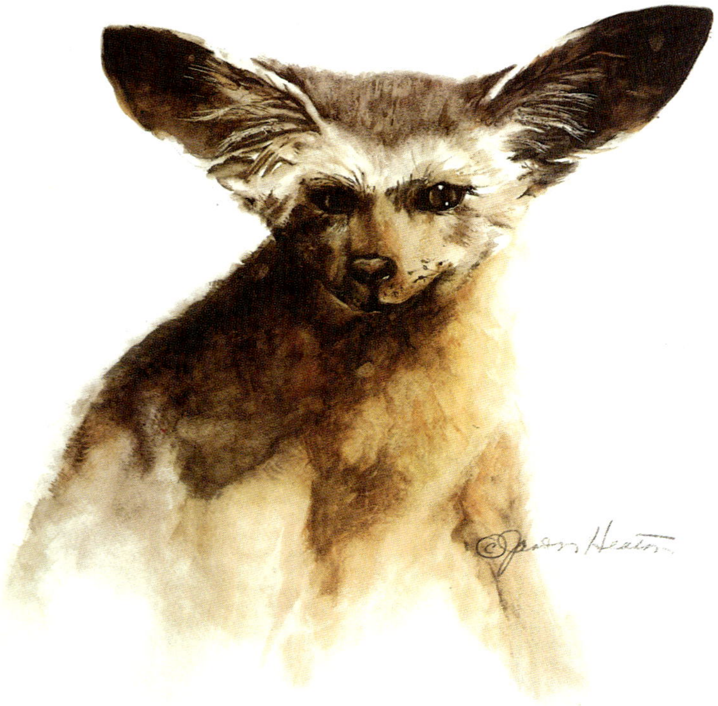

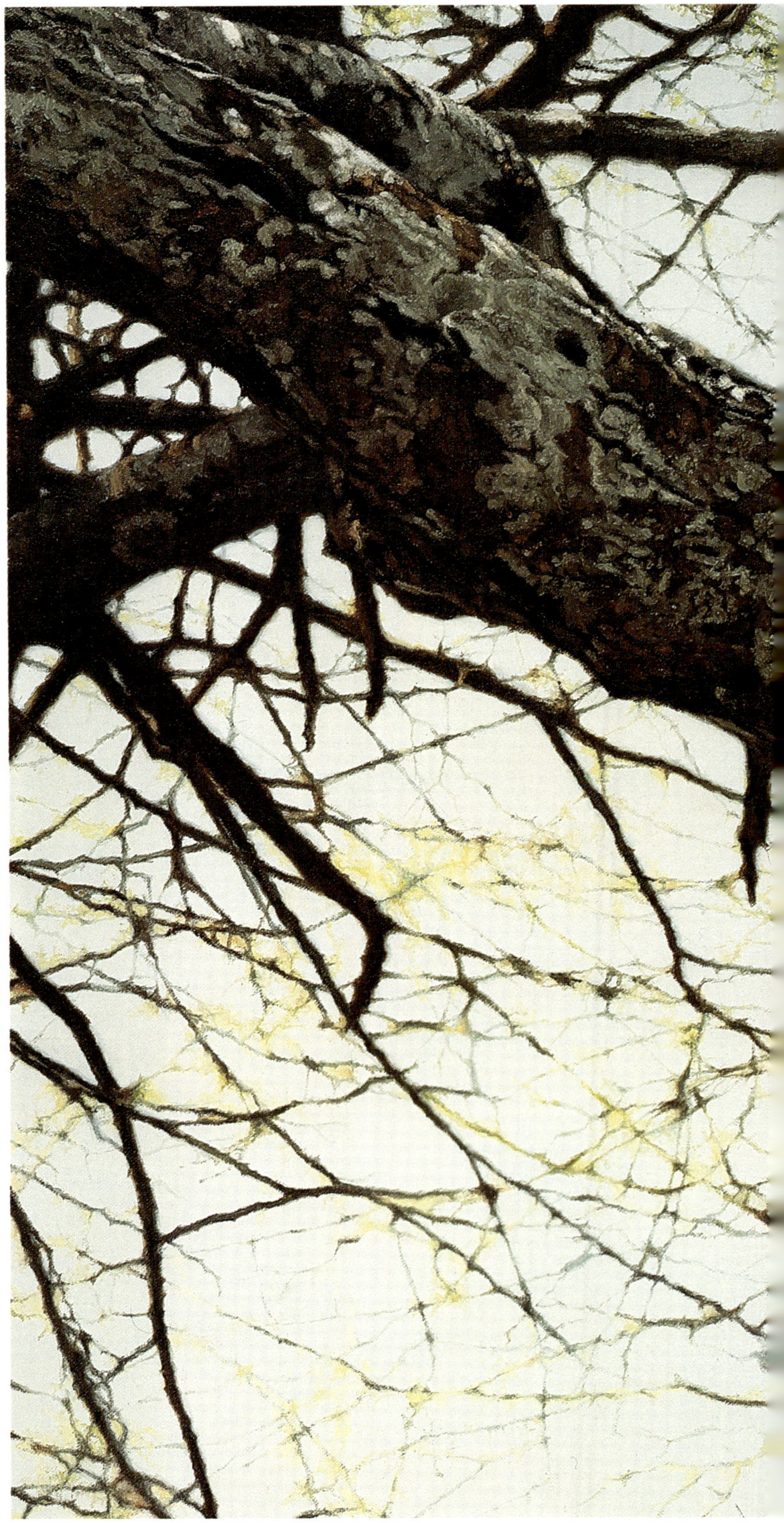

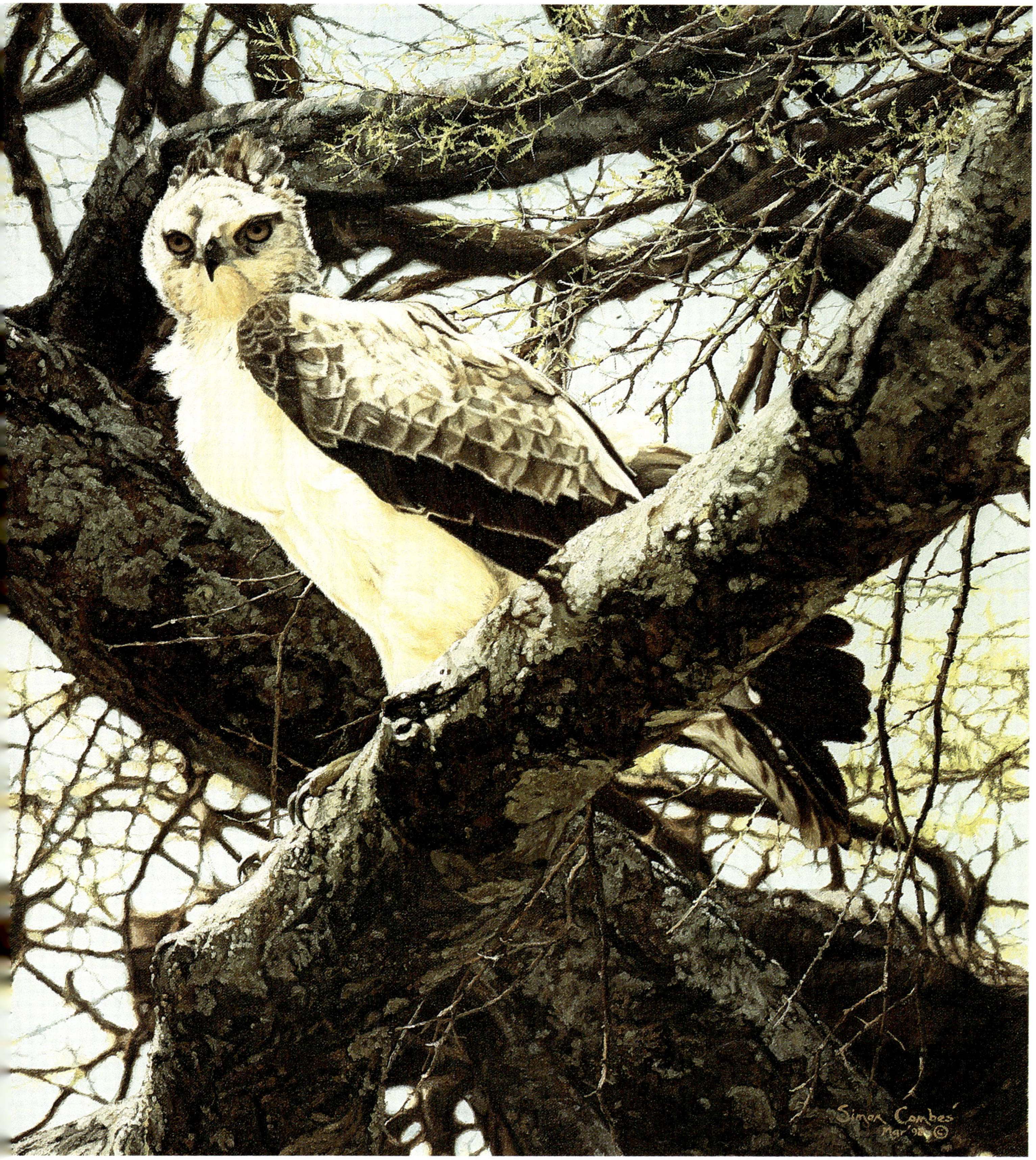

Most safari enthusiasts believe they can recognize all of Africa's powerful predators, but have a surprising blind-spot when it comes to birds of prey. Simon Combes' portrait is of an immature martial eagle, one of the largest and most powerful of African eagles. Martials spend much of the day soaring, on wings that span 9ft from tip to tip.

According to Combes, "Whoever named the martial eagle was right on target. Everything from its fierce yellow eyes to its supreme efficiency as a hunter are aptly applied to the word martial, with its connotations of conflict and attrition. I have watched these fearsome raptors kill mongooses, monkeys, gazelles and snakes, then attempting to carry their quarry into nearby trees but, more often than not, being unable to fly with the weight of it." Immature martial eagles retain the same markings until they are at least five years old, when they moult almost at once into full adult plumage.

YOUNG MARTIAL EAGLE
Simon Combes

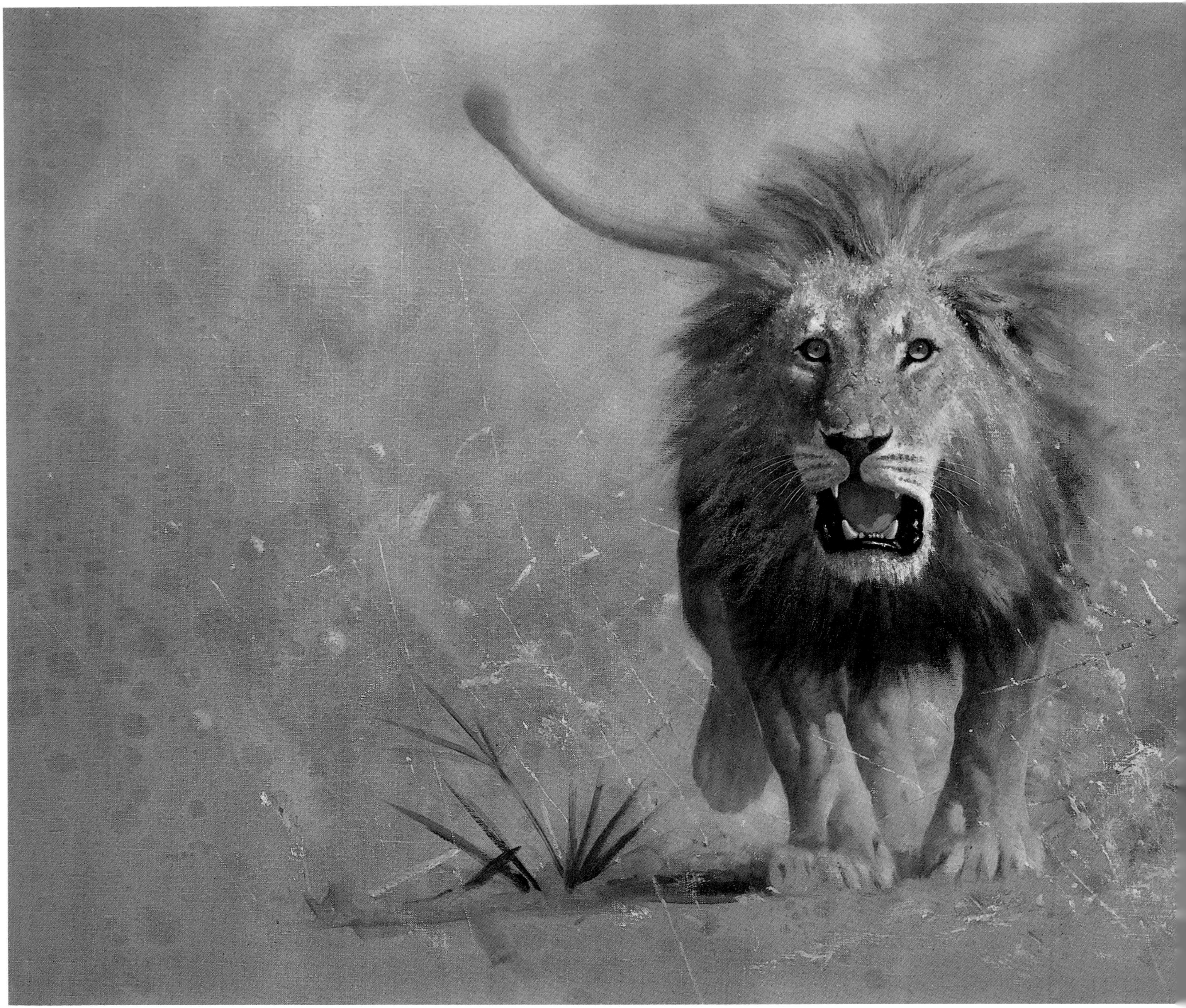

Just as the owl sketch was drawn from life, so too was this exciting oil of a charging lion. "He was mating, and definitely guarding his territory when I chanced upon him. What amazed me was his power and speed when he charged me, and also, to a lesser extent, what one actually sees in this sort of situation. I can remember the eyes; the muzzle; even the old battlescars on his nose; the mane, flowing as he came forward, and the teeth, definitely the teeth. I recall, too, the background, a brownish haze, whiplashed by the black-tipped tail, and then the growl . . . but that is *absolutely all*.

"It would have been nice to notice the beautiful scenery – the winding sand river, with its pools of water, leading back into the distant hills – and to hear the sound of hornbills and guineafowl, and the emerald-spotted wood dove. All this I absorbed a year later, when I stood on the spot where the lion charged me."

CHARGING LION
Michael Ghaui

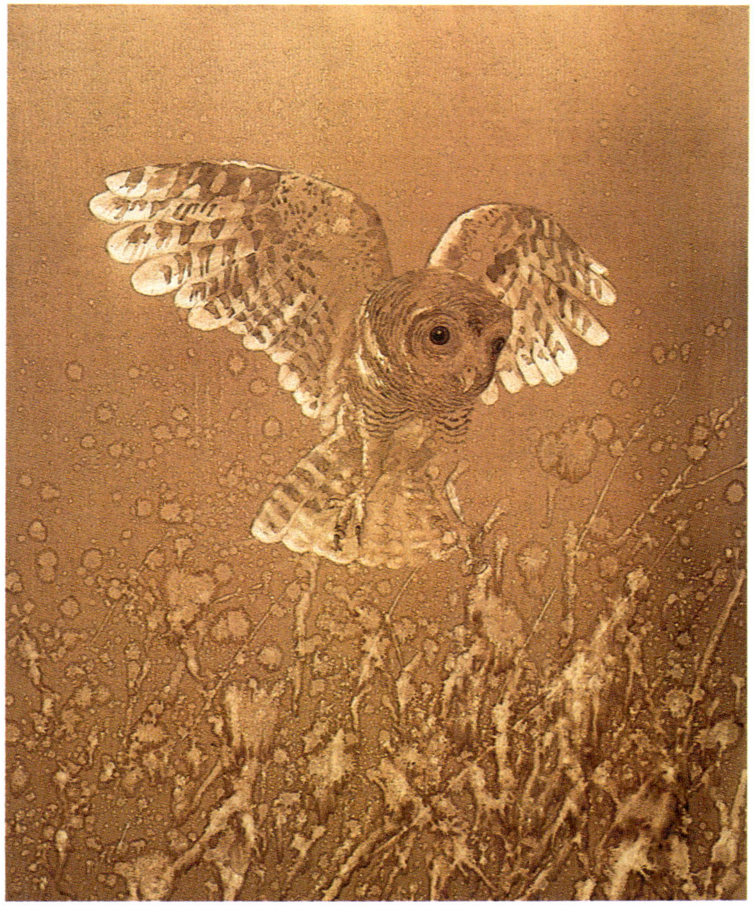

WOOD OWL STUDY
Michael Ghaui

Most films of African wildlife give a false impression: you are led to believe that death lurks behind each bush. What you are not told is that the cameraman followed the same pride of lions night and day for 18 months to capture the few minutes of hunting sequences which invariably dominate a 30-minute film. Bob Kuhn's exciting painting of lioness hunting impala is vibrant with action, though Kuhn admits to never having seen lions kill.

"On my numerous trips to East Africa, several of them two months long, I have spent a lot of time observing, photographing and sketching lions. I have witnessed their intense concentration when prey is sighted and serious hunting begins. I have seen them chase and miss. I have come across them squabbling over captured prey or sleeping off a gigantic feed. I have never seen the kill itself, but I know a lot about it. The much-maligned tube in our den has satisfied my need to witness this act of violence again and again, often in slow motion. If we who portray wildlife don't improve on our predecessors in the challenging business of portraying animals in action then shame on us."

HIT AND MISS
Bob Kuhn

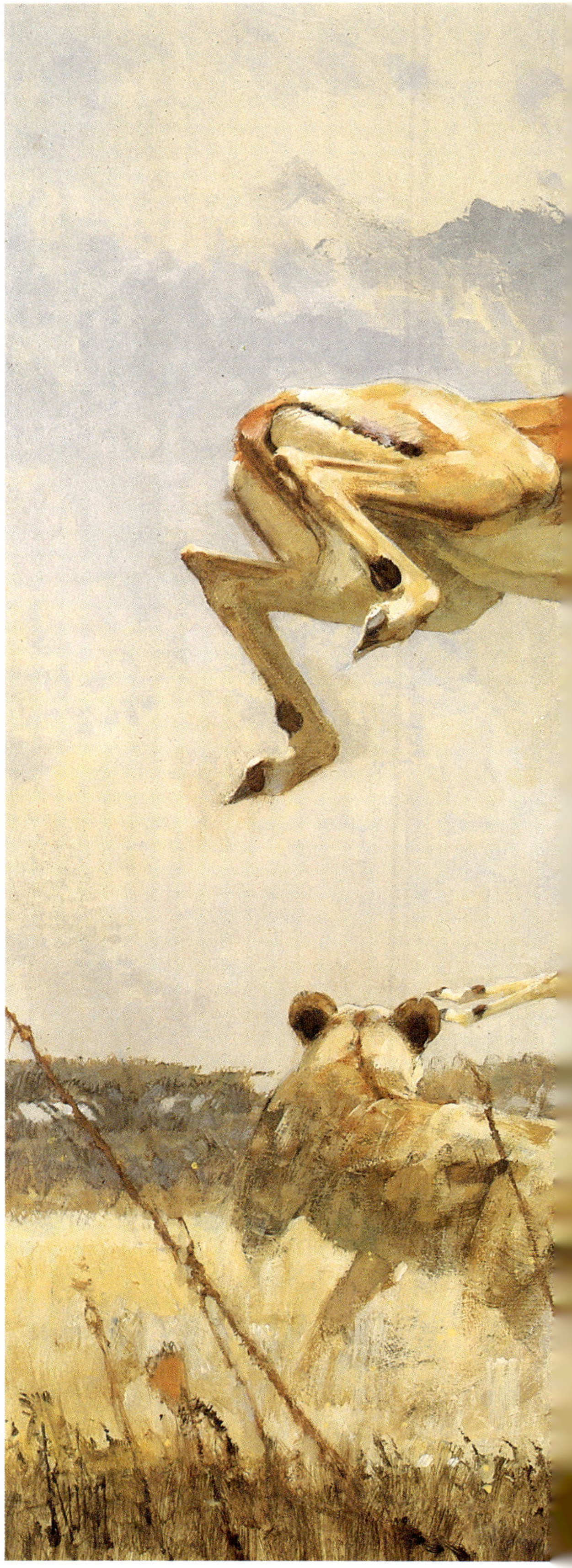

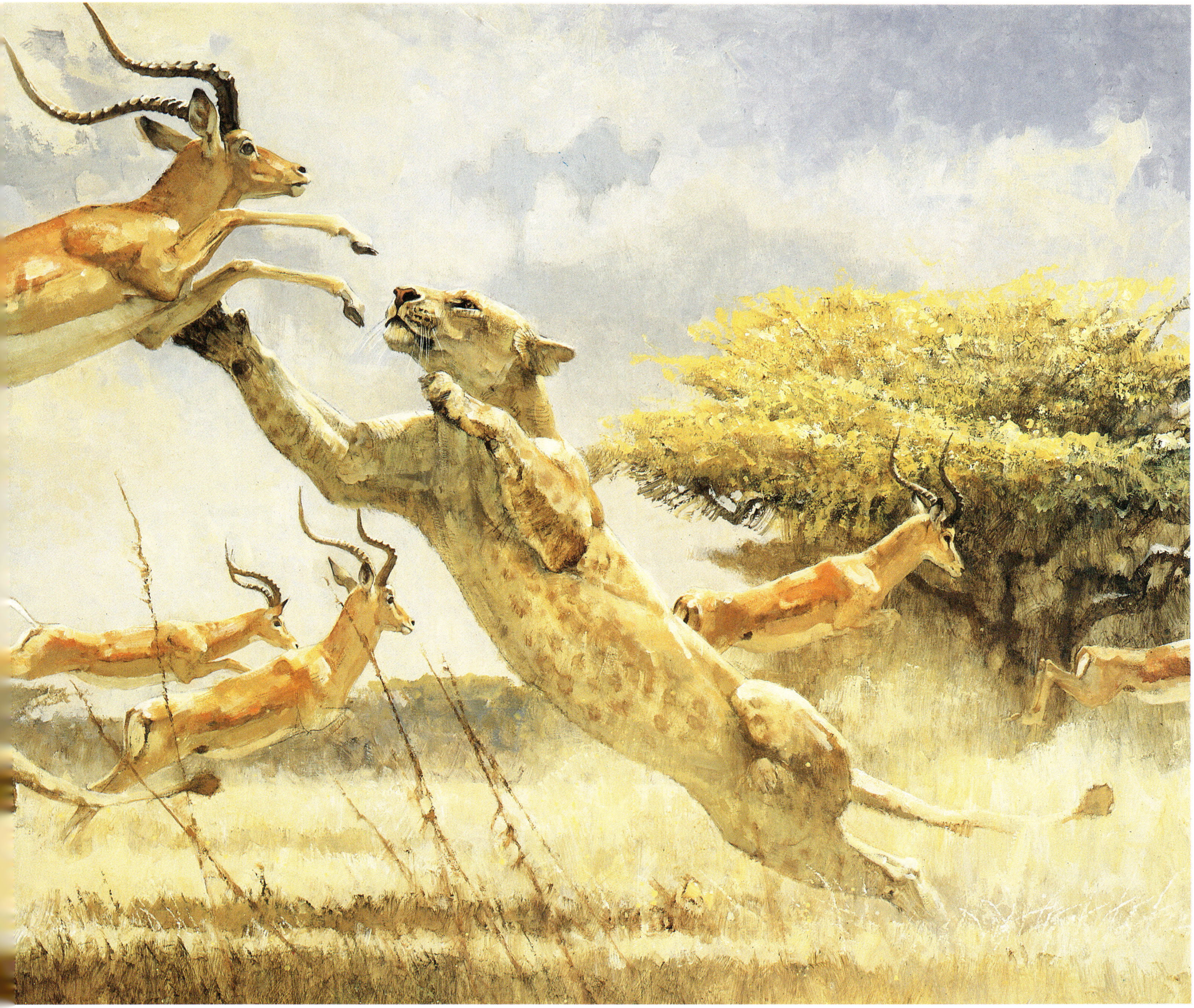

Wilhelm Kuhnert never had the luxury of studying slow-motion films of lions hunting, so his paintings lack the action of modern masters such as Kuhn. However, Kuhnert certainly knew his lions, as this study of a feeding pair shows so clearly. The composition is simple: two lions and a dead zebra, in an uncluttered savanna landscape. But both the lions have stopped feeding and are staring intently at an unseen intruder, adding atmosphere and tension to the painting. One must also remember that Kuhnert not only lacked the assistance of the long lens camera, but also travelled in East Africa in times of far simpler transport technology than that of today. His paintings are from a different era, but it is a mark of his greatness that current artists still strive to be compared with him.

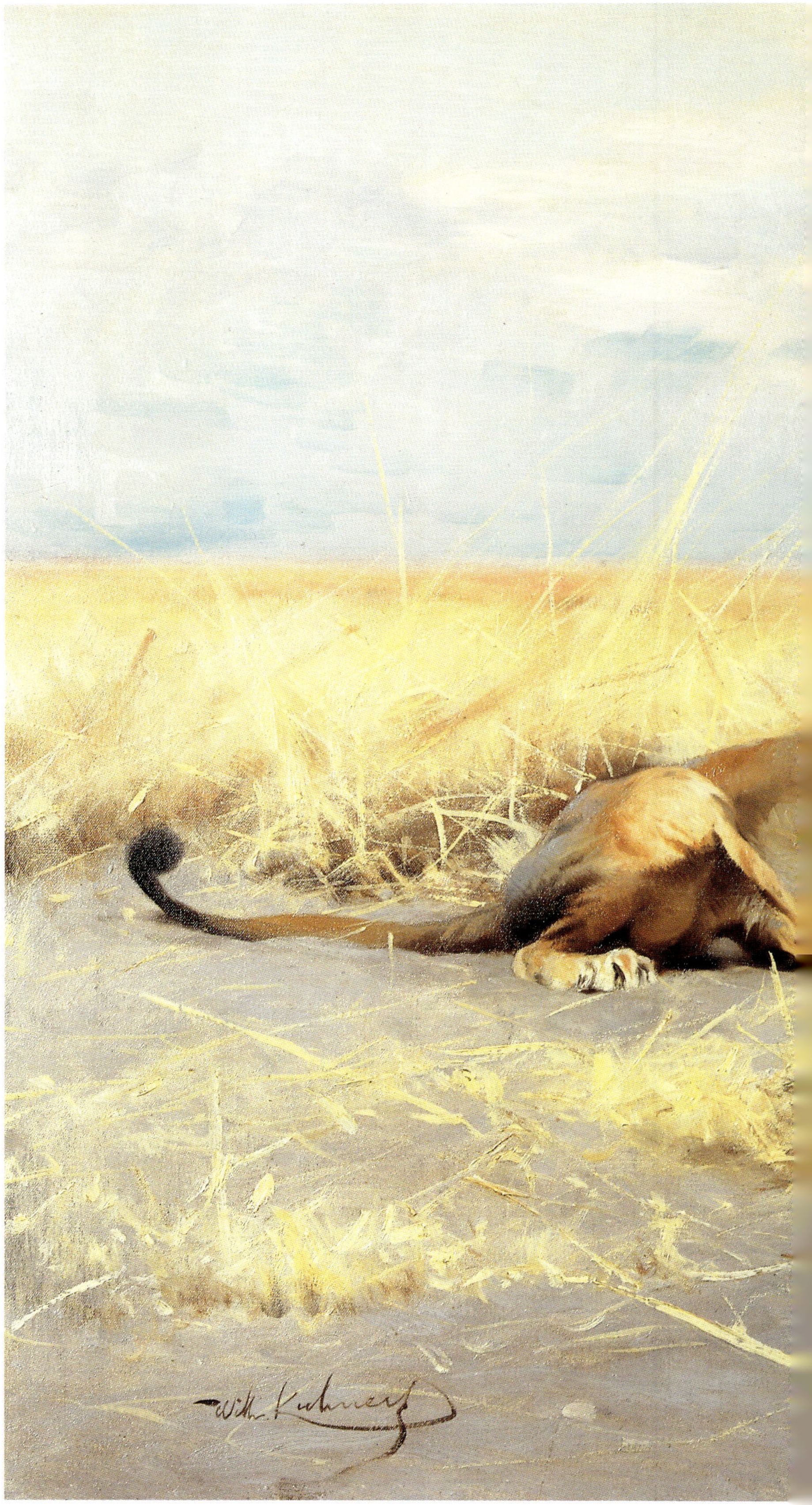

THE VICTIM: LIONS AND ZEBRA
Wilhelm Kuhnert

NAIROBI GAME PARK ON A DULL AFTERNOON
Rena Fennessey

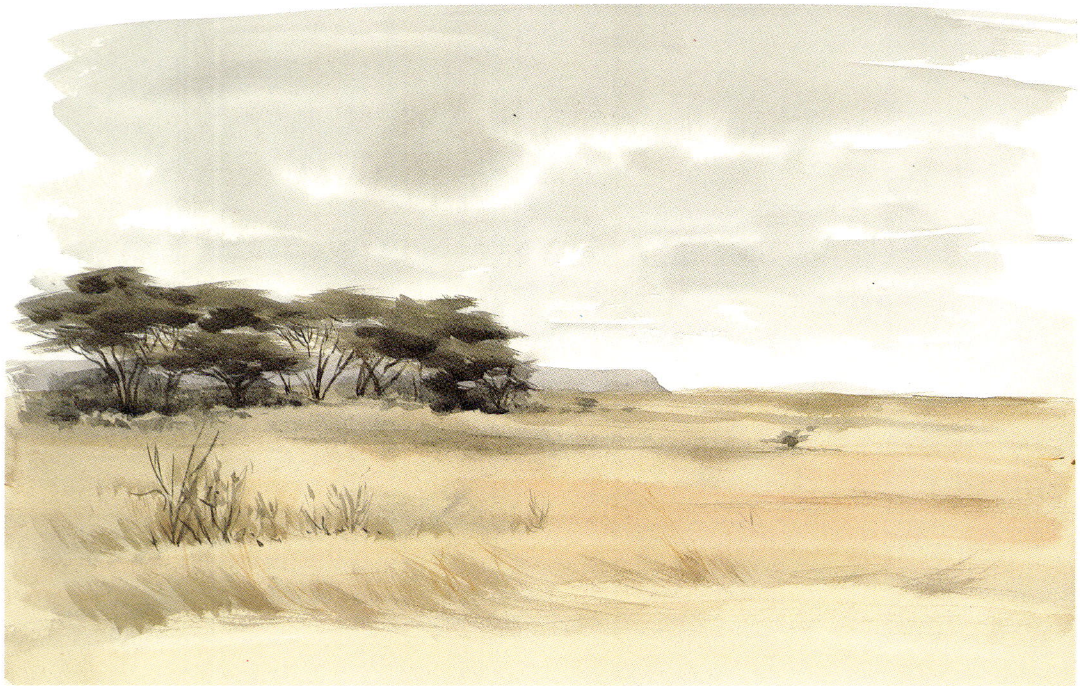

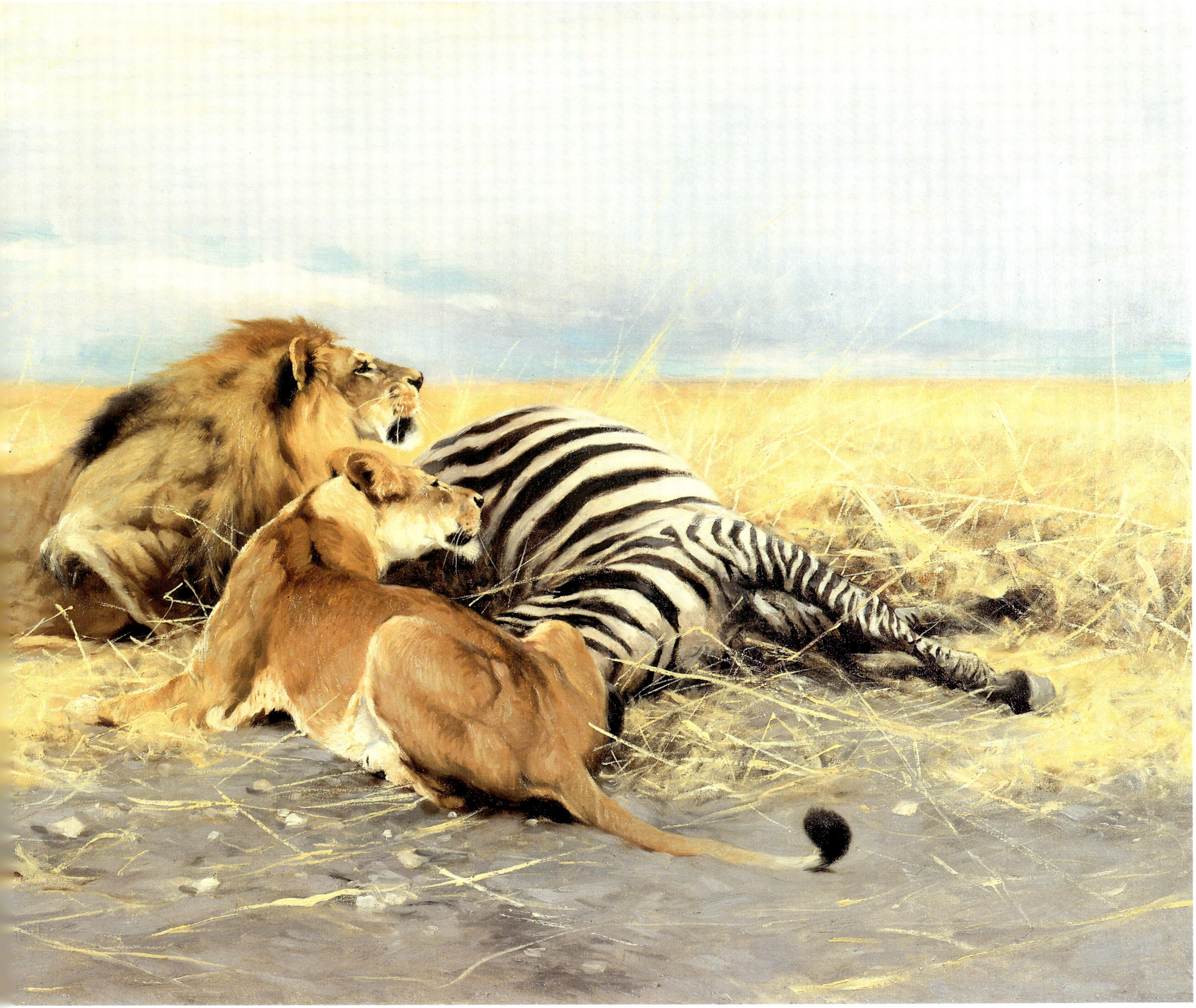

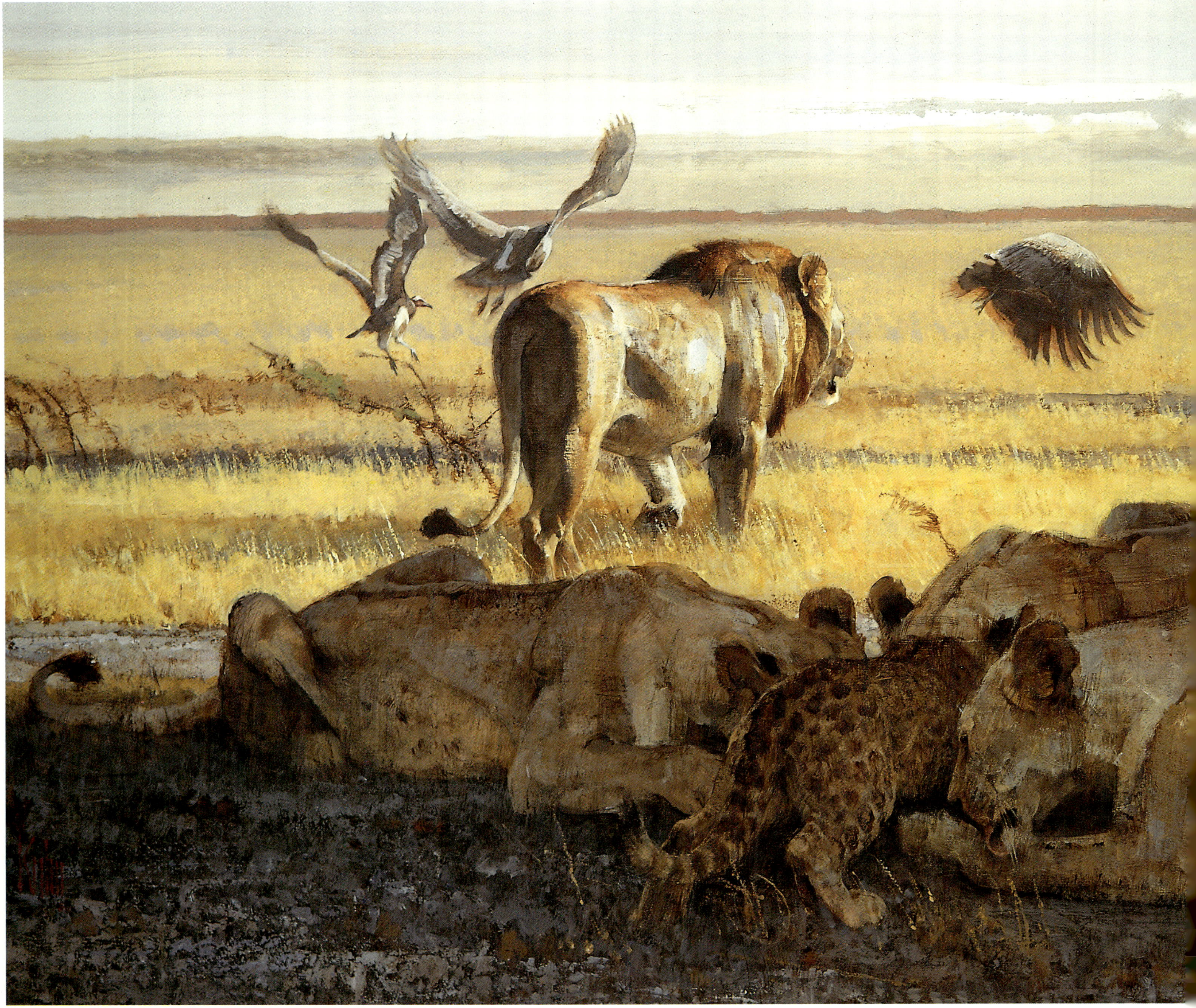

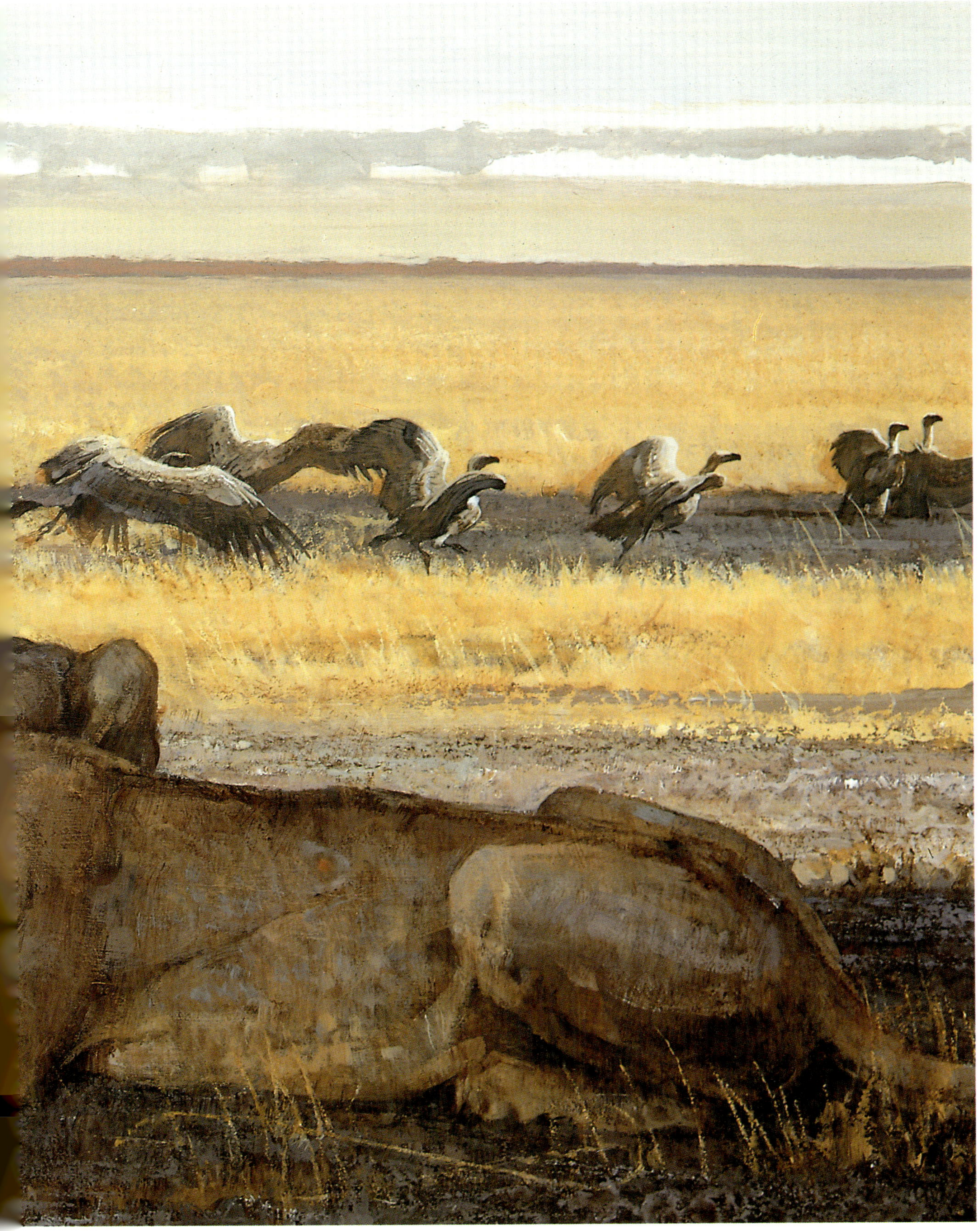

A lion's kill is just the first in a well-ordered sequence of events. First, the lion will feed, before permitting his wives and cubs to join in the feast. Bob Kuhn, creator of this evocative landscape, points out that "it's common knowledge that lions, for all their kingly virtues, are woefully lacking in gallantry. They will run their female consorts off of kills with no regard for the major role the lionesses usually play in putting meat on the table. When the males are stuffed to bursting, they will tolerate a timid approach from the ladies. . ."

However, they are less happy to tolerate the various scavengers sharing the spoils, and show their displeasure by chasing off jackals, hyenas and vultures. Here, the old male is making a token effort to see off an assortment of marabou storks and vultures. Their turn will come, but not just yet.

SLIM PICKENS
Bob Kuhn

Though birds often appear in Bob Kuhn's paintings, they rarely form the main subject. "I don't fancy myself as anything more than a journeyman bird painter," says Kuhn, who admits to a preference "for creatures with a leg at each corner". This approach contrasts strongly with that of fellow American Guy Coheleach, who is the most accomplished of bird artists, as this large (6ft by 3ft) work demonstrates. Fittingly titled "Attorneys and Bankers", it was painted after a period of legal turmoil in Coheleach's life, and it is easy to appreciate the analogy of title and subject.

Watching vultures feed is a fascinating, if gruesome, experience. There is a pecking order, with the larger species dominant over the smaller birds, but in what appears to be a mass free-for-all this can be difficult to observe. Here, Coheleach illustrates the two most numerous vultures of the East African plains: Rüppell's griffon vulture, and the slightly smaller white-backed vulture. The former has the longer neck, and so can penetrate deeper into the carcase, but is normally outnumbered at a kill by the white-backed. The Rüppell's griffon is easily identified by the pale edges to many of its body feathers, while the white-backed is a more uniform brown, with distinctive white back.

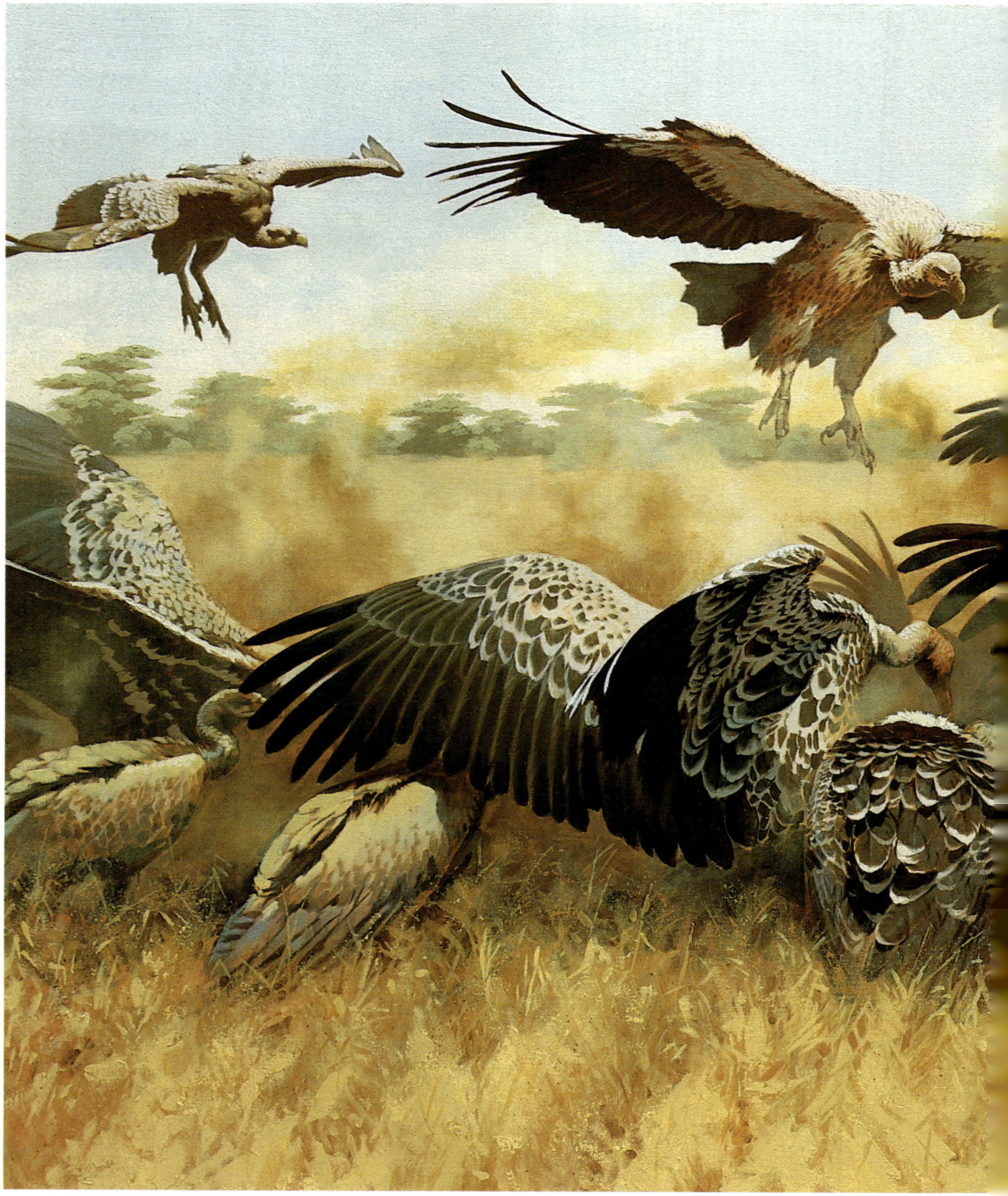

ATTORNEYS AND BANKERS
Guy Coheleach

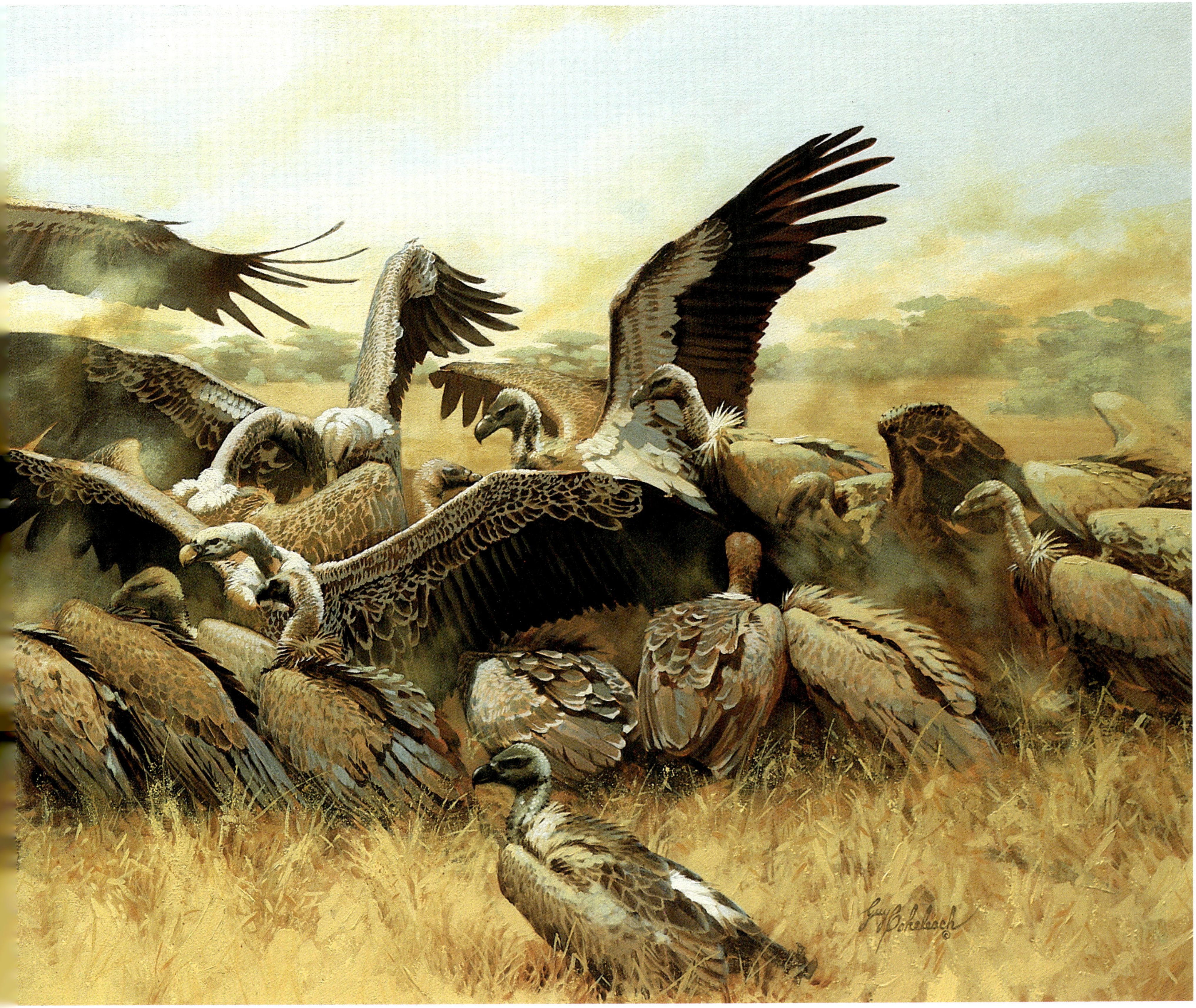

124 Considering their size and bulk, elephants are surprisingly swift movers, and a running herd can sustain a speed of up to 20mph for an hour at a time. Ghaui shows a breeding herd which has just winded him, the cows and calves "shambling off in a great hurry trying not to look too undignified. Tails and trunks flail in the air, with the odd hoot and bellow to let you know they are definitely not amused. A tiny calf, even at this age, will try to imitate its elders."

Elephants have an uncanny knack of shielding their babies from view, and even when fleeing from danger mothers stay in close contact with their offspring. Artists can overcome problems such as these; whereas I have numerous shots of baby elephants, largely obscured by their mother. At birth, elephants are about 3ft high at the shoulder, so the baby shown here is only a few weeks old. Despite its small size, it will have little difficulty in keeping up with the herd.

ON THE MOVE
Michael Ghaui

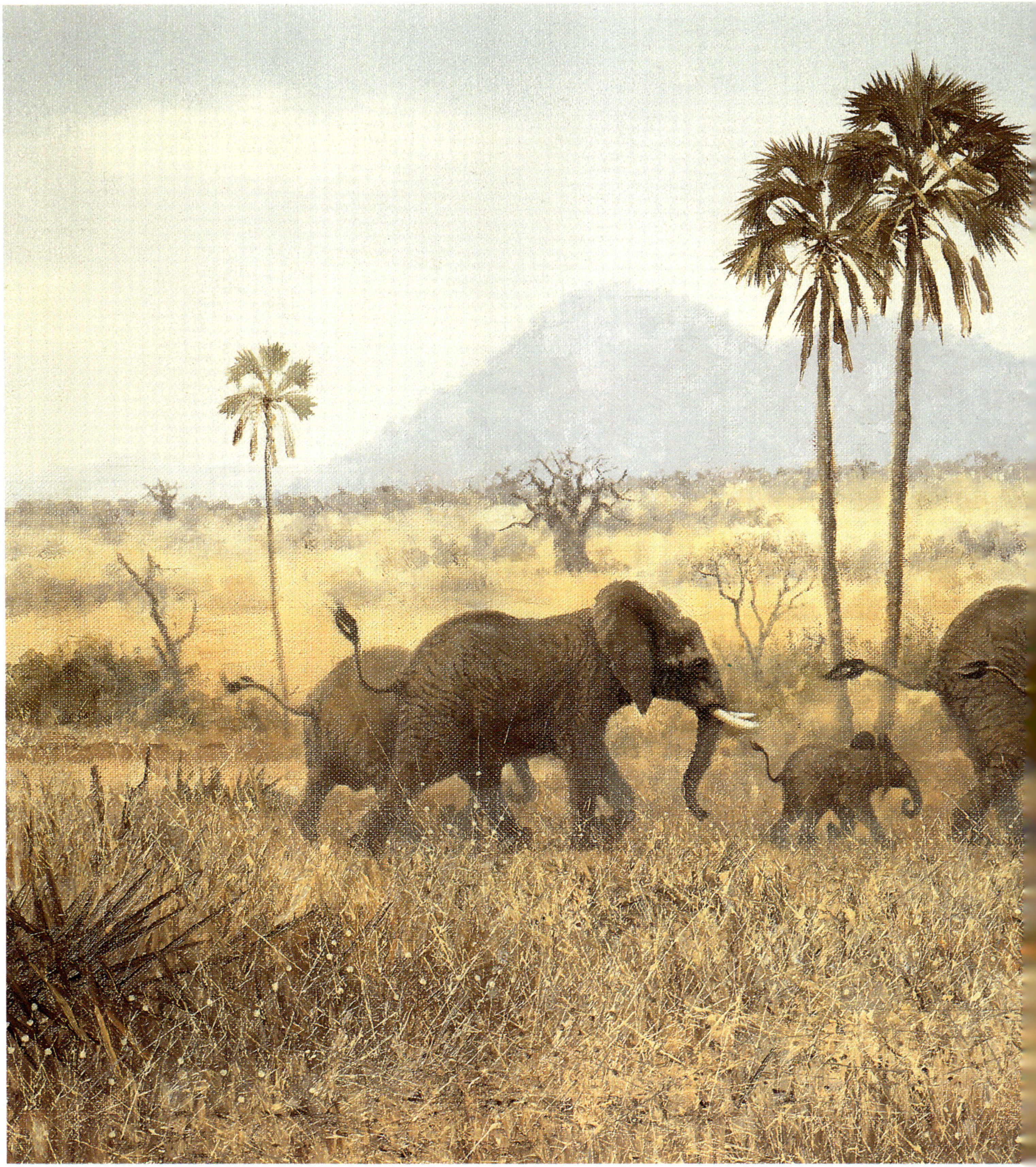

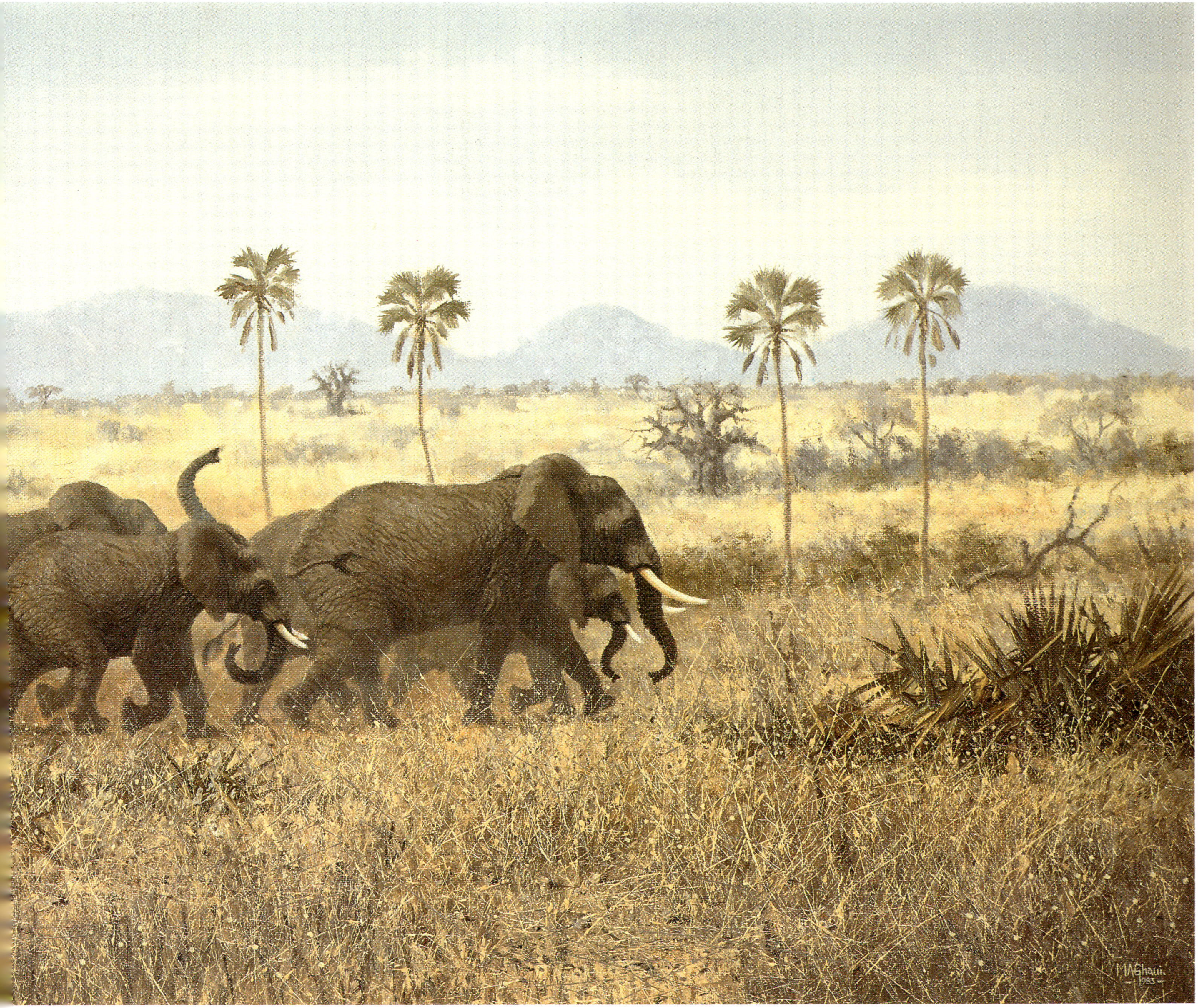
M.A.Ghani.
1983

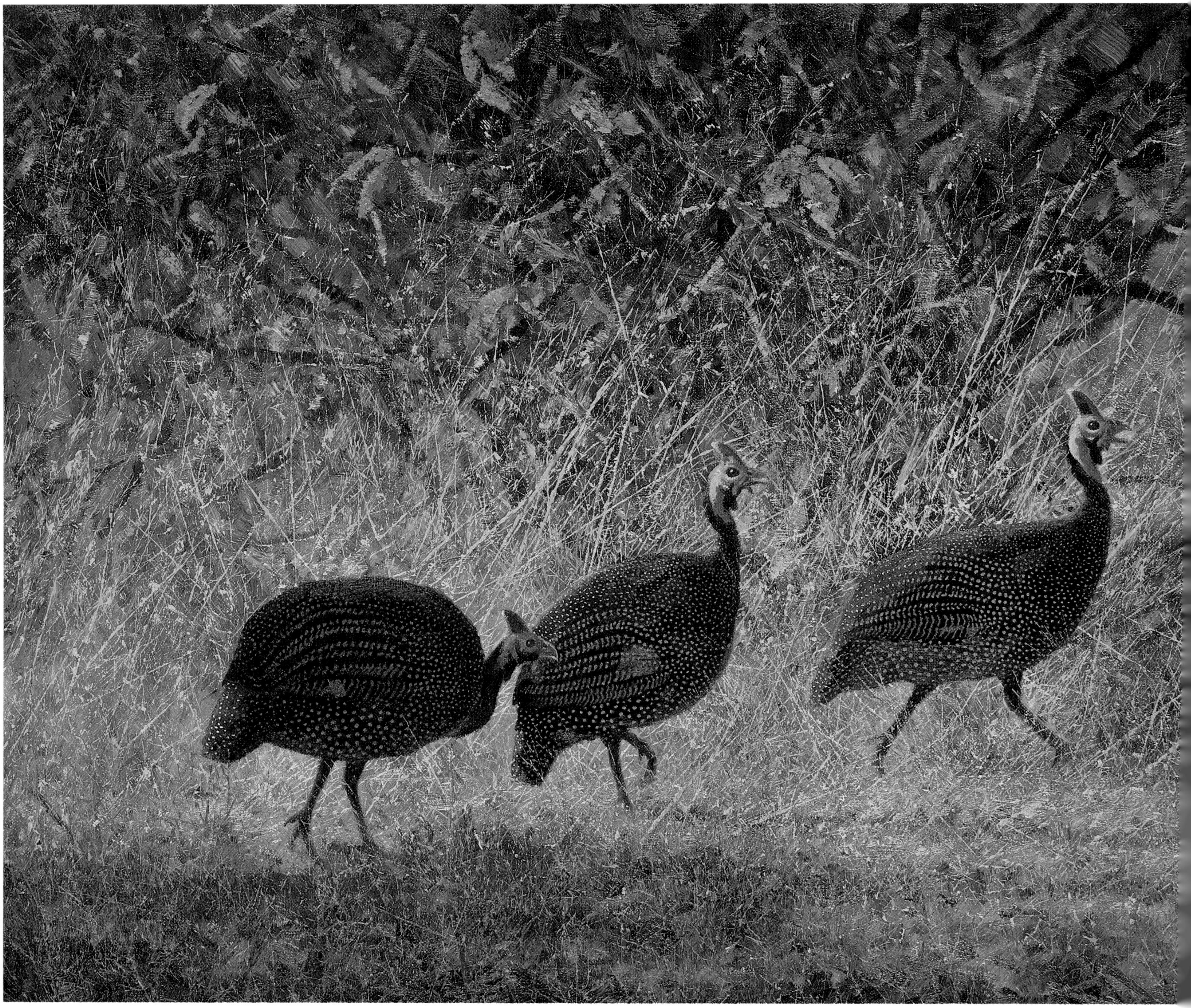

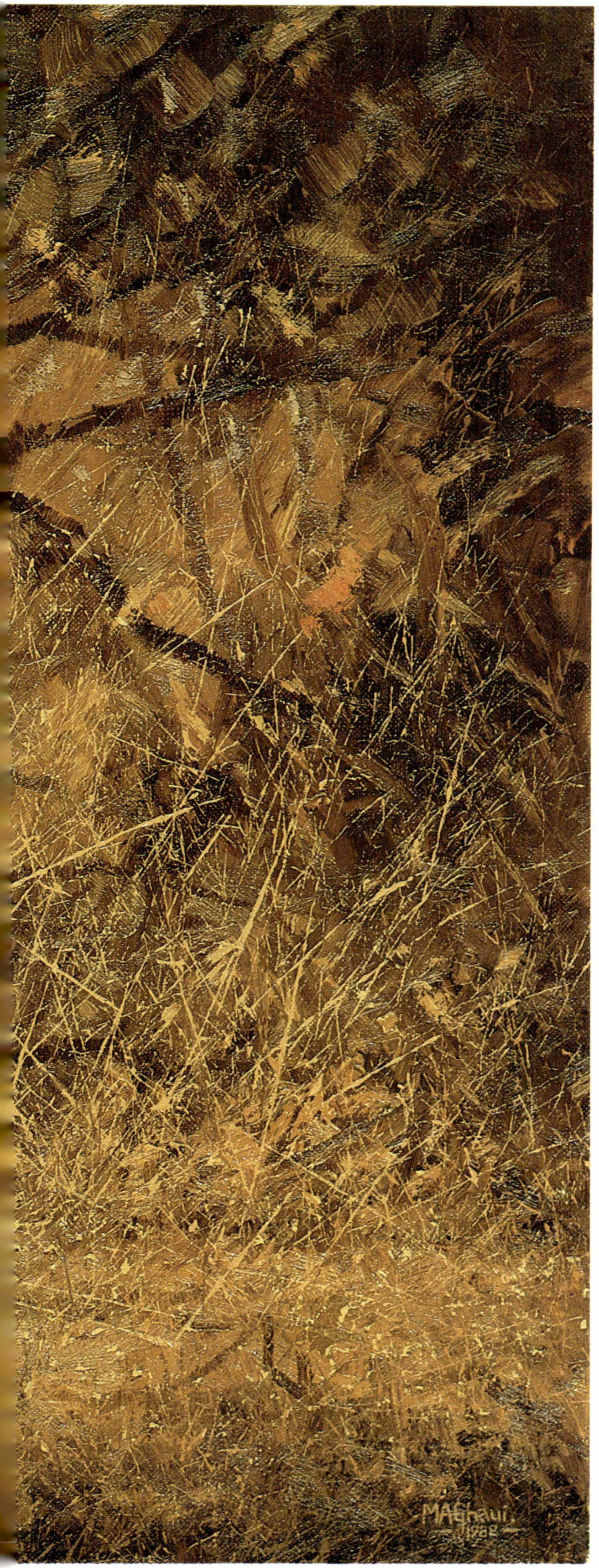

Helmeted guineafowl occur throughout the savannas of sub-Saharan Africa, from Senegal to Namibia and South Africa. Throughout this extensive range there is a small degree of geographical variation: Michael Ghaui's painting shows the subspecies *reichenowi* typical of Kenya and central Tanzania, with pale-blue facial skin and entirely red wattle. Domesticated guineafowl are descended from the West African subspecies, which has a smaller casque, or helmet.

For Ghaui, "there are one or two sounds that epitomize the African bush. The helmeted guineafowl, with its whistle and alarm call, is one of them. Not only this, but they are also beautiful birds, especially in the early morning or late afternoon when the colours of their neck and head are caught by the sun – an almost electric blue with a dash of red."

Guineafowl have three basic requirements: drinking water, cover and roosting sites. Where these exist, they can be abundant, despite the fact that many creatures, including man, prey upon them.

GUINEAS IN THE MORNING
Michael Ghaui

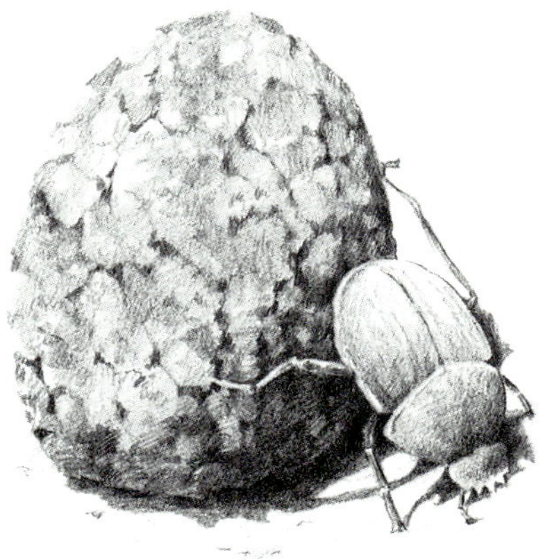

DUNG BEETLE
Gunnar Pettersson

128

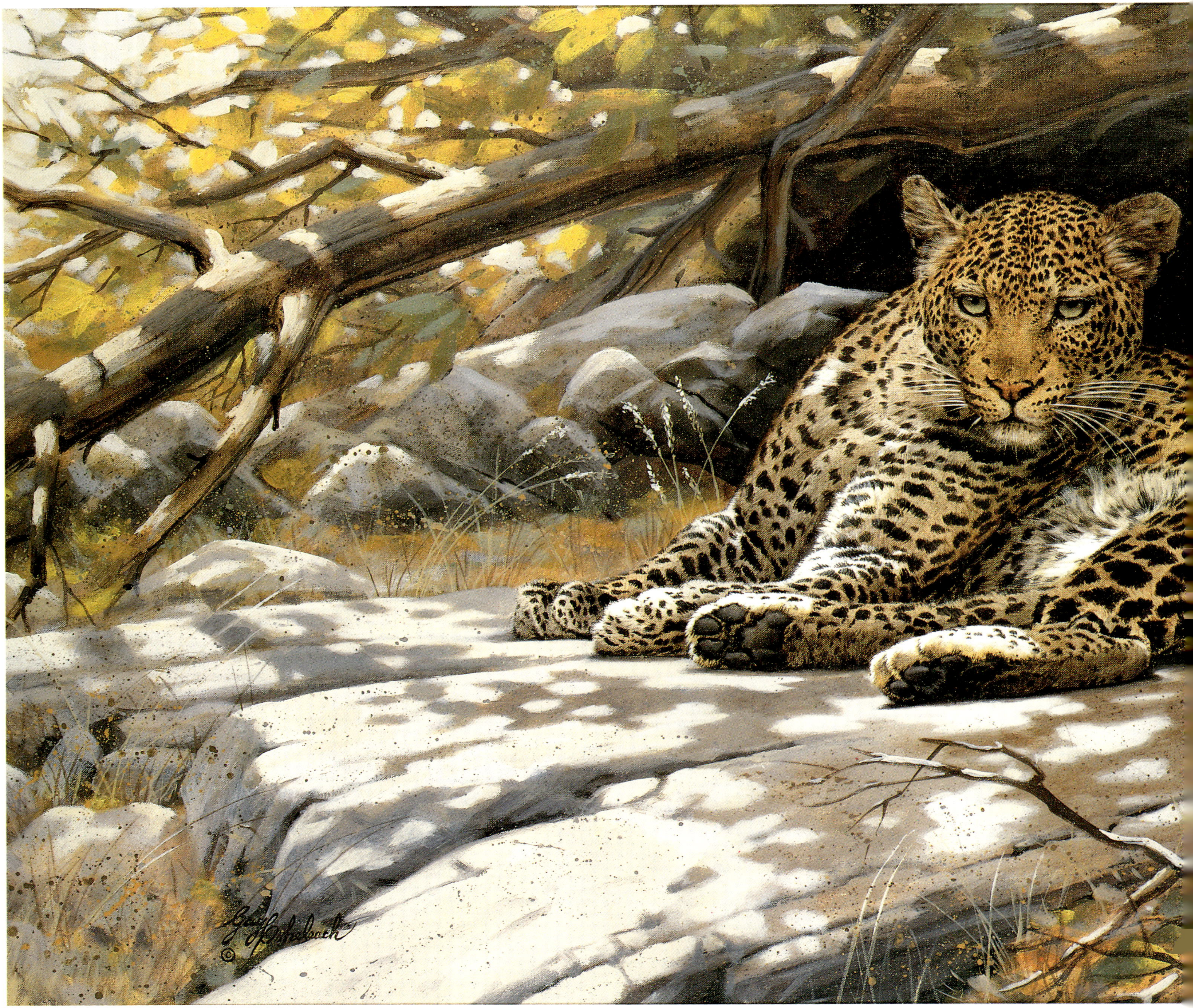

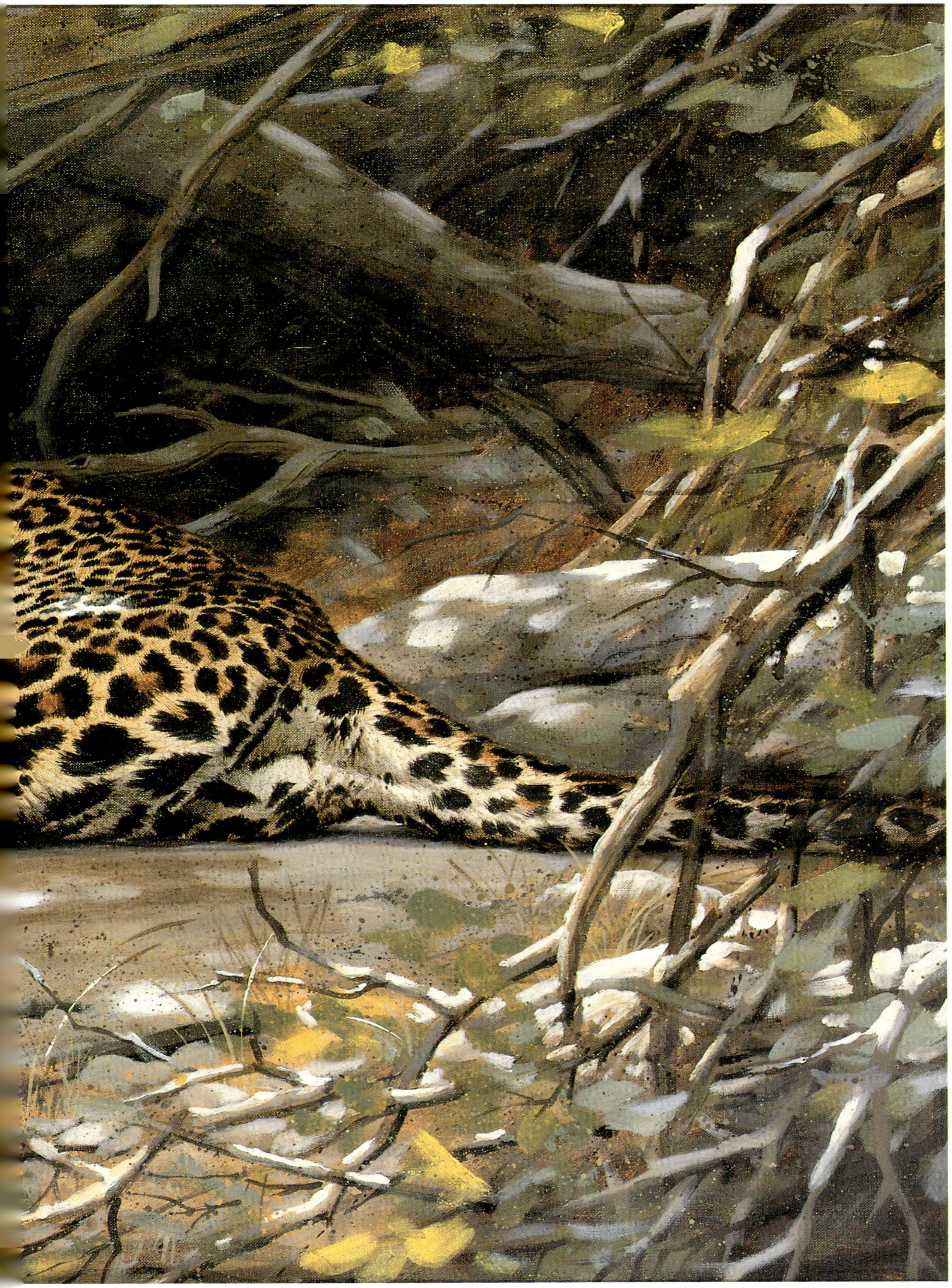

A leopard, resting in the middle of the day in a shelter of rocks and roots, has been alerted by something that requires closer attention. Guy Coheleach captures the sleepy, bored curiosity so typical of all cats with this pleasing oil which is in his book, *The Big Cats*.

Published in 1982, this is a serious natural history of the eight species of so-called big cat, ranging from the North American puma through to the snow leopard of the Himalayas, and including the African trio of leopard, lion and cheetah.

LEOPARD'S LAIR
Guy Coheleach

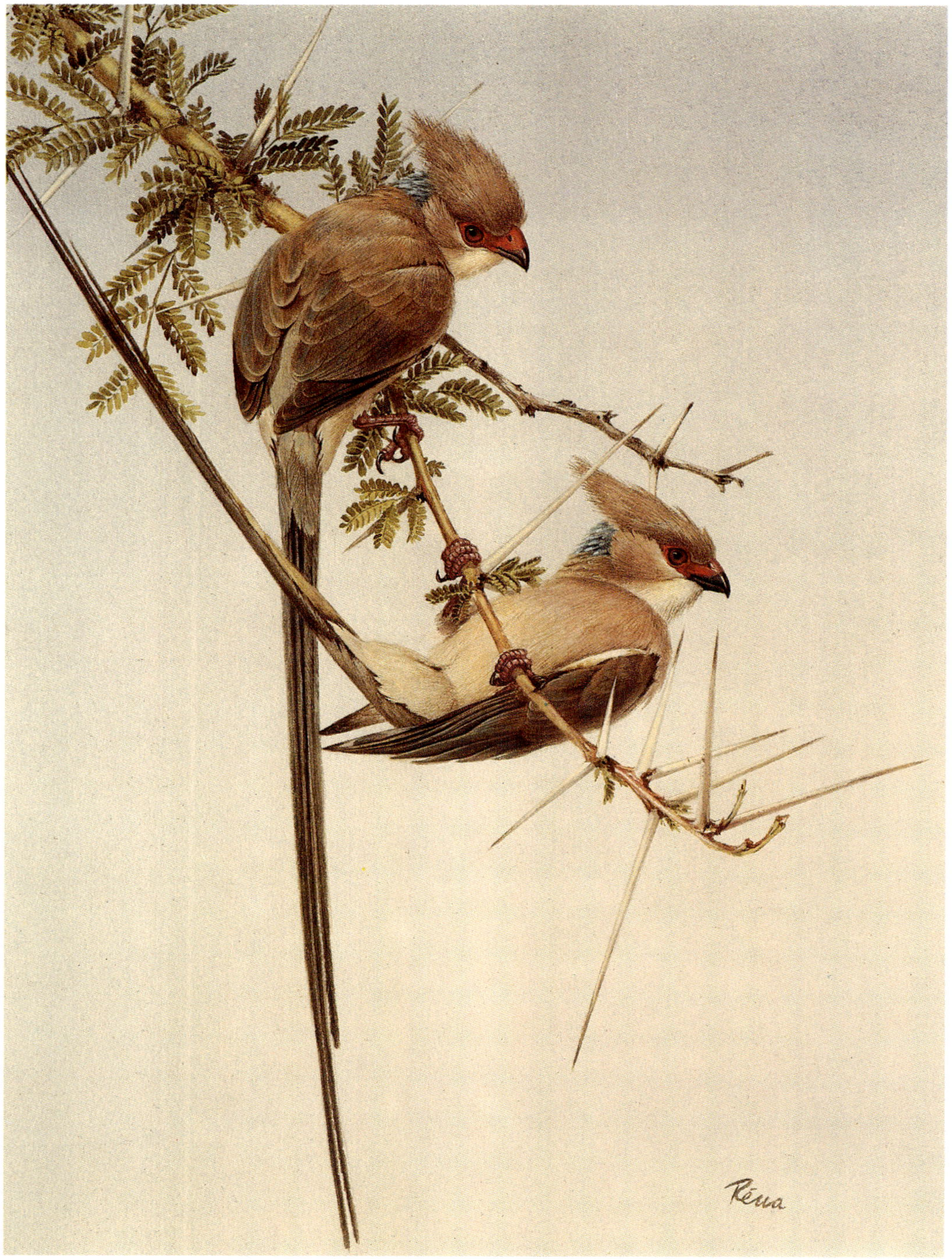

This delightful watercolour study of blue-naped mousebirds (*left*) was painted by Rena Fennesey for *Birds of the African Bush*, published by the Tryon Gallery and Collins in 1975. The text was contributed by that most eminent of African ornithologists, Leslie Brown. Both artist and author joined forces again to produce *Birds of the African Waterside*, published four years later.

Mousebirds are an exclusively African family: there are six species in all, of which the blue-naped is one of the most widespread. Mousebirds get their name from their habit of creeping about like mice inside thick cover. They are invariably found in small flocks, which draw attention to themselves with their long-drawn, mournful whistle, which sounds rather like *sueeeeee*. Shy and not easy to observe, they are attractive little birds, as Rena Fennessey's study shows so well.

MOUSE BIRDS
Rena Fennessey

Unlike greater kudus, lesser kudus (*right*) are both shy and elusive, and not easy to see. Robert Bateman painted this study from life, the result of a chance encounter in Kenya's Meru National Park. "The Land Rover we were in rounded a bend, and suddenly there was a male kudu staring right at us. A few moments later, another male emerged from the bush. In this painting, I've tried to recapture the moment when I first saw the kudus, including the soft browns and greys of the animals and the gentle slanting light that played over the whole scene."

MERU DUSK – LESSER KUDU
Robert Bateman

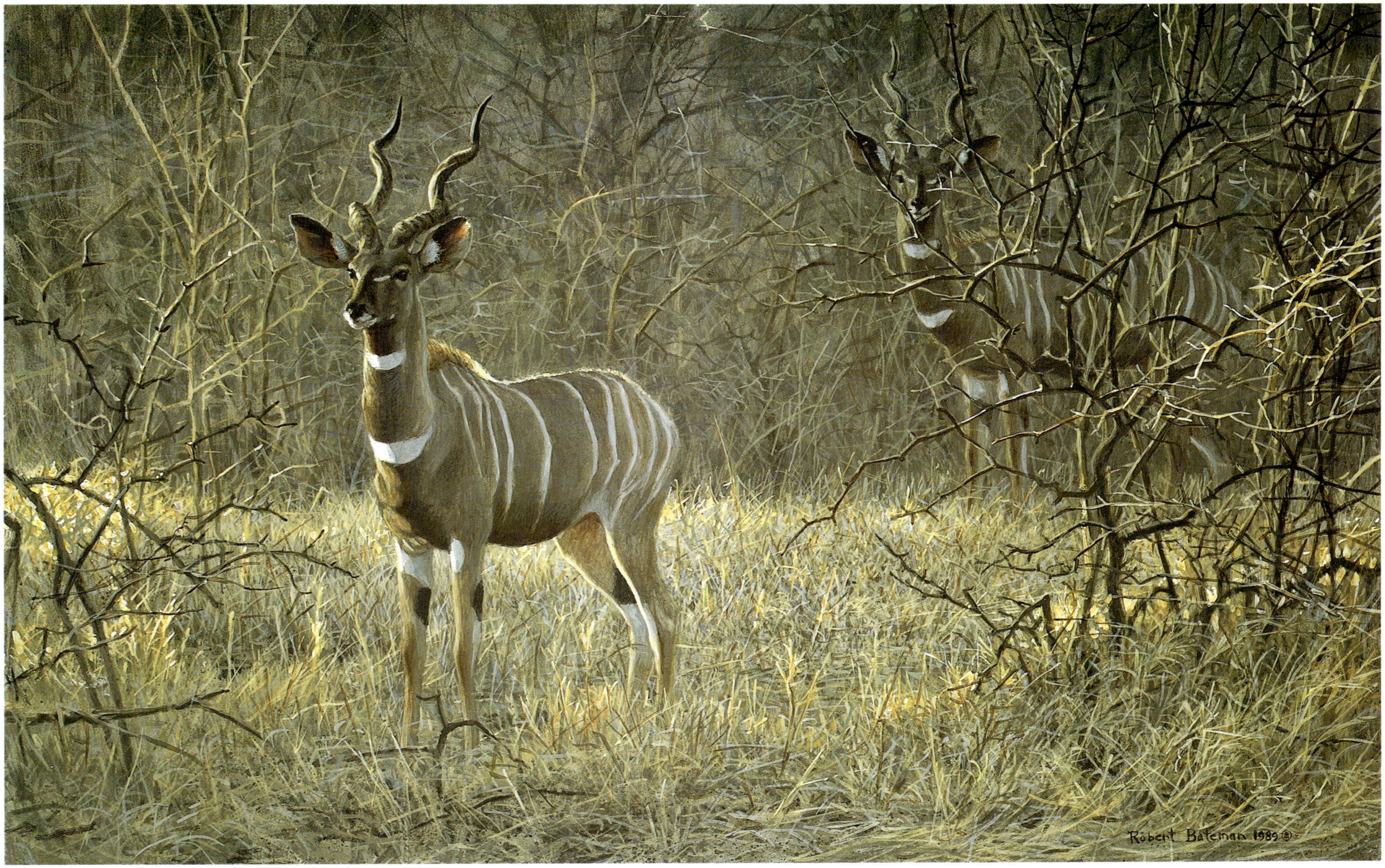
Robert Bateman 1989

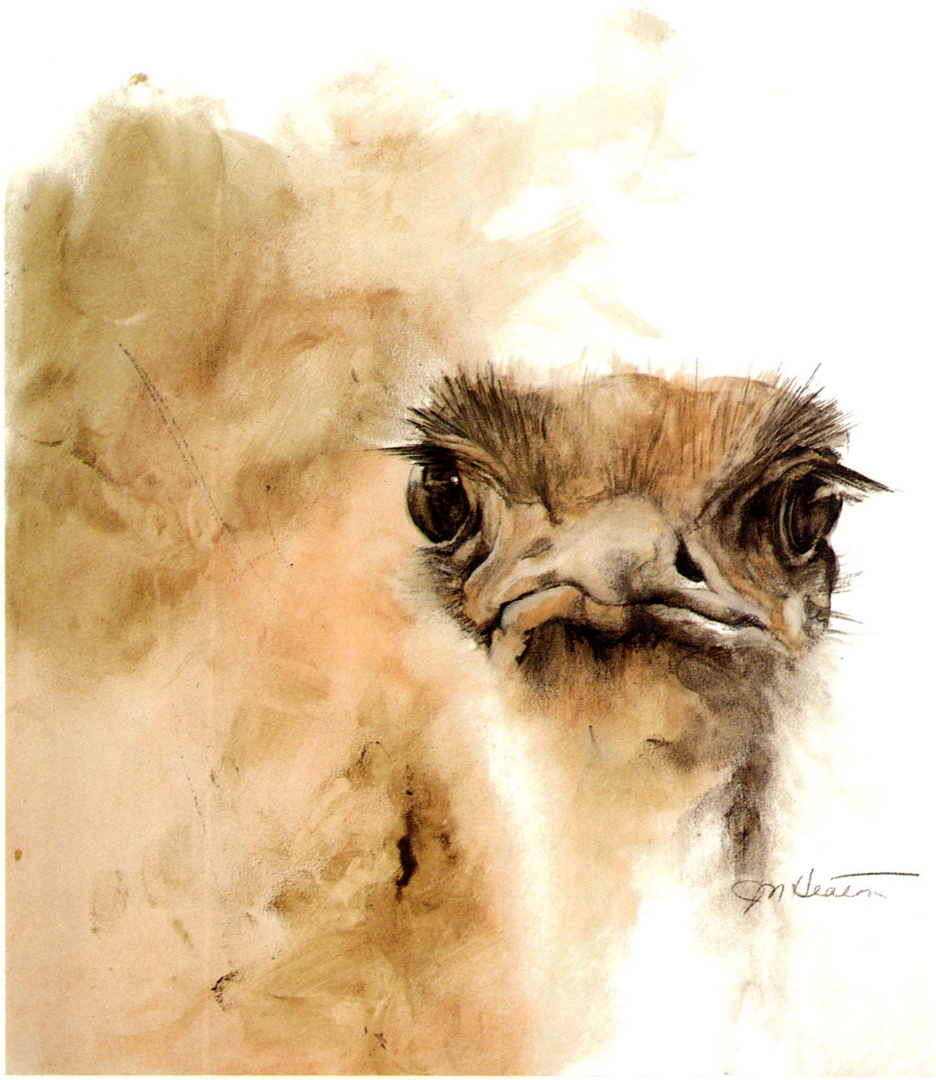

An ostrich (*left*), standing erect, has its eyes some 7ft or so above the ground, giving it a tremendous field of view. As a result, ostriches are able to spot danger long before the grazing animals around them. A running ostrich immediately alerts most antelopes, which may then bolt without establishing the original cause of the disturbance – false alarms are frequent.

OSTRICH
Janet Heaton

Greater kudu (*right*) do occur in open country, but as a rule they much prefer light forests and thick bush, where they can be surprisingly difficult to see, despite their size. This painting by Larry Norton depicts a family group of kudus in thick mopane woodland, and shows just how effective their camouflage is. Half close your eyes and you can hardly make out the animals, so effectively does their striped coat break up their outline.

Norton, who lives in Zimbabwe, is an up-and-coming young artist who recently had his first one-man exhibition at the Sportsman's Edge gallery in New York. Readers of this book may be interested to know that this gallery, and the Tryon gallery in London, are the places to go and see original paintings by many of the leading wildlife artists whose work is represented here.

GREY GHOSTS – GREATER KUDU
Larry Norton

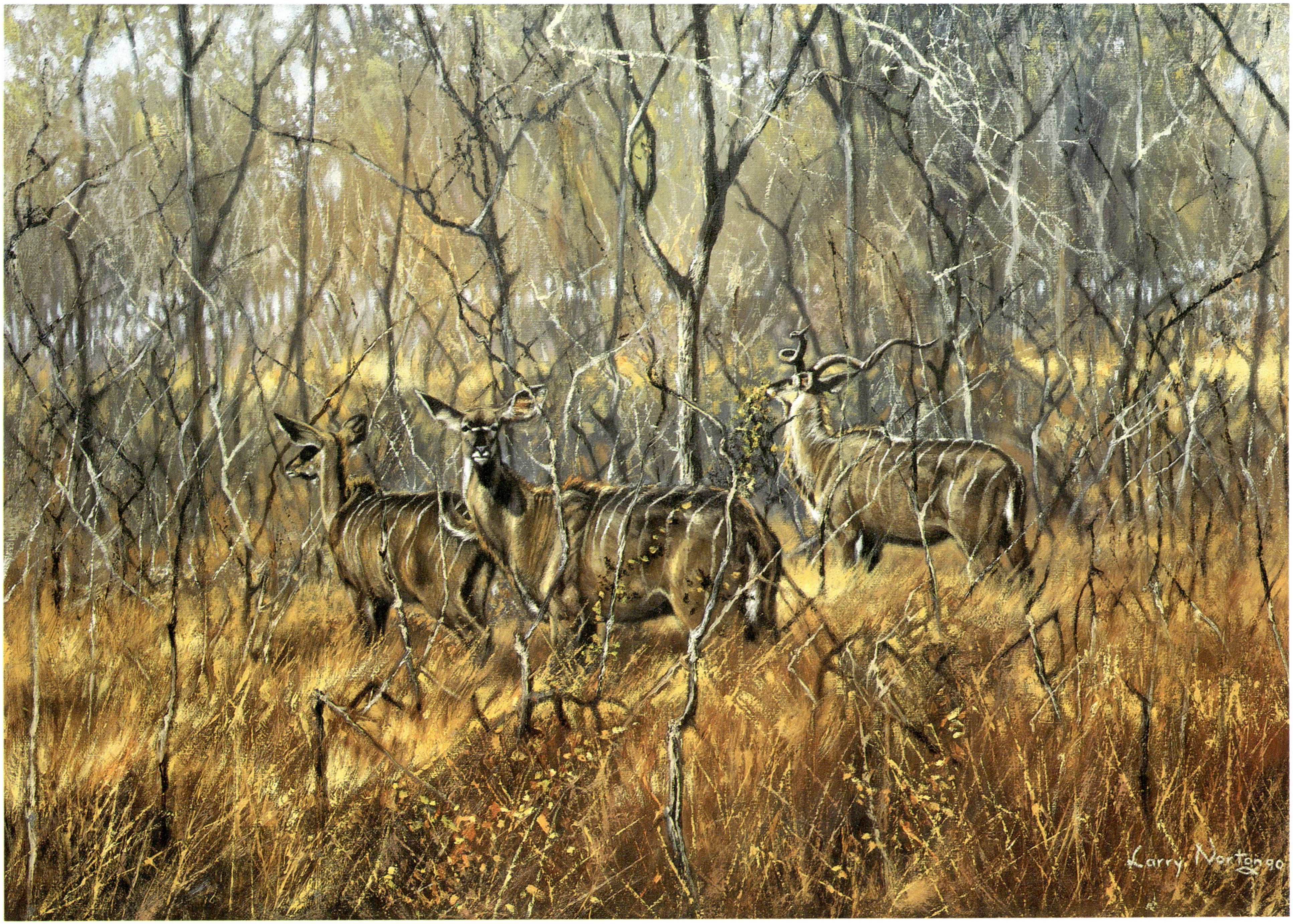
Larry Norton 90

134 A huge termite hill provides a perfect vantage point for a lioness, whose gleaming, golden hide shows she is in her absolute prime. Long ago, and for reasons unknown, the termites abandoned their massive castle. Since then it has been rounded by the rubbing of elephants, rhinos and a host of other animals; its chimneys long since knocked off, the remaining holes successively occupied by mongooses, birds and snakes. Now, the grassy extinct mound still rises above the surrounding plains, giving the ideal position from which the big cat can watch lazily for the tell-tale movement of potential prey in the tall grass.

ON TOP OF THE WORLD
Simon Combes

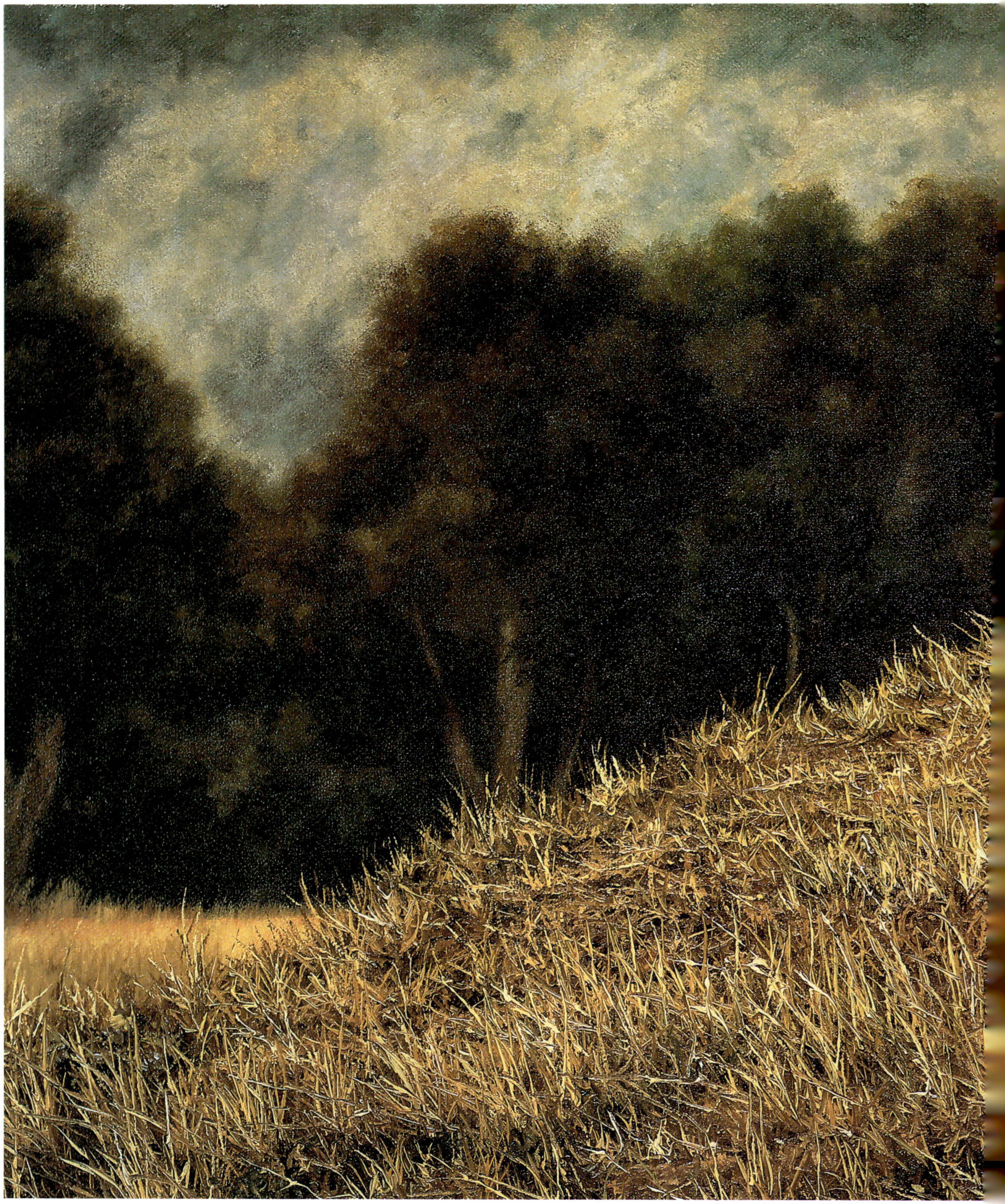

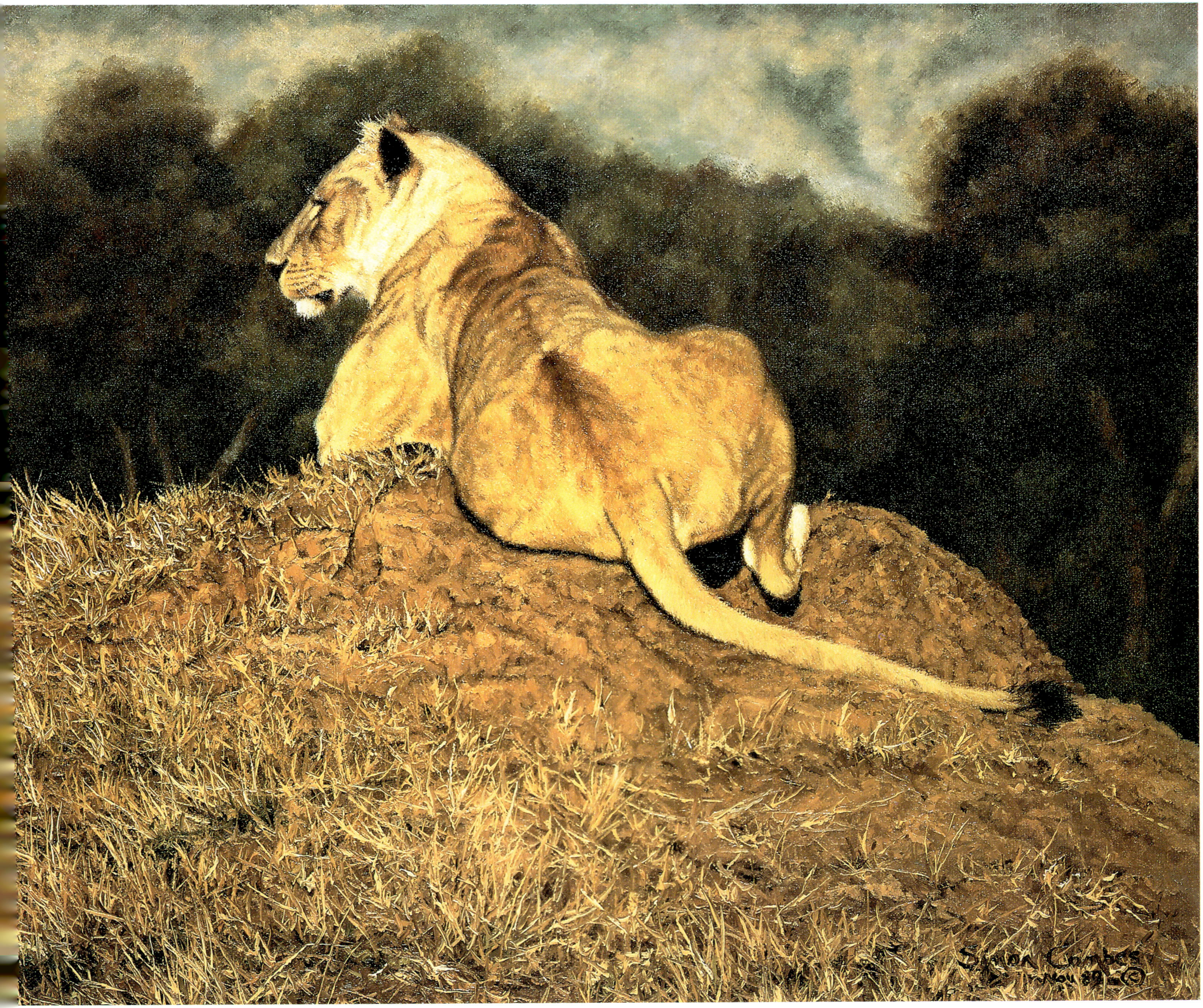

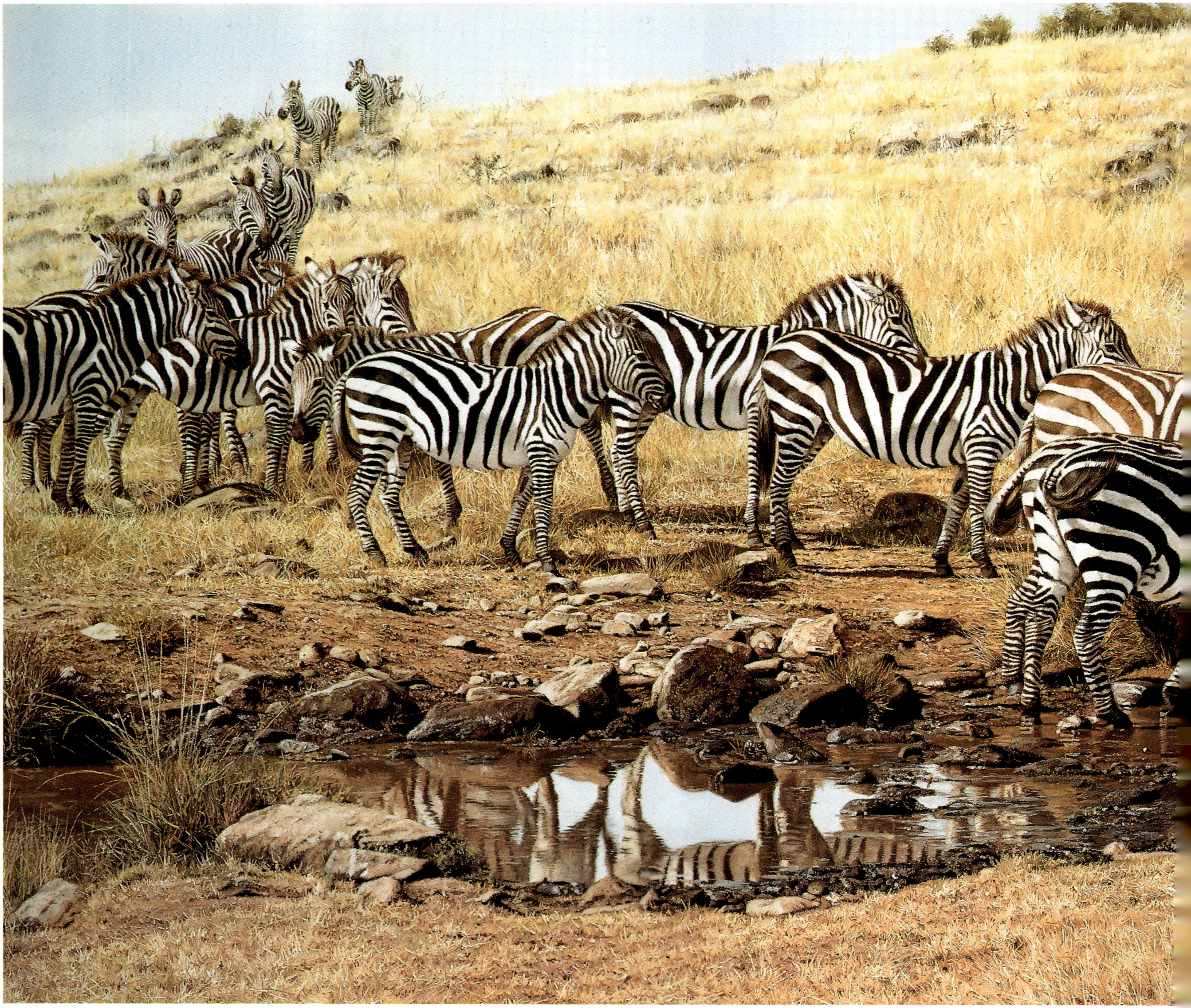

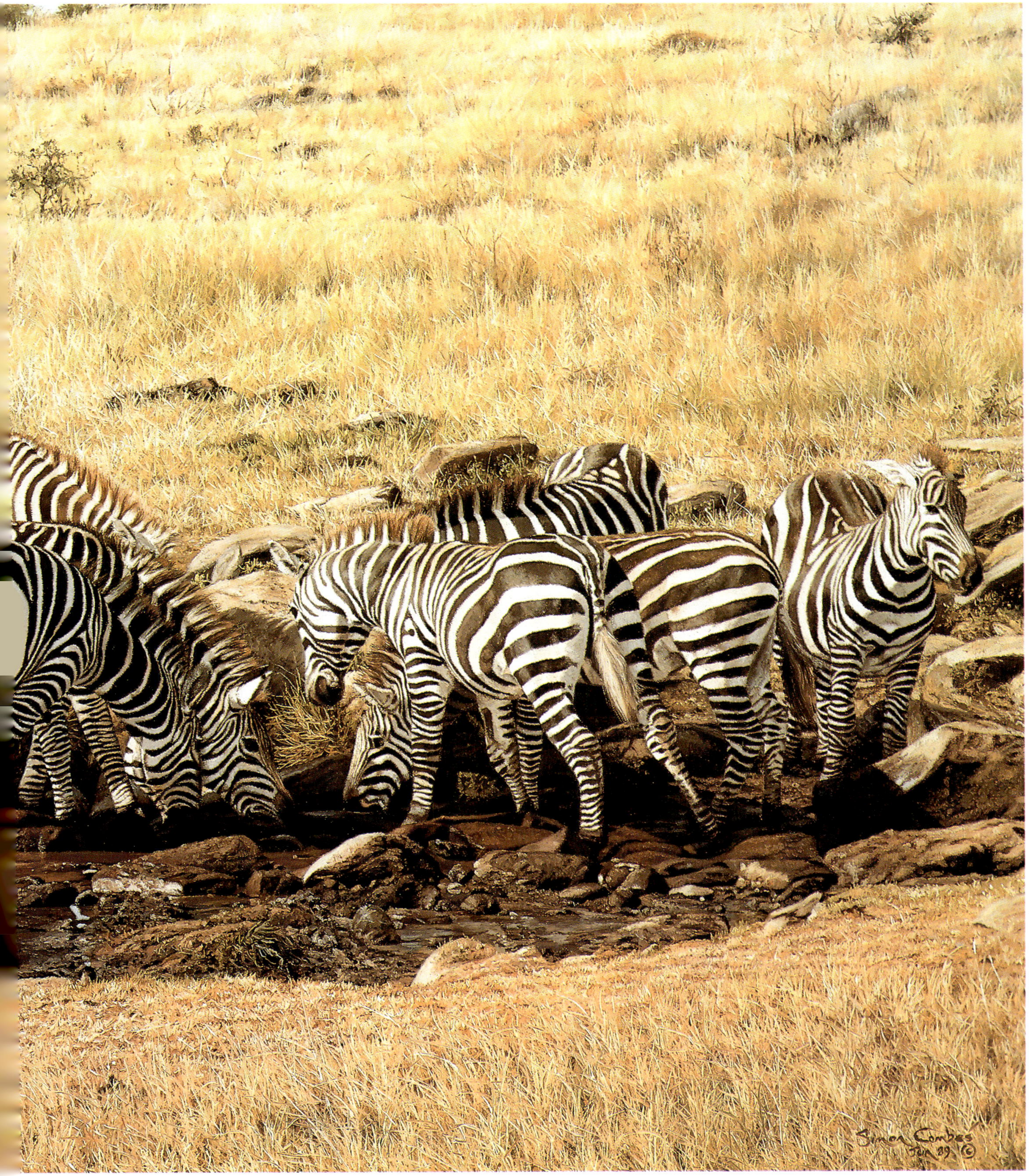

Zebras never wander far from water holes, for they like to drink every day, a ritual illustrated here by Simon Combes. "Having crossed the sun-parched grass of a hot Kenya plain, a herd of zebras reaches the cool waters of a spring seeping from a rocky hillside. This is the moment of greatest danger, when predators might lurk in the long grass, when the zebras are bunched together with their heads down to quench their long thirst, and when their hooves sink into the clinging mud, critically hampering a quick escape. Instinctively, therefore, they approach the water with great caution, all their senses alert. Only a few will drink at one time, the others patiently waiting and standing guard. Those with their heads lowered to the water show every muscle and sinew tensed for instant flight."

THE WATERING HOLE
Simon Combes

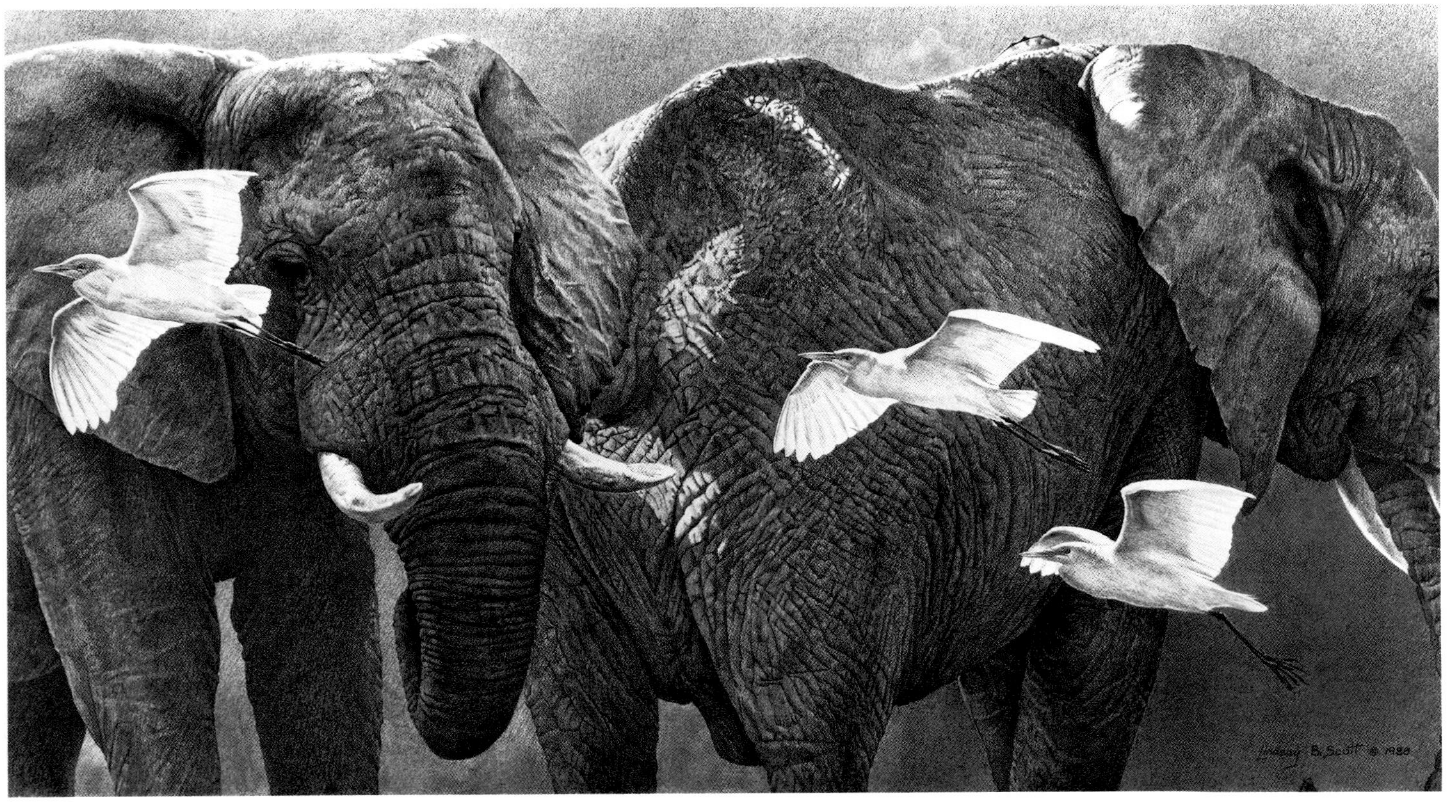

Born and raised in Zimbabwe, Lindsay Scott learned to appreciate wildlife at an early age. Seeing the work of Robert Bateman inspired her to paint her first wildlife piece although, unlike him and indeed most other wildlife artists, she prefers the control of pencil.

For Scott, there are two types of artist, those who paint and those who draw. She belongs to the latter school and is one of its finest advocates. She uses an HB pencil, often practising on a spare bit of paper before she tackles the final piece. "Getting a light, even touch with lead is one of the most difficult aspects of pencil drawing," says Scott. "It's almost like an opera singer doing scales to get in good voice. I cannot do pale areas first thing in the morning, for instance."

PASSING FLOCK
Lindsay B. Scott

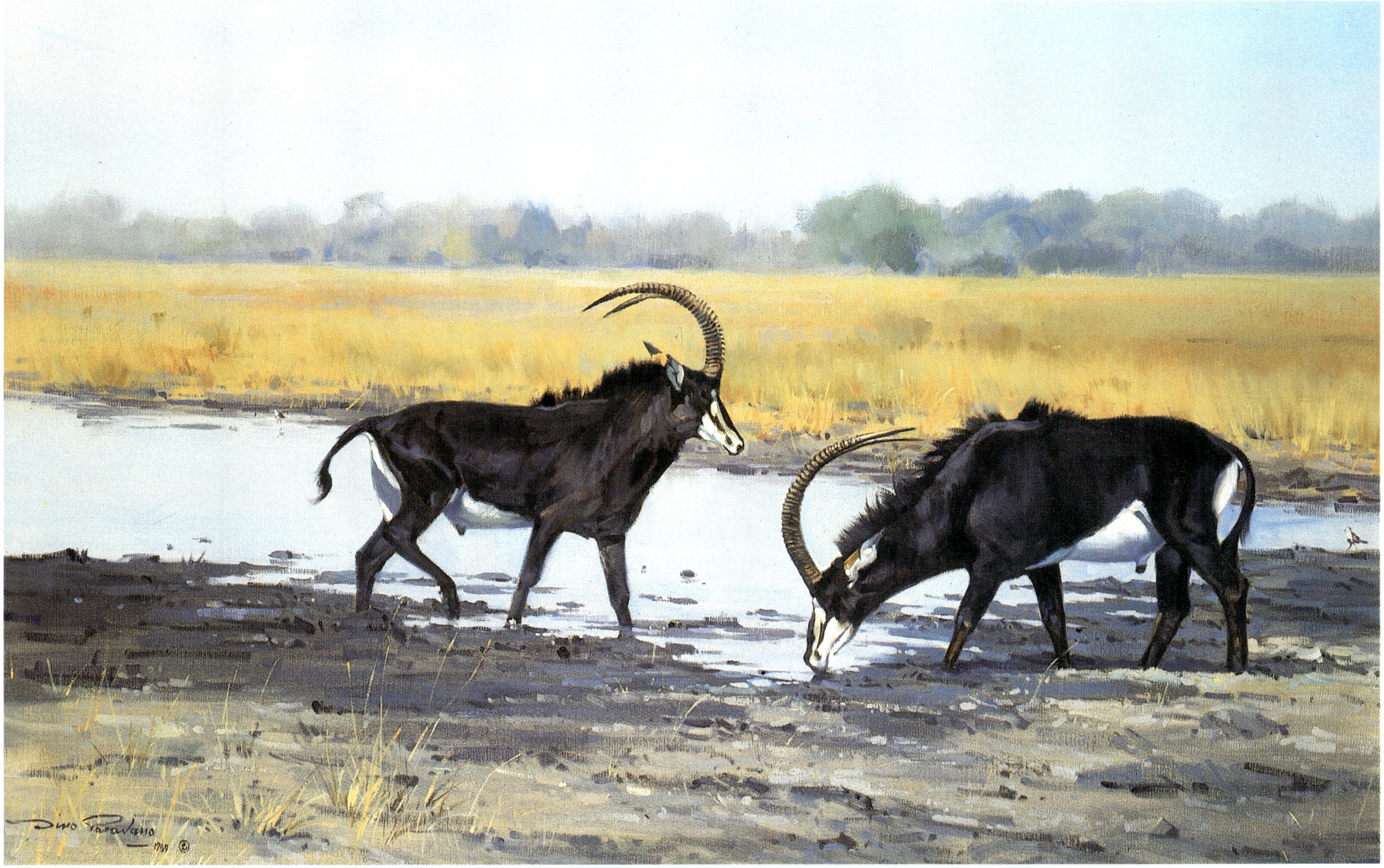

Dino Paravano's painting shows a pair of mature sable bulls at a water hole in Botswana's Chobe National Park, one of the best places to see this handsome antelope. Sable are powerfully built animals, extremely pugnacious, and well able to defend themselves against predators with their long, curved horns. As a result they are seldom attacked by lions, and approach water with rather more confidence than most antelope. They are often found in small herds, led by a master bull, but it is not unusual to find small parties of bulls, or solitary animals.

SABLES IN BOTSWANA
Dino Paravano

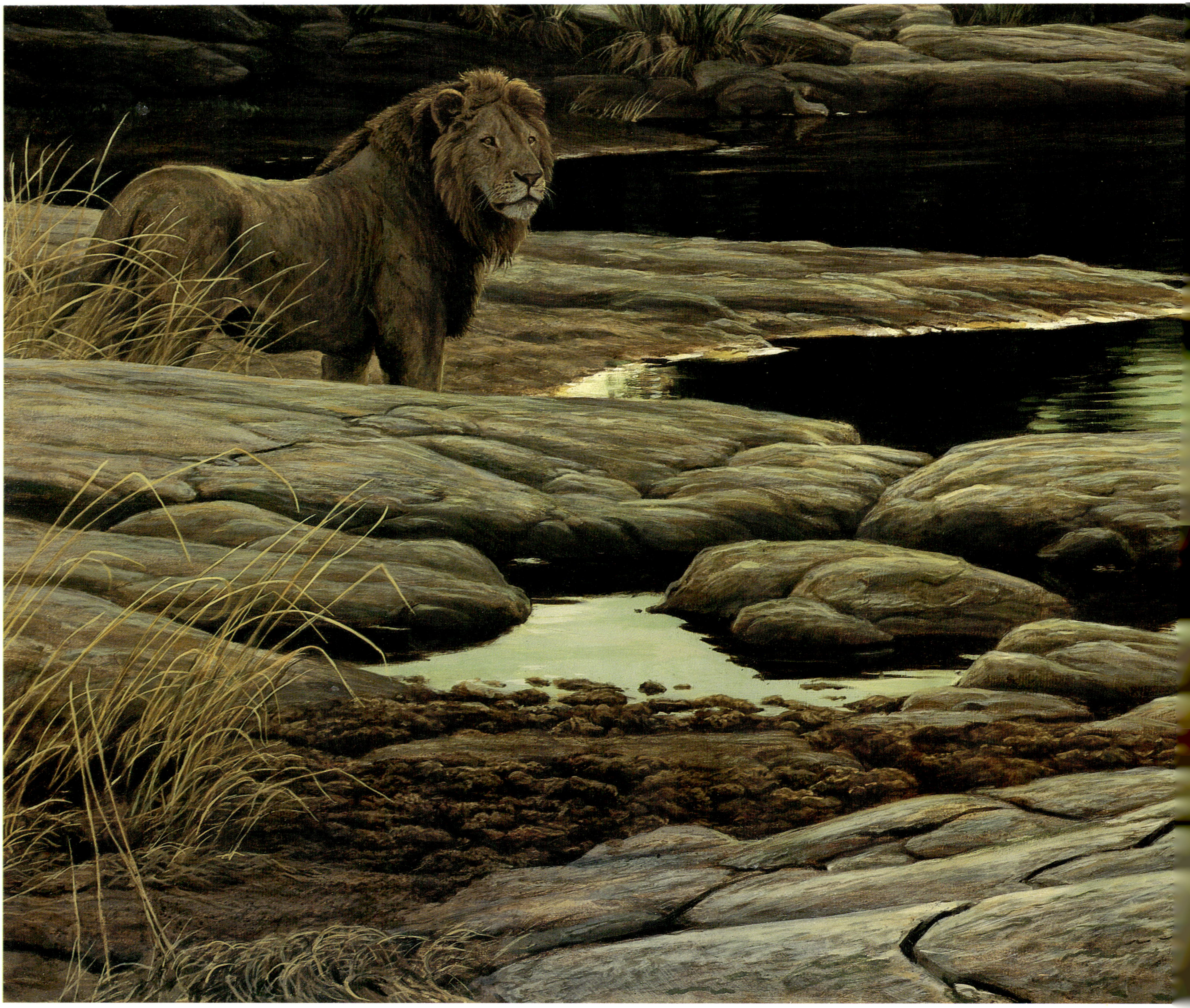

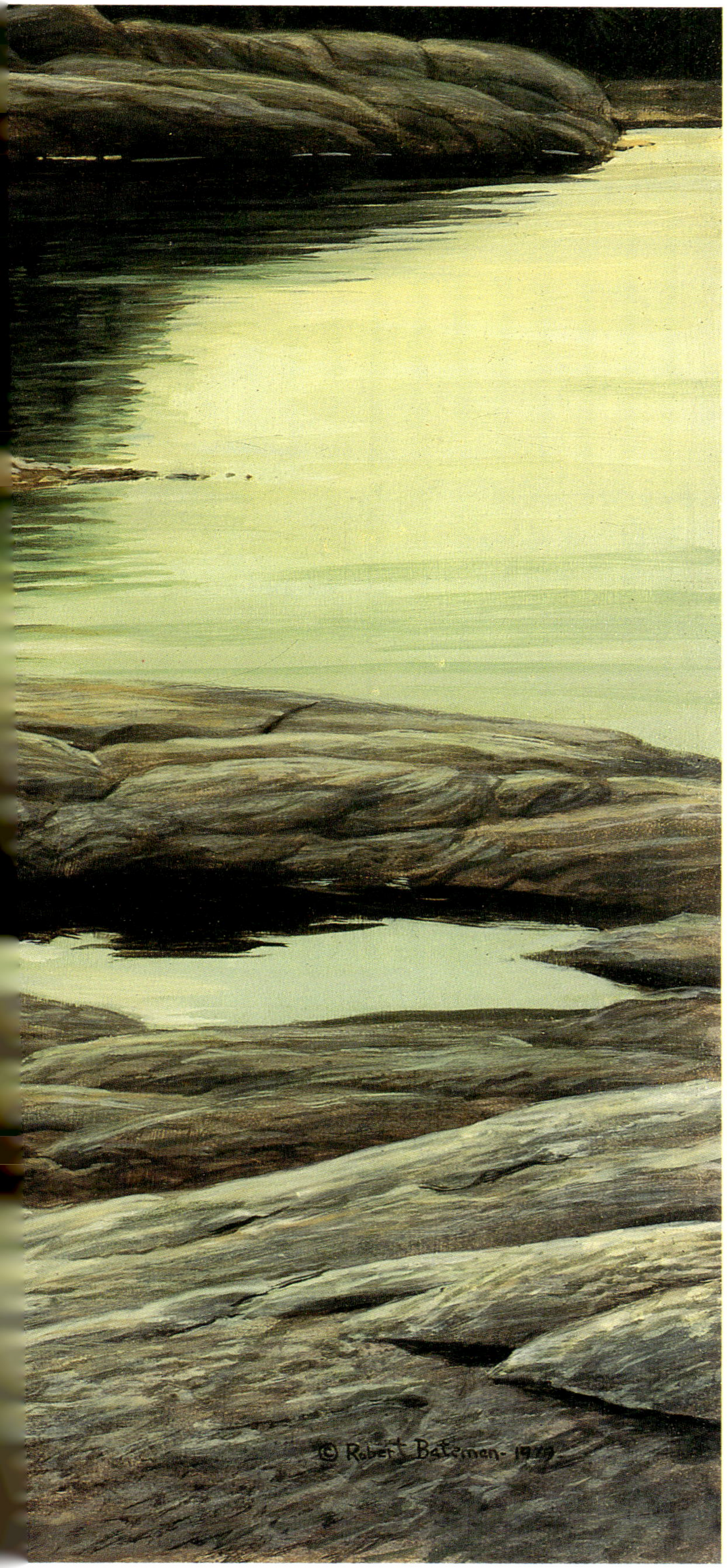

A fine lion strolls along a river bank at dusk. Though the lion completes the picture, it is the river which is really the subject. Bateman comments that he "liked the positive and negative shapes of the rocks and water and reflections. African rivers are subject to sudden floods. The ancient rocks are sculpted by the river. In the mud deposits are the texture of hoof prints of the grassland game. Perhaps they had just been drinking and have moved out at the lion's casual approach."

LION AT TSAVO
Robert Bateman

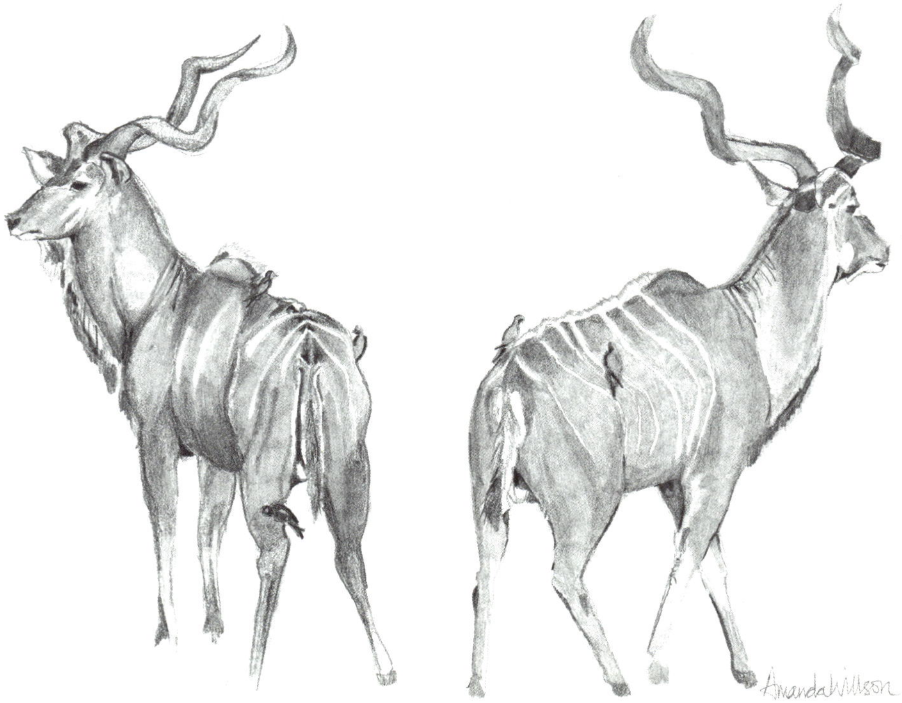

GREATER KUDU
Amanda Willson

The Letaba is one of the most scenic of the rivers which flow through Kruger National Park. Dino Paravano shows a panoramic view of the river, from the bank at the Letaba camp grounds. Elephants are plentiful here – in his 25 or so visits to the area, Paravano has never failed to see them.

Nearly all of South Africa's 8,000-odd elephants live in the Kruger, where periodic culls take place to keep the population stable. In 1990, the cull numbered 262. Nothing of the animals is wasted: the culled beasts are taken to the Kruger's own abattoir, where they are butchered, the meat cooked and canned. A sad end for such a large and intelligent animal, but at least the Kruger's elephant population is healthy, and largely untroubled by poaching.

ELEPHANTS AT LETABA
Dino Paravano

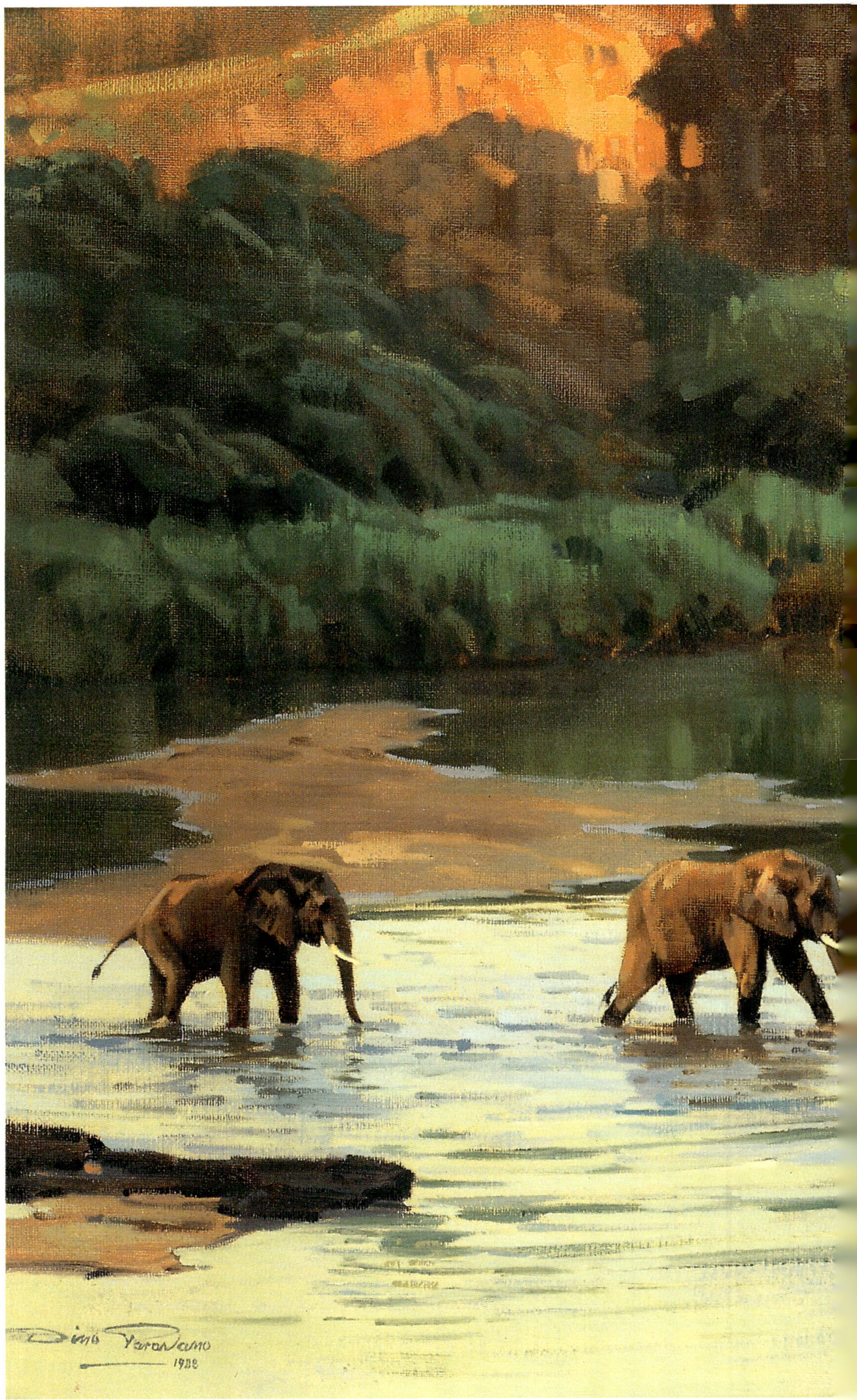

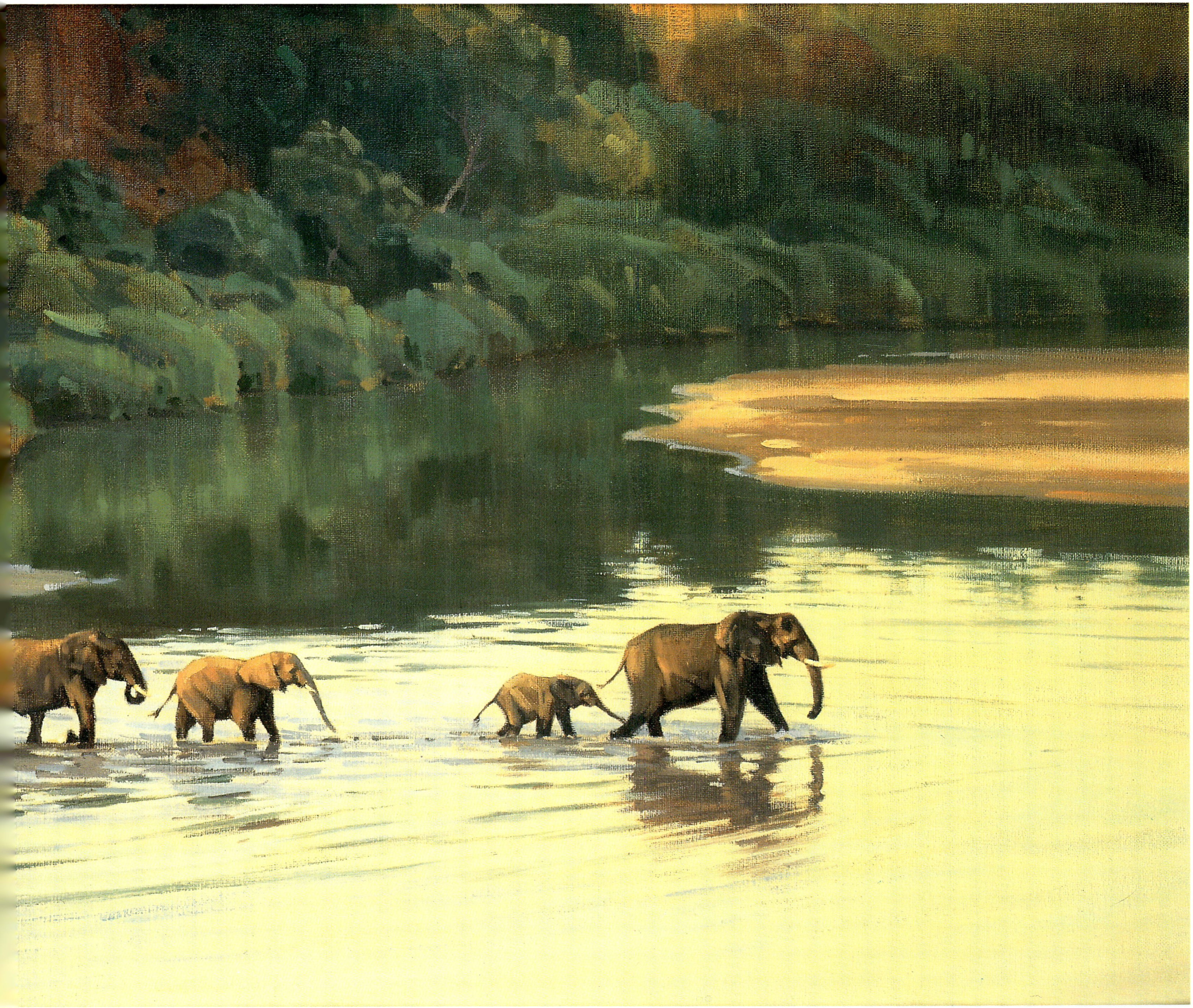

The rivers of Africa are great places for observing life. Big game country is usually quite arid and so the water courses are particularly important. It is here that many kinds of wildlife congregate.

Elephants at the water exhibit obvious pleasure. They wade, they splash, they drink, they squirt a shower bath with their trunks, they even lie down and roll. With their large body mass they have a heat control problem,

and their large ears are more for radiating heat than for listening.

In this painting a group of cow elephants and young have just entered the river. The dusty, dry hides will soon be criss-crossed with dark splashes. The little ones are timid and stay very close to their mothers.

Sandgrouse are dove-like ground birds of the arid bush country. These are Namaqua sandgrouse which sometimes gather in flocks of hundreds to land at the water's edge for a drink.

ELEPHANT HERD AND SANDGROUSE
Robert Bateman

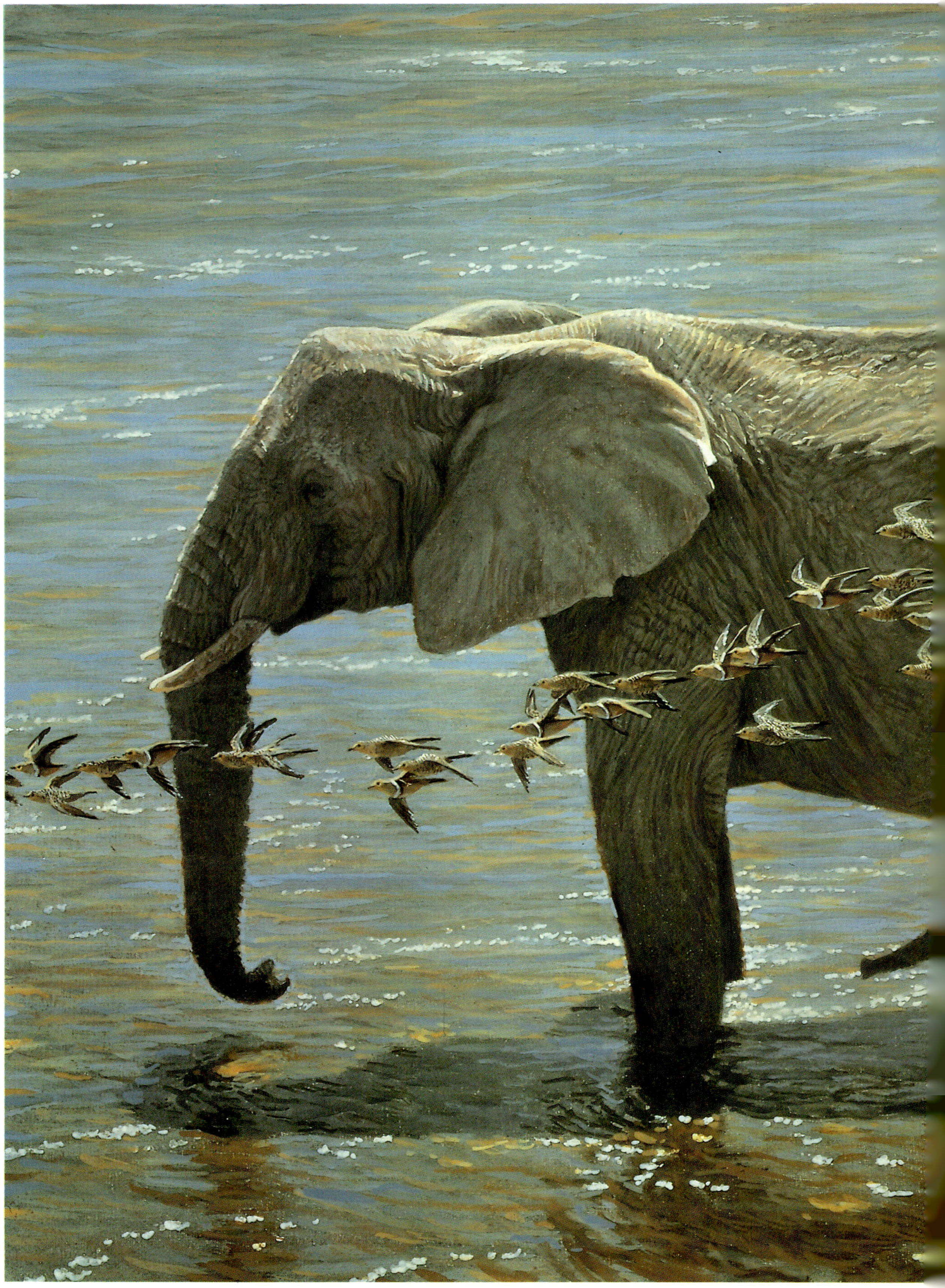

Guy Coheleach is one of the most versatile of artists, his work varying greatly depending on both medium and subject. "This is a fun painting and I enjoyed it," writes Guy Coheleach. "Everyone seems to like hippos, but the truth is they are one of the most dangerous animals in Africa. They account for more human deaths than anything else, with the possible exception of crocodiles."

HIPPO
Guy Coheleach

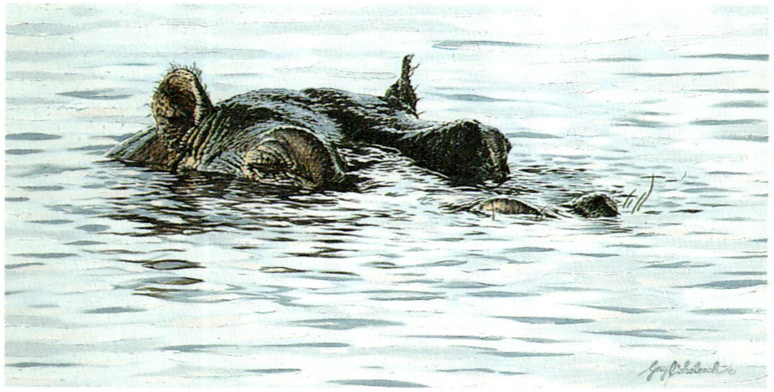

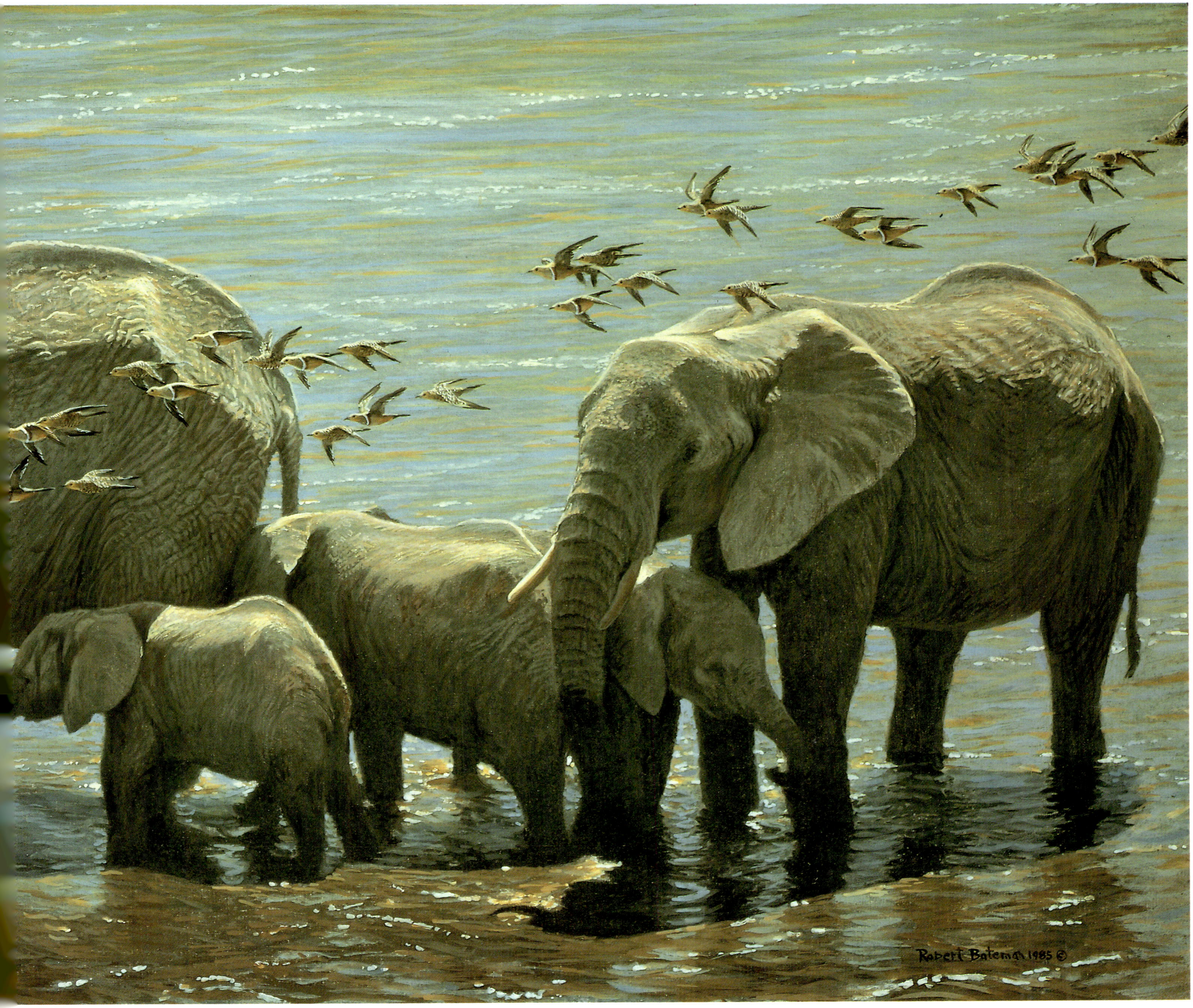
Robert Bateman 1985 ©

Hippos are the most gregarious of creatures, and are invariably found in groups which may number anything from five to 30 or more. Michael Ghaui shows here a herd of hippos disturbed from their midday siesta. "They aren't really sure what the problem is, or even if there is a problem at all – hence the half-hearted retreat into the water."

During the day, hippos are seldom found far from water. For the first part of the morning they usually stay submerged, except for ears, eyes and nostrils. By mid-morning, as the day gets hotter, they will come out to bask in the sun on the river bank, occasionally returning to the water to cool off.

They rarely feed during the day, but at night they will travel several miles to forage. Sometimes one encounters a hippo in the early morning, several miles from water, heading home after a night's foraging, looking for all the world like an overweight reveller after a night on the town. Such a large animal requires plenty of food, and they will eat as much as 130lb of vegetable matter – mainly grasses – in a night.

HIPPO POOL
Michael Ghaui

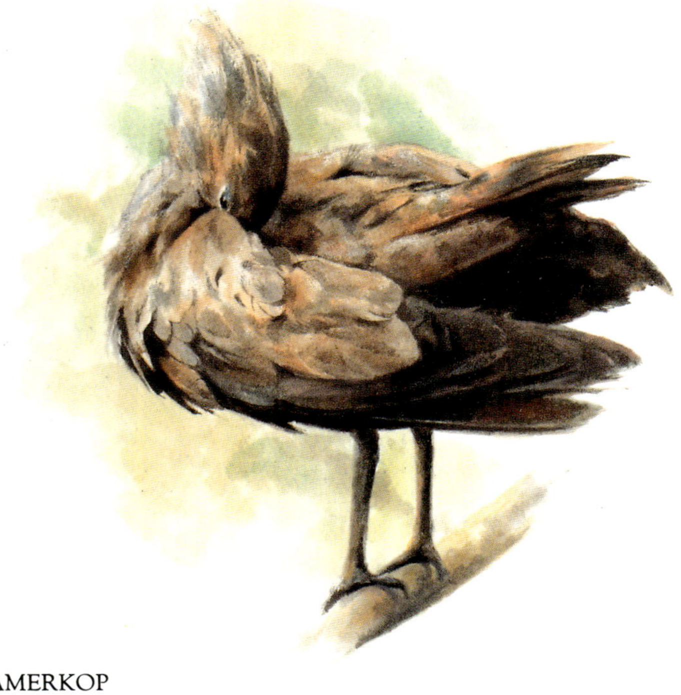

HAMERKOP
Mandy Shepherd

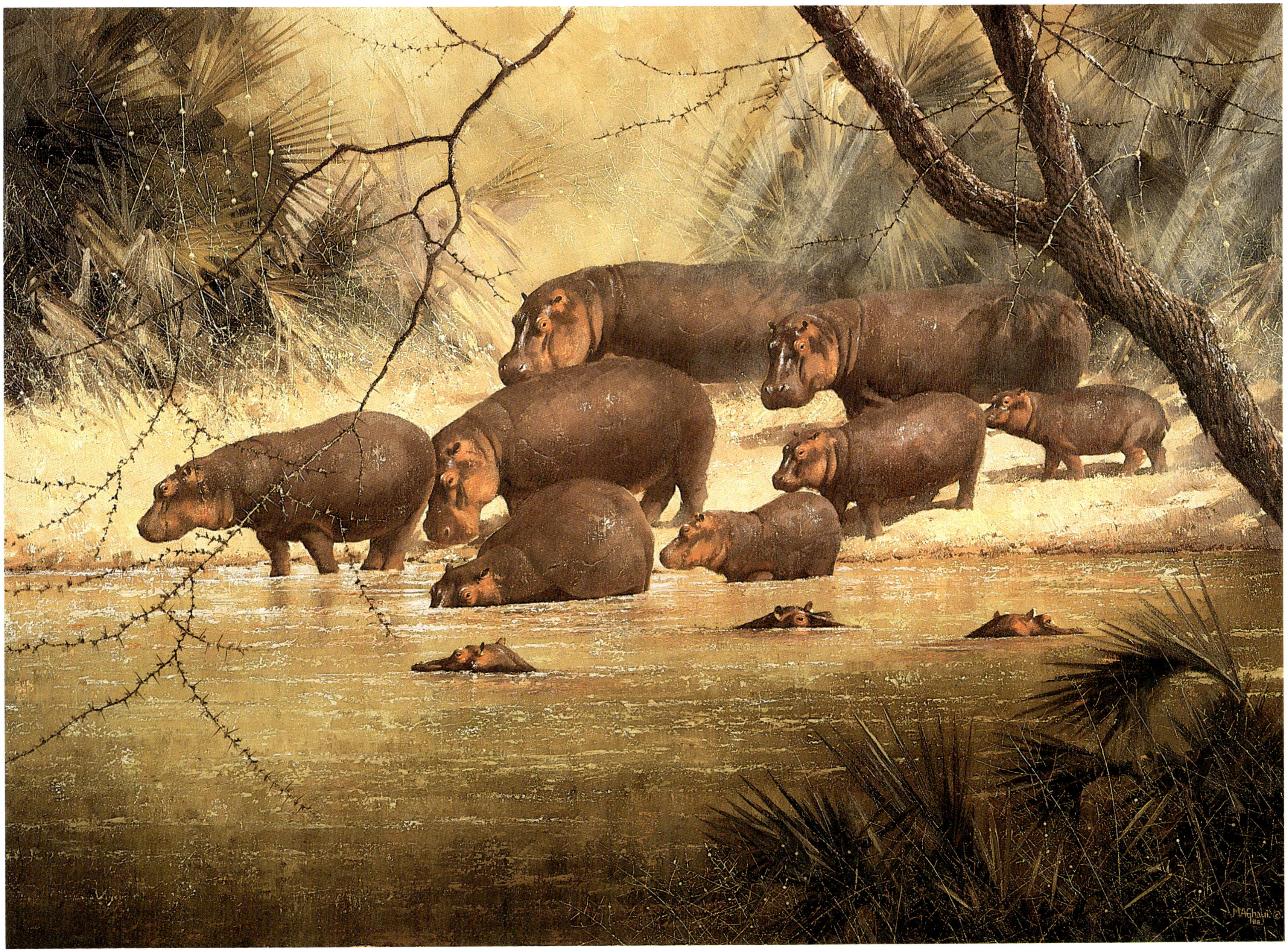

148

These four buffalo, at Mana Pools in Zimbabwe, are old bulls that have been forced out of the breeding herds. Donaldson reassuringly notes that "buffalo in a herd are generally not dangerous, and act in a similar way to a herd of domestic cattle. I have often walked near herds of buffalo, receiving no more than curious looks and inquisitive approaches. A wounded bull or a protective mother is, however, a completely different beast, and the animal is treated with great respect by the knowledgeable person.

"In the Mana Pools there is little to disturb the buffalo, save for an occasional right-of-way dispute with an elephant. Food and water are plentiful, and here they see out their days in the warm languid atmosphere of the Zambezi Valley. A good mudbath is a favourite pastime: apart from cooling them down, it provides a protective coating of mud to ward off insect bites."

BUFFALO – MANA POOLS
Kim Donaldson

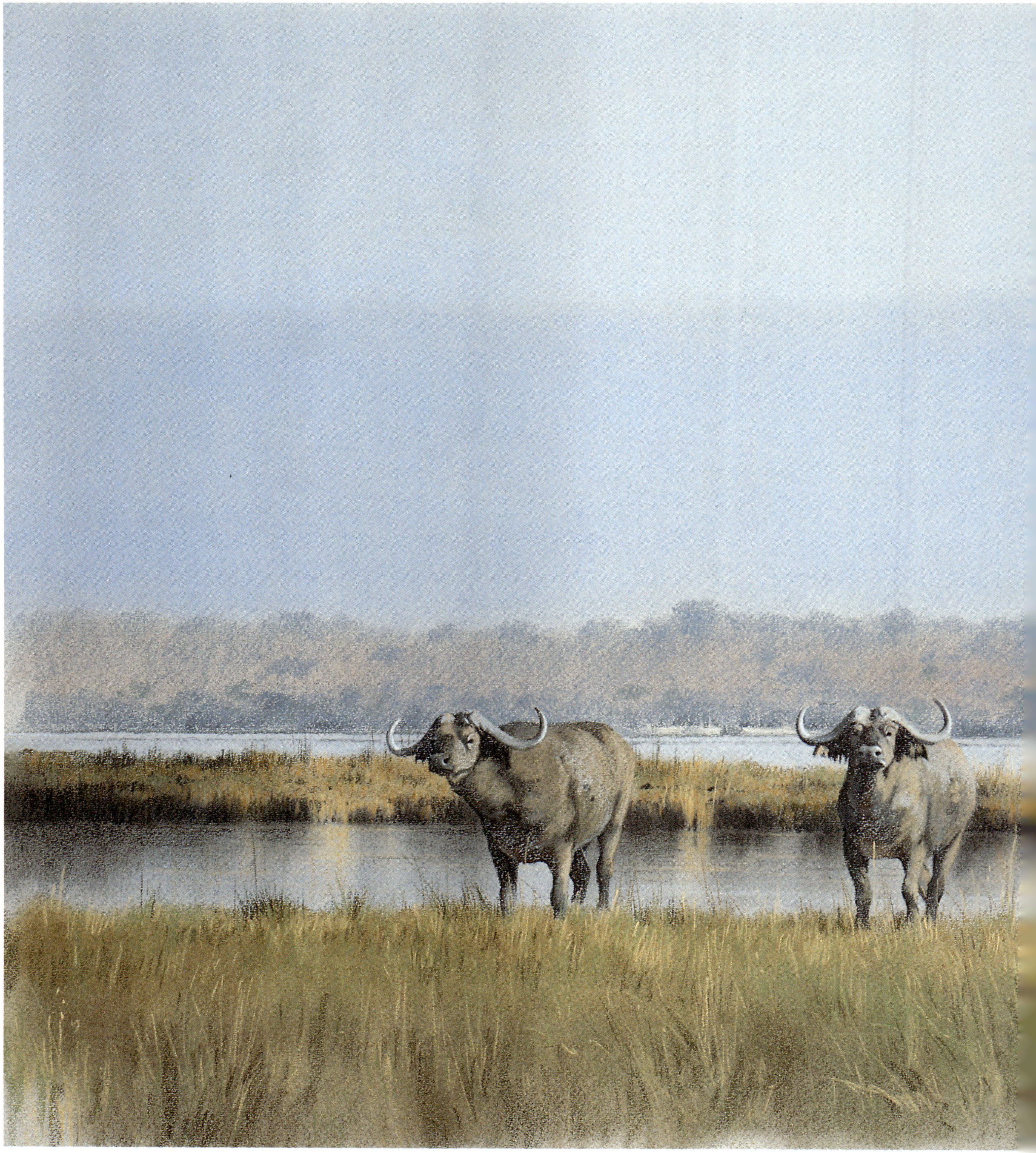

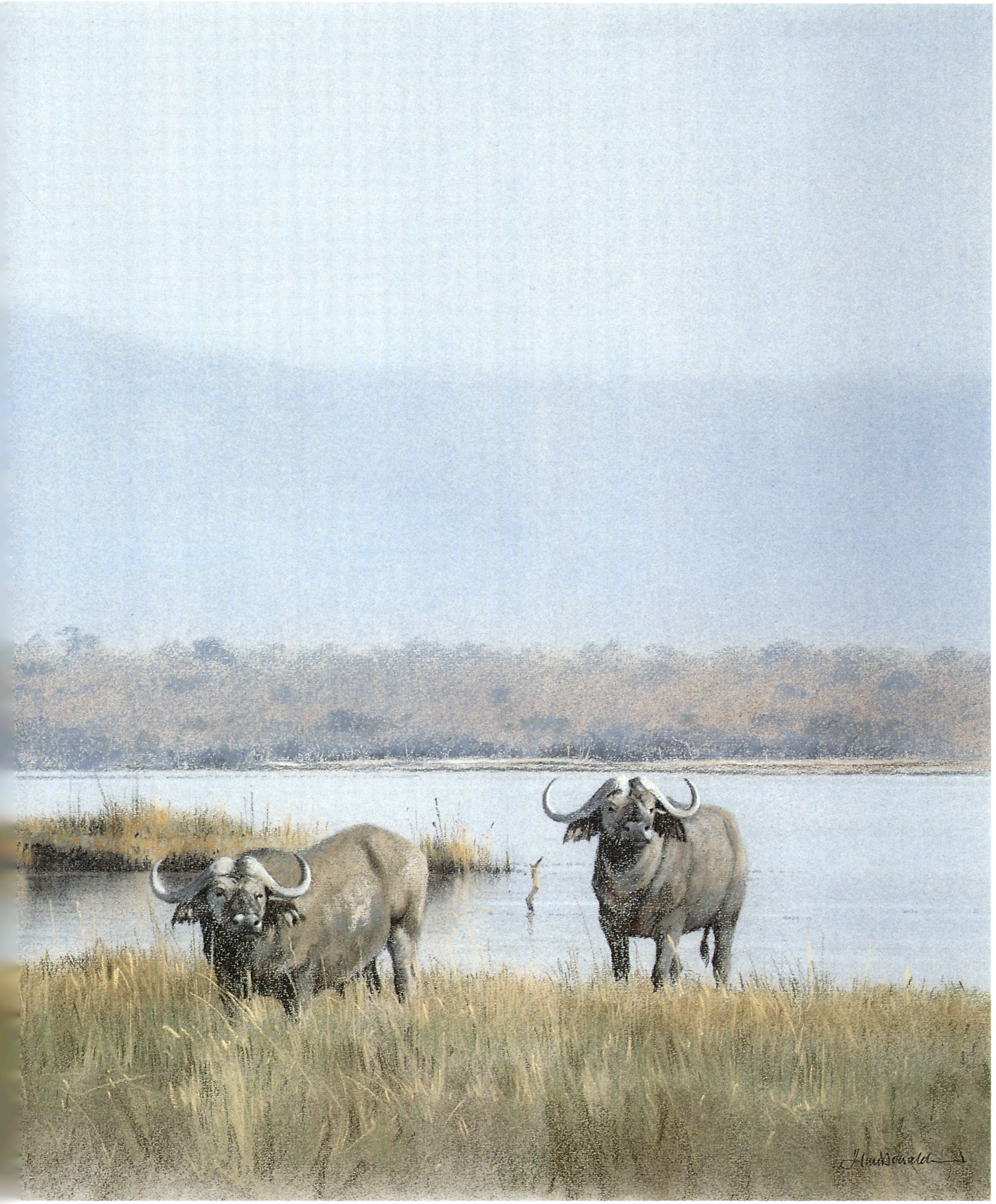

NYALA RAM
Kim Donaldson

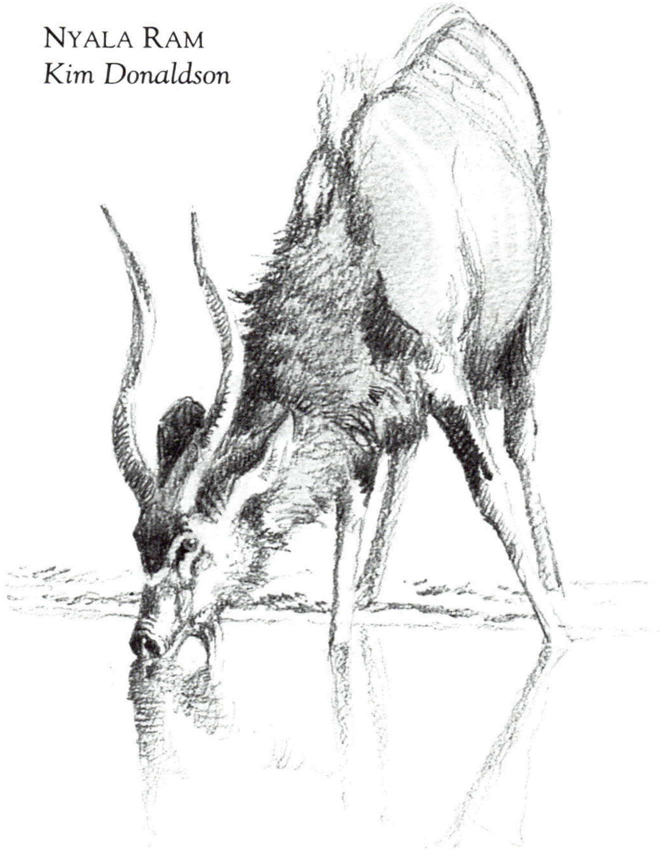

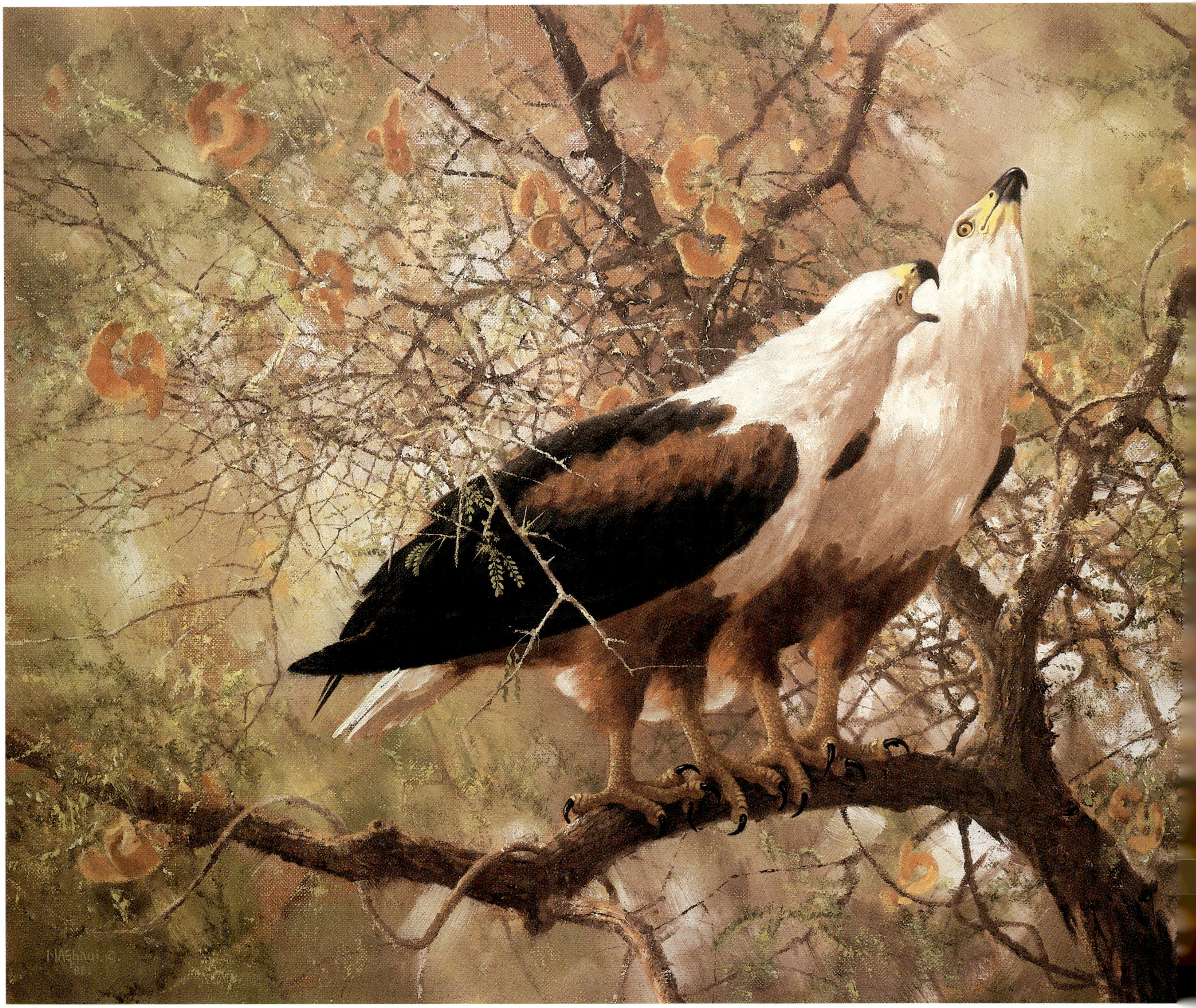
M.A.Ghaui. ©.
88.

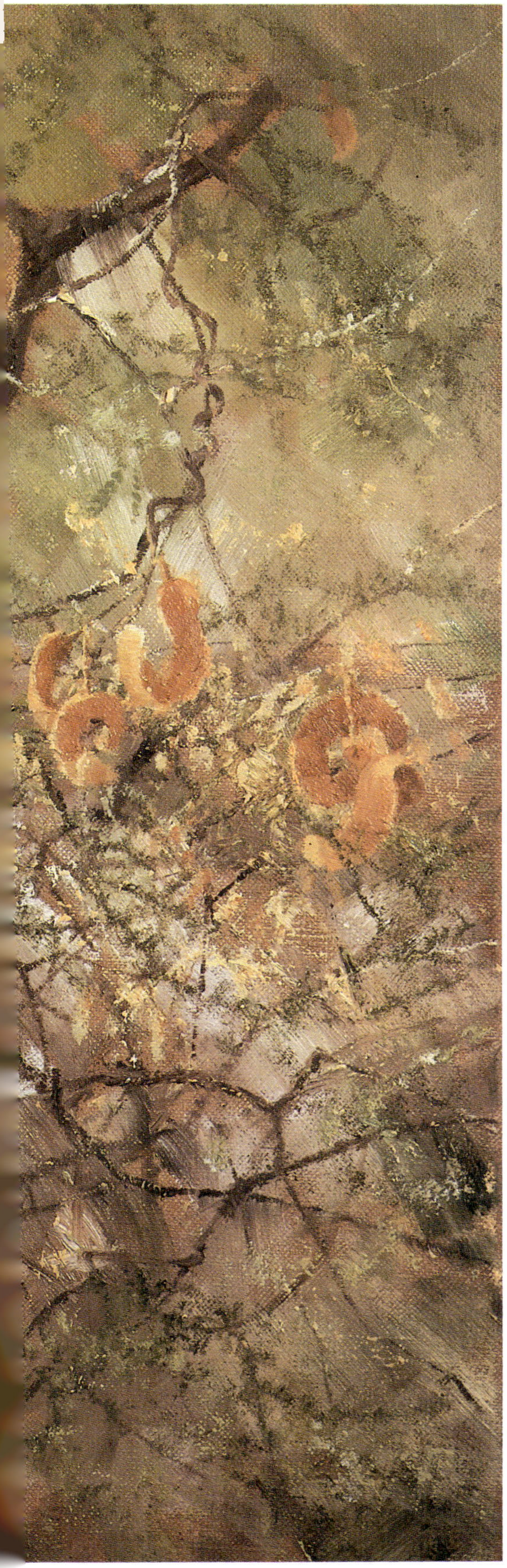

Fish eagles are the most familiar of African raptors, found on almost every river and lake south of the Sahara. They are difficult to overlook, for they are very noisy, calling at first light, and repeatedly again during the day. They call either from a perch, or while soaring, throwing their head back and uttering the loud, far-carrying series of yelps which is so often described as the Call of Africa. The female is more vociferous than the male, and it is often she who initiates duets, when the two birds call back and forth to each other.

With "Fish Eagle Duet" (*left*) Michael Ghaui has tried to create the illusion of sound. "When you look at this painting, I hope it will take you back to that distant lake shore or riverbank where you can hear that call – the sound of the African bush." Fish eagles are particularly common around Ghaui's home at Lake Naivasha.

FISH EAGLE DUET
Michael Ghaui

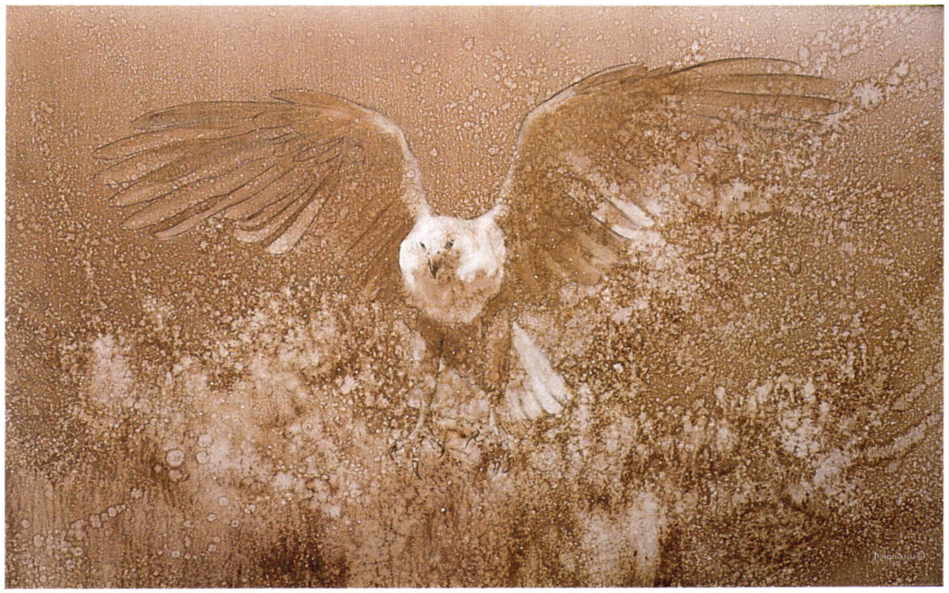

Watching a fish eagle plunge-diving is spectacular: the bird hitting the water, talons first, in a cloud of spray. If successful, the eagle will often pause on the water, with wings spread, before labouring away with its fish. As Michael Ghaui's title indicates, such hunting requires exceptional precision, and not every dive is successful. Nor should it be thought that plunge-diving is the fish eagle's usual way of catching fish, more often it plucks its prey from the surface of the water, hardly getting its feet wet in doing so.

Though fish are, hardly surprisingly, the eagle's main food, this powerful species is quite capable of killing adult flamingoes, or robbing birds as large as goliath herons and saddle-billed storks of their prey. Carrion is also taken, especially by young birds which will feed at kills of lions or hunting dogs. Here the tables may be turned, and the fish eagle robbed of its food by tawny or bateleur eagles.

PRECISION TIMING – FISH EAGLE
Michael Ghaui

152 My first African safari was to Botswana's Okavango delta, and this pastel by Dino Paravano brings back fond memories of that magic trip. Here we see a flock of great white egrets, flying low over a channel in the delta of the Okavango river. The white plumage of the egrets contrasts with the clear deep blue-grey autumn sky, while a line of papyrus completes the back-drop. Paravano paints in either oil or pastel, but he chose pastel for this because he felt that it would achieve a softer and more delicate result. It has certainly done so.

EGRETS IN FLIGHT
Dino Paravano

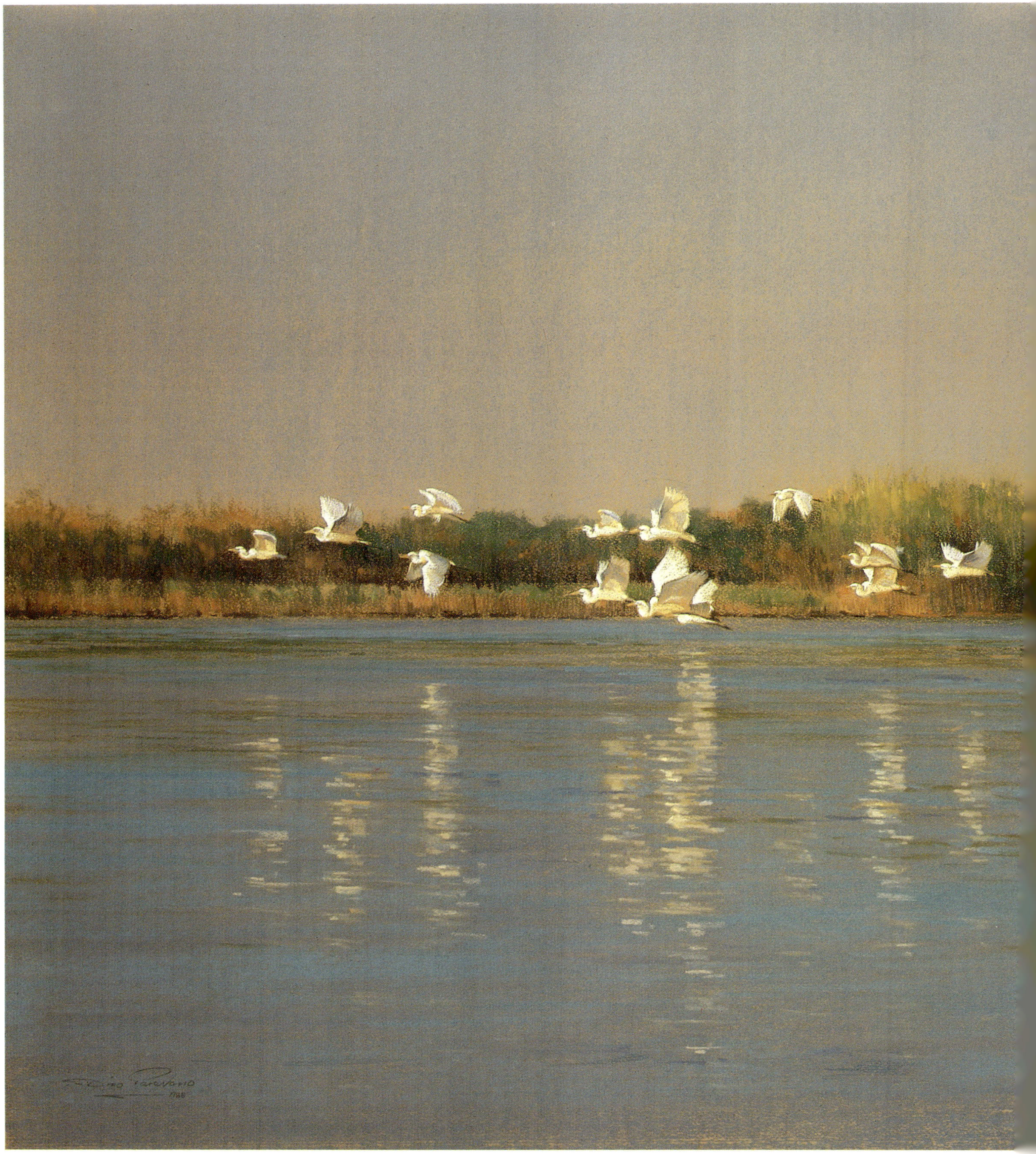

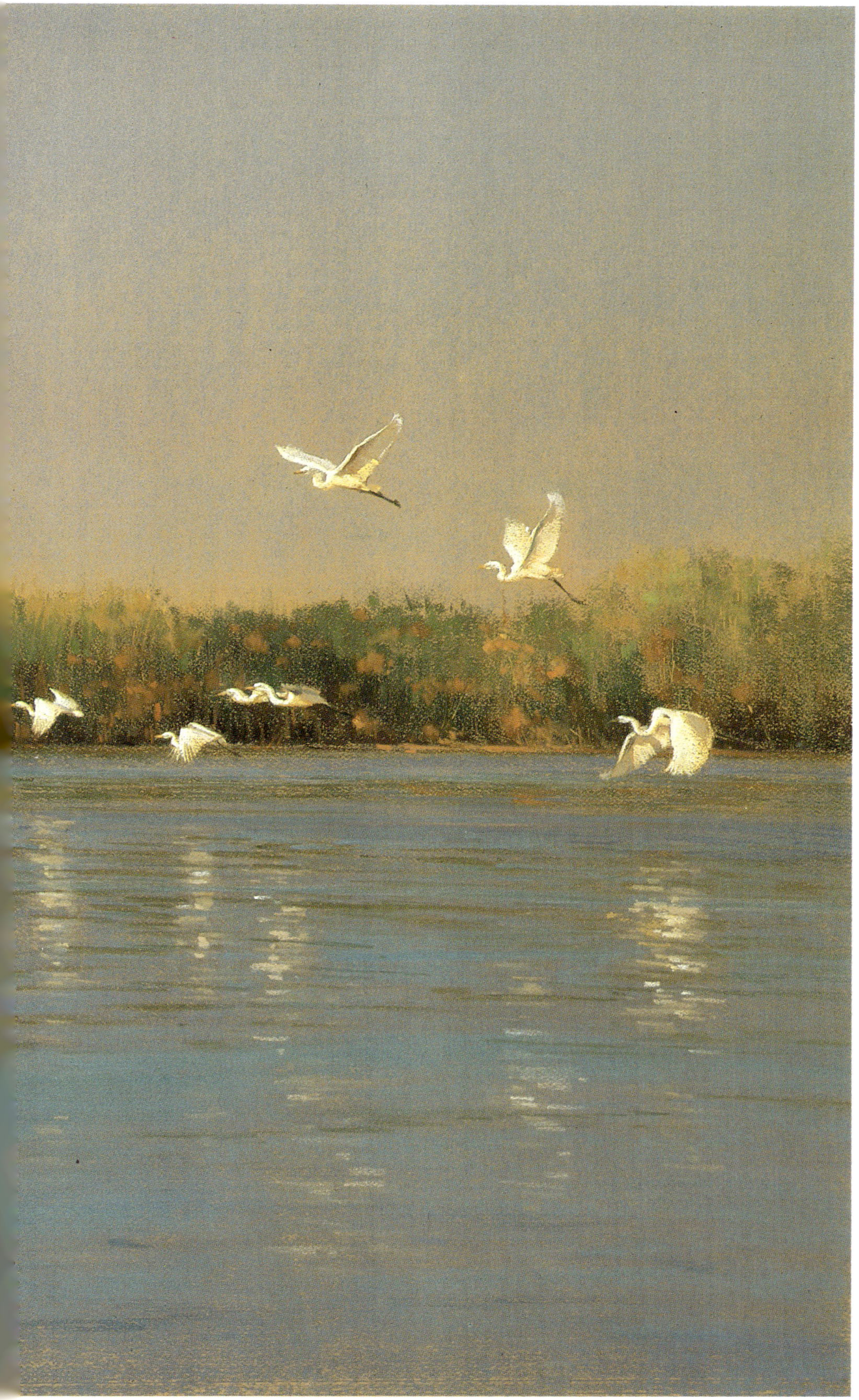

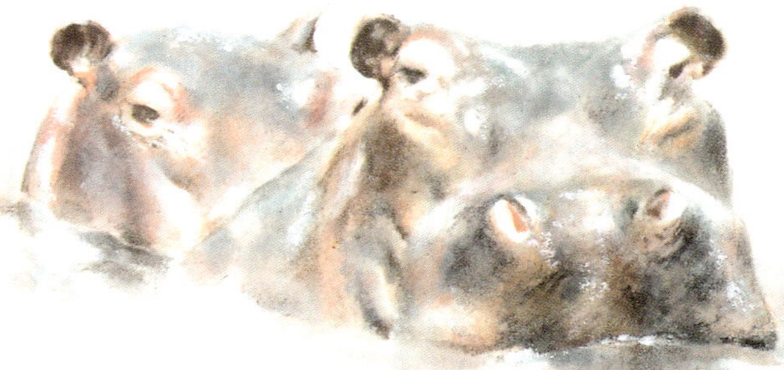

HIPPOS
Mandy Shepherd

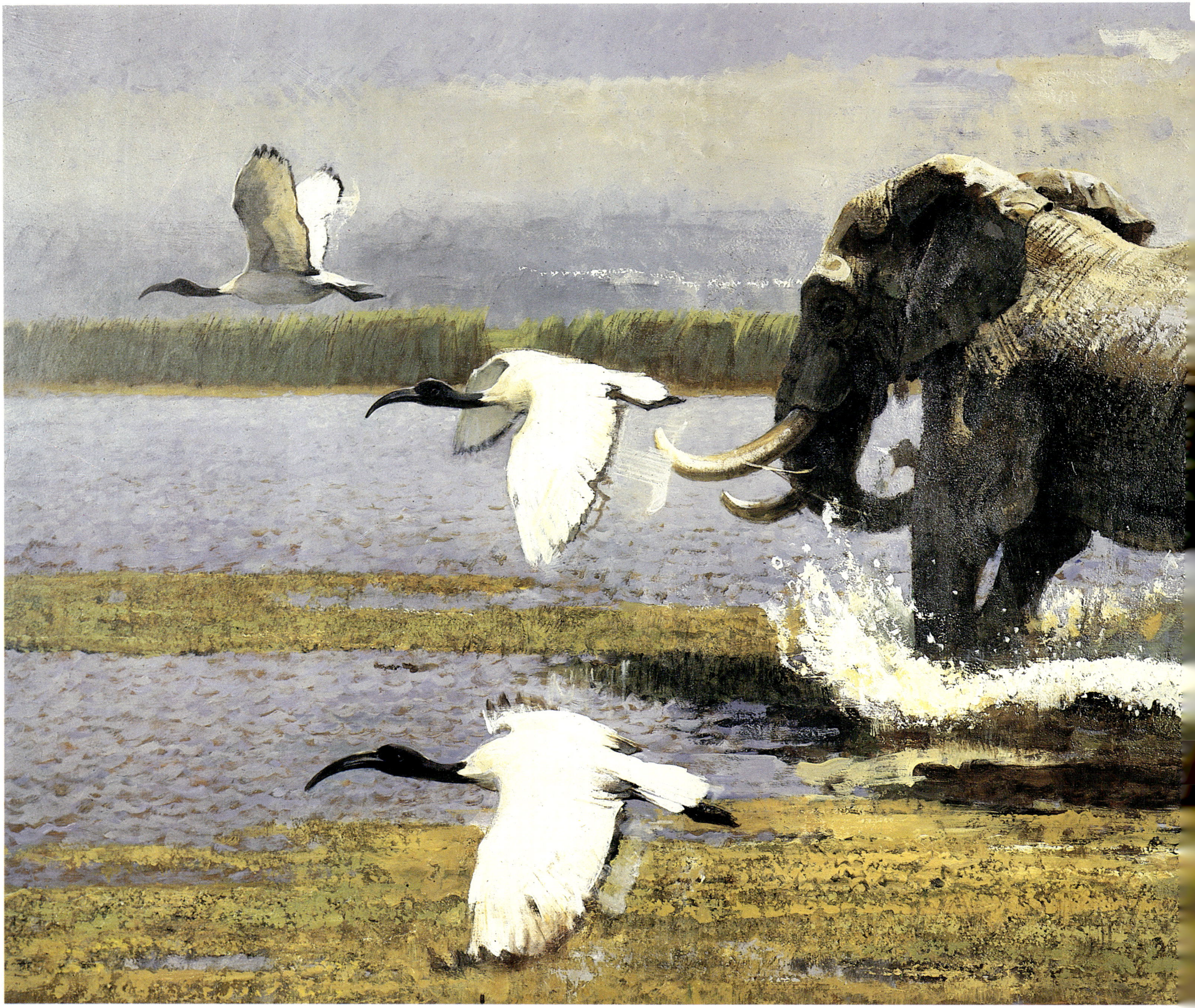

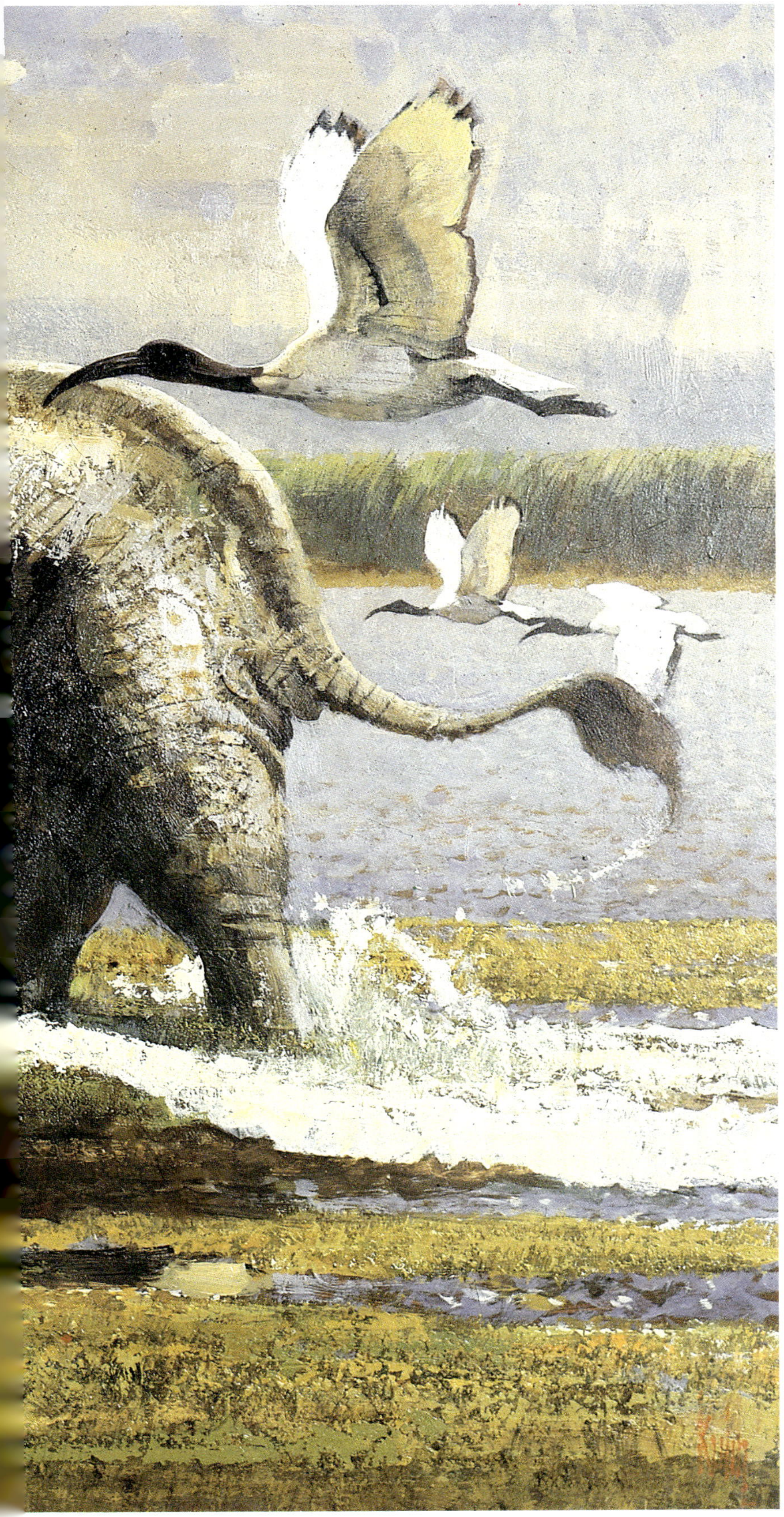

Bob Kuhn is fond of using the formula of powerful animals, splashing through water, disturbing birds as they go. Compare this elephant and ibis study, entitled "Aquacade", with "Buffalo Moving Out", and "Rhino Flushing Cattle Egrets" on pages 52/53. The artist explains that "While I'm not a bird painter *per se*, there are times when a flight of them (or even a few) adds drama and motion to a painting. In most cases I make use of symbiotic relationships – this is, a connection of bird and mammal where both derive some benefit, such as tick birds and Cape buffalo. In 'Aquacade', the lumbering elephant has to share billing with a flock of sacred ibis which happened to be using the same weed-filled watercourse. There is no special relationship between them, just a shared fondness for water. The important thing is that they add interest and contrast to the pageant."

AQUACADE
Bob Kuhn

156 Flamingoes (*right*) are such awkward birds that, despite their stunning colours, they are largely ignored by artists. The other problem is that they occur in such huge numbers, and dense flocks, that it is difficult, not to say tedious, for an artist to attempt to depict them. With "Pink Tranquillity", John Seerey-Lester has indeed captured the tranquillity of a flamingo lake albeit concentrating attention on a small, isolated flock. The birds depicted are lesser flamingoes, which can be readily identified from the greater flamingo not only by their smaller size, but their somewhat pinker plumage and dark maroon bills.

Flamingoes are highly specialized feeders. Their main food is microscopic blue-green algae, which they gather by walking or swimming in shallow water, scything their head and neck from side to side. Choppy water makes this difficult for them, so they tend to feed mostly at night, when there is invariably less wind. However, a flock of a thousand or more birds, packed closely together, will create local areas of calm where they can forage successfully.

PINK TRANQUILLITY – LESSER FLAMINGOES
John Seerey-Lester

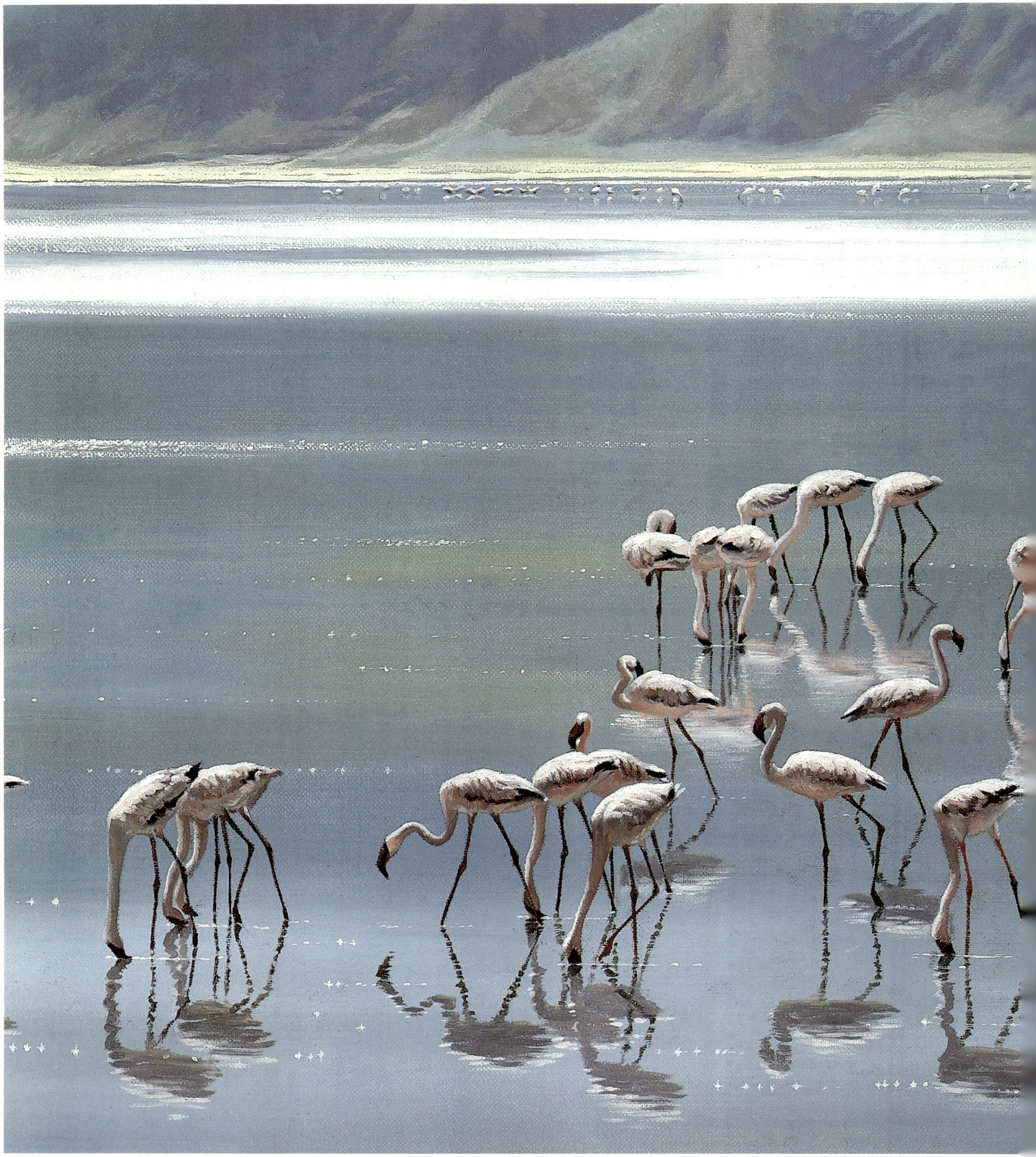

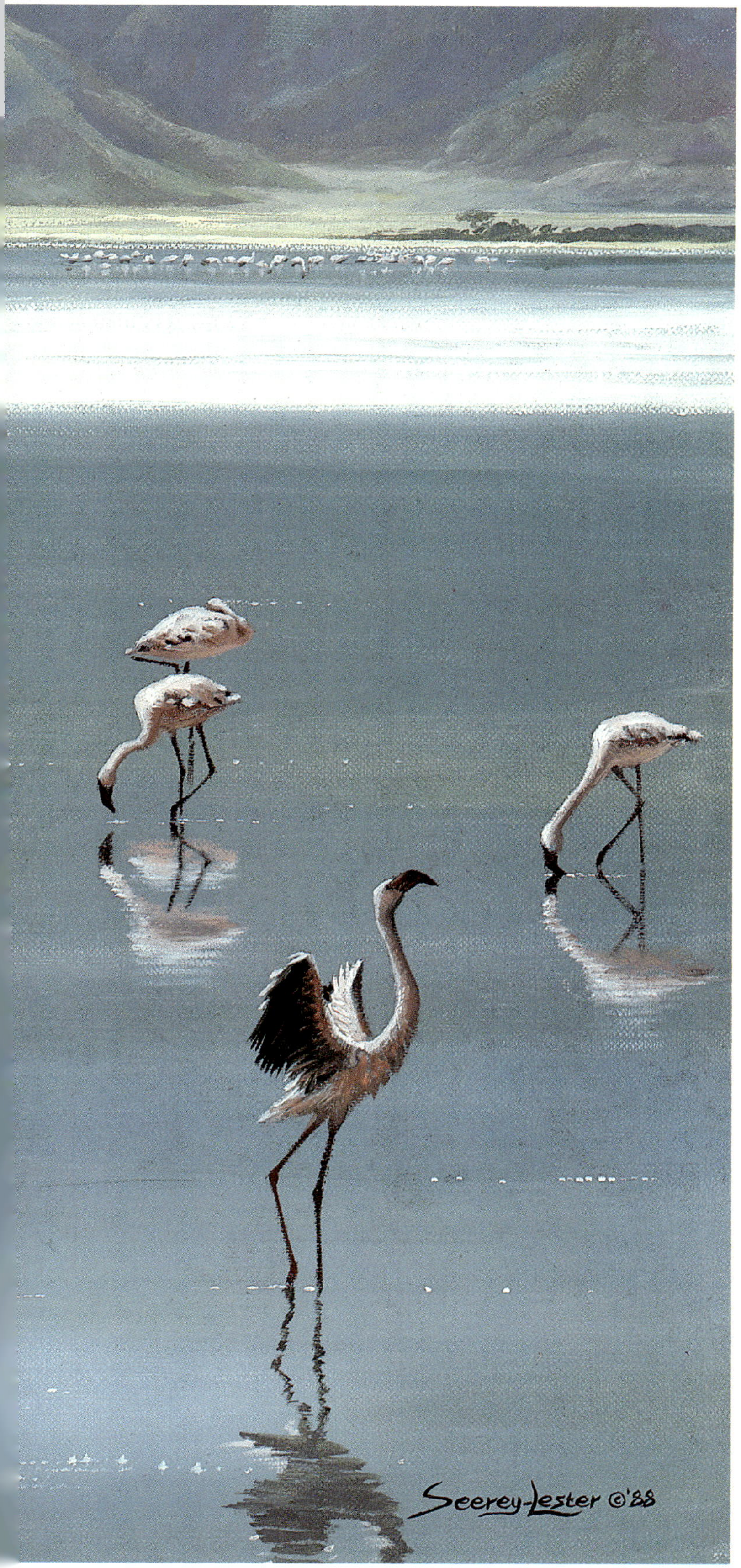

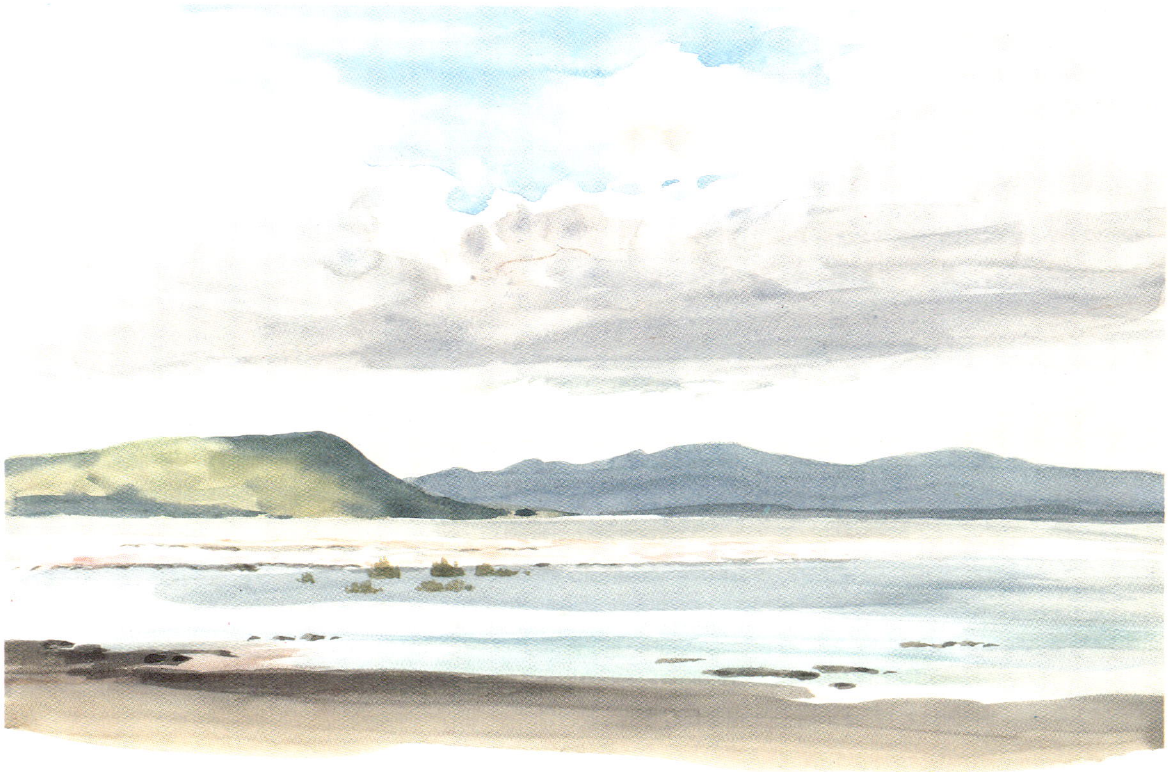

Lake Nakuru, seen here in a watercolour sketch by Rena Fennessey, often holds between two and three million lesser flamingoes, making it one of the greatest avian spectacles in the world. However, flamingoes are highly mobile, and at times they desert Nakuru completely, moving off to other Rift Valley lakes – possibly Bogoria to the north, or south to lakes Magadi or Natron. They rarely attempt to nest at Nakuru, though they frequently display there. The display is spectacular: hundreds or even thousands of birds will pack tightly together, necks raised vertically, feathers erected, marching as one. The display is a prelude to nesting, which does not necessarily take place at the same site.

FLAMINGOES ON LAKE NAKURU
Rena Fennessey

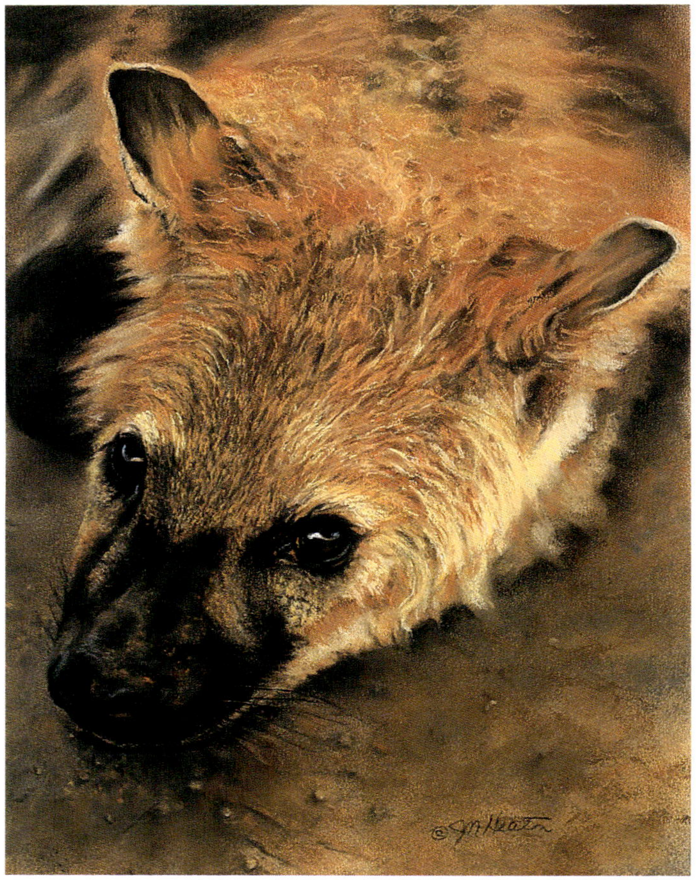

SPOTTED HYENA
Janet Heaton

The publishers of *African Wildlife in Art* would be interested to hear from picture owners and from those who may have suggestions for a further book on the subject.

INDEX

ACKNOWLEDGEMENTS

EGYPTIAN VULTURE
Kim Donaldson

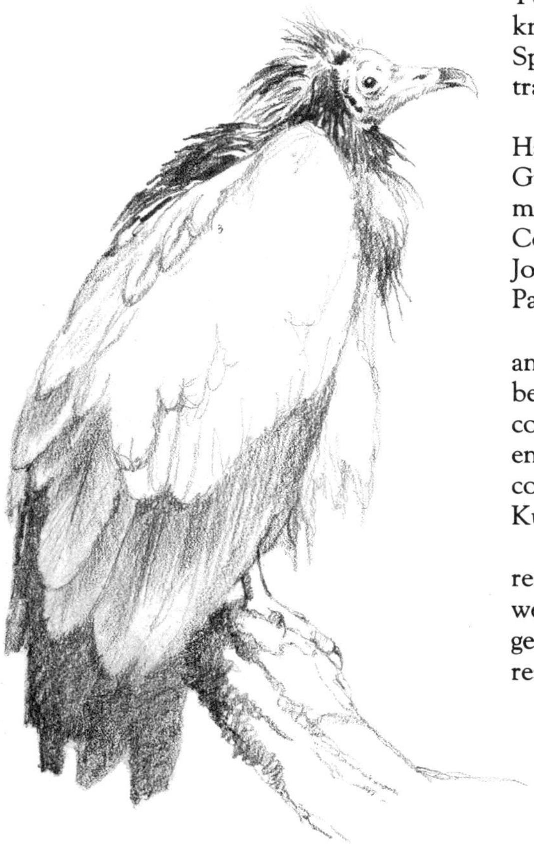

The publishers are grateful to Ken Modzelewski and Mary Nygaard of the Mill Pond Press, Florida, agents for a number of the artists whose work is featured in this book, for their practical help and for the wholehearted manner in which it was given.

We are indebted to Brian Booth of the Tryon and Moorland Gallery in London, and to Fred King of the Sportsman's Edge Gallery in New York, who have gone out of their way to advise and assist in every possible respect. The Greenwich Workshop, Dave Usher, Jack Innes and Ellen Woodward, have been equally generous and forthcoming, as has Kim Donaldson's agent, Peter Wilkins. We thank Mary Suffudy of Watson Guptill, for her counsel and for generously giving us a number of books for reference.

Nobody's enthusiasm has exceeded that of Kathy Kelsey Foley, Director of the Leigh Yawkey Woodson Art Museum in Wausau, Wisconsin, who has given us a number of leads, and helped us with transparencies. Likewise we are grateful to Julian Royle of W.R. Royle & Son Ltd. and to Nicholas Hammond, author of *Twentieth Century Wildlife Artists* (Croom Helm, 1986) whose specialized knowledge and suggestions have been a great help. The John L. Wehle Gallery of Sporting Art at the Genessee Country Museum in the States has supplied transparencies for several of the excellent pictures in their permanent collection.

Others who have assisted with transparencies, advice, or in other ways include Hansjorg Werner, Dieter Grimmig of Gallery "G" in Heidelberg, and Claus Goran Green of Bra Bocker, Sweden. Individuals who have helped us and to whom we are most grateful include Edward Bunting, David Burnett, Colin Church, David Coulson, Linda and Alec Emmott, Mike Fear, Harper Collins Publishers Ltd, Johnny Havelock, June Holloway, Jane Kay, John McNeillie, Nigel and Clare Partridge, Tony Talbot, Gordon Tregear, Frank Vernon and Vivien Ward.

We are particularly thankful to David Tomlinson for his interest and expertise and to his wife, Jan, for her hospitality. Right from the start of this project it became apparent that the artists themselves were enormously enthusiastic; their co-operation and assistance has made setting about it both rewarding and enjoyable. To single any of them out for special thanks is awkward, because we could happily have listed them all, but Simon Combes, Kim Donaldson, Bob Kuhn, Mike Ghaui, Donald Grant and Mandy Shepherd went the extra mile.

On a personal note, doing books about Africa wouldn't be the same if, for any reason, the publishers were to be permanently harboured in London. Once again we are beholden to Tony Duckworth of Funzi Island near Shimoni, Kenya, for generously hauling up the anchor; and to Bob, for keeping a close eye on things that really matter.

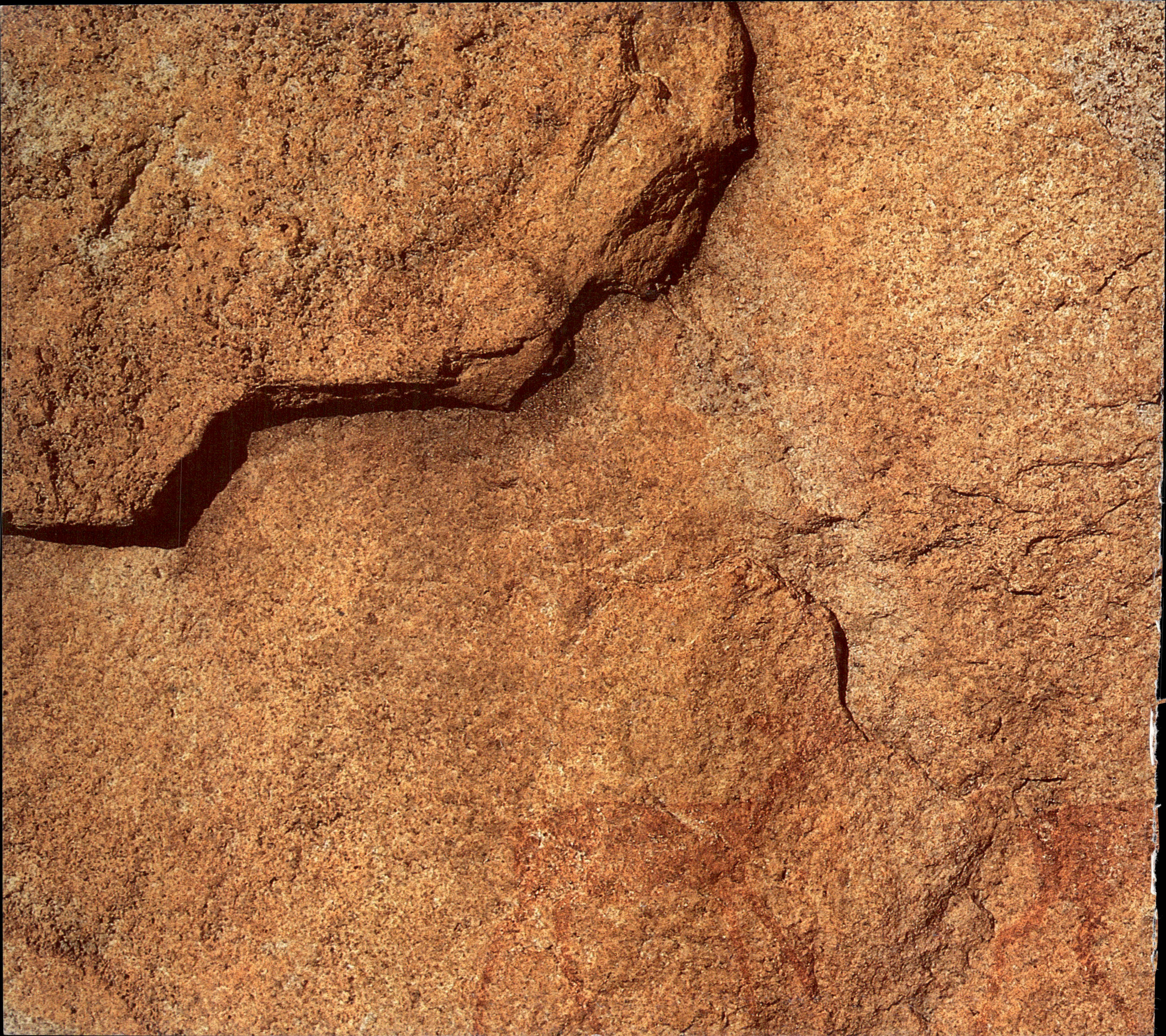